Professional SQL Server™ 2005 CLR Programming
with Stored Procedures, Functions, Triggers, Aggregates, and Types

Derek Comingore

Douglas Hinson

Wiley Publishing, Inc.

Professional SQL Server™ 2005 CLR Programming with Stored Procedures, Functions, Triggers, Aggregates, and Types

Published by
Wiley Publishing, Inc.
10475 Crosspoint Boulevard
Indianapolis, IN 46256
www.wiley.com

Copyright © 2007 by Wiley Publishing, Inc., Indianapolis, Indiana

Published simultaneously in Canada

ISBN-13: 978-0-470-05403-1
ISBN-10: 0-470-05403-4

Manufactured in the United States of America

10 9 8 7 6 5 4 3 2 1

1MA/RX/RR/QW/IN

For general information on our other products and services or to obtain technical support, please contact our Customer Care Department within the U.S. at (800) 762-2974, outside the U.S. at (317) 572-3993 or fax (317) 572-4002.

Library of Congress Cataloging-in-Publication Data
Comingore, Derek, 1978-
 Professional SQL server 2005 CLR programming : with stored procedures, functions, triggers, aggregates, and types / Derek Comingore and Douglas Hinson.
   p. cm.
 Includes indexes.
 ISBN-13: 978-0-470-05403-1 (paper/website)
 ISBN-10: 0-470-05403-4 (paper/website)
 1. SQL (Computer program language) 2. Database management--Computer programs. 3. Microsoft .NET Framework. I. Hinson, Douglas, 1968- II. Title.
 QA76.73.S67C655 2007
 005.75'85--dc22
                    2006031028

Wiley also publishes its books in a variety of electronic formats. Some content that appears in print may not be available in electronic books.

To my son, Derek Steven Comingore, and the next generation of programmers.

—Derek Comingore

To Misty, Mariah, and Kyle, for your love, support, and patience.

—Douglas Hinson

About the Authors

Derek Comingore is an independent consultant, trainer, and speaker specializing in SQL Server and .NET technologies. He has recently started two ventures, an online Microsoft community for colleagues to learn from one another, located at www.RedmondSociety.com, and a second for SQL Server consulting at www.SQLServerDBAs.com. Derek holds the MCAD/MCDBA Microsoft certifications, the Carnegie Mellon Personal Software Process (PSP) credential, and an AAS/BS in Computer Information Systems from University of North Dakota. Derek's blog is located at http://RedmondSociety.com/blogs/Derek.

Douglas Hinson has worked as an independent software and database consultant in the logistics and financial industries, with an extensive SQL Server background. He has coauthored several Wrox books, including *Professional SQL Server 2005 Integration Services*.

Credits

Executive Editor
Bob Elliott

Development Editor
Brian MacDonald

Technical Editor
Dan Meyers

Production Editor
Felicia Robinson

Copy Editor
Foxxe Editorial Services

Editorial Manager
Mary Beth Wakefield

Production Manager
Tim Tate

Vice President and Executive Group Publisher
Richard Swadley

Vice President and Executive Publisher
Joseph B. Wikert

Project Coordinators
Patrick Redmond
Ryan Steffen

Graphics and Production Specialists
Carrie A. Foster
Peter Gaunt
Denny Hager
Alicia B. South
Ronald Terry

Quality Control Technician
Laura Albert
John Greenough

Proofreading and Indexing
Techbooks

Contents

Contents

Contents

Contents

Contents

Contents

Acknowledgments

Books are a lot of work and they are not the sole creation of the authors. There are countless people involved in producing the work that you hold in your hands. So, first I wish to thank the core members of the "Pro SQL CLR" team, including Brian MacDonald, development editor; Bob Elliott, acquisitions editor; Dan Meyers, technical editor; and Douglas Hinson, coauthor. Brian MacDonald helped keep the book's schedule on track which was difficult as I had went through some huge changes in my personal life. Douglas Hinson, my coauthor, ended up writing an additional chapter to help me. Dan Meyers, a good personal friend of mine, provided us with stellar technical edits of the work. Dan is a Business Intelligence (BI) expert on the SQL Server platform, and I have meet few outside of Microsoft who have his knowledge of Analysis Services. And Bob Elliot, who provided me with the opportunity to lead this project. Like Brian, Bob keep me going when I thought I could not proceed any further; thank you.

Personally, I wish to thank my family. There is no dollar amount that can replace the feeling when another person believes in you and your capabilities; my family could not be any more supportive of my ambitions. And finally I wish to thank my son, who brings me more joy in life then anything else.

—*Derek Comingore*

First, I thank God for the continuous blessing of life. To my beautiful wife Misty, thank you for being so supportive and patient during this project. You are a wonderful wife and mother whom I can always count on. To Mariah and Kyle, thanks for getting Daddy out of the office to watch *Star Wars* and print Hello Kitty pictures. I love you both. To my parents, thanks for instilling in me the values of persistence and hard work. Thanks Jenny, for being my sister and my friend. Thanks to all my extended family for your love and support. Thanks, Brian for working your magic behind the scenes. And Dan Meyers, thanks for your time and attention for the technical editing on this book.

—*Douglas Hinson*

Introduction

"Host a .NET language routine in SQL Server?" If you picked up this book and are reading this introduction, you either saw the title and thought that very question, or you have already been trying to do just that and have some questions. Either way you will be satisfied with the content of this book. In SQL Server 2005, Microsoft's SQL Server Development Team introduced the capability to write code in a .NET language that could be compiled and run inside SQL Server. When should you consider doing this? How would you do this? What new capabilities does SQL CLR give you? What should you worry about? Like you, we were curious and felt compelled to dig into this new feature of SQL Server 2005, known as CLR Integration, or by its internal name, SQL CLR. New software architecture capabilities like this one require hours of deliberation to determine if and when to employ them. If you are a DBA or a developer and your team is thinking about using SQL CLR, this book will teach you what you need to know to make a decision about using SQL CLR in your solutions without having to learn the hard way.

Think about .NET code in the body of your T-SQL user-defined functions, procedures, and extended stored procedures and you'll start getting the picture of SQL CLR. Arrays, datasets, even object-oriented programming techniques that are available when you develop in .NET are just not possible in current T-SQL development. But this is only a start. SQL CLR opens up the ability to create user-defined types, triggers, user-defined table values functions, and user-defined aggregates using a .NET managed language. Programming using SQL CLR and .NET also opens up abilities to read and write to resources outside of SQL Server as well as tighter integration with XML, web services, and simple file and logging capabilities. These external activities are cool, but they create some security risks that you'll need to know how to lock down before you attempt to ask your DBA to deploy. Read up on how to lock down .NET assembly capabilities in Chapter 10 and you'll look like an expert.

Like you, we are both developers and DBAs that don't have time to learn something that we won't ever use. Typically, we leave the book open while we are building or debugging some code. We started digging into SQL CLR to see how it worked and whether we should even use it. We finished with the answers to these questions and an idea that we could write a book about SQL CLR that you'd leave open while you are learning. The best thing about it is you'll get hours and hours of experimentation boiled down into 11 real-world chapters. Use the time you save to decide how you can use SQL CLR in your next SQL Server development project.

Who This Book Is For

Are you a DBA who needs to get up to speed on the integration of .NET assemblies into SQL Server? Are you a developer who wants to see how far you can push coding in your favorite .NET language instead of T-SQL for complex cursor and looping tasks? Perhaps you are a software architect who needs an in-depth study of the new capabilities of SQL CLR both within the database and by interacting with external resources outside of SQL Server. If any of these descriptions sound familiar, this book is for you.

Learning new technology has always been demanding. Developers and architects have been more subject to Moore's law lately than the DBAs. First, we were hit with the whole idea of a unified .NET framework.

Then we endured a wild ride with the evolution from version 1.0 to the ultra-slick features of version 2.0. Now it's the DBAs' turn. The DBAs had a free ride for a while with SQL Server 2000, but now that SQL Server 2005 has arrived, we've got a short on ramp to get on the .NET superhighway. SQL Server 2005 is packed with new features. The more we use it, the more stuff we find in this release. The ability to code .NET in SQL Server was one of the features that grabbed our attention immediately. Now that we've had a chance to learn this new technology, we want to help you get up to speed on SQL CLR as soon as possible. Understanding what you can do and how to do it will be a little bit of a challenge, but read these chapters and you'll immediately see some new possibilities for your SQL Server development.

We approached the writing of this book for two distinct audiences: the developers and architects who are more familiar with .NET concepts, and DBAs, who are developers in their own right, but maybe a little behind on the .NET learning curve. Neither of these two audiences is expected to be beginners, so if you are just starting to learn database programming, this book may not meet your needs. You need a solid grounding in T-SQL to understand best where SQL CLR objects fit. If you already have some T-SQL coding experience as well as a little bit of .NET, you will be able to follow along as we introduce the technology and then immediately jump into coding our first SQL CLR stored procedure. If you are interested in a comparative analysis, you should start with Chapter 5, where we dig into the performance differences between T-SQL and SQL CLR. If you are just starting to look into SQL CLR, or if you've been using it for a while and you are stuck and looking for answers, you'll find something that will stick with you in these chapters.

How This Book Is Structured

When we first discussed putting a book together on SQL CLR we had only one goal: to put together not only a book on SQL CLR that you would bring to work but also one that you'd use continuously. If you are going to use it daily, we think that it not only has to answer the questions that you have when you start, questions about what SQL CLR is and how it works, but also be able to answer the questions that will you have two months from now. How does that impersonation stuff work again? How do you use the code access security model to restrict assemblies to creating files in only one directory? We think that a book worth using daily has to answer these questions. That's what we put together for this book: one small part reference manual and one big part here's-how-you-really-do-it.

Writing about SQL CLR and staying in the middle of the road between the developers and the DBAs is a tall task, especially when you consider the subject matter. SQL CLR spans two similar but completely different code camps: .NET framework-based coding and procedural T-SQL-based database coding. Either approach can solve problems, but to appreciate the appropriate use and capabilities of SQL CLR objects, you really need both a good understanding of the elegance of .NET coding capabilities and the raw crunching power of the SQL Server engine. We understand that not everyone gets to work in both worlds often enough to be able to make those finer connections. For those of you in this situation, you'll find attempts to bridge one side to another. For example, we may compare a .NET `ByRef` parameter to a T-SQL `INPUT OUTPUT` parameter to bring the two development environment concepts together.

We have structured our chapters in an attempt to interleave just enough background information to let us dive into the action. This is partly to keep with our theme of creating the book you'll keep on your desk but also to avoid what is commonly referred to as the "nap" effect. This is an unscientific phenomenon that occurs when you have to read through too much reference material and you wake up at 3:00 in the morning having fallen asleep with the TV still on. We want you reading with the computer on, not the TV. When you start working through the examples and see the magic for yourself, you'll start coming up with ideas on where you can use SQL CLR.

The chapters in this book start from ground zero, but in Chapter 2 you'll be creating a basic SQL CLR stored procedure. From there you'll come up for air to get a few .NET concepts in place and then you'll immediately put those new skills to work. After you've seen what you can do with SQL CLR, we'll step back and look at a comparison between SQL CLR and T-SQL to put some perspective on the hype. Then we'll dive into some more complex SQL CLR objects and explore the topic of replacing the soon-to-be extinct extended stored procedures. To round out the book, we've focused on some of the DBA concerns of SQL CLR particularly those related to security and administration. We hope you'll enjoy using this book as much as we do.

Chapter 1 introduces you to the concepts and architecture of SQL CLR.

Chapter 2 dives right in with the building of your first SQL CLR stored procedure. You'll learn where all the moving parts are and where the metadata is stored within SQL Server.

Chapter 3 covers the basics of the .NET namespaces. In T-SQL development, you have a limited function library. In .NET there are many ready-made objects that make programming easier and safer.

Chapter 4 shows you how to build all of the support SQL CLR objects.

Chapter 5 takes a step back to compare and contrast the capabilities of programming in T-SQL versus .NET languages. Here, we develop routines in both languages and perform benchmarking to determine where each technique excels.

Chapter 6 looks at replacing the common extended stored procedures using SQL CLR routines.

Chapter 7 uses the Problem/Design/Solution paradigm to show advanced examples of employing SQL CLR to fulfill business requirements.

Chapter 8 shows how you can use SQL CLR objects in external applications. It is one thing to build the SQL CLR object, but this chapter shows you how to interact with them.

Chapter 9 demonstrates some error-handling techniques in SQL CLR and compares the differences between T-SQL and .NET error handling.

Chapter 10 describes the security risks and details the process and procedures that administrators will need to know to safely manage SQL CLR deployments.

Chapter 11 details a case study of solving a business problem using T-SQL and SQL CLR to demonstrate advantages of deploying appropriate solutions in SQL CLR.

What You Need to Use This Book

To follow along with this book, you'll need a copy of SQL Server Express 2005 at a minimum. SQL Server Express is the free successor to MSDE (the older SQL Server 2000–based engine that had a workload governor on it to limit concurrent access). Get SQL Server Express at http://msdn.microsoft.com/vstudio/express/sql. In addition, there is a free management tool built explicitly for the Express edition called SQL Server Management Studio Express, which can also be found at http://msdn.microsoft.com/vstudio/express/sql.

Visual Studio 2005 is the preferred development environment to create, debug, and deploy your SQL CLR routines. However, Visual Studio 2005 is not required. You could use Notepad to create your source code, compile the source code with your managed language's corresponding command-line compiler, and then manually deploy to SQL Server. But practically speaking, you'll want the productivity advantages of using the Professional Edition of Visual Studio 2005 IDE to create, deploy, and debug your SQL CLR objects. Use either Visual Studio Professional Edition, Visual Studio Tools for Office, or Visual Studio Team System. We will be using the Professional Edition of Visual Studio 2005 for the creation of our code samples in this book.

Conventions

To help you get the most from the text and keep track of what's happening, we've used a number of conventions throughout the book.

> **Boxes like this one hold important, not-to-be forgotten information that is directly relevant to the surrounding text.**

Tips, hints, tricks, and asides to the current discussion are offset and placed in italics like this.

As for styles in the text:

❑ We *highlight* new terms and important words when we introduce them.

❑ We show keyboard strokes like this: Ctrl-A.

❑ We show file names, URLs, and code within the text like this: `persistence.properties`.

❑ We present code in two different ways:

Code examples are displayed like this.

```
In code examples we highlight new and important code with a gray background.
```

The gray highlighting is not used for code that's less important in the present context, or has been shown before.

Source Code

As you work through the examples in this book, you may choose either to type in all the code manually or to use the source code files that accompany the book. All of the source code used in this book is available for download at `http://www.wrox.com`. Once at the site, simply locate the book's title (either by using the Search box or by using one of the title lists), and click the Download Code link on the book's detail page to obtain all the source code for the book.

Because many books have similar titles, you may find it easiest to search by ISBN; this book's ISBN is 0-470-05403-4 (changing to 978-0-470-05403-1 as the new industry-wide 13-digit ISBN numbering system is phased in by January 2007).

Once you download the code, just decompress it with your favorite compression tool. Alternately, you can go to the main Wrox code download page at `http://www.wrox.com/dynamic/books/download.aspx` to see the code available for this book and all other Wrox books.

Errata

We make every effort to ensure that there are no errors in the text or in the code. However, no one is perfect, and mistakes do occur. If you find an error in one of our books, like a spelling mistake or faulty piece of code, we would be very grateful for your feedback. By sending in errata you may save another reader hours of frustration and at the same time you will be helping us provide even higher-quality information.

To find the errata page for this book, go to `http://www.wrox.com` and locate the title using the Search box or one of the title lists. Then, on the book details page, click the Book Errata link. On this page, you can view all errata that has been submitted for this book and posted by Wrox editors. A complete book list including links to each's book's errata is also available at `www.wrox.com/misc-pages/booklist.shtml`.

If you don't spot "your" error on the Book Errata page, go to `www.wrox.com/contact/techsupport.shtml` and complete the form there to send us the error you have found. We'll check the information and, if appropriate, post a message to the book's errata page and fix the problem in subsequent editions of the book.

p2p.wrox.com

For author and peer discussion, join the P2P forums at `p2p.wrox.com`. The forums are a web-based system for you to post messages relating to Wrox books and related technologies and interact with other readers and technology users. The forums offer a subscription feature to e-mail you topics of interest of your choosing when new posts are made to the forums. Wrox authors, editors, other industry experts, and your fellow readers are present on these forums.

At `http://p2p.wrox.com`, you will find a number of different forums that will help you not only as you read this book but also as you develop your own applications. To join the forums, just follow these steps:

1. Go to `p2p.wrox.com` and click the Register link.
2. Read the terms of use and click Agree.
3. Complete the required information to join as well as any optional information you wish to provide and click Submit.
4. You will receive an e-mail with information describing how to verify your account and complete the joining process.

You can read messages in the forums without joining P2P, but in order to post your own messages, you must join.

Introduction

Once you join, you can post new messages and respond to messages other users post. You can read messages at any time on the web. If you would like to have new messages from a particular forum e-mailed to you, click the Subscribe to this Forum icon by the forum name in the forum listing.

For more information about how to use the Wrox P2P, be sure to read the P2P FAQs for answers to questions about how the forum software works as well as many common questions specific to P2P and Wrox books. To read the FAQs, click the FAQ link on any P2P page.

Introducing SQL CLR

SQL Server's .NET integration is arguably the most important feature of SQL Server 2005 for developers. Developers can now move their existing .NET objects closer to the database with SQL CLR. SQL CLR provides an optimized environment for procedural- and processing-intensive tasks that can be run in the SQL Server tier of your software's architecture. Also, database administrators need a strong knowledge of SQL CLR to assist them in making key administrative decisions regarding it. If you ignore SQL CLR, you're missing out on the full potential SQL Server 2005 can offer you and your organization, thus limiting your effectiveness with the product.

SQL CLR is a very hot topic in the technical communities but also one that is frequently misunderstood. Unquestionably, there will be additional work devoted to SQL CLR from Microsoft and Paul Flessner (Microsoft's senior vice president, server applications), including the support of future database objects being created in SQL CLR. The book you are reading is your one and only necessary resource for commanding a strong knowledge of SQL CLR, including understanding when to use the technology and, just as importantly, when not to use it.

What is SQL CLR?

SQL CLR is a new SQL Server feature that allows you to embed logic written in C#, VB.Net, and other managed code into the body of T-SQL objects like stored procedures, functions, triggers, aggregates and types. Client applications interact with these resulting routines like they are written in native T-SQL. Internally, things like string manipulations and complex calculations become easier to program because you are no longer restricted to using T-SQL and now have access to structured .Net languages and the reuse of base class libraries. Externally, the logic you create is wrapped in T-SQL prototypes so that the client application is not aware of the implementation details. This is advantageous because you can employ SQL CLR where you need it without re-architecting your existing client code.

With SQL CLR, you are also freed from the constraint of logic that applies only within the context of the database. You can with appropriate permissions write logic to read and write to file systems, use logic contained in external COM or .Net DLLs, or process results of Web service or remoting methods. These capabilities are exciting and concerning, especially in the historical context of new feature overuse. To help you use this new feature appropriately, we want to make sure that you understand how it integrates with SQL Server and where this feature may be heading. In this chapter, we'll give you this type of overview. We'll spend the rest of the book explaining these concepts using real-world SQL CLR examples that you can use today.

The Evolution of SQL CLR

A few years ago, we came across a product roadmap for Visual Studio and SQL Server that mentioned a feature that was described as "creating SQL Server programming objects in managed languages." At the time, we could not comprehend how this feature would work or why Microsoft had chosen to do this. .NET 1.0 had just been released not, and to be able to use these compiled procedural languages to create database objects just did not "compute" to us.

At the time of this writing, the year is 2006 and Microsoft SQL Server 2005 has arrived with a big roar in the database market. *CLR Integration* is the official Microsoft term for the .NET Framework integration into SQL Server. *SQL CLR* was the original term used by Microsoft to refer to this technology and it continues to be used predominantly in the surrounding technical communities.

> **The Common Language Runtime (CLR) is the core of the Microsoft .NET Framework, providing the execution environment for all .NET code. SQL Server 2005 hosts the CLR, thus the birth name of the technology "SQL CLR," and its successor "CLR Integration."**

Pre-SQL Server 2005 Extensibility Options

Before SQL Server 2005, there was a handful of options a database developer could implement to extend beyond the boundaries of T-SQL. As we will discuss in this chapter, SQL CLR is almost always a better environment for these routines. The pre-SQL Server 2005 extensible options are:

❑ Extended Stored Procedures, C/C++ DLLs that SQL Server can dynamically load, run, and unload.

❑ sp_oa Procedures, OLE automation extended stored procedures. You can use these system procedures to invoke OLE objects. Even with the arrival of the SQL CLR technology there may be times when you still need to use these procedures for those situations in which you must use a Object Linking and Embedding (OLE) object.

Why Does SQL CLR Exist?

Dr. E. F. "Ted" Codd is the "father" of relational databases and thus Structured Query Language (SQL) as well. SQL is both an American National Standards Institute (ANSI) and International Organization for Standardization (ISO) standard. SQL (and its derivatives, including T-SQL) are set-based languages designed to create, retrieve, update, and delete (CRUD) data that is stored in a relational database management system (RDBMS). SQL was and still is the natural choice when you only require basic CRUD functionality.

There are many business problems in the real world that require much more than basic CRUD functionality, however. These requirements are usually fulfilled in another logical layer of a software solution's architecture. In today's current technical landscape, web services, class libraries, and sometimes even user interfaces fulfill the requirements beyond CRUD. Passing raw data across logical tiers (which sometimes can be physical tiers as well) can be undesirable, depending upon the entire solution's requirements; in some cases, it may be more efficient to apply data transformations on the raw data before passing it on to another logical tier in your architecture. SQL CLR allows the developer to extend beyond the boundaries of T-SQL in a safer environment than what was previously available, as just discussed. There are unlimited potential uses of SQL CLR, but the following situations are key candidates for it:

- ❑ Complex mathematical computations
- ❑ String operations
- ❑ Recursive operations
- ❑ Heavy procedural tasks
- ❑ Porting extended stored procedures into the safer managed code environment

The Goals of SQL CLR

The architects and designers of the CLR integration into SQL Server at Microsoft had a few objectives for the functionality:

- ❑ **Reliability:** Managed code written by a developer should not be able to compromise the SQL Server hosting it.
- ❑ **Scalability:** Managed code should not stop SQL Server from supporting thousands of concurrent user sessions, which it was designed to support.
- ❑ **Security:** managed code must adhere to standard SQL Server security practices and permissions. Administrators must also be able to control the types of resources that the CLR assemblies can access.
- ❑ **Performance:** Managed code being hosted inside SQL Server should execute just as fast as if the code were running outside of SQL Server.

Supported SQL CLR Objects

SQL CLR objects are the database objects that a developer can create in managed code. Originally, most people thought that SQL CLR would only allow the creation of stored procedures and functions, but luckily there are even more database programming objects supported. As of the RTM release of SQL Server 2005, you can create the following database objects in a managed language of your choice:

- ❑ Stored procedures
- ❑ Triggers (supporting both Data Manipulation Language [DML] and Data Definition Language [DDL] statements)

❑ User-defined Functions (UDF) (supporting both Scalar-Valued Functions [SCF] and Table-Valued Functions [TVF])

❑ User-defined aggregates (UDA)

❑ User-defined types (UDT)

Stored procedures are stored collections of queries or logic used to fulfill a specific requirement. Stored procedures can accept input parameters, return output parameters, and return a status value indicating the success or failure of the procedure. Triggers are similar to stored procedures in that they are collections of stored queries used to fulfill a certain task; however, triggers are different in that they execute in response to an event as opposed to direct invocation. Prior to SQL Server 2005, triggers only supported INSERT,UPDATE, DELETE events, but with SQL Server 2005 they also support other events such as CREATE TABLE.

Functions are used primarily to return either a scalar (single) value or an entire table to the calling code. These routines are useful when you want to perform the same calculation multiple times with different inputs. Aggregates return a single value that gets calculated from multiple inputs. Aggregates are not new with SQL Server 2005; however, the ability to create your own is new. User-defined types provide you with a mechanism to model your specific data beyond what the native SQL Server data types provide you with.

The .NET Architecture

The *assembly* is the unit of deployment for managed code in .NET, including SQL Server's implementation of it. To understand what an assembly is, you need a fundamental understanding of the CLR (which is the heart of the .NET Framework, providing all managed code with its execution environment). The CLR is the Microsoft instance of the CLI standard. The CLI is an international standard developed by the European Computer Manufactures Association (ECMA) that defines a framework for developing applications in a language agnostic manner. The CLI standard's official name is ECMA-335, and the latest draft of this standard, as of the time of this writing, was published in June 2005.

There are several key components of the CLI and thus the Microsoft implementation of it (the CLR and Microsoft Intermediate Language [MSIL] code):

❑ Common Type System (CTS)

❑ Common Language Specification (CLS)

❑ Common Intermediate Language (CIL)

❑ Virtual Execution System (VES)

❑ Just-in-Time compiler (JIT)

Figure 1-1 shows how these components work together.

CTS

The CTS defines a framework for both value types and reference types (classes, pointers, and interfaces). This framework defines how types can be declared, used, and managed. The CTS describes type safety, how types are agnostic of programming language, and high-performing code. The CTS is a core component in supporting cross-language interoperability given the same code base. In the Microsoft .NET context, this is implemented by the .NET Framework as well as custom types created by users (all types in .NET must derive from `System.Object`).

CLS

The CLS defines an agreement between programming language and class library creators. The CLS contains a subset of the CTS. The CLS serves as a baseline of CTS adoption for designers of languages and class libraries (frameworks). In the Microsoft.NET context, this could be any .NET-supported language including Visual Basic .NET and C#.

CIL

CIL is the output of a compiler that adheres to the CLI standard. ECMA-335 specifies the CIL instruction set. CIL code is executed by the VES (discussed shortly). In the Microsoft .NET context, this is the code you produce when you build a project in Visual Studio or via the command line using one of the supplied compilers such as VBC for Visual Basic .NET and CSC for C#. Microsoft Intermediate Language (MSIL) is the Microsoft instance of CIL.

VES

The VES is the execution environment for CIL code; the VES loads and runs programs written in CIL. There are two primary pieces of input for the VES, CIL/MSIL code and metadata. In the Microsoft .NET context, this occurs during the runtime of your .NET applications.

JIT

The JIT compiler is a subsystem of the VES, producing native CPU-specific code from CIL/MSIL code. As its name implies, the JIT compiler compiles CIL/MSIL code at runtime as it's requested, or just in time. In the Microsoft.NET context, this is during runtime of your .NET applications as you instantiate new classes and their associated methods.

How does the assembly fit into this CLI architecture? In the .NET context, it is when you compile your source code (this is what occurs "behind the scenes" when you build a project in Visual Studio as well) using one of the supported compilers, the container for your MSIL code is the assembly. There are two categories of assemblies in .NET: the EXE and the DLL (SQL CLR assemblies are always DLLs). Assemblies contain both the MSIL code and an assembly manifest. Assemblies can be either single-file- or multi-file-based. In the case of a single-file assembly, the manifest is part of the contents of the assembly. In the case of the latter, the manifest is a separate file itself. Assemblies are used to identify, version, and secure MSIL code; it is the manifest that enables all of these functions.

If you're a compiler guru or you just wish to learn more about the internal workings of Microsoft's CLR implementation of the CLI standard, Microsoft has made the Shared Source Common Language Infrastructure 1.0 Release kit available to the general public. You can find this limited open source version of the CLR at `www.microsoft.com/downloads/details.aspx?FamilyId=3A1C93FA-7462-47D0-8E56-8DD34C6292F0&displaylang=en`.

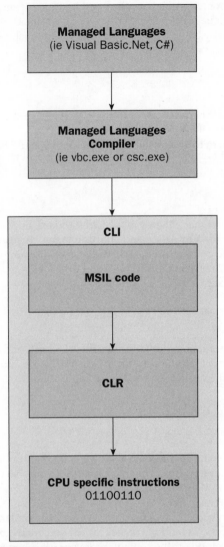

Figure 1-1

Managed Code and Managed Languages

Code that is executed inside the CLR is called *managed code*. Thus, the languages that produce this code are called managed languages. The languages are called *managed* because the CLR provides several run-time services that manage the code during its execution, including resource management, type-checking, and enforcing security. Managed code helps prevent you from creating a memory-leaking application. It is this "managed nature" of CLR code that makes it a much more secure environment to develop in than previous platforms.

Hosting the CLR

The CLR was designed from the beginning to be hosted, but only since the arrival of SQL Server hosting has the concept received so much attention. All Windows software today begins unmanaged, that is, running native code. In the future, the operating system will probably provide additional CLR services so that applications can actually begin as managed software as opposed to what we have today. Thus, in today's Windows environment any application that wishes to leverage the CLR and all its advantages must host it in-process, and this means invoking it from unmanaged code. The .NET Framework includes unmanaged application program interfaces (APIs) to enable this loading and initialization of the CLR from unmanaged clients. It is also worthwhile to mention that the CLR supports the notion of running multiple versions of itself side by side on the same machine, but a CLR host can only load one version of the runtime; thus, it must decide which version to load before doing so.

There are several pieces of software that you use today that host the CLR, including ASP.NET, Internet Explorer, and shell executables.

SQL CLR Architecture

SQL Server 2005 hosts the CLR in a "sandbox"-like environment in-process to itself, as you can see Figure 1-2. When a user requests a SQL CLR object for the first time, SQL Server will load the .NET execution engine `mscoree.dll` (which is the CLR) into memory. If you were to disable SQL CLR (see Chapter 2 for more details) at a later point in time, the hosted CLR would immediately be unloaded from memory.

This contained CLR environment aids SQL Server in controlling key CLR operations. The CLR makes requests to SQL Server's operating system (SQLOS) for resources such as new threads and memory; however, SQL Server can refuse these requests (for example, if SQL Server has met its memory restriction, and doesn't have any additional memory to allocate to the CLR). SQL Server will also monitor for long-running CLR threads, and if one is found, SQL Server will suspend the thread.

> **SQLOS is not a topic for the novice; we are talking about the "guts" of SQL Server here. SQLOS is an abstraction layer over the base operating system and its corresponding hardware. SQLOS enables SQL Server (and future server applications from Microsoft) to take advantage of new hardware breakthroughs without having to understand each platform's complexities and uniqueness. SQLOS enables such concepts as locality (fully utilizing local hardware resources to support high levels of scalability) and advanced parallelism. SQLOS is new with SQL Server 2005.**
>
> **If you wish to learn more about SQLOS you can visit Slava Oks's weblog at** `http://blogs.msdn.com/slavao`. **Slava is a developer on the SQLOS team for Microsoft.**

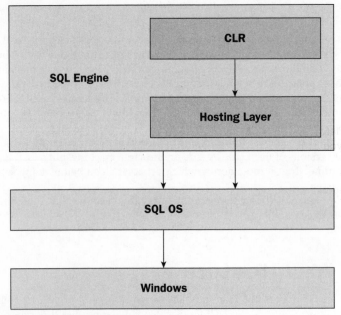

Figure 1-2: The SQL CLR Architecture

Application Domains

You can think of an application domain as a mini-thread, that is an execution zone. Application domains are managed implicitly by the CLR for you. Application domains are important because if the CLR code encounters a fatal exception, its corresponding application domain will be aborted, but not the entire CLR process. Application domains also increase code reliability, including the SQL Server hosting of it. All assemblies in a particular database owned by the same user form an application domain in the SQL Server context. As new assemblies are requested at runtime they are loaded into either an existing or new application domain.

The CLR Security Model

Microsoft's CLR security model is called code access security (CAS). The primary goal of CAS is to prevent unauthenticated code from performing tasks that should require preauthentication. The CLR identifies code and its related code groups as it loads assemblies at runtime. The code group is the entity that assists the CLR in associating a particular assembly with a permission set. In turn, the permission set determines what actions the code is allowed to perform. Permission sets are determined by a machine's administrator. If an assembly requires higher permissions that what it was granted, a security exception is thrown.

So how does the CLR security model apply to SQL CLR? There are two methods of applying security in SQL CLR, CAS permission sets and Role-Based Security (RBS) also known as Role-Based Impersonation (RBI), both of which can be used to ensure that your SQL CLR objects run with the required permissions and nothing more.

SQL CLR CAS Permission Sets

When you load your assemblies into SQL Server, you assign those assemblies a permission set. These permission sets determine what actions the corresponding assembly can perform. There are three default permission sets you can assign to your assemblies upon loading them into SQL Server (see Chapter 8 for more details):

❑ **SAFE** indicates that computational or string algorithms as well as local data access is permitted.

❑ **EXTERNAL_ACCESS** inherits all permissions from SAFE plus the ability to access files, networks, registry, and environmental variables.

❑ **UNSAFE** is the same as EXTERNAL_ACCESS without some of its restrictions and includes the ability to call unmanaged code.

RBS/RBI

RBS is useful when your SQL CLR objects attempt to access external resources. SQL Server will natively execute all SQL CLR code under the SQL Server's service account; this can be an erroneous approach to enforcing security because all users of the SQL CLR object will run under the same Windows account regardless of their individual permissions. There are specific APIs to allow SQL CLR developers to check and impersonate the user's security context (see Chapter 8 for more details).

RBS is only applicable when the user is logged in to SQL Server using Windows Authentication. If your SQL CLR code determines the user is using SQL Server Authentication, it will automatically deny them access to resources that require authentication.

Key SQL CLR Decisions

With the arrival of the SQL CLR technology, you're now faced with several key decisions to be made regarding when and how to use it. These key decisions are some of the hottest topics regarding the technology in the online and offline technical communities.

Using SQL CLR or T-SQL

The one decision always coming to the foreground is now, "Should I implement this object in T-SQL or managed code?" Do not discount T-SQL just because you now have a more secure alternative in SQL CLR. T-SQL has been greatly enhanced in SQL Server 2005. If you take away only one concept from this chapter, let it be that SQL CLR is not a replacement for T-SQL — SQL CLR complements T-SQL. The following table compares the various attributes of each environment.

Attribute	T-SQL	SQL CLR
Code Execution	Interpreted	Compiled
Code Model	Set-Based	Procedural-Based
Access to subset of the .NET Framework Base Class Libraries (BCL)	No	Yes
SQL Server Access	Direct Access	In-Process Provider
Support Complex types	No	Yes
Parameter Support	Input and Output Parameters	Input and Output Parameters

Be aware that the CLR natively does not support VarChar *or* Timestamp *datatypes.*

Based on this information, you can draw some general conclusions about when to use T-SQL for a solution and when to employ SQL CLR: In general, if you are performing basic CRUD functionality you should use traditional T-SQL for these tasks; for anything else, such as intensive cursor processing, accessing external resources, you should use SQL CLR.

Using SQL CLR or Extended Stored Procedures

Extended Stored Procedures (XPs) are typically written in C/C++ against the SQL Server Extended Procedure API, and produce a DLL that SQL Server can load, execute, and unload at runtime. XPs are notorious for causing memory leaks and compromising the integrity of the SQL Server process. In addition, XPs will not be supported in future versions of SQL Server. SQL CLR provides a much safer alternative to using XPs. We recommend that all new development that requires such functionality employ SQL CLR and not XPs. We also recommend that you immediately begin the process of converting your existing XPs to the CLR (see Chapter 4 for more details).

One of the strongest reasons to adopt SQL CLR is to port existing XPs to the safer environment of the CLR.

Using SQL CLR or OLE Automation Procedures

Since SQL Server 6.5 standard edition, SQL Server has supported the functionality of calling Component Object Model (COM) objects from within T-SQL; this feature is known as OLE Automation. OLE Automation is implemented in SQL Server using several XPs prefixed with sp_oa, oa meaning OLE Automation. By leveraging these XPs in your T-SQL code you can instantiate objects, get or set properties, call methods, and destroy objects.

Similarly to using XPs, the COM objects you invoke with sp_oa run in the same address space as the database engine, which creates the possibility of compromising the entire database engine. OLE Automation has been known to cause memory leaks too; there have been knowledge base articles from Microsoft about these XPs leaking memory natively without poor coding techniques. So again, the main benefit of SQL CLR as compared to older technologies is stability and security.

Using the Data Tier or Application Tier for Business Logic

Prior to SQL Server 2005, business logic would typically reside on another server in the form of a COM object or a web service. With the advent of SQL CLR middle-tier developers now have a choice regarding where they want their routines to "reside." When you're deciding where your business logic should be placed, there is one key issue you must consider: the cost of bandwidth versus the cost of computing resources. Generally speaking, you are going to want to consider leveraging SQL CLR for your business logic when your data access returns a lot of data. On the other hand, when your business logic returns minimal data, it probably makes more sense not to employ SQL CLR. Again, the key here is which resources do you have more of, and which resource do you wish to use to support your business logic processing? Maybe you have excessive amounts of bandwidth to spare, but your SQL Server's CPUs and memory are already maxed out. In this case, it may still make more sense to send a lot of data across the wire as you would have done previously.

The other consideration is whether or not you wish to keep your business logic close to the database to help promote its global use. Typically, developers will create a logical middle tier to encapsulate their business logic, but one drawback of this approach is that your business logic is not as "close" to the database it's accessing. If you were to employ SQL CLR for your business logic it would help, but not enforce, your middle-tier logics use. The bottom line here is that each environment and software solution is unique, but these are the issues you should be contemplating when making these crucial decisions.

SQL CLR Barriers of Entry

Not only are there crucial decisions that must be made about a new technology, but there are also barriers of entry in order to properly use and obtain the benefit provided by the technology. SQL CLR is no different in this aspect. There are security, implementation, performance, and maintenance tasks that should be addressed.

Security Considerations

We realize that security from a developer's standpoint is more of a nuisance and you'd rather leave this task to the DBAs. But our experience as DBAs tell us that security is a from-the-ground-up thought process with TSQL and even more so with SQL CLR. If you're a developer, we have some shocking news: you are going to have to understand SQL CLR security because it's very important in dictating what your assemblies are allowed to do. Organizations that are successful in deploying SQL CLR assemblies will foster teamwork between its DBAs and developers (more than the typical organization does).

As an example of the concepts that you'll be deciding about the security of SQL CLR code is how TSQL and SQL CLR will enforce and respect security between shared calls. *Links* or *Comingling* is the term assigned to the relationship formed between T-SQL and managed code calling one another. You should already be aware of CAS permission sets as they were briefly covered earlier in the chapter, as well as Role-Based Impersonation. You have also heard a bit about application domains; just be aware that application domains, in a security context, are important because they form a level of isolation for your managed code. So, if a piece of SQL CLR tries to perform an illegal operation, the entire application domain gets unloaded. Bottom line, security is always important, but in the SQL CLR context an open dialogue between both developers and DBAs is even more important. Chapter 9 will explore SQL CLR security in depth.

The DBA Perspective on SQL CLR

The DBA is typically very cautious about giving developers flexibility, as they should be. One piece of poorly written code could compromise the entire SQL Server instance executing it. As we previously mentioned, XPs are notorious for causing SQL Server problems, and this has contributed to DBAs enforcing strong policies on developers. After all, the DBA is ultimately responsible for the overall health of a SQL Server, and not the developers.

SQL CLR's arrival is forcing DBAs to consider the question of "should I enable this thing or not?" It has been our experience with SQL Server 2005 thus far that DBAs will leave this feature turned off unless it is explicitly required to fulfill certain requirements of the organization. SQL CLR is turned off, by default upon a fresh installation of SQL Server 2005, part of Microsoft's "secure by default" strategy.

Although leaving SQL CLR off is not necessarily a bad option, we also think enabling SQL CLR and restricting what your developers can do via CAS permissions is a better solution. By allowing (and even promoting) SQL CLR in your SQL Server environment, developers will have a safe, secure, and managed alternative to T-SQL with permissions designated by you. After reading this book, DBAs will be well equipped to be proactive about SQL CLR and at the same time be confident in what you are allowing your developers to do with the technology.

Implementation Considerations

Before you even think about using SQL CLR (whether you're a DBA or developer), you must learn either VB.NET or C#. This is not an option. VB.NET and C# are the only officially supported SQL CLR languages. (Managed C++ is somewhere in between not supported and supported, because it does have a Visual Studio template for SQL CLR projects, but it must also be compiled with a special /safe switch for reliability). We encourage you to explore using other managed languages for creating SQL CLR objects, but be aware that they are not officially supported as of the time of this writing.

Logically you're probably now wondering what we mean by officially supported managed languages. Remember, all managed code gets translated into MSIL, so really we are misleading you here. The language you choose is largely about a choice of syntax, but what is supported and not supported is what your managed code does and what types it uses. The reason VB.NET and C# are the officially supported managed languages for SQL CLR is that they have built-in project templates that are guaranteed to generate code that is safe for SQL CLR execution. If you create a new VB.NET/C# Database/SQL Server project, and select "Add Reference," you will notice that not all of the .NET Framework classes or types appear which brings us to the next implementation point. You do not have access to the complete .NET Framework Base Class Library (BCL) in SQL CLR, as most people presume. In reality, you have access to a subset of the BCL that adheres to the SQL Server host requirements.

Host Protection Attributes (HPAs) are the implementation for a CLR host's requirements, which determine what types can be used when the CLR is hosted as opposed to when the CLR is running natively. Additionally, HPAs become more important when coupled with the various CAS permission sets you can apply to your SQL Server assemblies. For now, just understand that there are CLR host requirements, which assist SQL Server in determining if it should allow the use of a particular type or not.

> *If you use an unsupported managed language to create an assembly that you then load into SQL Server as an UNSAFE assembly and that assembly does not adhere to the HPAs, the assembly could attempt an operation that could threaten the stability of the SQL Server hosting it. Any time the stability of*

SQL Server is threatened by an assembly, the offending assembly's entire application domain gets unloaded. This fact goes a long way in proving that stability was designed and implemented well in SQL CLR.

Finally, there is the relation of the CAS permission sets to implementation considerations (which we started to discuss above). The CAS permission set assigned to your SQL CLR assemblies will ultimately determine just how much you can do in the assembly. One of the most common questions about SQL CLR is whether you can call native code in a SQL CLR assembly. The answer is based on the permission set assigned to the assembly. In Chapter 3, we will thoroughly go through all of this material, but realize that if you assign the UNSAFE permission set to an assembly it can attempt practically any operation (including calling native code). Whether the host of the CLR executes "allows" it or not is another matter.

Performance Considerations

Performance is always important, but even more so when you're talking about code running inside of a relational database engine designed to handle thousands of concurrent requests. Consider these SQL CLR performance issues:

First and foremost, if your routine simply needs to perform basic relational data access, it will always perform better when implemented in T-SQL than in SQL CLR. If there is a "no brainer" performance decision relating to SQL CLR, it is when your code just needs to perform CRUD functionality, use T-SQL 100% every time.

Second, transactions are important for your SQL CLR performance considerations. By default, all SQL CLR code is enlisted in the current transaction of the T-SQL code that called it. Thus, if you have a long-running SQL CLR routine, your entire transaction will be that much longer. The point is, be very hesitant about creating long-running routines in SQL CLR (see Chapter 3 for more details on the handling of transactions).

Last, once you have elected to use SQL CLR for a particular routine, be aware of the various resources you have at your disposal to monitor SQL CLR performance (see Chapter 9 for more information). These resources include:

❑ System and Dynamic Management Views

❑ SQL Trace Events (captured with SQL Server Profiler or system stored procedures for custom monitoring needs)

❑ Performance Counters

Maintenance Considerations

If we had a dollar for every SQL Server instance we have worked on that was poorly maintained . . . we wouldn't be rich, but we'd be well off. Databases can easily become unwieldy beasts if you don't take a proactive approach to maintenance (this is usually the case when we work on SQL Server installations that did not have an official DBA assigned to them). SQL CLR assemblies and their related database objects are no different.

The DBA is usually the title of the person in an organization who is responsible for database maintenance, so naturally this aspect of SQL CLR is going to affect him or her more than the developer. If the

DBA chooses to enable SQL CLR in one of the SQL Servers, he or she should also be willing to keep track and monitor the inventory of SQL CLR assemblies. Not only would it be a serious security risk to allow developers to "push" SQL CLR assemblies to a production box without first consulting the DBA, but you could also end up with potentially hundreds of assemblies stored in your database that no one uses anymore or even knows their purpose.

SQL Server 2005 SQL CLR support

All nonportable editions of SQL Server 2005 support SQL CLR, including SQL Server Express. We also found that SQL Server 2005 Mobile does not offer similar functionality via hosting the .NET Compact Framework's CLR in-process on portable devices. We will be using the Express edition of SQL Server 2005 for the creation of our code samples in this book. SQL Server Express is the free successor to MSDE (the older SQL Server 2000–based engine that had a workload governor on it to limit concurrent access). SQL Server Express can be found at http://msdn.microsoft.com/vstudio/express/sql. In addition, there is a free management tool built explicitly for the Express edition called SQL Server Management Studio Express, which can also be found at http://msdn.microsoft.com/vstudio/express/sql. The following are the system requirements for SQL Server Express:

Resource	Required	Recommended
Processor	600-megahertz (MHz) Pentium III–compatible or faster processor	1–gigahertz (GHz) or faster processor
Operating System	Windows XP with Service Pack 2 or later Windows 2000 Server with Service Pack 4 or later Windows Server 2003 Standard, Enterprise, or Datacenter editions Windows Server 2003 Web Edition Service Pack 1 Windows Small Business Server 2003 with Service Pack 1 or later	N/A
Memory	192 megabytes (MB) of RAM	512 megabytes (MB)
Hard Disk Drive	Approximately 350 MB of available hard-disk space for the recommended installation	Approximately 425 MB of additional available hard-disk space for SQL Server Books Online, SQL Server Mobile Books Online, and sample databases
Display	Super VGA (1,024x768) or higher-resolution video adapter and monitor	N/A

Visual Studio 2005 SQL CLR support

Visual Studio 2005 is the preferred development environment to create, debug, and deploy your SQL CLR routines in, however Visual Studio 2005 is not required. You could even use Notepad to create your source code, compile the source code with your managed language's corresponding command-line compiler, and then manually deploy it to SQL Server. If you do wish to use Visual Studio 2005, you will need at least the Professional Edition of Visual Studio 2005 to be able to create, deploy, and debug your SQL CLR objects in Visual Studio. Thus, you need either Visual Studio Professional Edition, Visual Studio Tools for Office, or Visual Studio Team System. We will be using the Professional Edition of Visual Studio 2005 for the creation of our code samples in this book. The following are the requirements for Visual Studio 2005 Professional Edition:

Resource	Recommended
Processor	600 mHz
Operating System	Windows XP with Service Pack 2 or later
	Windows XP Professional x64 Edition (WOW)
	Windows Server 2003 with Service Pack 1
	Windows Server 2003 x64 Edition (WOW)
	Windows Server 2003R2
	Windows Server 2003R2 x64 Edition (WOW)
	Windows Vista
Memory	192 MB of RAM or more
Hard Disk	2 GB available
Drive	DVD-ROM drive

Required Namespaces for SQL CLR Objects

There are four namespaces required to support the creation of SQL CLR objects. The required namespaces are:

- ❑ System.Data
- ❑ System.Data.Sql
- ❑ System.Data.SqlTypes
- ❑ Microsoft.SqlServer.Server

All of these namespaces physically reside in the System.Data assembly. System.Data is part of the BCL of the .NET Framework and resides in both the Global Assembly Cache (GAC) as well as in the .NET 2 Framework directory: C:\WINDOWS\Microsoft.NET\Framework\v2.0.50727\System.Data.dll.

> System.Data *is automatically referenced for you when using Visual Studio 2005 for creating your SQL CLR objects. Also, the above-mentioned namespaces are automatically imported for you as well.*

Summary

In this introductory chapter, we have covered a lot of information that you need to comprehend before you begin creating your SQL CLR objects. You learned of the database objects you can create in the SQL CLR technology. We have shown the architecture of the .NET Framework and when it is being hosted by

SQL Server. We have addressed the biggest decisions developers and administrators have to make regarding SQL CLR. We also wanted to inform you that we are using SQL Server Express coupled with Visual Studio Professional for the production of this book's sample code, we choose these editions of the tools because they are the "lightest" editions of each product that support the SQL CLR technology, and we feel the vast majority of Microsoft developers use Visual Studio as opposed to the command-line compilers. Now that you have a strong foundation in how .NET and SQL CLR works, its time to begin creating your first SQL CLR objects. In Chapter 2, we are going to be covering how to create, deploy, and debug a managed stored procedure.

2

Your First CLR Stored Procedure

The ability to integrate the idiom of .NET programming via the CLR into the database world of SQL Server has generated many strong opinions for and against its use. Some purists have argued that a non-set-based programming approach has no place in the database arena. Some have worried that developers will overuse SQL Server Common Language Runtime (SQL CLR) routines to avoid learning the programmatic idioms of T-SQL. Others are concerned about the security and complexity and want to turn it off completely. Opening up SQL Server to capabilities beyond pure database operations will drive and is driving this discussion beyond the DBA community. Both DBAs and developers are exploring and taking sides on how to use these capabilities, and many issues are up for discussion. Who should build SQL CLR objects? Should only developers build SQL CLR routines, or only DBAs, or both? When is it appropriate to use a SQL CLR routine versus a T-SQL object? How do you build a SQL CLR stored procedure or user-defined function? These are just some of the questions you'll have as you start digging into extending SQL Server using SQL CLR. Before you drown in all the details of the philosophical, let's answer the question of how to create SQL CLR routines and obtain a good grounding in how they work inside SQL Server.

Our first task is to expose you to the technology, to show you the mechanics of hosting managed code into the SQL environment. Get your feet wet by walking through this how-to chapter to build some working CLR routines—namely user-defined function and stored procedures. In this chapter, you'll go through the creation of a basic SQL CLR stored procedure. We'll work manually at first using Notepad, without the Visual Studio environment. This will give you the blue-collar knowledge of how to put a SQL CLR object together from the ground up. You'll learn the inner workings of these new objects as well as gain an understanding of how the managed code fits into the SQL Server metadata. We'll start slow in case you're not yet familiar with the .NET environment. Then, we'll build the same project using the Visual Studio environment and get you up to speed on the improved 2005 integrated development environment (IDE). Finally, we'll give you an idea of how you'll need to approach your development processes to ease the pain of deployment later as you deploy into robust production environments. As with all technology, the key to using it appropriately is to understand how it works. This insight helps you learn what it can do, as well as its limitations. While this chapter won't answer all your questions, you'll get the basics of how to create and deploy some basic SQL CLR stored procedures and user-defined functions.

Setting Up SQL Server Express and the AdventureWorks Database

In this book, our examples are built using the .NET Framework 2.0 or higher. We will be using the AdventureWorks sample database for some examples, and for others we recommend that you create a sample database called CLRTESTDB. This can be done most easily by opening up SQL Server Management Studio and right-clicking the database node in the Object Explorer underneath your SQL Express server. Click New Database in the pop-up menu and then type the name **CLRTESTDB** into the Database Wizard and click OK to accept all the defaults. If you are using just the Visual Studio 2005 Professional product with SQL Server Express, or if you installed a copy of SQL Server 2005 using the default options, you may not have the AdventureWorks database installed. If you are using SQL Server Express, go to www.microsoft.com/downloads and search on AdventureWorksDB.msi for the download. Open the MSI by double-clicking it to activate the Windows installer that will extract the AdventureWorks_data.mdf and AdventureWorks_ldf into the file path C:\Program Files\SQL Server 2000 Sample Databases. Follow the instructions in the Readme file to run the installation scripts that will install the database.

If you installed SQL Server 2005 with the default options, you have two ways to get AdventureWorks up and running. You can download the AdventureWorksDB.msi and install it as well, or you can go to Control Panel ➪ Add Remove Programs and click the Change button. When the wizard comes up, click the link to add new components. You'll be asked to point to the setup.exe on the installation disk and then follow the Setup Wizard to add the AdventureWorks database.

> *A common issue is not being able to connect to the SQLExpress instance within Visual Studio Data Connections because of the instancing of the SQLExpress engine. To connect, use the server name* .\SQLEXPRESS *or replace the "." with your machine name.*

The Mechanics of a Creating and Deploying a CLR Routine

The procedural aspects of creating, deploying, and using a CLR-based routine in SQL Server will seem straightforward after you do a few of them. Figure 2-1 shows each step graphically. The steps are simply:

1. Create a public class using a .NET language using at least one static method as an entry point.
2. Compile the class into a .NET DLL file.
3. Load the DLL file into a target database using a new DDL CREATE ASSEMBLY T-SQL statement.

4. Wrap a DLL entry point in the loaded assembly with a T-SQL object using standard DDL T-SQL statements for the object type (stored procedure, function, trigger, and so on) with an additional reference to the loaded assembly.

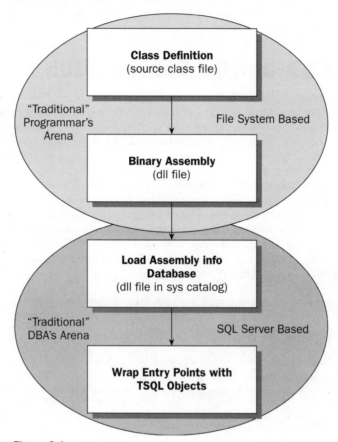

Figure 2-1

Figure 2-1 shows immediately that the biggest difference between using SQL-CLR- and T-SQL-based routines will at first center on who does what. The deployment aspect of SQL CLR routines is solidly in the court of the DBA. This is because they are usually the only roles with rights to move objects in and out of production databases. In terms of development, it will probably depend on the skill sets of the team. For pure T-SQL-based routines, it has traditionally been the responsibility of the developer to define the interface or prototype of the objects and the role of the DBA to develop and fine-tune the body of the routine. With the availability of SQL CLR, the DBA will need to be more involved in the design phase to ensure that the SQL CLR routines are used appropriately. Most DBAs are not going to be happy finding out at the end of a project that they are going to need to deploy SQL CLR objects that access the Internet or expose SQL Server entry points in web services. There may be nothing wrong with these type of deployments, but the DBA is going to want to be involved in these decisions early.

The development of the body, or the content of the managed code, may, in the short term, alternate between the developer and DBA roles. This may be an uncertain set of roles until DBAs and developers become familiar with the capabilities and limitations of the target .NET language being used in their shops. More likely is that the CLR routines will involve a closer working relationship between developer and DBA roles to make the use of these routines appropriate and will expand the skills levels of both roles.

Enabling CLR in SQL Server 2005

To get started, you'll need to enable the Common Language Runtime (CLR) feature for the SQL Server instance. As part of a more security-sensitive installation process, not all features are installed in SQL Server by default. This is a marked departure from previous SQL Server 2000 installations. Many shops that have made the transition to SQL Server 2005 have found that the installation process is more "fussy" then previously, but most agree that the tradeoff of knowing specifically what features are turned on makes for a safer, more secure platform. If you are an admin on your machine, navigate to Microsoft SQL Server 2005 ⇨ Configuration Tools ⇨ SQL Server Surface Area Configuration menu to invoke the Surface Area tool. The surface area tool is a Setup Wizard that walks you through administering features that you want to install or restrict. This tool has the ability to control local and remote servers, but the default startup points to the local environment. If you are walking through this chapter using a remote development server, click on the hypertext label *change computer* shown in the lower middle of Figure 2-2. Select the option of a remote computer, and type the name or IP address of the remote SQL Server you wish to add to the Surface Area Configuration Wizard.

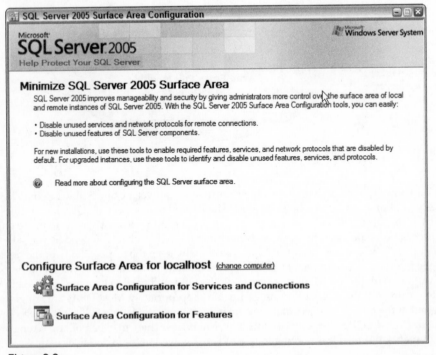

Figure 2-2

There two options in the wizard: to configure Services and Connections or to add or remove Features. Click the link titled Surface Area Configuration for Features. The tool will examine any SQL Server instances on the local host or a selected remote host to determine which features are available within each instance. If you have installed SQLEXPRESS, Navigate to this instance, find the feature named CLR integration, and click the check box to Enable CLR Integration. If you are using a server installation of SQL Server, navigate to that server instance instead. While you are here, notice the other features in the Surface Area tool that are not activated by default, most notably xp_CmdShell, which we will discuss later.

This is not the only way to set up CLR. If you do not have access to the Surface Area Configuration Wizard, or if you are going to create a T-SQL script to enable CLR integration, then open the Microsoft SQL Server Management Studio (SSMS). This tool is the new version of the Enterprise Manager and Query Analyzer rolled up into one interface. Open SSMS by navigating to Microsoft SQL Server 2005 ➪ SQL Server Management Studio. Connect to the SQL Server instance for which you just enabled CLR integration. In our examples, we'll be using SQLEXPRESS for our SQL Server instance unless otherwise stated. Click the New Query button in the toolbar to open a new T-SQL query window like the previous Query Analyzer. Use T-SQL and the sp_Configure stored procedure to set the feature called "clr enabled" to 1.

```
--Script to Enable CLR Integration
use master
go
sp_configure 'clr enabled', 1
go
reconfigure
go
```

If you've configured CLR properly, you should be able to verify this by executing the system stored procedure sp_configure with the feature parameter and without the setting:

```
--Show current configuration setting for CLR Enabled
sp_configure 'clr enabled'
...
(results)
name                       minimum     maximum     config_value run_value
-------------------------- ----------- ----------- ------------ -----------
clr enabled                0           1           1            1
```

The column labeled config_value indicates the current setting of the configuration. Because some configurations require a server restart, the column run_value indicates the configuration setting running on the server at the current time. The enabling (or disabling) of SQL CLR doesn't require you to restart SQL Server. This feature controls whether any code that accesses the .NET CLR is allowed to execute. If you have already loaded SQL CLR objects into a database and want to disable them from executing, disabling this setting will render them useless. SQL CLR routines called when the CLR Feature is disabled will generate an error similar to this:

```
Msg 6263, Level 16, State 1, Line 1
Execution of user code in the .NET Framework is disabled. Enable "clr enabled"
configuration option.
```

Note that you have to run the reconfigure command to update the run value after enabling or disabling CLR integration.

Creating Your First SQL CLR Routine without VS2005

Now that the server environment is ready, you can start creating your first SQL CLR routine. Although using Visual Studio 2005 would make the task far easier, you would miss some of the steps that happen for you automatically. We are going to work this example manually by keying items specifically into a text file to turn these contents into a SQL CLR routine. To keep things simple, you are going to start with a managed C# function that will accept no parameters and return an integer value. This way you can focus on the mechanics of implementing your CLR routine as both as a stored procedure and as a user-defined function, while avoiding, for now, the unnecessary complexities of things like SQL pipes and variable translations.

Since at this time SQL Server can only host one version of the .NET Framework, you may need to keep an eye on future .NET Framework upgrades and the effects that such upgrades may have on your compiled managed code. So, for the first project, you'll write something that will allow you to programmatically determine the version of the .NET CLR Framework running in SQL Server.

Coding the Class

Looking back at the CLR Programming Paradigm in Figure 2-1, you probably had a good idea that you'd be coding something in .NET. Did you realize that you were actually going to build a class? It seems strange to talk about building a class object to run in SQL Server, but a class is one of the basic building blocks for code development in .NET. A class in .NET is an organizational structure that can contain properties or attributes as well as implementation or code to perform specific tasks. An equivalent structure in the T-SQL world really doesn't exist. The closest comparison would be a combination of a user-defined type and a user-defined function. For practical purposes of building SQL CLR objects, you'll use a class structure to contain one or more function-like routines. You can expose these function-like routines with T-SQL object definitions to create SQL CLR stored procedures, user-defined functions, aggregates, and types.

To create your first SQL CLR class open up Notepad and create a file to be named `FirstCLRRoutine.cs`. Within the file, type the code below to create a class definition for a public class named `FirstCLRRoutines`. Save the file in a directory named `c:\prosqlclr\chapter2\FirstCLRRoutine.cs`. The file name does not have to match the class name. The code in notepad will ultimately look like the code shown here. Notice that a set of curly brackets (`{}`) frame the basic structure of the class. For T-SQL programmers these are the equivalent of `BEGIN` and `END` statements.

```
public partial class FirstCLRRoutines
{
    public static int GetCLRFrameworkMajorVersion()
    {
        return System.Environment.Version.Major;
    }
};
```

To figure out why you needed to type these lines specifically, let's walk through each line of this SQL CLR object. The first block defines the class:

```
public partial class FirstCLRRoutines
```

Consider a class in the same way you'd consider any variable or value type. Just as you would define a datatype like INT or VARCHAR in T-SQL, you have to start with a definition of your class. In T-SQL you'd set aside memory for an INT by declaring a variable like this:

```
--EXAMPLE T-SQL VARIABLE DECLARATION
DECLARE @MYINT AS INT
```

By comparison, the syntax of defining a type is reversed in .NET. The type definition of class comes before the variable name FirstCLRRoutines. The access modifier or the keyword public is added because external T-SQL code (that you'll be adding later) has to be able to access the class directly. There are some other keywords that can be used for classes within a SQL CLR routine, but for now, stick with public classes and we'll get into these variations later.

You may notice the partial keyword in a lot of the SQL CLR examples online and in this book. This keyword tells the compiler that multiple files may be used to implement a class. This feature is useful for splitting up large classes for team development, or to combine custom coded class parts with parts of a class generated using a code generator. The main reason you'll see this keyword is because Visual Studio uses it by default. Each managed object you build in a Visual Studio project gets its own class file, but they all have the same class name. Each new SQL CLR stored procedure added to a project will have the default class name of StoredProcedures. New SQL CLR UDFs have the default class name of UserDefinedFunctions. The compiler combines them by name at compile time into one class. Since this example class is only in one file, you can ignore the partial keyword, or even leave it out, and the code will still compile and work.

```
public static int GetCLRFrameworkMajorVersion()
```

This line of code is the start of a specific task that we want to perform within the class. This task, or function, is referred to as a *method*, and is a piece of code that can be called with parameters or without and may return an output of some type or not. SQL CLR class methods can return output parameters or rowsets. This example method returns an int value to correspond with the CLR Framework Major Version number. Again, if you are used to coding T-SQL, notice that the arguments are reversed. You provide the return value before the method name in opposition to T-SQL code requirements.

Notice that access modifier of this method is also public. Can it ever be private? What other options are there? There are other modifiers can be used on a method, but you've only got one choice if you want to expose the functionality of this .NET method as a SQL CLR routine — that option is public. If you did not declare the method public, you'd get an error. This error doesn't occur during the compile process for .NET (unfortunately), but later when you attempt to bind to the entry point in the loaded assembly in SQL Server. We'll take a look at this type of error later.

All SQL CLR methods that are going to be exposed as SQL CLR routines also have to be static (or shared in Visual Basic .NET). The static or shared keywords allow you to access the method without specifically creating an instance of the class. The method must also be static to give SQL Server a valid entry point to bind to the method. By creating a static method, the method can be called directly without first having to create a copy of the class. If you fail to designate a method as a static method in the class an error is raised during the binding of the routine to a T-SQL definition. We'll look at this type of error later as well.

```
return System.Environment.Version.Major;
```

This last line is the meat of the whole class. The intent is to report the current version of the CLR framework. Once you load this class into SQL Server, it will have access to the hosted CLR and .NET Base Class Libraries. These libraries contain classes and code functions that are reusable in your applications. Groups of these classes are called *namespaces*. In this line, we are using a namespace called System that contains a class named Environment. In the Environment class, there is a structure that stores the CLR version. A property of that structure called major reports the major version of the CLR. A common question is: How did you know to go through all of that to get the version number? You'll be surprised how quickly you catch on to the organizational structure of these default namespaces. However, if you can't remember or need help, use the Object Browser, Ctrl-Alt-J, to search keywords.

The final noteworthy item in this line is the last character (;). If you are coding SQL CLR routines in C#, you'll need to end each statement with a semicolon like this. It is a little confusing to determine which lines require this and which lines do not. If you remember to end all declarative statements with the semicolon, you'll get it straight quickly.

If you have not saved the Notepad contents as the class file c:\prosqlclr\chapter2\FirstCLR Routine.cs, do that now.

Compiling the .NET DLL

To see the compiling processes up close, use the Visual Studio 2005 command prompt to activate a command window. If you are new to .NET compilation, it matters whether or not you are using the Visual Studio 2005 command prompt or an operating system command window. The operating system command prompt will only work if you change your environment path variables to point to the directory containing either the C# (csc.exe) or VB.NET (vbc.exe) compiler. The preferred command line is located in Start ⇨ Program Files ⇨ Microsoft Visual Studio 2005 ⇨ Visual Studio Tools ⇨ Visual Studio 2005 Command Prompt. This command prompt is already preset to these environment paths, so when you type the compiler EXE names, this command windows "knows" where to find these compilers. Once in the command prompt, it is also easier to first change to the source directory of the class file. This keeps you from having to type out long path names. For this chapter, all code will be created in a directory named c:\prosqlclr\ in subdirectories named chapter2.

Compile the class by calling the C# or VB compiler passing in the class file name. Direct the compiled output into a library file or DLL by using the compiler option, /target:library or /t:library. Pressing Enter or executing this command will result in a compiled DLL binary file with the same name as your class file—except for the DLL ending. The full command will look like this:

```
Csc /t:library FirstCLRRoutine.cs
```

The output should look similar to Figure 2-3.

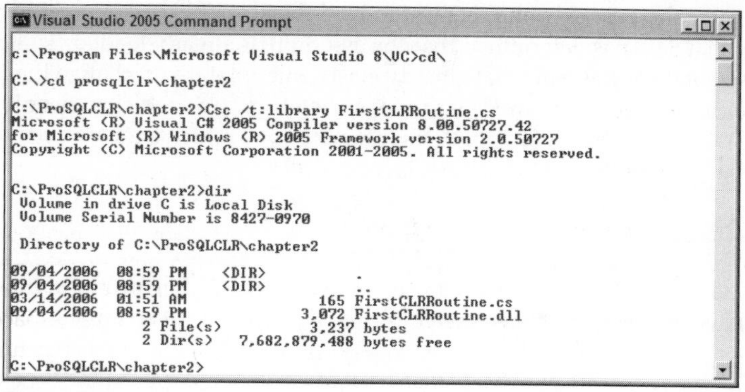

Figure 2-3

Creating the Assembly

If you completed the compilation of the class you now have a .NET DLL or an assembly named `first clrroutine.dll`. Normally you'd start with a *project* to create the original class, and you'd call the whole project an *assembly*. An assembly is just a bundle of types and classes that work together to form a logical unit of functionality. For this DLL to become usable as a SQL CLR object, you need to make the functionality available within SQL Server. To do this, you need to first load the DLL or assembly into SQL Server. Use the new Data Definition Language (DDL) statement CREATE ASSEMBLY to move a copy of the DLL into SQL Server metadata. To execute the DDL statement, you need at least a name for the assembly and the location of the compiled DLL. The assembly name can be any valid T-SQL object name. To be consistent with what you're going to do later, use the assembly name [Chapter2.FirstCLRRoutine]. The location can be either a local path or a UNC file path; for this example, the path will be c:\prosqlclr\chapter2\ firstclrroutine.dll. There are other default options to this DDL statement, most importantly relating to security, that we will discuss later.

Use SQL Management Studio or one of the command-line tools: SQLCMD.exe or OSQL.exe to execute the DDL statement. Using the recommended name and directory path, the DDL would look like the following:

```
USE CLRTESTDB  --This is our test database.
GO
CREATE ASSEMBLY [Chapter2.FirstCLRRoutine] FROM
'c:\prosqlclr\chapter2\firstclrroutine.dll'
```

Here's the interesting part: You can also load the assembly again in another database. Try just changing the script above to USE another database on your server. The assembly will load again successfully. Although CLR routines are frequently compared to extended stored procedures, this is one important difference. Extended procedures can only be loaded in the Master database. SQL CLR assemblies can be loaded in multiple databases on a server. However, this may not be a great thing, and we'll discuss the issues later in Chapter 9.

If you try to rename the assembly and attempt to load the assembly back into either database, you'll get an error stating that SQL has determined that the assembly is already loaded. That will keep you from loading the assembly using a name that already exists, but what if you change the content in the class or recompile the class with a new method? If you're curious, go back and change only the body not the interface of the `GetCLRFrameworkMajorVersion` method to return a minor version integer instead of a major version integer like this:

```
return System.Environment.Version.Minor;
```

Recompile the class with the same `firstclrroutine.dll` name. Regardless of how you try to reload the assembly or DLL, even using a different assembly name, you will get an error similar to the following:

```
Msg 10326, Level 16, State 2, Line 1
Two versions of assembly '[Chapter2.FirstCLRRoutine], version=0.0.0.0,
culture=neutral, publickeytoken=null, processorarchitecture=msil' cannot coexist in
database 'CLRTESTDB'. Keep one version and drop the other.
```

This is a nice double-check for the DBAs when loading assemblies. You may not be able to easily inspect all the details of the functionality in a DLL, but at least the database engine can determine that the DLL has changed. SQL Server can do this through some specialized metadata and a feature of .NET called reflection. Reflection allows assemblies to be programmatically inspected for features and other aspects of interface implementation. Now, the only issue that you'll have to worry about as a DBA is multiple versions of a CLR routine running in different databases. If you can load the assembly, it is now available to SQL Server. To make it available as a SQL CLR object, you need to create a T-SQL-like face for your .NET functions.

Choosing between User-Defined Functions and Stored Procedures

Our final step is to create a T-SQL object prototype that will conceptually wrap the assembly and the one method or entry point in this example with a T-SQL definition or *interface*. Imagine creating a T-SQL stored procedure that instead of executing a SELECT or INSERT statement, it executed a method or function in a .NET assembly. This is exactly what you are going to do. This step essentially results in the creation of a SQL object that you can interact with in the same way as if the logic task had been coded in T-SQL. From a developer's perspective, this is a beautiful thing, especially if the body of the method contains complicated logic involving arrays or loops that the programmer may not be comfortable programming in T-SQL.

Now your only decision is what type of SQL object you are going to use. The T-SQL object you choose to create will depend on how you intend to use it. A common question revolves around when to use a stored procedure and when to use a user-defined function. There are several things to consider, but you can boil them down to these few issues:

❑ Are you going to perform any Data Manipulation Language (DML actions like UPDATE, DELETE, or SELECT INTO? What about Data Definition Language (DDL) statements? If so, use stored procedures, because these actions are not allowed in user-defined functions.

❑ Are you going to use scalar results "in-line" in set operations or constraints? If so, use user-defined functions.

❑ Are you going to use the results as a table in a FROM statement? If so, use user-defined functions.

These are the most common decision points. Most everything else you can do in either object type, but even with the guidelines we are providing here, there are exceptions. For example, technically, it is possible to run an extended stored procedure from a user-defined function that will perform DML or DDL activity. But there's also something to be said about what's expected and what's considered a common practice. The following table is intended as a quick reference to help you decide whether to implement a SQL object from the manage code functions in the assembly as a stored procedure or a user-defined function.

If You Are . . .	Use This T-SQL Definition
Updating data	Stored Procedure
Updating schemas	Stored Procedure (use sp_ExecuteSQL)
Returning Scalar Results INT	User-Defined Function/Stored Procedure
Returning Scalar Results other than INT	User-Defined Function
Returning Multi-Column Results	Table-Valued Function/Stored Procedure
Returning Result of One-column Calculation	User-Defined Aggregate
Using the results in a FROM statement	Table-Valued Function

Creating the T-SQL Stored Procedure

In this example, your .NET assembly method GetCLRFrameworkMajorVersion is returning an integer. In the previous decision matrix, both the User-Defined Scalar Function and Stored Procedure objects can support a return variable of type integer. Since either would work, you'll first implement this method as a stored procedure and later you'll implement it as a user-defined function. To create the stored procedure, use the enhanced DDL statement for CREATE PROCEDURE with the additional new argument EXTERNAL NAME, which allows the proc to reference an external assembly:

```
EXTERNAL NAME assembly_name.class_name.method_name
```

The important part here is that the assembly name must match the name of the assembly that was loaded in SQL Server. Once the assembly is loaded and named in the CREATE ASSEMBLY DDL, the .NET assembly or DLL is no longer needed. You can physically remove the file from the server and the assembly and still create a SQL CLR object with the assembly, as long as it is loaded, or hosted, in SQL Server. If you've chosen an assembly name with special characters or spaces in it, you'll need to delimit the name with brackets ([ ]) or quotation marks (" ").

All you have to do now is execute a well-formed DDL statement to create a new SQL CLR stored procedure. Run this script in your test database to complete your first CLR routine. Here's the code:

```
CREATE PROCEDURE mspGetCLRFrameworkMajorVersion
AS
EXTERNAL NAME
[Chapter2.FirstCLRRoutine].[FirstCLRRoutines].[GetCLRFrameworkMajorVersion]
```

Earlier we talked about why it is important that your .NET class methods be public. If the class method were not public, you'd get an error that would look similar to this:

```
Msg 6574, Level 16, State 1,Stored Procedure mspGetCLRFrameworkMajorVersion, Line 1
Method, property or field 'GetCLRFrameworkMajorVersion' of class 'FirstCLRRoutines'
in assembly '[Chapter2.FirstCLRRoutine]' is not public.
```

Attempting to bind a T-SQL prototype to a nonstatic method in the class would also generate the following error during the binding process:

```
Msg 6573, Level 16, State 1, Stored Procedure GetCLRFrameworkMajorVersion, Line 1
Method, property or field 'GetCLRFrameworkMajorVersion' of class 'FirstCLRRoutines'
in assembly 'myFirstCLRRoutines' is not static.
```

Now that you've compiled, loaded, and bound the T-SQL prototype to your assembly method, the SQL CLR stored procedure is ready to use just like any other T-SQL stored procedure, Run the following test code in the SSMS query window to experience using your first SQL CLR stored procedure.

```
DECLARE @VERSION_MAJOR INT;
EXEC @VERSION_MAJOR = mspGetCLRFrameworkMajorVersion
SELECT @VERSION_MAJOR as SqlCLRVersion
```

The results should look something like this:

```
SqlCLRVersion
-------------
2
```

How SQL Server Manages Assemblies

You've now coded your first SQL CLR routine and implemented it as a stored procedure. Do you remember having to load the assembly into SQL Server? What did SQL Server do with your assembly? Open up the Microsoft SQL Server Management Studio, or alternatively you can use the Server and Data Connections Explorer in Visual Studio, and connect to your instance of SQLEXPRESS. Expand the nodes in the object explorer to look like Figure 2-4.

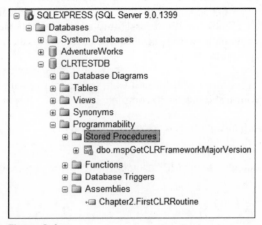

Figure 2-4

This Object Explorer contains categories of object types for each database. Previously in the SQL Server 2000 version of this Object Explorer, stored procedures and functions were displayed in the root. Now in SQL Server 2005, they are moved to a new grouping category titled Programmability. Under this node, you'll find the assemblies for each database. Does this mean that you are storing the contents of the assembly like you store stored procedures in the syscomments table? Or are you just storing the local path to the assembly? Actually, SQL Server loads the whole assembly into the system tables in the database. Want to prove it? Go ahead and delete the FirstCLRRoutine.dll in your compile path, and rerun the test query. You'll see that the test query still returns the current CLR .NET framework version.

The user-defined, system, and aggregate functions, as well as the triggers, types, and assemblies are also grouped under the Programmability node. Notice that your first example SQL CLR stored procedure is stored under the Stored Procedures node.

Assembly Metadata

If you think that SQL Server must have stored that DLL byte code somewhere, you'd be right. Although you might expect that SQL Server would store this information in the usual metadata storage locations for stored procedure and user-defined functions, it does not. SQL Server 2005 stores the assemblies byte for byte in new metadata tables. However, information about other internal SQL object dependencies is stored in the normal metadata for dependencies. In other words, the assembly itself is treated as a new entity in SQL Server, but the T-SQL definitions to expose the .NET methods are treated just like any other T-SQL object for metadata storage. In fact, SQL Server 2005 has completely altered how it uses metadata from its 2000 counterpart. The physical location for many of the system tables that were previously stored in the master database is in a new database called resource that is not visible within the SSMS interface. The actual location of this database is c:\program files\microsoft sql server\ mssql.1\mssql\data\mssqlsystemresource.mdf. The system objects, like sysobjects, that you can get to in SQL Server 2005 are actually views. You can dig into more about these details in the Books Online, but for the assemblies, there are some new system views specifically for examining stored metadata — including the binary assembly itself.

System View	Stored Information
Sys.Assemblies	Assembly Name, CLR Name, .NET Assembly Version, Permissions, IsVisible Flag, Create_Date, ModifyDate
Sys.Assembly_Files	Original Load Location, Content
Sys.Assembly_Modules	Implemented Class and Method Names
Sys.Assembly_References	Relationship References between Assemblies
Sys.Module_Assembly_Usages	Links from SQL Objects to Assemblies

Select all columns and rows from the sys.assemblies view to see the assembly name and .NET assembly version of your first CLR routine. An example of the metadata you might see is shown in Figure 2-5.

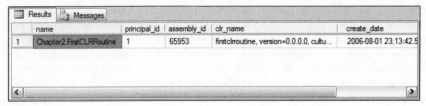

Figure 2-5

Where is the actual DLL code? Select from the `sys.assembly_files` view to look at the information stored about the files in the assembly. The content column shown in Figure 2-6 contains the actual binary content for your first CLR routine DLL, `firstclrroutine.dll`. One of the things you should notice in these two views is the detailed information that SQL Server is storing about the assembly. Since SQL Server knows the physical name of the DLL, you can now see how it was able to provide loading errors when you tried changing the class object or loading the assembly more than once.

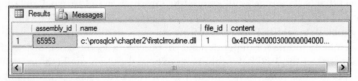

Figure 2-6

If SQL Server has a copy of the DLL in the database, this means that when you back up the database, the assembly is backed up as well. This also means that you can either copy content from server to server or extract this content back into a DLL file and move the DLL to another server. You can exploit this capability to store files and associate them with an assembly and establish a DBA best practice by also storing the original C# or VB.NET class file with the compiled assembly. To store the original class file in the metadata system tables, use an `ALTER` statement with the assembly name and class file path to add the class file, like this:

```
ALTER ASSEMBLY [Chapter2.FirstCLRRoutine]
ADD FILE FROM 'c:\prosqlclr\chapter2\FirstCLRRoutine.cs'
```

If you run this T-SQL and requery the `sys.assembly_files` view, you'll now see the additional content, as shown in Figure 2-7.

	assembly_id	name	file_id	content
1	65953	c:\prosqlclr\chapter2\firstclrroutine.dll	1	0x4D5A9000030000000400...
2	65953	c:\prosqlclr\chapter2\FirstCLRRoutine.cs	2	0x7075626C696320706172...

Figure 2-7

Extracting Assembly DLL and Source Code

Now that the source is stored with the assembly, DBAs are no longer held hostage over source code that is stored and maintained (and perhaps not properly labeled or versioned) outside their area of control. This is particularly advantageous for resolving production issues when you need to know what is happening when an assembly method is generating an error. Without the source loaded in the server, first you'd need to know where the code is located, and second you'd need to have access to retrieve the code to review it. It is much easier to be able to pull that code right out of the database to review. To extract small source objects like this one, you can convert the content column to a VARCHAR or NVARCHAR data type of MAX size and simply view it in the SSMS query window. To get the best results, change the query window to output the query using the Results to Text option. Set this option using Query ⇨ Results to ⇨ Results to Text. Note that the length of the data you can see in the query analyzer is limited to 8192 characters — and you have to go to Tools ⇨ Options ⇨ Query Results ⇨ SQL Server ⇨ Results to Text to set that number of characters. Normally the default is a max column width of 256, and the column will appear to be truncated if you leave this default set. Running the following query with the query results output to TEXT will export this small source file into the query window from the metadata:

```
SELECT CONVERT(varchar(MAX), content)
FROM sys.assembly_files f
INNER JOIN sys.assemblies a
ON f.assembly_id = a.assembly_id
  WHERE a.name = 'Chapter2.FirstCLRRoutine'
  AND f.name like '%.cs'
```

The results should look like your original .NET source file:

```
public partial class FirstCLRRoutines
{
    public static int GetCLRFrameworkMajorVersion()
    {
        return System.Environment.Version.Major;
    }
};

(1 row(s) affected)
```

The most foolproof and easy way to extract both the DLL and the sources files from the metadata back to their original files is to use an SSIS package with an Export Column transformation. This transformation automatically handles dealing with the casting issues associated with binary or blob-typed data. Figure 2-8 shows such a package recreating the original DLL and source files. The package uses the name and content columns to regenerate the original files. See the online code for this chapter at www.wrox.com to download a working SSIS package for this project. Also, see Chapter 6 of *Professional SQL Server 2005 Integration Services*, by Brian Knight, et al. (Wiley, 2006) for more information on using SSIS packages and Export Column transformations. Regardless of which method you use, it is nice to know that you've got recovery options if the original .NET source or DLL is lost or unavailable.

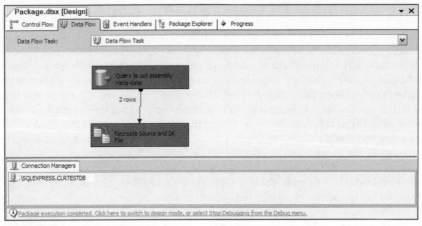

Figure 2-8

Creating Your First CLR User-Defined Function

Many of the examples you find on the Internet and in Books Online show one assembly containing one class object and one method as in the previous example. That is purely for ease of explanation. An assembly can contain many classes, and each class can contain many methods. You may also create many T-SQL objects with different names to implement any one .NET method in an assembly. Earlier, you looked at a decision matrix to determine whether to implement the GetCLRFrameworkMajorVersion method as a stored procedure or a user-defined function. Because this method returns an INT, you determined that either T-SQL object would work. Now you'll implement it again as a SQL CLR user-defined function.

The assembly is already loaded, so you don't need to compile and reload the assembly. You only need to create a T-SQL object that will bind to the GetCLRFrameworkMajorVersion method of the assembly. The DDL is the same as for a normal T-SQL user-defined function with an addition of the EXTERNAL NAME argument. You'll notice that this deviation is similar to what we had to do with the stored procedure. The code to create the user-defined function is here:

```
CREATE FUNCTION [dbo].[mfnGetCLRFrameworkMajorVersion]()
RETURNS [int]
AS
EXTERNAL NAME
[Chapter2.FirstCLRRoutine].[FirstCLRRoutines].[GetCLRFrameworkMajorVersion]
```

To use this new SQL CLR UDF, run the following test query, including the parentheses. The current CLR version is "2." It should be the same for you as well (perhaps higher). If it is not, you may want to revisit the installation portion of this chapter, because SQL Server doesn't allow loading of a CLR Framework below version 2.0.

```
SELECT SqlCLRVersion=[dbo].[mfnGetCLRFrameworkMajorVersion]()
```

The results look like this:

```
SqlCLRVersion
-------------
2
```

If you go back to the Programmability node in the test database Object Explorer, and expand the Stored Procedures node, you'll see the addition of your new CLR function. Since your user-defined function results in a scalar return value (an integer), the function is found under the Scalar-valued Functions node.

Using Visual Studio to Create a CLR Routine

You've built this SQL CLR stored procedure and user-defined function once the hard way, so at this point you should have a good understanding of the mechanics behind the scenes. Now let's move up to life as it was intended. Start your Visual Studio 2005, and wait for the fans to stop humming (this thing uses some resources, doesn't it?). Start a new project by selecting File ⇨ New Project from the Visual Studio menu. In the New Project Wizard on the left in the tree view control, expand the node corresponding to your .NET development language. Select a Database project type and the SQL Server Project template. Your New Project Wizard should look similar to Figure 2-9. Its actual look will depend upon which .NET language you have defined for your default.

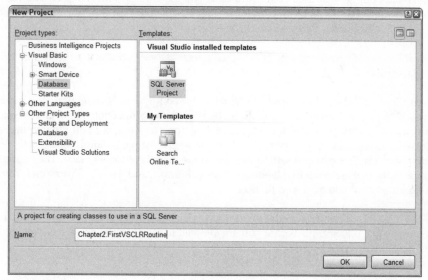

Figure 2-9

Change the name to Chapter2.FirstVSCLRRoutine. Once you provide the name and click OK, you'll be prompted for a SQL Server connection, similar to Figure 2-10.

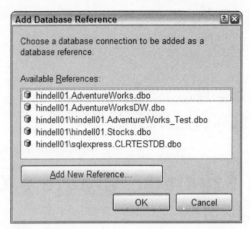

Figure 2-10

CLR Assemblies run in-process with SQL Server 2005, so a connection is not typically needed to access a database when the assembly is used. However, the project does needs the server reference to access the SQL Server during development time to retrieve the assembly and namespace references in the CLR hosted on that server. DBAs can use this fact to lock down SQL Server, so that no SQL CLR development can occur on a server without proper authority. We cover this technique in Chapter 10. The server connection data source is also used for the auto-deployment that makes working in Visual Studio much nicer than hand-coding these SQL CLR routines as you did earlier in this chapter. The database reference also is used in the Server Explorer to enable viewing T-SQL objects and performing queries possible right in the IDE, eliminating the need to use SQL Server Management Studio for most tasks.

> *If you are having trouble connecting to the SQLExpress database engine, try using the convention* `.\SQLExpress`.

If this is the first .NET database project that you have used for a new connection, you may get a prompt asking you if you wish to enable SQL/CLR debugging on the connection. Answer Yes, since this is a good idea while you are in a development phase. Just don't forget to turn off the debugging aspects when you move your DLLs into production. You can easily change the build options by right-clicking on the properties of your project and setting options in the Build and Deploy tabs. The configuration combo box allows for the options of Active (Debug), Debug, Release, and All Configurations. You want this to be set to Release when you go to production.

Visual Studio 2005 is different from the previous versions in that it doesn't automatically require you to save the project to a physical file before you are allowed to work on the project. Save the blank project now into the `c:\prosqlcls\chapter2\` directory.

Creating the Class

When the project is loaded, right click on the project and add a new item of type User-Defined Function. In the dialog that appears, name the class file `GetCLRFrameworkMajorVersion`. Notice that when the class file is created, the template internally creates a class name named `UserDefinedFunctions`. If you add another User-Defined Function class to the project, it would have the same class name too. This is by design. Partial classes enable the Visual Studio IDE to provide code templates for each method individually and then the .NET compiler merges the methods together into one object. This allows for simplicity in programming, since you only need to reference the one merged class, and simplifies sharing production code references across multiple developers on a project.

We don't need partial class support for this projects, so rename this class from UserDefinedFunctions to FirstCLRRoutines for the purposes of matching the class definition of your manual version of the same routine change the return to an int instead of a string. Add the body to the function to return the Major component of the CLR Framework version. The finished C# code should look like this:

```
using System;
using System.Data;
using System.Data.SqlClient;
using System.Data.SqlTypes;
using Microsoft.SqlServer.Server;

public partial class FirstCLRRoutines
{
    [Microsoft.SqlServer.Server.SqlFunction]
    public static int GetCLRFrameworkMajorVersion()
    {
        // Put your code here.
        return System.Environment.Version.Major;
    }
};
```

One thing that is different in this version from your manually created class is the addition of the series of using statements at the top of the class. C# uses a using statement and VB.NET uses the imports statement to create references to external namespaces. If you have ever coded with languages that use include files, this concept will be familiar to you. If you have not, these entries specifically point to code libraries that are intended to be part of your current code. They allow you to refer to the Environment class without having to prefix the class with the System namespace to which the class belongs. We've left this extended reference in the code above to remain consistent to our original manual example. All the rest of the code is the same thing that you had in the manual example. The only other real difference is the additional line above the function declaration.

```
[Microsoft.SqlServer.Server.SqlFunction]
```

This peculiar syntax is known officially as a *function attribute*. You'll also hear it informally referred to as a decoration. The attribute informs Visual Studio and the compiler that this method should be implemented as a SQLFunction. You could restate the attribute as simply [SqlFunction] because the code contains a reference already to the namespace Microsoft.SqlServer.Server in the using statements at the top. Either way, these attributes play an important role in deployment and in performance as they provide something similar to T-SQL Index hints. We'll get into that later, but for now the most important thing this attribute does is enable the auto-deployment processes in Visual Studio to deploy this C# method using the current database connection as a SQL user-defined function.

Deploying the Class

Deployment is where the attribute pays for itself. Previously you had to load the assembly and then create a T-SQL function prototype. This required some knowledge of how to get around with SQL Server Management Studio. To see what this little attribute can do, compile the project by clicking the Build menu and selecting the option to Build or Rebuild the current project. What this does is compile the class object into an assembly just as you did manually in the command window. The next thing you have to do is deploy the assembly. If you want to see what the auto-deployment and build processes are doing for you, click Start ⇨ Programs ⇨ SQL Server 2005 ⇨ Performance Tools ⇨ SQL Profiler and open up the SQL Profiler. Since the SQL Profiler can monitor all T-SQL activity, turning the SQL Profiler on before deploying allows you to monitor the activity of the deployment. Click Build ⇨ Deploy current project to have the automated processes duplicate your manual actions of loading the assembly and creating the T-SQL entry points around the C# methods. The output of the compiler process is:

```
Time Elapsed 00:00:00.15
Drop assembly: Chapter2.FirstVSCLRRoutine.dll ...
------ Deploy started: Project: Chapter2.FirstVSCLRRoutine, Configuration: Debug
Any CPU ------
Deploying file: Chapter2.FirstVSCLRRoutine.dll, Path:
C:\prosqlclr\chapter2\Chapter2.FirstVSCLRRoutine\Chapter2.FirstVSCLRRoutine\obj\
Debug\Chapter2.FirstVSCLRRoutine.dll ...
Deploying file: Chapter2.FirstVSCLRRoutine.pdb, Path:
C:\prosqlclr\chapter2\Chapter2.FirstVSCLRRoutine\Chapter2.FirstVSCLRRoutine\obj\
Debug\Chapter2.FirstVSCLRRoutine.pdb ...
Deploying file: Properties\AssemblyInfo.cs, Path:
C:\prosqlclr\chapter2\Chapter2.FirstVSCLRRoutine\Chapter2.FirstVSCLRRoutine\
Properties\AssemblyInfo.cs ...
========== Build: 1 succeeded or up-to-date, 0 failed, 0 skipped ==========
========== Deploy: 1 succeeded, 0 failed, 0 skipped ==========
```

The important thing to notice here is that the DLL is named using the project name. That's because Visual Studio uses the assembly name when compiling the DLL, and the assembly name defaults to the project name. You can change the name of the assembly by changing the AssemblyTitle property in the AssemblyInfo class in the project. If you had named your project FirstCLRRoutine and method mfnGetCLRFrameworkMajorVersion, which is the same as the manually created assembly, you would have received an error during deployment that looked like the following:

```
Error    1    The assembly module 'mfnGetCLRFrameworkMajorVersion' cannot be re-
deployed because it was created outside of Visual Studio.  Drop the module from the
database before deploying the assembly. Chapter2.FirstCLRRoutine.
```

This is because the assembly FirstCLRRoutine already exists and redeploying that assembly affects a dependency that already exists.

Visual studio also uses that [sqlFunction] attribute with the data connection to deploy the project. To get an idea of what is going on, look at the output in the SQL Profiler, shown in Figure 2-11.

In the highlighted row, Visual Studio executed a CREATE FUNCTION TSQL DDL statement because of the [sqlFunction] .NET function attribute. Notice that unlike the manual example, where you specifically named the function mfnGetCLRFrameworkMajorVersion, Visual Studio simply uses the function name. If you want to maintain any naming standard, those standards will have to extend into your .NET managed source code, so name your methods accordingly.

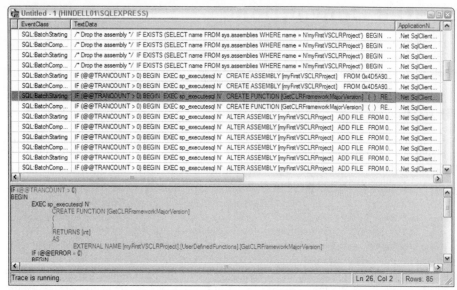

Figure 2-11

What the Auto-Deployment Process Does

Visual Studio's auto-deployment process completed each of the following tasks for you automatically:

- ❑ Checked for an existing assembly and dropped it

- ❑ Created the assembly and loaded the DLL file into SQL metadata

- ❑ Created a T-SQL Function prototype to access our DLL entry point

- ❑ Executed a series of ALTER Assembly statements to load all the files related to the project

This auto-deployment feature is going to provide a productivity boost to the developer that will be repeatedly coding and deploying to a development or a test environment. On one hand, this is great, but on the other hand, just the whole concept of being able to build and deploy to a production server should set off a few alarms. In the real world, thanks to good common sense, and now Sarbanes-Oxley, not many of us will be deploying straight to a production environment. As you may imagine, with the new surface area configuration controls, the DBAs can control the access rights of those who are even allowed to load a piece of .NET into production. It is to your advantage to understand all the mechanics that are going on underneath the covers. To get code in production, you'll have to provide the DLL, the code, and the scripts to a change control role to implement. This was our reasoning for making you go through the manual steps to creating and deploying your first CLR routine. You should now have a pretty good idea of how these parts work together and be able to implement a CLR Routine either by using the Visual Studio Environment or by running manual T-SQL scripts.

Suggested Conventions

We always approach this topic with care when it comes to recommending specific naming or coding conventions, since it much of this type of information is relative to the personal style of the programmer and that varies widely. We'll explain what we are using, and you can take it from there.

Assemblies

Name your assemblies the same as your namespace using Pascal case, no underscores. Use your company name. Visual Studio creates the assembly name as the .NET project name by default. This is important because as you increase the number of managed code assemblies you will be able to find things intuitively, because you are following the architecture of the development .NET assemblies.

Classes

Leave the managed code class names as they are auto-generated, unless you have some managed code assemblies with more than 10 public methods. Otherwise you'll have to remember to change the class name each time you generate a new class. Visual Studio by default creates partial classes with the names `StoredProcedures`, `UserDefinedFunctions`, and `Triggers`. These are descriptive enough, unless you have more than 10 of each.

If you do decide to specifically name your classes, use Pascal case, no underscores, or leading characters like "c" or "cls" to designate that this is a class. Classes should also not have the same name as the namespaces to which they belong. Remember also to rename the template-created class to be consistent if you create more than one class. Otherwise, you'll have a class with your custom name and a class using the Visual Studio default name.

Structures

Visual Studio doesn't provide any good names for structures like user-defined aggregates or types. These should follow the rules for classes and should be descriptive of what they represent.

Class and Structure Functions or Methods

Visual Studio auto-deploys class methods as T-SQL objects using the method name. Our suggestion here is to name your functions and methods keeping that in mind. Although it is easy to look at the dependencies of a T-SQL object to determine whether the object is based on a CLR assembly or if it is a T-SQL coded object, naming your CLR objects with a prefix of "m" makes the determination immediately visible. If your method is intended to be a user-defined function, prefix the method with something like "mfn". Prefix stored procedure methods with "msp". Prefix triggers methods with "mtg".

SQL CLR Object Type	Object Name

User-Defined Functions	`mfnCalculateFutureValue`
	`mfnGetEmployees`
	`mfnIsValidEmail`

SQL CLR Object Type	Object Name

Stored Procedures	`mspProcessLockboxUnmatched`
	`mspMakeHtmlListofManagedRoutines`
	`mspIndustryGroupsShowTop30`

The main reason we like naming these T-SQL definitions using these conventions is that it is difficult for DBAs, when troubleshooting issues in production, to determine at a glance whether the object is built with T-SQL or .NET. Although as you can see in Figure 2-12, the SQL CLR stored procedures get a special icon to indicate that they are .NET-based, but the SQL CLR UDFs are not indicated in any special way.

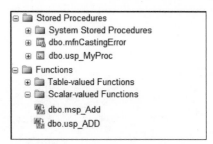

Figure 2-12

However, it is easy if you have a consistent naming convention to look in the object explorer in SMSS to determine that the `msp_Add` object is a managed code or SQL CLR UDF and the `usp_Add` object is a T-SQL version of the same function. Until someone comes up with a way to put different icons on all the objects, or adds the ability to right-click on any object and script the implementation details into a query window, regardless of whether that code is in .NET or T-SQL, you are going to need a quick way to identify them on sight.

Removing SQL CLR Objects

Removing the good work that you have done is also part of the development lifecycle. Unfortunately, there is no Visual Studio wizard to help with this task. Basically you have either use the right-click options in the Object Explorer or grab an open query window in SSMS connected to the database that you deployed the assembly and code some T-SQL. Before you do either, you need to know the impact of removing the assembly.

Reviewing Assembly Dependencies

Having more than one dependent SQL object bound to an assembly could cause some unintended consequences if you removed an assembly. Because the CLR routines are implemented through T-SQL object prototypes, SQL Server treats them as if they are T-SQL objects, and they are. This means that the dependency relationships are also stored in the metadata for each database, like regular T-SQL objects. To verify this, in the SQL Management Studio Object Explorer, right-click on the Chapter2.FirstCLRRoutine assembly icon under the programmability node in your test database and select View Dependencies. You should see a form similar to the one shown in Figure 2-13.

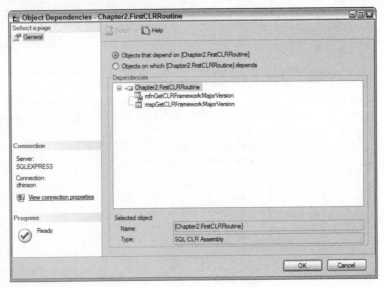

Figure 2-13

This object dependencies view is also made available through a Show Dependencies button if you attempt to delete an Assembly. The ability to wire these SQL CLR routines into the same infrastructure as the T-SQL objects keeps the administration burden familiar, so you can continue to troubleshoot as you would normally.

Dropping an Assembly

To delete an assembly, you must first walk backward through the installation process before you can remove an assembly that has any T-SQL object or references. The steps are simple:

1. Drop any T-SQL object definitions or entry points that are using the assembly.

2. Drop the assembly. This is as simple as issuing the following T-SQL command:

```
DROP ASSEMBLY Chapter2.FirstCLRRoutine
```

Both of these actions will remove all metadata in SQL Server.

Summary

In this chapter, we took an approach of breaking down the process of mechanically building a CLR routine to explore how you can create managed code and host that code in a SQL Server environment. In the process, we've covered how to approach building a basic class both using the low-tech Notepad environment and using Visual Studio 2005. The idea was to help you understand all the great things that the auto-build-and-deployment processes are doing underneath the covers. We first built a basic assembly from the class and then created two separate T-SQL implementations of the one .NET method. We built both a basic stored procedure and a user-defined function, and then peeked under the covers in the SQL Server meta-data to see how the managed routines are implemented. We hope that you feel up to speed on these basic mechanics of using SQL CLR. Now that you've got the basics down, continue to Chapter 3 to get some practical examples and to dig into the details of security and other aspects of SQL CLR development that we were not able to cover in this quick overview.

3

SQL CLR Structure and Common Tasks

In Chapter 1, we provided you with a solid foundation in CLR and SQL CLR architecture, as well as introducing you to the supported objects you can create using SQL CLR technology. In Chapter 2, you saw the first two examples of SQL CLR objects via a managed stored procedure and function (using a standard text editor as well as Visual Studio 2005). You should now have a good foundation in the basics of SQL CLR. In this chapter, we'll introduce you to the structure of SQL CLR code and teach you how to perform a variety of common tasks in those objects. You'll learn how to detect whether SQL CLR is available and how to perform data access, return result sets, and implement transactions.

SQL CLR Code Structure

SQL CLR objects can be divided into two categories based on code structure. The first category is the objects that are implemented as public, static methods (or shared methods, in Visual Basic.NET), which you saw in Chapter 2. This category includes functions, stored procedures, and triggers. As we mentioned in the previous chapter, because these objects use partial classes, you can choose to either create multiple SQL CLR objects in a single class file or use a separate partial class files for each object. The following code demonstrates how you can create two stored procedures in the same C# class file:

```csharp
public partial class StoredProcedures
{
    [Microsoft.SqlServer.Server.SqlProcedure(Name="uspInsertCustomer")]
    public static void uspInsertCustomer()
    {
        // Put your code here
    }
```

```
    [Microsoft.SqlServer.Server.SqlProcedure(Name = "uspUpdateCustomer")]
    public static void uspUpdateCustomer()
    {
        // Put your code here
    }
};
```

The second category of SQL CLR objects are those that are implemented as entire classes. This category of objects includes user-defined aggregates and types.

Type is short and synonymous for data type. A type in SQL Server is always a "value type," that is, you declare a variable of that type and then use it. In Microsoft .NET, a type can be either a value type or a "reference type." In .NET, value types work much the same that they do in SQL Server; however, reference types must be instantiated first and should also be "cleaned up" after you're done using them. In a nutshell, you can think of value types as traditional data types and reference types as classes in an object-oriented platform. Under the hood of .NET's CLR, every type is implemented as a class, but to the user (programmer) a subset of them appears to behave as a traditional data type.

When you're programming the class-based objects, you will have to create several required methods based upon which SQL CLR object you are creating. For example, if you are creating an aggregate, you must ensure that your class meets the aggregation contract. In a nutshell, the aggregation contract consists of four methods that you must define, Init(), Accumulate(), Merge(), and Terminate(). What follows is the aggregate template:

```
[Serializable]
[Microsoft.SqlServer.Server.SqlUserDefinedAggregate(Format.Native)]
public struct uda_Template
{
    public void Init()
    {
        // Put your code here
    }

    public void Accumulate(SqlString Value)
    {
        // Put your code here
    }

    public void Merge(uda_Template Group)
    {
        // Put your code here
    }

    public SqlString Terminate()
    {
        // Put your code here
        return new SqlString("");
    }

    // This is a place-holder member field
    private int var1;

}
```

For user-defined types (UDTs) you must create a public static (shared) Null() method, a public static (shared) Parse() method, a public ToString() method, and the class must contain a default public constructor that has no arguments (because overrides are allowed to accept parameters). The UDT must provide data items as public fields and properties. In addition, the maximum serialized size of a UDT must no exceed 8,000 bytes.

The following is the UDT template:

```
[Serializable]
[Microsoft.SqlServer.Server.SqlUserDefinedType(Format.Native)]
public struct udt_Template : INullable
{
    public override string ToString()
    {
        // Replace the following code with your code
        return "";
    }

    public bool IsNull
    {
        get
        {
            // Put your code here
            return m_Null;
        }
    }

    public static udt_Template Null
    {
        get
        {
            udt_Template h = new udt_Template();
            h.m_Null = true;
            return h;
        }
    }

    public static udt_Template Parse(SqlString s)
    {
        if (s.IsNull)
            return Null;
        udt_Template u = new udt_Template();
        // Put your code here
        return u;
    }

    // This is a place-holder method
    public string Method1()
    {
        //Insert method code here
        return "Hello";
    }

    // This is a place-holder static method
```

```
public static SqlString Method2()
{
    //Insert method code here
    return new SqlString("Hello");
}

// This is a place-holder field member
public int var1;
// Private member
private bool m_Null;
}
```

SQL CLR Common Tasks

Now that you are familiar with the structure of SQL CLR routines, we need to discuss the code you will be writing inside these structures. There are virtually an unlimited number of tasks you could perform in SQL CLR routines, but we have identified the most common ones:

❑ Using SQL CLR data type classes

❑ Detecting SQL CLR availability

❑ Performing data access

❑ Returning resultsets and messages

❑ Programming transactions

Using SQL CLR Data Type Classes

When you first start creating SQL CLR routines, more than likely you will use the native CLR types. In case you are not aware of these types, Microsoft .NET has several "base" data types, like all major programming platforms. These "base" types reside in the System namespace; thus, to declare a variable of type string you would reference the System.String class. This concept works just fine except for the "minor" issue that CLR and SQL Server types are quite different. NULLvalues, precision, and overflows are some of the major differences between native CLR types and SQL Server types.

Because of these differences between the two platforms, there is a new namespace called SqlTypes that belongs to the System.Data assembly. When you are storing data into variables that are either originating from or destined to go into SQL Server, you should use the classes found in this namespace. In addition, if you use the native CLR types, they will be implicitly converted to their corresponding SqlTypes class, thus producing a performance penalty. In short, use the types found in the SqlTypes namespace for your SQL CLR routines, except for those variables that will not be used to interact with SQL Server.

NULL Values

One of the biggest differences between the native CLR types and SQL Server types is that SQL Server types support the notion of a NULL value. Every SqlType class has an IsNull property, which can be used in your code to detect if the variable or parameter contains a NULL value. Also, be aware that you cannot directly assign the value of NULL to a SqlType in managed code.

To demonstrate this, try to return the result of a compare operation between an input of type `SqlInt32` and the value of 1 without calling the `IsNull` property. You will be passing in a NULL value to the procedure. The result of executing it in SQL Server Management Studio is shown in Figure 3-1.

```
public partial class StoredProcedures
{
    [Microsoft.SqlServer.Server.SqlProcedure]
    public static void usp_SqlTypesNull(SqlInt32 oInt)
    {
        SqlContext.Pipe.Send(Convert.ToString((oInt.Value == 1)));
    }
};
```

Figure 3-1

This time, you'll need to check the parameter's `IsNull` property before you attempt to evaluate its value.

```
public partial class StoredProcedures
{
    [Microsoft.SqlServer.Server.SqlProcedure]
    public static void usp_SqlTypesNull(SqlInt32 oInt)
    {
        if (oInt.IsNull == false)
        {
            SqlContext.Pipe.Send(Convert.ToString((oInt.Value == 1)));
```

```
        }
        else
        {
            SqlContext.Pipe.Send("INPUT WAS NULL");
        }
    }
};
```

This code returns results that look like Figure 3-2.

Figure 3-2

SqlTypes versus SqlDbType

There is an enumeration called SqlDbType that resides in the System.Data namespace. This enumeration contains members that also represent the types found in SQL Server. An *enumeration* in .NET is a set of related constants contained in an enumerator list. Every constant defined in the enumerator list is known as an *enumerator member*. The enumerator members map to types and their values. Enumerations are useful data structures because they provide the developer with a mechanism to logically group together related types and values.

So, when should you use the SqlTypes and the SqlDbTypes? Use the SqlDbType members exclusively for SqlParameter type declarations. For all other SQL Server interactions, use the classes found in the SqlTypes namespaces. The following example demonstrates how to use both the SqlTypes and the SqlDbType members.

```
public partial class StoredProcedures
{
    //proc takes an input of type SqlInt32
    [Microsoft.SqlServer.Server.SqlProcedure]
    public static void usp_SqlTypesVsSqlDbTypes(SqlInt32 iID)
    {
        using (SqlConnection oConn =
            new SqlConnection("context connection=true"))
        {
            SqlCommand oCmd =
                new SqlCommand("SELECT * FROM " +
                "Production.ProductCategory " +
                "WHERE ProductCategoryID = @ID", oConn);
            oCmd.Parameters.Add("@ID", SqlDbType.Int).Value = iID;
            oConn.Open();
            SqlContext.Pipe.ExecuteAndSend(oCmd);
            oConn.Close();
        }
    }
};
```

Handling Large Objects

If you need to pass a large object (LOB) from SQL Server to a SQL CLR routine, you should use the SqlBytes or SqlChars classes. The SqlBytes class maps to the varbinary(max) data type in SQL Server, and the SqlChars type maps to the nvarchar(max) type in SQL Server. These SqlTypes allow you to stream the large values from SQL Server to the hosted CLR as opposed to copying the entire value into the CLR space.

Detecting SQL CLR Availability

If you are writing managed code explicitly for SQL Server, detecting SQL CLR availability is pointless, but if you are writing classes that will be used both inside and outside SQL Server, you can reference the IsAvailable property of the SQLContext object. IsAvailable, returns a boolean value indicating if the managed code is being hosted by SQL Server or not. A *property* is a characteristic of a class (or object) that it belongs to. If you have created a car class, Color would be a candidate for a property. In .NET, properties can be read-only, write-only, or both (the default and most common).

For example, in-process connections (which we'll discuss in the next section) are not available to managed code running natively. The following example shows how you can use the IsAvailable property. This code detects to see if CLR is available:

```
public partial class StoredProcedures
{
    [Microsoft.SqlServer.Server.SqlProcedure]
    public static void uspIsAvailable()
    {
        //is code hosted by SQL Server?
        if (SqlContext.IsAvailable == true)
        {
            using (SqlConnection oConn = new
                SqlConnection("context connection=true"))
```

```
        {
            //perform work
        }
    }
    else
    {
        using (SqlConnection oConn =
            new SqlConnection("Data Source=.;" +
                "InitialCatalog=AdventureWorks;" +
                "Integrated Security=True;"))
        {
            //perform work
        }
    }
};
```

Take a look at the `if` statement from this code:

```
if (SqlContext.IsAvailable == true)
```

If the `SqlContext.IsAvailable` property returns `true`, you know that your code is being hosted by SQL Server, and you can specify the connection with `"context connection=true"`, which we'll discuss in the next section . If not, you use code in the `else` block, where you'll have to specify the connection parameters.

Performing Data Access

When you create your SQL CLR objects, you are going to need to access the hosting SQL Server and potentially additional data sources. Accessing the hosting SQL Server is known as an *in-process connection* because the connection is to the database engine that is running in the same process. If you require access to external data sources, for the most part, you will accomplish this is the same manner that you always have from managed code; however, be aware there are security implications you must consider, which we'll cover in Chapter 10.

In-Process Connections

One of the first questions people have about the SQL CLR technology is how does it access the hosting SQL Server and is it faster than a typical client database connection? To connect to a hosting SQL Server from a SQL CLR routine, you simply assign a string value of `"context connection=true"` to the SQLConnection class's connection string property. When you use an in-process connection you are implying that all data access be wrapped in the same transaction as the calling code, use the same set options, temporary object availability and so on.

```
public partial class StoredProcedures
{
    [Microsoft.SqlServer.Server.SqlProcedure]
    public static void uspContextConnection()
    {
        using (SqlConnection oConn =
            new SqlConnection("context connection=true"))
```

```
        {
            SqlCommand oCmd = new SqlCommand("SELECT * FROM " +
                "HumanResources.Employee", oConn);
            oConn.Open();
            SqlContext.Pipe.ExecuteAndSend(oCmd);
            oConn.Close();
        }
    }
};
```

Notice the new connection string value we used:

```
using (SqlConnection oConn = new SqlConnection("context connection=true"))
```

When you pass in a string value of `context connection=true` or `context connection=yes` you are stating that you wish to use an in-process connection.

The traditional database connection carries with it some "weight," which is the protocol and transport layer. In-process connections bypass all of this overhead and connect directly to the hosting database engine. So yes, in-process connections are faster than a traditional client database connection.

Accessing External Resources

SQL CLR code will always execute under the security context of the SQL Server service account, by default. While this is fine for in-process connections, it is not fine when you want to access external resources. You have two options for accessing external resources from a security perspective. You can simply assign permissions for the external resource to the SQL Server service account and then access the resource under the default security context. This solution is not a "best practice" and should only be used as a last resort as opposed to the second solution: You can impersonate the caller's identity and attempt access under that user's security context .

> SQL CLR assemblies requiring impersonation must be assigned either the EXTERNAL_ACCESS OR UNSAFE permission set.

When you use impersonation in your SQL CLR routines, you use the `SqlContext.WindowsIdentity` property to obtain the current security context. You will then call the identity's `Impersonate` method to begin security impersonation. The following code demonstrates this concept by connecting to a local SQL Server Express instance. Notice that you must call the Identity's `Undo` method, which stops impersonation, before returning the results back to the client via the `SqlContext.Pipe.Send` method, which we'll discuss in the next section. If you do not call `Undo()` before returning results back to the client, a runtime error will be thrown when you attempt to execute the routine.

You may notice that in the following example we make use of the `try/catch/finally` syntax. In .NET (SQL Server 2005 now has its own implentation of these statements too, discussed in Chapter 9) you place all of your code in the `try` block, your exception handling code goes in the `catch` block, and any code you wish to always execute regardless of whether or not an error occurs should go into the `finally` block. If you use the `try/catch/finally` syntax in a SQL CLR routine, you should use the `System.Data.SqlClient.SqlException` class as the type for the exception in the `catch` block's paranthesis. In typical .NET development, you would use the `System.Exception` class instead.

We also use the `ToString()` method in the following example. .NET is an advanced object-oriented development platform. Its Base Class Library is built in a hierarchical manner where there are lower-level classes that other classes are built upon in turn. `System.Object` is the ultimate base (low-level) class in the .NET Base Class Library. Every class in the Base Class Library is ultimatly based upon it. Without going into more advanced object-oriented concepts such as inheritence, in a nutshell, the `System.Object` class contains a method called `ToString()`, which means that all "consuming" (high-level) classes also have the same method.

```
public partial class StoredProcedures
{
    [Microsoft.SqlServer.Server.SqlProcedure()]
    public static void usp_ExternalConnection()
    {
        WindowsIdentity newIdentity = null;
        WindowsImpersonationContext newContext = null;

        try
        {
            //impersonate the caller
            newIdentity = SqlContext.WindowsIdentity;
            newContext = newIdentity.Impersonate();

            if (newContext != null)
            {
                using (SqlConnection oConn =
                    new SqlConnection("Server=.\\sqlexpress;" +
                        "Integrated Security=true;"))
                {
                    SqlCommand oCmd = new SqlCommand("SELECT * FROM " +
                        "AdventureWorks.HumanResources.Employee", oConn);
                    oConn.Open();
                    SqlDataReader oRead =
                        oCmd.ExecuteReader(CommandBehavior.CloseConnection);

                    //revent security context
                    newContext.Undo();

                    //return results
                    SqlContext.Pipe.Send(oRead);
                }
            }
            else
            {
                throw new Exception("user impersonation has failed");
            }
        }
        catch (SqlException ex)
        {
            SqlContext.Pipe.Send(ex.Message.ToString());
        }
        finally
        {
            if (newContext != null)
            {
```

```
                    newContext.Undo();
                }
            }
        }
    };
```

Returning Resultsets and Messages

The SqlContext object represents the context of the caller. You have already seen a few examples of this object in this chapter, specifically, its Pipe property that returns resultsets back to the caller, and its WindowsIdentity property that returns the caller's current security context. In this section, we are going to focus on the most useful aspect of the SqlContext object, is the returning of resultsets and messages to the client. The SqlPipe object facilitates returning of results back to the client. You can access the SqlPipe by referencing the SqlContext.Pipe property.

In .NET, a method is said to be *overloaded* when it has more than one signature for a method. A *signature* in turn is the combination of a method's parameter types and inputs or outputs. This means that you have two different methods with the same name, but different parameters, and the two methods might do very different things. Overloading a class's method can be beneficial because it allows the developer to specify different sets of parameters. The following is a simple class that contains an overloaded method called Add().

```
namespace chapter3
{
    public class clsMath
    {
        static public int add(int iFirstNum, int iSecondNum)
        {
            return (iFirstNum + iSecondNum);
        }

        static public int add(int iFirstNum, int iSecondNum, int iThirdNum)
        {
            return(iFirstNum + iSecondNum + iThirdNum);
        }
    }
}
```

The SqlPipe has three overloaded methods of the Send() method, as follows:

```
void Send(SqlDataReader reader)
void Send(SqlDataRecord record)
void Send(string message)
```

We will use the third overload to create the famous "hello world" example. This third overload sends a simple string message. Here is "hello world" in SQL CLR:

```
public partial class StoredProcedures
{
    [Microsoft.SqlServer.Server.SqlProcedure]
    public static void uspHelloWorld()
    {
```

```
        SqlContext.Pipe.Send("hello world from SQL CLR");
    }
};
```

If you run this code in SQL Server Management Studio, you should see results similar to those in
Figure 3-3.

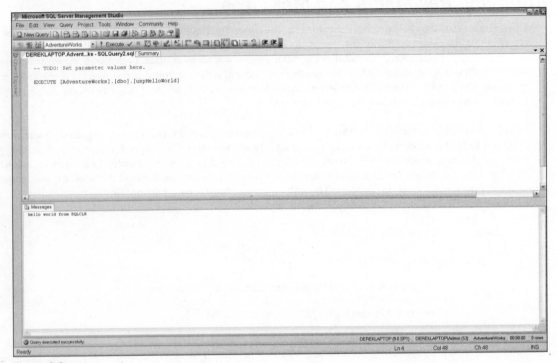

Figure 3-3

The second overload of the `Pipe.Send()` method is important because it represents performing a unique
task in your SQL CLR routines, to create and return dynamic records. You use the `SqlDataRecord` class
in conjunction with the `SqlMetaData` class to return dynamic resultsets in SQL CLR routines. Before we
show you an example of using these classes, we'll discuss them.

To enable constructing records and returning them in your SQL CLR routines, you need a mechanism
that represents the attributes of a given row and its columns. This is where the `SqlMetaData` class
comes into play. You use the `SqlMetaData` class to describe a single column in a row, and thus an array
of `SqlMetaData` objects represents a record.

Arrays are a simple data structures (or data type) used in modern programming platforms, including .NET.
Arrays store the same type of data in concurrent locations within itself that are referenced by an Index. So,
using the car class example, you could create an array to store several instances of your car class.

We are not going to explore every property of the `SqlMetaData` class, but a few of the more common ones
are `DbType`, `Max`, and `Name`. There are also two public methods in the `SqlMetaData` class. The `Adjust()`
method is used for changing a `SqlMetaData` object to accommodate a value that was assigned to it. There

is also the `InferFromValue()` method that is used to instantiate a new instance of the `SqlMetaData` class from it's supplied parameter. We will be using the `InferFromValue()` method in the example below because it provides a very easy way to create a new instance of the `SqlMetaData` class.

The second class that enables dynamic resultsets is the `SqlDataRecord`. `SqlDataRecord` objects can contain only one record. The `SqlDataRecord` class contains two public properties and several public methods. The two properties are read-only, `FieldCount` and `Item`. `FieldCount` is self-explanatory as it returns the number of columns in the record. Item returns the value of the column that you pass into it either using an index location or the column name. While the `SqlDataRecord` does contain several public methods, there are a handful that you are going to use a lot, specifically the `Get_DataType()` and `Set_DataType()` methods. In the following example, we use the `GetInt32()` method to return the field's value as a 32-bit integer.

```
public partial class Chapter3
{
    [Microsoft.SqlServer.Server.SqlProcedure()]
    public static void uspSqlDataRecord_SetGet()
    {
        try
        {
            //declare local variables
            int i = 0;
            string sFirstName = "Douglas";

            //create metadata via InferFromValue() method
            SqlMetaData oMetaID = SqlMetaData.InferFromValue(i, "ID");
            SqlMetaData oMetaFirstName =
                SqlMetaData.InferFromValue(sFirstName, "FirstName");
            SqlMetaData[] oMetaArray =
                new SqlMetaData[] { oMetaID, oMetaFirstName };

            //create model row, used for the SendResultsStart() method
            SqlDataRecord oModelRow =
                new SqlDataRecord(oMetaArray);

            //create records
            SqlDataRecord oFirstRecord =
                new SqlDataRecord(oMetaArray);
            oFirstRecord.SetSqlInt32(0, 1);
            oFirstRecord.SetSqlString(1, "Derek");

            SqlDataRecord oSecondRecord =
                new SqlDataRecord(oMetaArray);
            oSecondRecord.SetSqlInt32(0, 2);
            oSecondRecord.SetSqlString(1, "Douglas");

            SqlContext.Pipe.Send(oFirstRecord.GetInt32(0).ToString());
            SqlContext.Pipe.Send(oFirstRecord.GetSqlString(1).ToString());
        }
        catch (SqlException ex)
        {
            //return exception message
            SqlContext.Pipe.Send(ex.Message.ToString());
        }
    }
};
```

The result of this code should look like Figure 3-4.

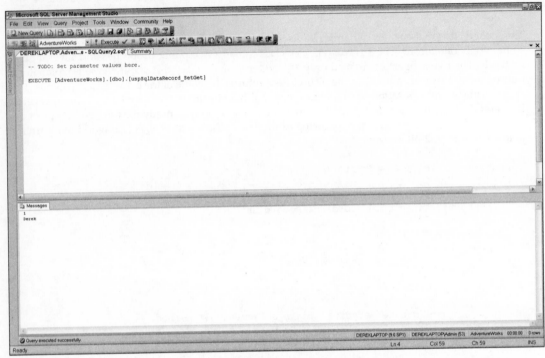

Figure 3-4

The final method you have for returning messages and resultsets is the pipe's `ExecuteAndSend()` method. This method takes an input of type `SqlCommand`. The `SqlCommand` class resides in the `System.Data.SqlClient` namespace, thus its fully-qualified location in the Framework is `System.Data.SqlClient.SqlCommand`. The `SqlCommand` class represents a T-SQL statement or stored procedure to execute against a Microsoft SQL Server. You can only use the `ExecuteAndSend()` method with command objects that are using an in-process connection. In the following sample, we create an instance of the `SqlCommand` class, assign it a T-SQL query, and execute it using an in-process connection.

> *As discussed in Chapter 2, in .NET a namespace is a logical grouping of related classes. In Chapter 7, you'll see how the Base Class Library is physically implemented by several "system" assemblies (.dlls) which are logically are organized into namespaces. You can also create your own user-defined namespaces to arrange your .NET routines into more logical collections.*

```
public partial class Chapter3
{
    [Microsoft.SqlServer.Server.SqlProcedure()]
    public static void uspSqlPipe_ExecuteAndSend()
    {
        using (SqlConnection oConn =
            new SqlConnection("context connection=true"))
        {
            try
```

```
        {
            //open in-process connection
            oConn.Open();

            //initialize command
            SqlCommand oCmd = new SqlCommand(
            "SELECT LoginID, Title FROM HumanResources.Employee" +
            " WHERE SalariedFlag = 0;", oConn);

            //execute command and return results
            SqlContext.Pipe.ExecuteAndSend(oCmd);
        }
        catch (SqlException ex)
        {
            //return exception message
            SqlContext.Pipe.Send(ex.Message.ToString());
        }
        finally
        {
            oConn.Close();
        }
    }
  }
};
```

This code returns results that look like Figure 3-5.

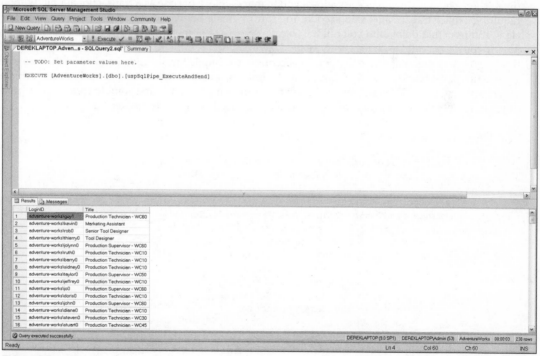

Figure 3-5

Programming Transactions

The System.Transaction namespace is new in the .NET 2.0 Framework. Although transactions have a scope beyond that of SQL CLR, they do play a role in the technology. Probably the most common use of the transactions namespace in SQL CLR routines is to mark blocks of code as an implicit transaction. In general, you should favor implicit transactions in your SQL CLR routines, but we will cover how to create both implicit and explicit transactions in this section.

Implicit Transactions

If you intend to use the TransactionScope class (or any other class in the System.Transactions namespace), you must manually add a reference to the System.Transactions assembly in your SQL CLR projects. When you create a new database project in Visual Studio, the System.Transactions assembly is not referenced by default. Once you've done that, you can begin to create implicit transactions.

To manually add a reference in your SQL CLR projects, perform the following tasks:

1. Display Solution Explorer by selecting View/Solution Explorer from the menu.
2. Right-Click on the References node and select Add Reference.
3. Under the default tab of SQL Server, you should see System.Transactions listed; select it and click on the OK button.

You'll often want blocks of code to either fully commit or roll back, a feature that is also known as atomicity. The easiest way to accomplish this is to employ the TransactionScope class in your SQL CLR routines. The TransactionScope class allows you to mark a block of code as a transactional unit, without requiring explicit transaction creation code. You simply create a new instance of the TransactionScope class, and from that point until you call the object's Complete() method, all code forms one transactional unit. If you do not call the Complete() method, an exception is thrown. Furthermore, once you do call the Complete() method, if an exception has occurred, the implicit transaction is rolled back. If no exception occurred, the transaction is committed. In the following code, a transaction named oTran is created to wrap two separate T-SQL statements into one logical transaction. We first want to create a new product category for mobile devices, and we then wish to create a subcategory for PocketPCs.

```
public partial class StoredProcedures
{
    [Microsoft.SqlServer.Server.SqlProcedure]
    public static void uspSimpleTransactionScope()
    {
        //create an instance of the TransactionScope class
        TransactionScope oTran = new TransactionScope();

        using (SqlConnection oConn =
            new SqlConnection("context connection=true;"))
        {
            try
            {
                //open inprocess connection
                oConn.Open();

                //first step of transaction
                SqlCommand oCmd =
```

```
                new SqlCommand("INSERT Production.ProductCategory " +
                  "([Name]) SELECT 'Mobile Devices'", oConn);
                oCmd.ExecuteNonQuery();

                //second step of transaction
                oCmd.CommandText = "INSERT " +
                  "Production.ProductSubcategory SELECT " +
                  "ProductCategoryID,'PocketPCs',NewID(),GetDate() " +
                  "FROM Production.ProductCategory " +
                  "WHERE [Name] = 'Mobile Devices'";
                oCmd.ExecuteNonQuery();
            }
            catch (SqlException ex)
            {
                //display error message
                SqlContext.Pipe.Send(ex.Message.ToString());
            }
            finally
            {
                //commit or rollback the transaction
                oTran.Complete();

                oConn.Close();
            }
        }
    }
    //clean up transaction object
    oTran.Dispose();
    }
};
```

You should always ensure that you call the `Dispose()` method when you are finished using the `TransactionScope` object, because the `Dispose()` method marks the end of the transaction's scope. To help ensure that you always call the `Dispose()` method, Microsoft recommends that you create your `TransactionScope` objects in a `using` construct. In the following code, we have changed the structure of the code to implement the `using` statement for the `TransactionScope` class.

```
public partial class StoredProcedures
{
    [Microsoft.SqlServer.Server.SqlProcedure]
    public static void uspSimpleTransactionScope()
    {
        //create an instance of the TransactionScope class
        using (TransactionScope oTran = new TransactionScope())
        {
            using (SqlConnection oConn =
                new SqlConnection("context connection=true;"))
            {
                try
                {
                    //open inprocess connection
                    oConn.Open();

                    //first step of transaction
                    SqlCommand oCmd =
```

```
                        new SqlCommand("INSERT " +
                        "Production.ProductCategory " +
                        "([Name]) SELECT 'Mobile Devices'", oConn);
                    oCmd.ExecuteNonQuery();

                    //second step of transaction
                    oCmd.CommandText = "INSERT " +
                        "Production.ProductSubcategory SELECT " +
                        "ProductCategoryID,'PocketPCs',NewID()" +
                        ",GetDate() FROM Production.ProductCategory " +
                        "WHERE [Name] = 'Mobile Devices'";
                    oCmd.ExecuteNonQuery();
                }
                catch (SqlException ex)
                {
                    //display error message
                    SqlContext.Pipe.Send(ex.Message.ToString());
                }
                finally
                {
                    //commit or rollback the transaction
                    oTran.Complete();

                    oConn.Close();
                }
            }
        }
    }
};
```

Implicit Transaction Promoting

When you use the `TransactionScope` class in SQL CLR, routines, the code is executed as a local transaction. By default, if you were to open a second database connection to a remote server, the transaction would automatically be promoted to a fully distributed transaction (which uses more system resources). This concept of automatic transaction promotion is advantageous because your transactions stay "light" unless they need to become fully distributed. In the following code we promote our implicit transaction by opening a second, remote database connection.

Distributed Transactions require the Microsoft Distributed Transaction Coordinator (MSDTC) service to be running on the host machine.

```
public partial class StoredProcedures
{
    [Microsoft.SqlServer.Server.SqlProcedure]
    public static void usp_Distributed_Transaction()
    {
        using (TransactionScope oTran =
            new TransactionScope())
        {
            using (SqlConnection oConn =
                new SqlConnection("context connection=true"))
            {
                using (SqlConnection oRemoteConn =
```

```csharp
                new SqlConnection("Data Source=.\\sqlexpress;" +
                    "Initial Catalog=AdventureWorks;" +
                    "Integrated Security=True"))
        {
            try
            {
                //open the connection
                oConn.Open();
                oRemoteConn.Open();

                //define command objects
                SqlCommand oCmd =
                    new SqlCommand("INSERT " +
                        "Production.ProductCategory " +
                        "([Name]) SELECT 'Pen Drives'"
                        , oConn);
                SqlCommand oRemoteCmd =
                    new SqlCommand("INSERT " +
                        "Production.ProductCategory " +
                        "([Name]) SELECT 'Pen Drives'"
                        , oRemoteConn);

                //fire off commands
                oCmd.ExecuteNonQuery();
                oRemoteCmd.ExecuteNonQuery();
            }
            catch (SqlException ex)
            {
                //display error message
                SqlContext.Pipe.Send(ex.Message.ToString());
            }
            finally
            {
                //commit or rollback the transaction
                oTran.Complete();

                oConn.Close();
                oRemoteConn.Close();
            }
        }
    }
  }
 }
};
```

If you do not want the remote server's connection enlisted in the current transaction (thus promoting it) you can use the Enlist keyword in the remote server's connection string. Enlist is set to true by default, so you need to explicitly use the keyword only if you want it turned off. The server must be remote; you cannot use the Enlist keyword with a context connection.

```csharp
using (SqlConnection oRemoteConn =
    new SqlConnection("Data Source=.;Initial Catalog=AdventureWorks;" +
    "Integrated Security=True;Enlist=false;"))
{
}
```

TransactionScope Options

A *constructor* is a special method of a class used for creating an instance (or object) of it. A class's constructor must have the same name as the owning class. Constructors can be overloaded, and if a constructor has no arguments, it is called a default constructor. You will typically perform any initialization work in a class's constructor such as assigning variables initial values. The constructor of the `TransactionScope` object can optionally take an input of type `TransactionScopeOption`. You can use the `TransactionScopeOption` enumeration for specifying how you want your new implicit transaction to treat any current transactions, otherwise known as an *ambient transaction*. There are three options available as represented by the enumeration's members.

- ❏ `Required`: This is the default; the new transaction joins an ambient transaction if it exists; or else creates a new transaction.

- ❏ `RequiresNew`: Always creates a new transaction.

- ❏ `Suppress`: Does not participate in an ambient transaction if it exists, and it does not create a new transaction.

The following code sample shows a nested `TransactionScope` example, with the second `TransactionScope` creating a new transaction context even though it is inside of a parent transaction.

```
//first transaction
using (TransactionScope oOuterTran = new TransactionScope())
{
    try
    {
        using (SqlConnection oConn = new SqlConnection("context
                                                    connection=true"))
        {
            //perform first transaction's work
            oConn.Open();
            SqlCommand oCmd = new SqlCommand("insert Production.ProductCategory
                                ([Name]) select 'Monitors'", oConn);
            SqlContext.Pipe.ExecuteAndSend(oCmd);

            //second transaction
            using (TransactionScope oInnerTran = new
                    TransactionScope(TransactionScopeOption.RequiresNew))
        }
    }
}
```

Setting TransactionScope Timeout

Several of the `TransactionScope` class's overloaded constructors include a `timeout` parameter. You can use any of the `TimeSpan` class's static "From" methods to specify a timeout in your choice of time interval. Setting a timeout on your transactions can be useful when you are performing work with resources that may be used concurrently by other entities; the timeout will prevent waiting for long periods of time or deadlocks. In the following code we purposely exceed the explicit timeout setting which results in an exception being thrown.

```
public partial class StoredProcedures
{
    [Microsoft.SqlServer.Server.SqlProcedure]
```

```
public static void uspTransactionScopeTimeout()
{
    using (TransactionScope oTran =
        new TransactionScope(TransactionScopeOption.Required,
            System.TimeSpan.FromSeconds(5)))
    {
        using (SqlConnection oConn =
            new SqlConnection("context connection=true"))
        {
            try
            {
                //perform transaction's work
                oConn.Open();
                SqlCommand oCmd =
                    new SqlCommand("WAITFOR DELAY '00:00:07' " +
                        "INSERT Production.ProductCategory " +
                        "([Name]) SELECT 'Keyboards'",
                        oConn);
                SqlContext.Pipe.ExecuteAndSend(oCmd);
            }
            catch (SqlException ex)
            {
                //return error message to user
                SqlContext.Pipe.Send(ex.Message.ToString());
            }
            finally
            {
                //complete the second transaction
                oTran.Complete();
            }
        }
    }
};
```

Setting the TransactionScope Isolation Level

Not only can you specify the transaction behavior and timeout, but you also can set the isolation level of the transaction. Isolation levels dictate how your transactions behave in regard to volatile data (data that is currently being altered by another transaction). Unlike the previous transaction settings the isolation level cannot be directly passed into the TransactionScope class's constructors. To specify the isolation level, you must first create an instance of type TransactionOptions, and set its IsolationLevel property. Then pass the TransactionOption object into one of the TransactionScope class's constructors. You set the isolation level property with one of the members of the IsolationLevel enumeration:

❑ Serializable: This is the default; volatile data can be read but not modified.

❑ Chaos: Volatile data from higher isolated transactions cannot be modified.

❑ ReadCommitted: Volatile data can be modified but not read.

❑ ReadUncommitted: Volatile data can be modified and read.

❑ RepeatableRead: Volatile data can be read but not modified.

❑ Snapshot: Volatile data can be read, and throws an exception if the transaction attempts to modify data that has been changed since it was initially read.

❑ Unspecified: The transaction's isolation level cannot be determined.

The following example creates an instance of the TransactionOptions type, sets its IsolationLevel and Timeout properties, and then passes it into the TransactionScope class's constructor. This code shows demonstrates one method of setting a transaction various properties, including the isolation level.

```
public partial class StoredProcedures
{
    [Microsoft.SqlServer.Server.SqlProcedure]
    public static void usp_TransactionIsolationLevels()
    {
        //specify transaction options with the TransactionOptions type
        TransactionOptions oTranOptions =
            new TransactionOptions();
        oTranOptions.IsolationLevel =
            System.Transactions.IsolationLevel.RepeatableRead;
        oTranOptions.Timeout =
            System.TimeSpan.FromSeconds(5);

        using (TransactionScope oTran =
            new TransactionScope(TransactionScopeOption.Required,
                oTranOptions))
        {
            using (SqlConnection oConn =
                new SqlConnection("context connection=true"))
            {
                try
                {
                    //perform transaction's work
                    oConn.Open();
                    SqlCommand oCmd =
                        new SqlCommand("INSERT " +
                            "Production.ProductCategory " +
                            "([Name]) SELECT 'Mice'", oConn);
                    SqlContext.Pipe.ExecuteAndSend(oCmd);
                }
                catch (SqlException ex)
                {
                    //return error message to user
                    SqlContext.Pipe.Send(ex.Message.ToString());
                }
                finally
                {
                    //complete the second transaction
                    oTran.Complete();
                }
            }
        }
    }
};
```

Explicit Transactions

Instead of using the `TransactionScope` class for creating transactions implicitly, you can create them explicitly with the `CommitableTransaction` class. Explicit transactions require more code, but offer you the advantage of greater flexibility too. The biggest difference you will notice when using explicit transactions is that you must call the `Commit()` method when your transaction code complete successfully or you need to call the `RollBack()` when your code generates an exception. When you use explicit transactions with SQL Server connections, you will pass the `CommitableTransaction` object to the connection's `EnlistTransaction()` method. The following example uses three separate inserts into the AdventureWork's `Production.ProductCategory` table. The third `insert` statement is invalid thus rolling back the entire transaction.

```
public partial class StoredProcedures
{
    [Microsoft.SqlServer.Server.SqlProcedure]
    public static void usp_ExplicitTransaction()
    {
        //Create a committable transaction
        System.Transactions.CommittableTransaction oTran =
            new CommittableTransaction();
        using (SqlConnection oConn =
            new SqlConnection("context connection=true"))
        {
            try
            {
                SqlCommand oCmd = new SqlCommand();

                //Open the SQL connection
                oConn.Open();

                //Give the transaction to SQL to enlist with
                oConn.EnlistTransaction(oTran);

                oCmd.Connection = oConn;

                //first insert
                oCmd.CommandText = "INSERT Production.ProductCategory"
                    + " ([Name]) SELECT 'Laptops'";
                SqlContext.Pipe.ExecuteAndSend(oCmd);

                //second insert
                oCmd.CommandText = "INSERT Production.ProductCategory"
                    + " ([Name]) SELECT 'Servers'";
                SqlContext.Pipe.ExecuteAndSend(oCmd);

                //third insert
                oCmd.CommandText = "INSERT Production.ProductCategory"
                    + " ([Name]) SELECT 'Desktops'";
                SqlContext.Pipe.ExecuteAndSend(oCmd);

                //inform caller of rollback
                SqlContext.Pipe.Send("COMMITING TRANSACTION");

                //commit xact
```

```
                          oTran.Commit();
                      }
                  catch (SqlException ex)
                  {
                      //inform caller of rollback
                      SqlContext.Pipe.Send("ROLLING BACK TRANSACTION DUE " +
                          "TO THE FOLLOWING ERROR " + ex.Message.ToString());

                      //rollback xact
                      oTran.Rollback();
                  }
                  finally
                  {
                      oConn.Close();
                      oTran = null;
                  }
              }
          }
      };
```

Accessing the Current Transaction

You may want to access the current transaction (also called the ambient transaction) your SQL CLR code is executing inside of if you need to detect various attributes regarding the transaction your code is executing inside of. You can programatically detect the isolation level, creation time, distributed transaction ID, local transaction ID, and the status of the current transaction. The following example returns all of the ambient transaction's available properties.

```
public partial class StoredProcedures
{
    [Microsoft.SqlServer.Server.SqlProcedure]
    public static void uspAmbientTransaction()
    {
        //specify transaction options with the TransactionOptions type
        TransactionOptions oTranOptions =
            new TransactionOptions();
        oTranOptions.IsolationLevel =
            System.Transactions.IsolationLevel.ReadCommitted;
        oTranOptions.Timeout =
            System.TimeSpan.FromSeconds(5);

        using (TransactionScope oTran =
            new TransactionScope(TransactionScopeOption.Required,
            oTranOptions))
        {
            using (SqlConnection oConn =
                new SqlConnection("context connection=true"))
            {
                try
                {
                    //perform transaction's work
                    oConn.Open();
                    SqlCommand oCmd =
                        new SqlCommand("INSERT " +
```

```
                            "Production.ProductCategory ([Name]) SELECT"
                            + " 'Monitors'", oConn);
                    SqlContext.Pipe.ExecuteAndSend(oCmd);

                    //gets the current transaction
                    System.Transactions.Transaction oAmbient =
                        System.Transactions.Transaction.Current;

                    //return transaction information
                    SqlContext.Pipe.Send(
                        oAmbient.IsolationLevel.ToString());
                    SqlContext.Pipe.Send(
                        oAmbient.TransactionInformation.CreationTime.ToString());
                    SqlContext.Pipe.Send(oAmbient.TransactionInformation.
                                        DistributedIdentifier.ToString());
                    SqlContext.Pipe.Send(oAmbient.TransactionInformation.
                                        LocalIdentifier.ToString());
                    SqlContext.Pipe.Send(
                        oAmbient.TransactionInformation.Status.ToString());
                }
                catch (SqlException ex)
                {
                    //return error message to user
                    SqlContext.Pipe.Send(ex.Message.ToString());
                }
                finally
                {
                    //complete the second transaction
                    oTran.Complete();
                }
            }
        }
    }
};
```

Transaction Lifetimes

When you begin a transaction in a SQL CLR routine, you must perform a commit or rollback inside the same SQL CLR routine. Transactions started in external routines cannot be committed or rolled back inside a SQL CLR routine. Overall, the idea is that CLR code cannot manipulate the transaction state it is executing inside of.

Summary

Now, you not only have a background in how SQL CLR works, but you also know how to perform common tasks in your SQL CLR routines.

In the next chapter, we will be exploring each supported SQL CLR object in detail. SQL CLR supports stored procedures, functions, triggers, types, and aggregates. It is truly amazing how many objects support being created in managed code for a V1 technology.

Creating SQL CLR Objects

You have now seen some of the database objects you can create with the SQL CLR technology. In addition, you know how to perform some of the most common tasks in these routines. In this chapter, we will take a more thorough look at each database object supported by SQL CLR. You may notice that the examples in this chapter are very limited, and that is intentional, so that you can get used to how the objects work in isolation. Later in the book we will provide advanced examples of effectively using SQL CLR in the real world.

Managed Stored Procedures

Stored procedures are probably the most-used database object in SQL Server from a developer's perspective, so it only makes sense to cover this object first. Stored procedures consist of T-SQL code that gets executed in a procedural manner (procedural implies that one query gets executed after another in the procedure). You can use stored procedures to return results and messages to the client. Stored procedures support input and output parameters as well as a return values. Some of the reasons for using stored procedure are to enforce security, support modular programming, reduce network traffic, and cache execution plans after the first request.

Managed stored procedures have all of the same benefits as T-SQL-based procedures. Managed procedures are compiled by the hosted CLR; they are not interpreted by the Query Optimizer like traditional T-SQL statements. Managed stored procedures also have the ability to leverage the rich classes you have access to in the available subset of the .NET Framework.

Managed Code

In Chapter 3, we mentioned that there are two types of structure used for creating your SQL CLR objects, depending on whether you wish to create static methods or complete classes/structures. Managed stored procedures fall into the first category of structure, and are implemented as public static methods, as the following code shows:

```
public partial class StoredProcedures
{
    [Microsoft.SqlServer.Server.SqlProcedure]
    public static void usp_BlankProc1()
    {
        // Put your code here
    }
};
```

Because each method represents a stored procedure, you can have multiple procedures in one class. The following example shows three stored procedures being defined in one class.

```
public partial class StoredProcedures{
    [Microsoft.SqlServer.Server.SqlProcedure]
    public static void usp_BlankProc1()
    {
        // Put your code here
    }

    [Microsoft.SqlServer.Server.SqlProcedure]
    public static void usp_BlankProc2()
    {
        // Put your code here
    }

    [Microsoft.SqlServer.Server.SqlProcedure]
    public static void usp_BlankProc3()
    {
        // Put your code here
    }
};
```

If you were to comment out one of these procedures and then issue another Deploy command in Visual Studio, you would find that the commented out procedure no longer exists in the database. This is because Visual Studio removes all previous SQL CLR objects associated with the assembly you are redeploying.

The SqlProcedure Attribute

SQL CLR attributes are used for two primary purposes: they are used by Visual Studio to know what type of object you wish to create when deploying your code, and they have optional parameters you can use to set various attributes regarding your SQL CLR module(s).

We will demonstrate the first purpose of SQL CLR attributes with the SqlProcedure attribute. Remove the attribute from the third method in the previous example, as shown in the code below, and then select Build ➪ Deploy from Visual Studio's menu bar.

```
public partial class StoredProcedures
{
    [Microsoft.SqlServer.Server.SqlProcedure]
    public static void usp_BlankProc1()
    {
```

```
        // Put your code here
    }

    [Microsoft.SqlServer.Server.SqlProcedure]
    public static void usp_BlankProc2()
    {
        // Put your code here
    }

    public static void usp_BlankProc3()
    {
        // Put your code here
    }
};
```

When you deploy the changed code, you will notice that you now only have the first two stored procedures registered, as shown in Figure 4-1.

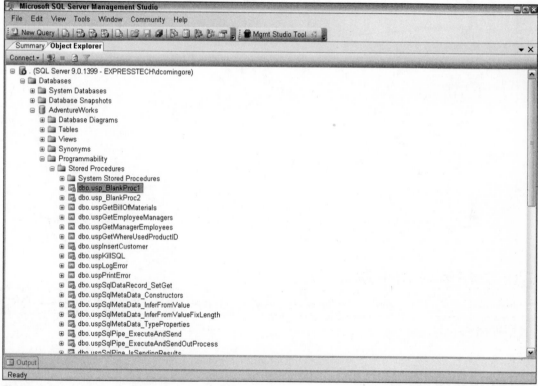

Figure 4-1

In addition to informing Visual Studio to create the procedure for a given method, the `SqlProcedure` attribute has an optional setting for overriding the name of the method as the stored procedure's name when it is deployed. The following example renames the method as `usp_HelloWorld`, while its original method is still named `usp_BlankProc1`.

```
public partial class StoredProcedures
{
    [Microsoft.SqlServer.Server.SqlProcedure(Name = "usp_HelloWorld")]
    public static void usp_BlankProc1()
    {
        // Put your code here
        SqlContext.Pipe.Send("HELLO WORLD FROM SQL CLR");
    }
};
```

Now when you view your stored procedures, you'll find an entry for `usp_HelloWorld` as opposed to `usp_BlankProc1`, as shown in Figure 4-2.

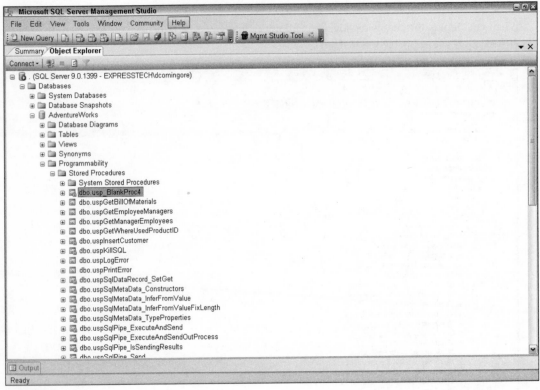

Figure 4-2

Parameters

Just like regular stored procedures, managed stored procedures support both input and output parameters. *Input parameters* are used for passing a value into the procedure, while *output parameters* are used for the inverse, to return a value to the calling code from the procedure. Do not confuse output parameters with return values (we discuss return values in the section below). As we discussed in Chapter 3, you should use the SqlType classes as opposed to the native CLR classes for parameters. Declaring a procedure's parameters simply requires you to define the type of the parameter and the parameter's name. The following code example has two input parameters defined for the procedure, a SqlInt32 type named iCnt and a SqlString named sName.

```
public partial class StoredProcedures
{
    [Microsoft.SqlServer.Server.SqlProcedure]
    public static void usp_ProcParms(SqlInt32 iCnt, SqlString sName)
    {
        SqlContext.Pipe.Send("FirstParm:" + iCnt.ToString());
        SqlContext.Pipe.Send("SecondParm:" + sName.ToString());
    }
};
```

The following is an example of using output parameters in your procedures. In this case, the SqlString variable sName is designated as an output parameter using the out keyword.

```
public partial class StoredProcedures
{
    [Microsoft.SqlServer.Server.SqlProcedure]
    public static void usp_ProcOutParm(SqlInt32 iCnt, out SqlString sName)
    {
        sName = "Derek";
        SqlContext.Pipe.Send("FirstParm:" + iCnt.ToString());
    }
};
```

When you run this code, you should get a similar result to that shown in Figure 4-3.

If you wish to specify a default value for a parameter used by a managed stored procedure, you must be aware of a few things. First, you cannot specify default parameter values in the managed code itself. A common "wish list" item for SQL CLR in its current implementation is to be able to set a default parameter value in your managed code and then during the Deploy operation from Visual Studio and have it map everything correctly for you. Second, to facilitate a default parameter value, you must go into SQL Server Management Studio and issue an ALTER PROCEDURE statement with a default parameter value specified. In the following ALTER PROCEDURE statement, we have added a default value for the parameter @iCnt. See the following sections for more information on the ALTER PROCEDURE statement.

```
ALTER PROCEDURE [dbo].[usp_ProcParms]
    @iCnt [int] = 1,
    @sName [nvarchar](4000)
WITH EXECUTE AS CALLER
AS
EXTERNAL NAME [Chapter4].[StoredProcedures].[usp_ProcParms]
GO
```

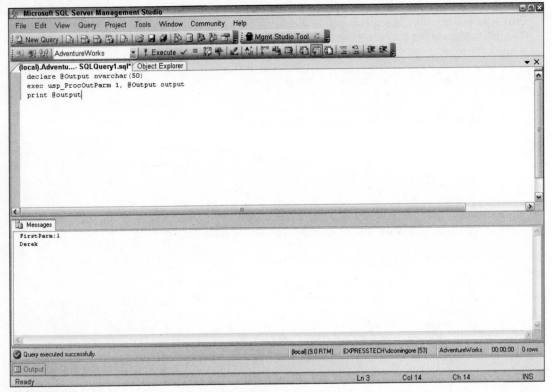

Figure 4-3

Return Values

Return values (also known as return codes) are used by stored procedures to inform the calling code of its execution status. In T-SQL you use the RETURN keyword followed by a 0 to indicate success (0 is also the default return value of a procedure) and a nonzero value to indicate an error has occurred. As with T-SQL, in a SQL CLR procedure, you use the return keyword followed by an integer value. When you want a managed procedure to return a value, you must change the method's return type to SqlInt32 or System.Int32. Unlike a T-SQL based procedure, where you can get a default return value of 0 without writing explicit return statements, in SQL CLR procedures you must set the return type or you will get compile (build) errors. The following example below features a static method, but notice its return type is SqlInt32.

```
public partial class StoredProcedures
{
    [Microsoft.SqlServer.Server.SqlProcedure]
    public static SqlInt32 usp_ReturnValue(SqlInt32 iDivisor)
    {
        try
        {
            //perform work here
            SqlInt32 iResult = 10/iDivisor;
```

```
            return (0);
        }
        catch (Exception ex)
        {
            //perform cleanup here
            return (1);
        }
    }
};
```

Now issue the following T-SQL to execute the procedure:

```
declare @Return int
exec @Return = usp_ReturnValue 0
print @Return
```

You get a return value of 1 because you cannot divide by 0. Notice that the `SqlException` class in isn't used in the `catch` block. You cannot use the `SqlException` class here because the scope of the exceptions it can catch does not include divide-by-zero errors. The `System.Exception` class handles a larger scope of exceptions than the `SqlException` class does, but for most SQL CLR routines, the `SqlException` class is the preferred type to use.

Creating, Altering, and Dropping Managed Stored Procedures

You can also work with managed stored procedures inside SQL Server with the CREATE, ALTER, and DROP Procedure statements. If you used Visual Studio to deploy the managed stored procedure, you will just need to use the Alter and Drop Procedure statements (assuming you wish to work with the procedures outside of Visual Studio after their initial deployment). In this section, we'll work through creating, altering, and finally dropping a managed stored procedure using the example from the previous section (`usp_ReturnValue`).

If you have not already done so, build your assembly in Visual Studio using the Build menu. Next, start up Management Studio and create a new query window using the database of your choice to house the new assembly. If you execute the following code (the path attribute may be different for your configuration), the assembly will be created in the database. This code was generated using Template Explorer's Create Assembly template, and we just filled in the blanks.

Template Explorer is a window you can display in SQL Server Management Studio by selecting View ⇨ Template Explorer. Template Explorer is very useful as it contains several templates of T-SQL arranged by the database object the template is for. There is a node or folder called Assembly in Template Explorer that contains two templates, a Create Assembly and a Drop Assembly.

```
--=============================================================
-- Create Assembly Template
--=============================================================
IF EXISTS(
  SELECT *
    FROM sys.assemblies
    WHERE name = N'Chapter4'
```

```
)
DROP ASSEMBLY Chapter4;
GO

CREATE ASSEMBLY Chapter4
FROM N'C:\Documents and Settings\dcomingore\My Documents\Visual Studio
2005\Projects\Chapter4\SqlServerProject4\bin\Release\Chapter4.dll'
WITH PERMISSION_SET = Safe;
GO
```

This Create Assembly Template will work just fine unless the assembly you want to create already exists, and contains registered SQL CLR objects (dependencies) such as a registered stored procedure. The Create Assembly template does not take dependencies into account as of this time. We will not be covering CREATE ASSEMBLY again in the other examples in this chapter because it is a redundant step. Now that the assembly has been uploaded into your database, you can create the database objects based upon it.

To create a SQL CLR stored procedure, we need to use the CREATE PROCEDURE T-SQL statement. CREATE PROCEDURE will typically be followed with AS BEGIN...END with the T-SQL code being between the BEGIN and END keywords. To create a managed stored procedure, you simply omit the BEGIN and END keywords and replace them with a new extension of CREATE PROCEDURE called EXTERNAL NAME.

In the following code you create a new managed stored procedure based on the uploaded assembly:

```
CREATE PROCEDURE [dbo].[usp_ReturnValue]
WITH EXECUTE AS CALLER
AS
EXTERNAL NAME [Chapter4].[StoredProcedures].[usp_ReturnValue]
GO
```

Notice what follows the EXTERNAL NAME clause. You specify a static method in a loaded assembly (meaning the assembly has already been stored in the database) for your procedure to be based upon EXTERNAL NAME that adheres to the convention:

```
[assembly_name].[class_name].[method_name].
```

If you have a managed stored procedure that contains parameters, you define the parameters in the CREATE PROCEDURE statement. Following the CREATE PROCEDURE statement, you list the parameters delimited by commas. First is the parameter's name, which must be started with an @ sign and then the name of the parameter. Following the parameter's name, you need to designate indicating which SQL Server type the parameter is to be based upon. The parameters in a CREATE PROCEDURE statement must correspond to the managed code's methods' parameters both in terms of count and compatible data types. The following code shows how to correctly define parameters in a CREATE PROCEDURE statement that maps to a managed routine:

```
CREATE PROCEDURE [dbo].[usp_Parms]
  @iFirstParm [int],
  @sSecondParm [nvarchar](4000)
WITH EXECUTE AS CALLER
AS
EXTERNAL NAME [Chapter4].[StoredProcedures].[uspParms]
GO
```

To update a managed stored procedure, you use the ALTER PROCEDURE T-SQL statement. If you need to change the managed code behind a procedure, you can issue an ALTER ASSEMBLY statement (rebuild in Visual Studio) after you have updated your code and both the assembly and the procedure that is based upon it have been "refreshed." The following code demonstrates a "refresh" of a managed stored procedure:

```
ALTER ASSEMBLY [Chapter4]
FROM 'C:\Documents and Settings\Administrator\My Documents\Visual Studio
2005\Projects\Chapter4\Chapter4\bin\Release\Chapter4.dll'
```

You cannot change a stored procedure from managed to T-SQL or vice versa using the ALTER PROCEDURE *statement.*

To remove (or drop) a managed stored procedure from a database, you use the DROP PROCEDURE statement. DROP PROCEDURE is simply followed by the schema and name of the procedure you wish to drop.

```
DROP PROCEDURE [dbo].[usp_Parms]
```

Managed Functions

Although stored procedures are the most popular programming objects in SQL Server, they are not the most useful in terms of CLR integration. Functions are the quintessential programming object in SQL CLR; they are the containers for intense processing logic that can take advantage of the CLR's Base Class Library and its precompiled nature. In SQL Server 2005, functions accept input parameters and return either a scalar value or a table. We'll discuss both types in this section.

When using Scalar-Valued Functions, you will typically pass in a column from a table into the function, thus you are executing managed code several times over for just one SELECT query. Within this context you can really begin to reap some performance benefits from compiled, managed code as opposed to the interpreted T-SQL language. In fact, generally speaking, it is the Scalar-Valued Functions that have the potential to provide you with the most benefit from a performance perspective out of all the supported SQL CLR objects/routines.

Scalar-Valued Functions

Scalar-Valued Functions (SVFs) return a single value. SVFs can return any scalar type, excluding varchar, char, rowversion, text, ntext, image, timestamp, table, or cursor. SVFs can be either *deterministic* or *nondeterministic*. A function is considered to be deterministic if it returns the same value given the same input(s). For example, the ABS() built-in function is deterministic because it will always return the same value given the same input:

```
--Deterministic Function Example
SELECT ABS(-1) AS ABS_Value
```

Nondeterministic functions, on the other hand will rarely return the same value given the same input(s). An example of this is the @@CONNECTIONS built-in function, which returns the number of attempted connections since SQL Server was last started:

```
--NonDeterministic Function Example
SELECT @@CONNECTIONS AS AttemptedConnections
```

A function's "determinism" is important because it dictates whether or not a function's result can be indexed. One example of this technique is the creation of a computed column based on an SVF. If the computed column is using a deterministic function, it can index the computed column's results; however, if the function being referenced is nondeterministic, its results cannot be indexed. We will discuss the importance of a function's determinism more in the "SqlFunction Attribute" section.

A computed column is one that holds the result of an expression as opposed to storing raw data. These expressions can reference other fields in the same table, functions, constants, and variables, all connected by any valid SQL Server operator, like this:

```
CREATE TABLE [dbo].[ComputedColumnExample]
(
    [ID] INT IDENTITY,
    [WidgetPackageCount] INT,
    [WidgetsPerPackage] INT,
    [WidgetsInStock] AS ([WidgetPackageCount] * [WidgetsPerPackage])
)
```

Managed Code

Creating an SVF is straightforward. Just as with a managed stored procedure you use a public static method (or a shared method in VB.NET). Unlike managed stored procedures, these methods are decorated with the SqlFunction attribute. In the following code we create a basic addition function:

```
public partial class UserDefinedFunctions
{
    [Microsoft.SqlServer.Server.SqlFunction()]
    public static SqlInt32 udf_Add(SqlInt32 iFirstNum, SqlInt32 iSecondNum)
    {
        //returns the result of the addition
        return (iFirstNum + iSecondNum);
    }
};
```

As with managed stored procedures, you can have multiple managed SVFs defined in one logical class. And also as with managed stored procedures, SVFs can take advantage of partial classes.

SqlFunction Attribute

You declare a method in managed code as a function using the SqlFunction attribute. The SqlFunction attribute has properties that are applicable to Scalar-Valued Functions, and others that are applicable to Table-Valued Functions (TVFs; see the "Table-Valued Functions" section for more). If you reference properties that are meant for TVFs in an SVF, or vice versa, they are simply ignored. We will now review those SqlFunction attribute parameters that are specific to SVFs.

For SVFs, you have the Name parameter which serves the same purpose as it does for managed stored procedures, to override a method's name for the database module. You also have the IsDeterministic, IsPrecise, SystemDataAccess, and UserDataAccess parameters. IsDeterministic indicates if your function will always return the same value given the same input(s). IsDeterministic has a default value of false. The `IsPrecise` parameter indicates if your function contains imprecise computations such as floating point operations. `IsPrecise` has a default value of false.

`SystemDataAccess` indicates if your function will be accessing SQL Server system catalogs. You assign this parameter a value from the `SystemDataAccessKind` enumeration (which contains two members, `NONE` and `READ`). False is the default value of the `SystemDataAccess` parameter. `DataAccess` is similar to `SystemDataAccess`; however, with this parameter you are indicating if your function's code accesses user data as opposed to system data. You assign the `DataAccess` parameter a value from the `DataAccessKind` enumeration (which also contains the `NONE` and `READ` members).

All of these parameters (excluding the `Name` parameter) have one common goal: to determine if your SVF(s) can be used in computed columns and indexes. Be aware though that the `SystemDataAccess` and `DataAccess` parameters are used independently as well for allowing data access in your functions. If you wish to create computed columns and index their results, you must ensure that your SVFs exhibit the following behaviors:

❑   Must be deterministic

❑   Cannot perform user or system data access

When you create a traditional T-SQL-based scalar function, SQL Server will implicitly determine for you whether the function can be used for computational and persisted (indexed) usage. In the context of SQL CLR, however, SQL Server is unaware of what your managed code is doing, so you need a mechanism that allows the developer to designate these key behaviors of scalar functions. When you assign these parameters, you are basically telling SQL Server how deterministic and precise your function's code is.

Do not incorrectly assign the values for `IsDeterministic` *and* `IsPrecise`. *Doing so can potentially lead to corrupted computed columns and indexed views.*

At this point, we are going to show you an example of how you can use the `SqlFunction` parameters to facilitate a computed column and index referencing your SVF. First, create a new SVF:

```
public partial class UserDefinedFunctions
{
    [Microsoft.SqlServer.Server.SqlFunction(IsDeterministic=true,IsPrecise=true)]
    public static SqlInt32
        udf_WidgetsInStock(SqlInt32 iPackageCount, SqlInt32 iWidgetsPerPackage)
    {
        //returns the result of the addition
        return (iPackageCount + iWidgetsPerPackage);
    }
};
```

Build and deploy your new managed function from Visual Studio 2005. Now, create a new user table based on the SVF.

```
CREATE TABLE [dbo].[ComputedColumnExample2]
(
    [ID] INT IDENTITY,
    [WidgetPackageCount] INT,
    [SpareWidgets] INT,
```

```
        [WidgetsInStock]
            AS ([dbo].[udf_WidgetsInStock]
                ([WidgetPackageCount],[SpareWidgets])) PERSISTED
)
GO
CREATE CLUSTERED INDEX pri_idx
    ON [dbo].[ComputedColumnExample2]([ID])
GO
CREATE NONCLUSTERED INDEX sec_idx
    ON [dbo].[ComputedColumnExample2]([WidgetsInStock])
GO
```

Parameters

You have already seen several examples of SVFs accepting input parameters. To specify an input parameter for a function, you simply declare its type and the parameter's name. Functions can accept up to 1,024 parameters. If you wish to assign a default value to one or more of your function's parameters, you must first deploy the function to SQL Server and then run an ALTER FUNCTION statement as follows:

```
ALTER FUNCTION
    [dbo].[udf_AddTwoNums](@iFirstNum [int] = 1, @iSecondNum [int] = 1)
RETURNS [int] WITH EXECUTE AS CALLER
AS
EXTERNAL NAME [Chapter4].[UserDefinedFunctions].[udf_AddTwoNums]
GO
```

Notice the "= 1" part of the code. We added these defaults before running the ALTER FUNCTION statement. Now that the function has been assigned defaults for its two input parameters, you can call it with the following code. You use the DEFAULT keyword to specify that you wish to use the parameter's default value.

```
SELECT [dbo].[udf_AddTwoNums](DEFAULT,DEFAULT)
```

Creating, Altering, and Dropping, Managed Scalar-valued Functions

The T-SQL for creating SVFs in SQL Server is simple; you use the CREATE FUNCTION statement. You specify the type to be returned and the managed code that implements your function in the EXTERNAL NAME clause. In the following code, we assume an assembly has already been loaded into the database and you simply wish to create the T-SQL "wrapper" function around it.

```
CREATE FUNCTION [dbo].[udf_AddTwoNums](@iFirstNum [int], @iSecondNum [int])
RETURNS [int] WITH EXECUTE AS CALLER, RETURNS NULL ON NULL INPUT
AS
EXTERNAL NAME [Chapter4].[UserDefinedFunctions].[udf_AddTwoNums]
GO
```

You may have noticed the RETURNS NULL ON NULL INPUT function option we used in the previous code; this option is only available for SVFs (both T-SQL and CLR SVFs). The option can contain one of the following two string literals:

❑ RETURNS NULL ON NULL INPUT

❑ CALLED ON NULL INPUT

You cannot specify SCHEMABINDING *or* ENCRYPTION *function options for SQL CLR SVFs, because these are T-SQL-only function options.*

These NULL INPUT options dictate how your SVFs should handle the situation of having NULL input parameters. As such they are quite self-explanatory; the first option will return NULL automatically, while the second option will not automatically return a NULL result and will attempt to execute the code with the NULL inputs being supplied.

To change or alter an existing scalar-valued function, you use the ALTER FUNCTION statement. For example, you might want to change how your managed SVF handles NULL inputs. The following code uses the ALTER FUNCTION statement to change how the managed SVF handles NULL inputs.

```
ALTER FUNCTION
    [dbo].[udf_AddTwoNums](@iFirstNum [int] = 1, @iSecondNum [int] = 1)
RETURNS [int] WITH EXECUTE AS CALLER, CALLED ON NULL INPUT AS
EXTERNAL NAME [Chapter4].[UserDefinedFunctions].[udf_AddTwoNums]
GO
```

ALTER FUNCTION *cannot be used to changed an SVF to a TVF or vice versa.*

If you no longer require a particluar function, you can remove it from the database (though its assembly will still exist) by using the DROP FUNCTION statement. The following code removes your previously created SVF, udf_AddTwoNums:

```
DROP FUNCTION [dbo].[udf_AddTwoNums]
```

Table-Valued Functions

Table-Valued Functions (TVFs) return a table as opposed to a scalar value. Managed TVFs return this tabular data by using a steaming mechanism; this ensures that each row is made available for consumption as soon as it materializes. TVFs also support both input and output parameters. You will use the same SqlFunction attribute when creating managed TVFs that you used for created SVFs, but with different parameters. When we first started creating TVFs, we had to do it a few times to grasp what was happening, but it's not really that difficult.

Managed Code

Creating a TVF function requires a little more work than creating a SVF function. You create TVFs by defining two methods in a class. The first method is the function's entry point, and the second one is for populating the result set the TVF is to return (known as the FillRow method). The entry-point method is the method that Visual Studio creates when you add a new function in Solution Explorer. You need this entry-point method to return a type of IEnumerable, so the first thing you will want to do is change the method's return type to IEnumerable. You must do this because IEnumerable provides an iteration mechanism over a collection of types.

Now, we must focus our attention on the FillRow method. This FillRow method will be called for each iteration of the IEnumerable type. At this point, let us explain a bit more about what is going on in these functions. As you will see in the "SqlFunction Attribute" section, you must specify an existing method's name for the `FillRowMethodName` parameter. By doing this, you are essentially hooking up the `FillRow` method to the entry-point method, meaning that you are declaring that once the entry-point's work is done and it returns a type of `IEnumerable`, it then passes the `IEnumerable` object to the `FillRow` method for each item in the `IEnumerable` object. There are a few more things you must do, but this accounts for the majority of creating managed TVFs. As with managed stored procedures and SVFs, you can have multiple managed TVFs defined in one logical class. And also like the other routines, TVFs can take advantage of partial classes. The following code shows a TVF that parses a text file and returns the individual items:

```
namespace SQL CLRRoutines.FileIO
{
    sealed public partial class TableValuedFunctions
    {
        [Microsoft.SqlServer.Server.SqlFunction(FillRowMethodName=
            "tvf_ParseFile_FillRow", + "TableDefinition="Item NVARCHAR(4000)")]
        public static IEnumerable tvf_ParseFile(String FilePath, char Delimiter)
        {
            //declare local variables
            String[] sItems;
            System.IO.StreamReader oSR;

            //does file exist?
            if (File.Exists(FilePath))
            {
                //open file
                oSR = System.IO.File.OpenText(FilePath);

                //parse file
                sItems = oSR.ReadToEnd().Split(Delimiter);

                //close file
                oSR.Close();

                //return items
                return(sItems);
            }
            else
            {
                throw new System.Exception("FILE NOT FOUND");
            }
        }

        private static void tvf_ParseFile_FillRow(Object obj, out SqlString sItem)
        {
            //convert object
            String sTemp = (string)obj;

            //assign value to field
            sItem = sTemp;
        }
    }
};
```

SqlFunction Attribute

The `SqlFunction` attribute contains two parameters specific to TVFs, `FillRowMethodName` and `TableDefinition`. `FillRowMethodName` is used to declare which method in your function's class will be used for populating the rows of the table you want it to return. The `TableDefinition` parameter is used to describe the returning table's definition. Both parameters are mandatory for creating TVFs. To see the TVF parameters being used look at the above example.

Parameters

There are no major differences between SVF and TVF parameters functionally.

Creating, Altering, and Dropping Managed TVFs

You create a managed TVF manually using the same `CREATE FUNCTION` statement you use to create a SVF. The difference here is that for TVFs we use a `RETURNS TABLE` statement, as opposed to, say, `RETURNS INT`. The table definition you place in the `RETURNS TABLE` parameter must be the same SQL Server types used by your assembly's `FillRow()` method. The following code first creates a managed TVF, then alters it, and finally drops it.

```
/****** Object:  UserDefinedFunction [dbo].[tvf_ParseFile]    Script Date:
08/13/2006 05:12:31 ******/
CREATE FUNCTION [dbo].[tvf_ParseFile](@FilePath [nvarchar](4000), @Delimiter
[nchar](1))
RETURNS  TABLE (
    [Item] [nvarchar](4000) COLLATE Latin1_General_CS_AS NULL
) WITH EXECUTE AS CALLER
AS
EXTERNAL NAME
[RedmondSocietycom].[SQLCLRRoutines.FileIO.TableValuedFunctions].[tvf_ParseFile]
GO
ALTER FUNCTION [dbo].[tvf_ParseFile](@FilePath [nvarchar](4000), @Delimiter
[nchar](1))
RETURNS  TABLE (
    [Item] [nvarchar](4000) COLLATE Latin1_General_CS_AS NULL
) WITH EXECUTE AS CALLER
AS
EXTERNAL NAME
[RedmondSocietycom].[SQLCLRRoutines.FileIO.TableValuedFunctions].[tvf_ParseFile]
GO
DROP FUNCTION [dbo].[tvf_ParseFile]
```

Managed Triggers

Triggers are simply stored procedures that are fired in response to events occurring in the database rather than by direct invocation. For example, suppose that you have a `Users` table, and there are semi-frequent changes made to the data in the table. These changes are originating from a front-end intranet application where certain key personnel have the ability to update user's information. The only problem with this data changing is that the users themselves are not being notified when something on their account changes. To remedy this, you need some T-SQL to "fire" after these changes occur that would send an e-mail message alerting the user of their account status. It is situations like these where triggers can be a good fit.

There are two primary types of triggers. The first is the type that fire in response to data-altering statements (INSERT, UPDATE, and DELETE), which are called Data Manipulation Language (DML) triggers. When you create the trigger, you specify the exact event(s) the trigger should fire for. The second type, which fire in response to object inventory statements (CREATE, ALTER, DROP, etc.) are known as Data Definition Language (DDL) triggers. As with DML triggers, when you create the trigger, you will assign it specific events to fire for. DDL triggers have a few basic uses, but the primary usage is for SQL Server object auditing and inventory tracking. Neither type of trigger supports parameters or return values.

Triggers usually fire after the event that causes their execution, and this is the behavior of the AFTER and FOR keywords (which are synonymous). With DML triggers, you also have the option of using the INSTEAD OF keyword, which is a DML trigger that executes in place of the data altering event that caused it to fire. When you create a trigger, you specify this firing behavior with the FOR, AFTER, or INSTEAD OF keywords. DDL triggers are brand new with SQL Server 2005. Before SQL Server 2005, if you wanted DDL functionality you would have had to create a "regular" DML trigger on a system table, such as sysobjects, which is heavily advised against.

At this time, you cannot create an INSTEAD OF *DDL trigger.*

Most people will have a handful of fairly common questions once they have been exposed to triggers. Can triggers be nested (meaning, can one trigger fire another)? Can triggers not only cause a different trigger to fire, but can they also cause themselves to fire? Can you have more than one trigger designated for the same event on the same object (table or view)? Furthermore, can you control their "firing order"?

The answer is that the FOR and AFTER triggers can be nested by default. There is a server-level setting that controls whether FOR and AFTER triggers can be nested. This setting is on by default, but here's how to turn it off:

```
 sp_configure 'nested triggers', 0;
GO
RECONFIGURE;
GO
```

INSTEAD OF triggers can always be nested, regardless of the "nested triggers" setting. You can nest triggers up to 32 levels, at which point the entire trigger execution context gets canceled. The second question we mentioned above is actually what is known as trigger recursion. Yes, by default you can have a trigger fire that causes a different trigger to fire on another table/view, and then the second trigger causes the original to fire again by updating the original's underlying table/view. What we just described is called *indirect recursion*, meaning that you didn't directly cause the trigger to fire itself. *Direct recursion* is when you have a trigger that gets fired off and then performs an operation on its own underlying table/view to fire itself off again. Direct recursion is only enabled if a particular database-level setting called RECURSIVE_TRIGGERS is used. If you set this option on, you are allowing both direct and indirect trigger recursion to occur in the particular database you set it in (the setting is off by default). The following code demonstrates how to turn on the RECURSIVE_TRIGGERS database setting:

```
ALTER DATABASE AdventureWorks
    SET RECURSIVE_TRIGGERS ON
```

Finally, in regard to recursive triggers, be aware that if you turn this setting off (again the default), then you are only disallowing direct recursion scenarios, the indirect recursion scenarios are still enabled. To disable both direct and indirect recursion, you must turn off the "nested triggers" server-level setting discussed earlier. We know the enabling and disabling of recursive triggers can be a little confusing, so the following are the actions and their results for enabling and disabling trigger recursion. We are looking at the tasks from a disabling perspective, but you only need to reverse the tasks for enabling them:

❑   To completely disable all trigger recursion, set the 'nested triggers' server-level setting off/0.

❑   To disable direct trigger recursion and leave indirect recursion enabled, set the RECURSIVE_TRIGGERS database-level setting off/0.

The next common question is: Can I have more than one trigger defined for the same event on the same table or view? It depends on the trigger type you are creating. You can only have one INSTEAD OF trigger defined for a given event on a given table or view. With FOR and AFTER triggers, you can specify multiple triggers for the same event and object. Which leads to the final common question: Can I set the "firing order" if I am allowed to have multiple triggers firing for the same event(s)? You can set the first and last trigger only; all others are "on their own" when it comes to who fires before whom. To set the first or last FOR or AFTER trigger use the following code (these are custom triggers I have created):

```
USE AdventureWorks;
GO
sp_settriggerorder @triggername= 'dbo.UpdateEmployee1', @order='First', @stmttype =
'UPDATE';
GO
sp_settriggerorder @triggername= 'dbo.UpdateEmployee2', @order='Last', @stmttype =
'UPDATE';
GO
```

Performance is always crucial, but in the context of triggers it is even more so. You need to remember that a trigger is going to (usually) fire after an event, which means that you need to pay attention to your trigger's workload and ensure that the trigger completes fairly quickly. Triggers participate in the same transaction context they are fired in. You don't want a one-second transaction actually taking five seconds to complete because of a poorly performing trigger.

Finally, there is the subject of returning resultsets from triggers. We'll be brief on this topic: don't do it. In SQL Server 2005, you can in fact return custom result sets from a trigger, but in future versions of the product, this functionality will be off by default. There is a server-level setting used to control this behavior called "disallow results from triggers." The following code sets this server-level option on to disable triggers from returning results:

```
sp_configure 'show advanced options', 1;
GO
RECONFIGURE;
GO
sp_configure 'disallow results from triggers', 1;
GO
RECONFIGURE;
GO
```

SqlTriggerContext Class

The most noticeable difference between managed triggers and the other SQL CLR objects is the availability of the `SqlTriggerContext` class. The `SqlTriggerContext` class provides contextual information for triggers at runtime. `SqlTriggerContext` provides the following functionality in managed triggers:

❑ Provides the columns that have been updated via an `Update` statement

❑ Provides the actions that caused the trigger to fire

❑ Access data regarding database objects that have been created, altered, or dropped (DDL trigger)

The first major use of the `SqlTriggerContext` is detecting which action caused the trigger to fire. This can be useful when you have a trigger that fires in response to more than one event. And be aware that by *event*, we are including DDL events, such as `Create Role`. The following is the sample table we are going to use for this example (and several others in this chapter).

```
CREATE TABLE [dbo].[Test](
  [ID] [int] NULL,
  [FirstName] [varchar](50) COLLATE SQL_Latin1_General_CP1_CI_AS NULL
)
```

On INSERT and UPDATE (DML) we want a trigger to fire and perform different logic based on which event caused it to fire. Do not concern yourself with the `SqlTrigger` attribute yet, as we will be covering that momentarily. We first store an instance of type `SqlTriggerContext` by accessing the `TriggerContext` property of `SqlContext`. Then we look at the `TriggerAction` property to determine which action caused the trigger to fire. And from there we simply return a message to the user informing them that this action requires processing logic.

Returning messages and resultsets from triggers is generally bad practice, as we discussed earlier; however, we are returning content from the sample triggers in this chapter to help convey how they work, for learning and demonstration purposes only.

```
public partial class Triggers
{
    // Enter existing table or view for the target and uncomment the attribute line
    [Microsoft.SqlServer.Server.SqlTrigger(Name = "udt_DMLTrigAction", Target =
      "Test", Event = "FOR INSERT,UPDATE")]
    public static void udt_DMLTrigAction()
    {
        SqlTriggerContext oTrigContext = SqlContext.TriggerContext;
        if (oTrigContext.TriggerAction == TriggerAction.Insert)
        {
            SqlContext.Pipe.Send("INSERT PROCESSING LOGIC GOES HERE");
        }
        else if (oTrigContext.TriggerAction == TriggerAction.Update)
        {
            SqlContext.Pipe.Send("UPDATE PROCESSING LOGIC GOES HERE");
        }
        else{
            SqlContext.Pipe.Send("ACTION COULD NOT BE DETECTED");
        }
    }
};
```

Everything is now in place for you to test the trigger. Choose the Deploy command from Visual Studio, and run the following T-SQL:

```
INSERT Test SELECT 1,'Douglas'
GO
UPDATE Test SET id = 2 WHERE id = 1
```

You should see results similar to Figure 4-4.

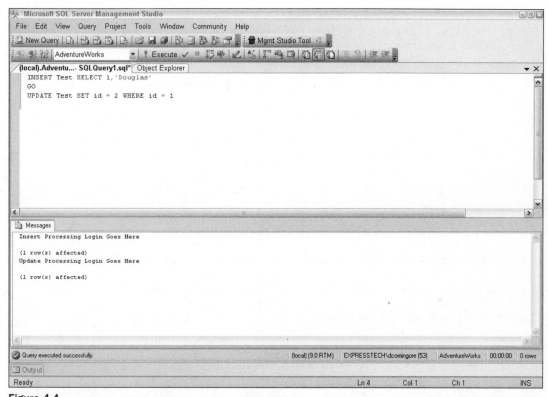

Figure 4-4

Accessing the Virtual Inserted and Deleted Temporary Tables

You have access to the `Inserted` and `Deleted` tables in managed triggers just as with a regular T-SQL trigger. You will use a context (in-process) connection and then simply query the temporary `Inserted` or `Deleted` tables. And as with T-SQL triggers you cannot modify the data contained in these temp tables. The following example shows a DML trigger for Updates on the same Test table we used in the previous example.

```
public partial class Triggers
{
    // Enter existing table or view for the target and uncomment the attribute line
```

```
[Microsoft.SqlServer.Server.SqlTrigger(Name = "udtDMLVirtualTables",
        Target = "Test", Event = "FOR UPDATE")]
public static void udtDMLVirtualTables()
{
    using (SqlConnection oConn = new SqlConnection("context connection=true;"))
    {
        //query the virtual Inserted table
        SqlCommand oCmd = new SqlCommand("SELECT * FROM Inserted", oConn);
        try
        {
            oCmd.Connection.Open();
            SqlContext.Pipe.ExecuteAndSend(oCmd);
        }
        catch (SqlException e)
        {
            SqlContext.Pipe.Send(e.Message.ToString());
        }
        finally
        {
            if (oCmd.Connection.State != ConnectionState.Closed)
            {
                oCmd.Connection.Close();
            }
        }
    }
};
```

Deploy the trigger to your desired SQL Server, and execute the following T-SQL to fire the trigger:

```
UPDATE Test SET ID = 4 WHERE ID = (SELECT MAX(ID) FROM Test)
```

You will see results similar to Figure 4-5.

Enabling and Disabling Triggers

Another aspect of triggers is that you can both disable and enable them, including DDL triggers. By default (after CREATE TRIGGER), all triggers are enabled, and for most SQL Server installations, the triggers never get disabled. But there are situations when disabling a trigger can be quite useful, For example, assume that you have a table with a FOR INSERT DML trigger attached to it. For some reason, all of your recent INSERTS into this table are not persisting. In this scenario, by disabling the attached trigger, you can immediately either eliminate or conclude that the trigger is the cause of the problem. The best part about this was that no SQL scripts were required, meaning that you didn't have to save the trigger's script somewhere first, then DROP the trigger and then recreate the trigger. You just disabled and then reenabled it!

In the following example, we first disable our sample trigger and then we reenable it using T-SQL:

```
DISABLE TRIGGER [dbo].[udt_DMLTrigAction] ON [dbo].[test];
GO
ENABLE TRIGGER [dbo].[udt_DMLTrigAction] ON [dbo].[test];
```

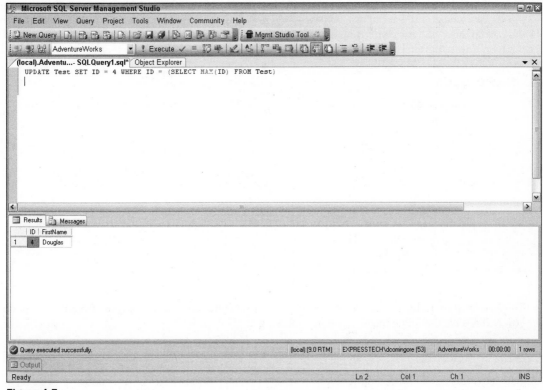

Figure 4-5

You can also enable or disable groups of triggers at the database and server levels, as shown here:

```
--disable/enable all triggers for current database
DISABLE TRIGGER ALL ON DATABASE;
GO
ENABLE TRIGGER ALL ON DATABASE;
GO
--disable/enable all triggers for entire server
DISABLE TRIGGER ALL ON ALL SERVER;
GO
ENABLE TRIGGER ALL ON ALL SERVER;
```

You can also enable or disable triggers using SQL Server 2005 Management Studio.

Managed DML Triggers

Why would you want to use the CLR for a DML trigger? The cases are definitely limited; however, there are times that business requirements dictate that certain events occur outside of a database once a particular record has been modified. Be aware though that if you have a DML trigger that needs to contain intense processing, it would be better to wrap that functionality up into a managed function as opposed to creating the entire DML trigger in managed code. Again, functions are the best SQL CLR routine for those cases where you want to use the processing power of precompiled managed code. Remember that the performance of your DML triggers is of the utmost importance as these "procedures" will be fired for every insert, update, or delete.

Managed Code

A DML trigger is implemented as a public static method that you decorate with the `SqlTrigger` attribute, like this:

```
public partial class Triggers
{
    // Enter existing table or view for the target and uncomment the attribute line
    [Microsoft.SqlServer.Server.SqlTrigger(Name = "udtDMLVirtualTables",
    Target = "Test", Event = "FOR UPDATE")]
    public static void udt_DMLVirtualTables()
    {
        SqlContext.Pipe.Send(SqlContext.TriggerContext.IsUpdatedColumn(0)
        .ToString());
    }
}
```

You also must mark the method as returning `void`; if you attempt to return a value from the method, you will receive the following error upon deploying:

```
"CREATE TRIGGER failed because method 'udtDMLVirtualTables' of class 'Triggers'
in assembly 'Chapter4' returns 'nvarchar', but CLR Triggers must return void."
```

SqlTrigger Attribute

The `SqlTrigger` attribute has three parameters that you can set, two of which are required. The first is the `Name` parameter. As you are aware, this is the standard `Name` parameter, which is available in all of the SQL CLR attributes. `Name` is optional, but be aware that if you do not assign it, the method's name will be used as the SQL CLR object's name.

`Target` and `Event` are the two required parameters of the `SqlTrigger` attribute. You must assign both of these events before you deploy your managed trigger. `Target` is simply the table that the trigger will be assigned to, and `Event` is where you list the events that the trigger should fire for. For a DML trigger, your event is going to be either FOR or INSTEAD OF, followed by the desired events INSERT, UPDATE, or DELETE. The following is an example of a DML managed trigger that fires INSTEAD OF a typical UPDATE event. Here is the code to implement the trigger:

```
public partial class Triggers
{
    // Enter existing table or view for the target and uncomment the attribute line
    [Microsoft.SqlServer.Server.SqlTrigger(Target = "Test", Event = "FOR UPDATE")]
    public static void udt_DMLVirtualTables()
    {
        using (SqlConnection oConn = new SqlConnection("context connection=true;"))
        {
            //query the virtual Inserted table
            SqlCommand oCmd = new SqlCommand("SELECT * FROM Inserted", oConn);
```

```
        try
        {
            oCmd.Connection.Open();
            SqlContext.Pipe.ExecuteAndSend(oCmd);
        }
        catch (SqlException e)
        {
            SqlContext.Pipe.Send(e.Message.ToString());
        }
        finally
        {
            if (oCmd.Connection.State != ConnectionState.Closed)
            {
                oCmd.Connection.Close();
            }
        }
    }

  }
}
```

If you run the following T-SQL, you should see that the update never actually commits because of the INTEAD OF trigger.

```
UPDATE Test SET ID = 5 WHERE ID = (SELECT MAX(ID) FROM Test)
GO
SELECT * FROM Test
```

Creating, Altering, and Dropping Managed DML Triggers

To create a managed DML trigger manually, you use the CREATE TRIGGER statement with the EXTERNAL NAME clause. When you use the manual method of creating your managed DML triggers, you are essentially providing the same information as if you were using the SqlTrigger attribute with the Visual Studio deploy feature. The following code shows how to create a standard managed DML trigger using T-SQL:

```
CREATE TRIGGER [dbo].[udt_DMLVirtualTables] ON [dbo].[Test]  FOR UPDATE AS
EXTERNAL NAME [Chapter4].[Triggers].[udt_DMLVirtualTables]
```

If you right-click on a trigger (or any SQL CLR object for that matter) that was deployed from Visual Studio 2005 and select Script ⇨ Create, you will notice that the generated T-SQL includes some calls to a system stored procedure called sp_addextendedproperty. This system procedure creates extended properties. Extended properties are a feature of SQL Server 2005 that you can use to annotate your database objects with additional information (metadata). You can then use this metadata in some useful method of consumption. For more information on extended properties use the keyword "Extended Properties" in Books Online's Index.

Use the ALTER TRIGGER statement for changing assigned events and targets (tables or views). If you are pushing updates of your trigger's managed code you only need to call the ALTER ASSEMBLY statement, and not ALTER TRIGGER, to perform a "refresh" of the managed code base. The following code assigns a second event to the trigger:

```
ALTER TRIGGER [dbo].[udt_DMLVirtualTables] ON [dbo].[Test]  FOR UPDATE,INSERT AS
EXTERNAL NAME [Chapter4].[Triggers].[udt_DMLVirtualTables]
```

We use the DROP TRIGGER statement to remove a managed trigger from a database:

```
DROP TRIGGER [dbo].[udtInsteadOfUpdate]
```

Removing the T-SQL trigger does not remove the underlying assembly in the database.

Managed DDL Triggers

Managed DDL triggers have many applications. The primary use is for auditing purposes, but there are others, such as automatically checking in the T-SQL definition of a new object into an external source code repository. DDL triggers cannot fire INSTEAD OF a DDL event, and they cannot issue a ROLLBACK statement either. Thus, if you need to prevent the DDL event from persisting in the database you must use a T-SQL-based trigger.

Managed Code

There are no differences between a managed DML trigger's code and a managed DDL trigger's code.

SqlTrigger Attribute

As with managed DML triggers, you must supply values for both the Target and Event parameters. DDL triggers simply require different values for these two attributes. Target can be either "all server" or "database" because DDL events are monitored at either the entire server or database level. The Event can be either an individual server-level event or an entire event group. Event groups are logical groups of server and database level events. Finally, you cannot autodeploy a managed DDL trigger that has server-level scope from Visual Studio. The following example demonstrates this point:

```
public partial class Triggers
{
    // Enter existing table or view for the target and uncomment the attribute line
    [Microsoft.SqlServer.Server.SqlTrigger(Target = "all server", Event =
            "FOR DDL_SERVER_LEVEL_EVENTS")]
    public static void udt_DDLServerAutoDeploy()
    {
        // Replace with your own code
        SqlContext.Pipe.Send("DDL TRIGGER FIRED");
    }
};
```

Now select Build ⇨ Deploy from the Visual Studio main menu. You should receive the following error:

```
'The method "ddltrigger" in class "triggers" marked as a server-level trigger
cannot be auto deployed because server-level trigger deployment is not supported.'
```

Creating, Altering, and Dropping Managed DDL Triggers

Manually creating a DDL trigger is a bit different from manually creating a DML trigger. Here, we want to go ahead and show you the full syntax of the CREATE/ALTER/DROP TRIGGER statements for DDL triggers.

```
CREATE TRIGGER trigger_name
ON { ALL SERVER | DATABASE }
```

```
[ WITH <ddl_trigger_option> [ ,...n ] ]
{ FOR | AFTER } { event_type | event_group } [ ,...n ]
AS { sql_statement  [ ; ] [ ,...n ] | EXTERNAL NAME < method specifier >  [ ; ] }
```

The first difference is that instead of following the ON clause with a table name, you must specify either ALL SERVER or DATABASE. Therefore, whenever the event_type or event_group (event groups were discussed above) occurs within the database or the entire server, the DDL trigger will fire. Next are the events the trigger fires on. Instead of (no pun intended) assigning the trigger to INSERT, UPDATE, or DELETE, you will be assigning the trigger to CREATE X, ALTER X, or DROP X, where X is the database object type (assembly, for example). You can assign a DDL trigger to an entire grouping of related DDL events, for example DDL_LOGIN_EVENTS. The ALTER statement for a DDL trigger contains the same syntax as that of the CREATE:

```
ALTER TRIGGER trigger_name
ON { DATABASE | ALL SERVER }
[ WITH <ddl_trigger_option> [ ,...n ] ]
{ FOR | AFTER } { event_type [ ,...n ] | event_group }
AS { sql_statement [ ; ] | EXTERNAL NAME <method specifier> [ ; ] }
```

The DROP statement for a DDL trigger is consistent with a DROP for a DML trigger except for the ON clause, which indicates the scope of the DDL trigger you are dropping.

```
DROP TRIGGER trigger_name [ ,...n ]
ON { DATABASE | ALL SERVER }
[ ; ]
```

Managed Aggregates

User-defined aggregates (UDAs) are a new feature with SQL Server 2005. In SQL Server 2000, if you wanted to provide your own aggregate, you would have to employ T-SQL cursors to loop through the rows and add each value into your aggregate. This method of using T-SQL cursors to support custom aggregates is not a very good solution because cursors are inherently slow, and it opens up the possibility of the developer writing nonoptimal code for the iteration of the records. With SQL Server 2005, you can create custom aggregates without having to create the iteration code. By the way, you cannot create UDAs in T-SQL. UDAs must be defined in a managed assembly. UDAs do not support parameters, because they can only accept the column of data you are passing in to accumulate. When you are referencing your UDA in T-SQL, you must prefix with it's schema as well.

There are a few limits to UDAs in their first implementation. Size is the first limit: UDAs have an 8,000-byte limit. If an instance of your UDA exceeds 8,000 bytes, an exception will thrown. The other main concern is that UDAs cannot ensure that the data will be passed to it in any particular order. If you want to create a UDA that is sensitive to the order of data being passed into it use another tier of your application, not the database.

Managed Code

You use a class or structure to implant a managed UDA. By default, when you add a new aggregate to your database project in Visual Studio, it will be created with a template based on a structure. This structure comes already adhering to the aggregation contract. The aggregation contract specifies that any CLR class or structure intended to server as an aggregate must adhere to the following requirements:

- ❑ It must be decorated with the SqlUserDefinedAggregate attribute.

- ❑ It must implement the required aggregation methods (Init, Accumulate, Merge, and Terminate).

Understanding these four methods that make up the aggregation contract are key to creating UDAs in SQL Server 2005:

- ❑ Init() is the initial entry-point into the UDA from a T-SQL query. This method should contain your UDA's initialization code.

- ❑ Accumulate() is called for each value that gets passed into the aggregate, adding the value passed into it to the running aggregate.

- ❑ Merge() is called when multiple processors are executing your UDAs in parallel (parallelism) to combine or merge their results.

- ❑ Terminate() is called after all of the incoming rows have been aggregated and (if parallelism was employed) the parallel aggregates have been merged as well. This method returns the final aggregated value to the caller and is the exit point of the UDA.

You are probably curious (as we were initially) about the implication of this "group" entity mentioned in these definitions. If SQL Server is running on a multiple-CPU-based machine, it can split up the cost of a query by employing parallel execution plans. If one of the parallel plans happen to contain a UDA, you must consider the effects of this, which is the reasoning behind the Merge() method.

Here is a sample UDA, uda_CountOfNegatives:

```
[Serializable]
[Microsoft.SqlServer.Server.SqlUserDefinedAggregate(Format.Native)]
public struct uda_CountOfNegatives
{
    //class fields
    private SqlInt32 iNumOfNegatives;

    public void Init()
    {
        this.iNumOfNegatives = 0;
    }

    public void Accumulate(SqlInt32 Value)
    {
        if ((Value) < 0)
        {
            this.iNumOfNegatives += 1;
        }
    }

    public void Merge(uda_CountOfNegatives Group)
    {
```

```
            this.iNumOfNegatives += Group.iNumOfNegatives;
        }

        public SqlInt32 Terminate()
        {
            return ((SqlInt32)this.iNumOfNegatives);
        }
    };
```

Not that your new UDA is created, you can test it with the following code:

```
UPDATE Test SET ID = 1
GO
SELECT dbo.uda_CountOfNegatives(ID) AS CountOfNegatives
FROM Test
GO
UPDATE Test SET ID = -1
GO
SELECT dbo.uda_CountOfNegatives(ID) AS CountOfNegatives
FROM Test
GO
```

Your results should be similar to those in Figure 4-6.

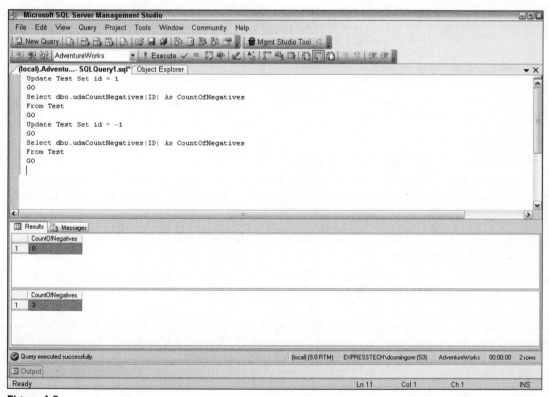

Figure 4-6

The first method in the UDS is the `Init()` method, which here just initializes a class field member to a value of 0. Basically, you are resetting the counter, if you will. The `Accumulate()` method, simply checks whether the incoming value is less then 0, and if so, it increments the counter (iNumOfNegatives). The `Merge()` method accumulates all of the groups (only applicable when running parallel execution plans); this step ensures that you have all of the passed-in values accounted for even when running on multi-CPU-based machines. Last, the `Terminate()` method is used for returning the final accumulated value to the caller.

SqlUserDefinedAggregate Attribute

The first parameter of the `SqlUserDefinedAggregate` attribute, Format, is required. Format is used to specify how you intend to serialize your class or structure. By default, you will be using the `Format.Native` serialization; however, if your UDA will be using reference types (as opposed to value types) then you will need to specify your own serialization format. For these cases, you will specify `Format.UserDefined` for the Format parameter. For more information on user-defined UDA formats, see "Attributes for SQL Server Projects and Database Objects."

The remaining parameters are optional and default to FALSE. These parameters are used by the Query Processor to determine the most efficient execution plan to use for the aggregate. Before we review each of them, we'll discuss the `IsInvariantToOrder` parameter first. `IsInvariantToOrder` is reserved for future use so that your UDAs can be sensitive to the order of data being passed into them, which they currently cannot. The other parameters are for production usage at this time, and they are:

❑   `IsInvariantToDuplicates`, which determines if your UDA will return the same result regardless of duplicate values being passed into it

❑   `IsInvariantToNulls`, which determines if your UDA will return the same result regardless of NULLs being passed into it

❑   `IsNullIfEmpty`, which determines if your UDA should return a NULL value when no rows have been passed into it

Creating, Altering, and Dropping UDAs

Unlike the managed functions and procedures, UDAs must contain the `SqlUserDefinedAggregate` attribute. So, the only way of using Visual Studio that would manually create a UDA is to perform the following steps:

1.   Build your database project's resulting assembly with the `SqlUserDefinedAggregate` attribute included.

2.   Issue a CREATE ASSEMBLY statement to load the assembly into the database.

3.   Issue a CREATE AGGREGATE statement to register your UDA.

Another interesting fact about UDAs is that you cannot change them using the traditional ALTER statement. This is because UDAs can only be built using the CLR; thus, you must DROP them and recreate them (which Visual Studio does automatically for you via the deploy option). If you wish to update the UDA's underlying code, you can simply execute an ALTER ASSEMBLY and the UDA's code base will be "refreshed." The final note is that if you have any T-SQL-based objects (views, procedures, and so on) that contain a reference to a UDA and the object has the schema binding option set, the DROP AGGRE-GATE statement will not execute. The following code manually creates a UDA and then removes it:

```
USE [AdventureWorks]
GO
CREATE AGGREGATE [dbo].[udaCountNegatives]
(@Value [int])
RETURNS[int]
EXTERNAL NAME [Chapter4].[udaCountNegatives]
GO
DROP AGGREGATE [dbo].[udaCountNegatives]
GO
```

Managed Types

SQL Server has supported the concept of user-defined types (UDTs) for some time. The idea is to create a more customized data type for your specific needs, and the result is a more consistent database. A classic example of this is the telephone number. In most databases, this entity is created as a varchar/nvarchar data type, possibly with an input mask associated with it to enforce consistency. This will suffice just fine so long as every instance of telephone number uses the same base type and input mask. But we all know that in the real world this is not the case; John will have his version of the phone number in one table, while Sally will have her own version of it in another table. This is the key reason for employing UDTs— enforcing data consistency and integrity throughout a database.

In comes SQL Server 2005 with its SQL CLR technology; now you can leverage this platform to extend the range of UDTs. Why would you want to create a managed UDT? First, managed UDTs can expose public properties and methods just like any other .NET type. The second and more obvious reason is that UDTs no longer need to be based on SQL Server native types.

Managed UDTs can be based on a class as opposed to a structure, but there is no gain in doing this and it requires an additional attribute (StructLayout). Generally speaking, you should use a struct for your UDTs unless you have a specific reason not to. UDTs are serialized by SQL Server, so you can implement your own serialization, or you can use the default format just like that of UDAs. Managed UDTs must implement the INullable interface (which only requires an IsNull property to be defined), be deco-rated with the SqlUserDefinedType and Serializable attributes, contain certain methods, and have one property. The required members of a UDT are as follows:

❑ The ToString() method, used to convert a type's value to a string representation

❑ The Parse() method, used when values are assigned to an object based on the UDT

❑ The Null property returns a NULL representation of the UDT

Managed Code

The code that implements a UDT is straightforward. You should use a structure with the required mem-bers and attributes. You can add additional properties and methods to your structure, but make sure that you decorate those members with the SqlMethod attribute. The following code creates a social security number UDT:

```
[Serializable]
    [Microsoft.SqlServer.Server.SqlUserDefinedType(Format.Native)]
    public struct udt_SSN : INullable
    {
        /////////////////////////////////////////////////////////////Methods
        public override string ToString()
        {
            return (this.iFirst3.ToString() + "-" + this.iSecond2.ToString() + "-"
                        + this.iThird4.ToString());
        }

        public static udt_SSN Parse(SqlString s)
        {
            if (s.IsNull)
                return Null;
            udt_SSN u = new udt_SSN();

            //let us use a try/catch block to return a more user-friendly error msg
            //regardless of the actual error that occurs
            try
            {
                //split the SSN on the '-'
                string[] arrNums = s.Value.Split("-".ToCharArray());
                if (Int32.Parse(arrNums[0]) <= 728)
                {
                    u.iFirst3 = Int32.Parse(arrNums[0]);
                    u.iSecond2 = Int32.Parse(arrNums[1]);
                    u.iThird4 = Int32.Parse(arrNums[2]);
                }
                else
                {
                    //invalid SSN
                    throw new Exception("INVALID SOCIAL SECURITY NUMBER, FIRST
                        THREE NUMBERS MUST BE LESS THEN 728");
                }
            }
            catch (Exception e)
            {
                if (e.Message.ToString() == "INVALID SOCIAL SECURITY NUMBER, FIRST
                        THREE NUMBERS MUST BE LESS THEN 728")
                {
                    throw e;
                }
                else
                {
                    throw new Exception("INPUT STRING WAS NOT IN CORRECT FORMAT");
                }
            }
            return (u);
        }

        /////////////////////////////////////////////////////////////Properties
        public bool IsNull
        {
```

```
        get
        {
            // Put your code here
            return bNull;
        }
    }

    public static udt_SSN Null
    {
        get
        {
            udt_SSN h = new udt_SSN();
            h.bNull = true;
            return (h);
        }
    }

    //Return The First Three Digits
    public int FirstThree
    {
        get
        {
            return (this.iFirst3);
        }
    }

    //Return The Second Two Digits
    public int SecondTwo
    {
        get
        {
            return (this.iSecond2);
        }
    }

    //Return The Last Four Digits
    public int LastFour
    {
        get
        {
            return (this.iThird4);
        }
    }

    /////////////////////////////////////////////////////////Fields
    //number locations in SSN format
    private int iFirst3;
    private int iSecond2;
    private int iThird4;

    //isnull member
    private bool bNull;
}
```

The `Parse()` method is the entry point into a UDT from SQL Server. When you declare a variable of UDT type, SQL Server simply creates a NULL reference. When you assign a value to the variable, SQL Server actually creates an instance of your UDT. The assignment of a value occurs though the `Parse()` method. So, within this method you should write all of your validation logic.

The `ToString()` method is used to return the current value of the UDT. Regardless of the type you use to internally persist the UDT's value, `ToString()` will return it as a string value to the calling T-SQL. You have to create a public `IsNull` property that returns the value of the private variable `bNull`. This is done so that calling T-SQL code can determine if the UDT is NULL or not. The following code first declares a variable of type `udt_SSN`, then calls its `IsNull` property, assigns the variable a value, and calls the `IsNull` property one more time:

```
DECLARE @SSN [dbo].[udt_SSN]
SELECT @SSN.IsNull AS [ISNULL]
SET @SSN = '111-11-1111'
SELECT @SSN.IsNull AS [ISNULL]
```

The results of this test look like Figure 4-7.

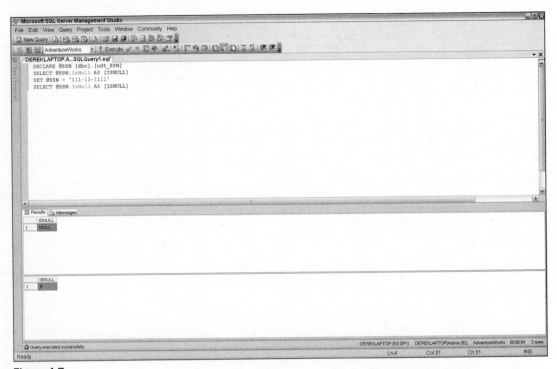

Figure 4-7

SqlUserDefinedType Attribute

Format is the only required parameter of the SqlUserDefinedType attribute (unless you specify UserDefined for the Format parameter, in which case the MaxByteSize is also required), and determines the type of serialization that will be used. The remaining optional parameters are:

- ❑ IsByteOrdered, which indicates that SQL Server can order the UDT's value based on binary serialized order.

- ❑ IsFixedLength, which indicates that every instance of the UDT is the same fixed length.

- ❑ MaxByteSize, which indicates the maximum size (in bytes) of your UDT.

- ❑ Name, which simply renames the UDT when registered by Visual Studio.

- ❑ ValidationMethodName, which indicates the method used to perform validation on the UDT during conversations. The method this maps to should return a Boolean value.

The maximum size of any UDT is 8,000 bytes.

Creating, Altering, and Dropping UDTs

Like UDAs, there is no ALTER TYPE statement, only CREATE and DROP. Similarly to removing UDAs, you cannot remove any UDT that is serving as the base type for a column or variable. The following code creates and then drops a UDT:

```
USE [AdventureWorks]
GO
CREATE TYPE [dbo].[udtPhoneNumber]
EXTERNAL NAME [Chapter4].[udtPhoneNumber]
GO
DROP TYPE [dbo].[udtPhoneNumber]
GO
```

Summary

In this chapter, we showed you the basics of creating each supported SQL CLR routine. Armed with the knowledge of this chapter and the previous one, you can begin to use the technology effectively. As you are now aware, each supported SQL CLR routine has its own unique traits and behaviors, but the development process used for all of them is pretty much the same.

In the next chapter, we will be comparing and contrasting T-SQL and SQL CLR. While there are some similarities between the two, in general the Common Language Runtime is a completely different beast from the set-based relational SQL Server engine.

5

Comparing T-SQL with Managed Code

Just hearing about the capability to code stored procedures and user-defined functions in a .NET language of your choice got the attention of more than a few developers. This is evident in the fact the .NET developers have frequently outnumbered DBAs and architects in Microsoft webcasts and other conference sidebars. The buzz from the developers is about leveraging existing knowledge to do more — specifically, extending the use of .NET programming into the database. The angst from the DBAs is about whether or not .NET database programming will replace the need for T-SQL. Just how far can you go in abstracting working with a database to a pure programmatic idiom, and is it a good idea? Feeding the angst, and on the horizon, is Microsoft's new language integrated query (DLINQ) that promises to remove the need to know even the most basic T-SQL. Whether it does remains to be seen.

This all sounds too familiar. Only a few years ago, Oracle shipped version 8i with the ability to integrate Java into the database. At that release, there were developers who wanted to use Java for everything, and DBAs who worried that it would be used for everything. Now, just a few short years later, these two capabilities coexist. Now it's just Microsoft's turn, and those of us who use their products to go through the same transition. Things will settle down once we get an understanding of where the use of SQL CLR is appropriate.

Beyond the hype and hyperbole, DBAs and T-SQL-based developers are paying attention. A few are weighing in heavily. However, their perspective is, and will be, developed cautiously. These voices will be heard. It will just take time. Unlike the Oracle DBAs, they have the added burden of being responsible for troubleshooting assemblies that can be built in several .NET languages, not merely one Java language. It is important to them that the use of SQL CLR be reliable and easy to maintain. One thing is certain: Choosing to use SQL CLR doesn't absolve you from needing to have at least a basic working knowledge of T-SQL.

That's where this chapter comes in. Since we've been working with these managed code routines as well as using T-SQL, we can help get right to the issues of using SQL CLR. What is the difference between T-SQL and SQL CLR from a coding, capability, and performance standpoint, anyway? Why and when should you consider using SQL CLR? To answer these questions we'll follow a classic compare-and-contrast examination for categories of syntactical, organizational, capabilities, and performance in both T-SQL and SQL CLR.

Syntactic Comparisons

First, let's separate and agree on the parts. SQL is the ANSI-compliant query language used to extract information from an RDBMS engine — SQL Server 2005 for our purposes. Coding in T-SQL is the flavor of ANSI SQL and the language that we use within the operating system of SQL Server. SQL CLR then is the method we use to code to the .NET CLR where SQL Server is the host (similar to how ASP.NET is hosted in IIS and IIS is hosted in Windows).

What's the hammer-and-nails difference between coding an algorithm in T-SQL and a .NET language? Well, if you are a .NET developer, the first obvious difference is a lack of IntelliSense. The T-SQL editor experience comes without any autocomplete capabilities that are available in the Visual Studio IDE — a big disappointment in the SQL2005 release. Overall, the T-SQL development environment is not as rich of an experience as coding solutions in Visual Studio. This is a matter of what you are used to using. Case-sensitivity and the whole world of the Base Class Libraries (BCL) may be an issue for you if you are accustomed to coding in T-SQL and are just starting to build SQL CLR routines. The other differences we'll be able to see with some examples. We'll first compare some of the syntactical differences.

> *We've been using a utility from Red-Gate Software, SQL Prompt , that approximates the IntelliSense experience in SQL Server. You can download this utility for free from* www.red-gate.com.

Variable Declaration and Scope

A variable in T-SQL is private by design. In T-SQL jargon, variables are *local*, meaning they're scoped to the current *batch*, or set of T-SQL statements run simultaneously. Variables are defined with a DECLARE statement, and the name has to start with the @ sign. You can define more than one variable with a single DECLARE statement, even different types. Bet you won't see this in a .NET language:

```
DECLARE @myCnt Int, @myVal varchar(10), @myAmt money
```

T-SQL variables are also subject to some automatic *casting* or data type conversion. How many times have you generated an error like the following in T-SQL while querying a VARCHAR field that you thought was numeric? The same thing can happen to variables within a stored procedure.

```
SELECT * FROM person.address WHERE postalcode = 98011
...
Msg 245, Level 16, State 1, Line 1
Conversion failed when converting the nvarchar value 'K4B 1T7' to data type int.
```

What about default values? In T-SQL, all variables have the default value of NULL when they're declared. In fact, unless you are defining a parameter, you can't assign a default to a variable.

Consequently, the extra step of using the SET statement is often forgotten. We can't tell you how many logic errors we've seen that look like the following example:

```
DECLARE @MYINT INT
SET @MYINT = @MYINT + 1
IF @MYINT > 0
  PRINT '@MYINT HAS INCREMENTED'        /*Never fires since MYINT IS NULL*/
```

The intent of the code is to increment the integer and then later evaluate that the counter has been incremented. It will never print the message because NULL + {any number} = NULL.

In the .NET languages, you can declare variables that are public or private to the body of the class where they are defined. The methods in SQL CLR are static, so you need to be careful with variables that are not scoped to individual methods. There are some differences and design limitations in simply hosting previously coded .NET assemblies with public and private variables into SQL CLR. In Chapter 2, you learned that managed code methods must be static to give SQL Server a valid entry point to bind to the method. Now these static methods that define your managed stored procedure names will affect how the class is able to interact with public and private variables. The following code shows the impact with just a simple C# stored procedure class having one public and one private variable.

```
public partial class StoredProcedures
{
    private int ValPublic = 0;
    public int ValPrivate = 0;

    [Microsoft.SqlServer.Server.SqlProcedure]
    public static void msp_myStoredProcedure()
    {
        //FIRST SOME CALCULATION HERE
        ValPublic = ValPublic++;
        ValPrivate = ValPrivate++;
    }
};
```

It may look OK, but when you compile you'll get a similar error for both assessors of each of the variables:

```
An object reference is required for the nonstatic field, method, or property
'StoredProcedures.ValPublic' myStoredProcedure.cs
```

This is because the variables ValPublic and ValPrivate are instance members. Following the C# language specification, they cannot directly be referenced from a static method. To accomplish this example, you can either change the declaration of the variables to be static or create an instance of the class to reference the instance variables like the body of msp_myStoredProcedure that follows. The point here is to dispel the notion that you can take just any .NET code and load it into SQL CLR.

```
public static void msp_myStoredProcedure()
{   //FIRST SOME CALCULATION HERE
    //CREATE AN INSTANCE OF THE CLASS SO INSTANCE VARIABLES CAN BE USED
    StoredProcedures mySp = new StoredProcedures();
    mySp.ValPrivate = mySp.ValPrivate++;
    mySp.ValPublic = mySp.ValPublic++;
}
```

For more information, see topic 17.5.2, Static and instance members, in the C# Language Specification standards document.

An advantage of coding in .NET is that you're working with variables that are more *type safe*. This means that the compiler is going to keep you honest with your use of data types. The degree to which this is enforced depends upon whether you use C++, C# or VB.NET. The type-safe capabilities will allow you to catch the unintentional conversions during compile time instead of deep into the testing processes. The issue we have with T-SQL in forgetting to assign a default value to a variable is not possible in .NET. The compilers either warn, or outright don't compile, if you fail to provide an assignment. Just don't get too complacent, because the .NET compiler can only validate your .NET code. Remember that typical database interactive code contains T-SQL, and at this point the IDE doesn't validate whether the T-SQL will work or not until run time. We'll get into that more in the Syntax checking section.

Automatic Variables and System Functions

In T-SQL, there are several built-in system functions that act like variables. Some of the more commonly used are @@IDENTITY, @@TRANCOUNT, @@ROWCOUNT, @@SERVERNAME, @@SERVICENAME, and @@VERSION. These variables are commonly used in T-SQL programming to get information from the database about data-centric activity.

When you are coding a stored procedure that has some logic dependent upon the results of an UPDATE, DELETE, or SELECT statement, the value of @@ROWCOUNT can validate that something happened or didn't happen. From the @@ROWCOUNT value, you can determine the next logical step, or if you should treat the action as a failure. A use of the @@SERVERNAME variable in a stored procedure in combination with a set of stored "known" server names can determine if the procedure should use a block of code that should only run in a production environment, or skip that code block.

These variables themselves are not readily available in the Microsoft.SQLServer.Server assembly like you might think. For most, but not all there are perfectly good replacements for them. Determining a count of affected rows is as easy as retrieving the return value of the sqlCommand object's ExecuteNonQuery method. The sqlConnection exposes a property for the server version that is equivalent to the numeric portion of what you'd find in @@VERSION. Some variables, like @@SERVERNAME, can't be found. However, if you really need them, you can use a data reader to select the variables as you would in SQL Server and bring them into your managed code environment.

```
[Microsoft.SqlServer.Server.SqlProcedure]
public static void msp_Show_SqlServerName_Example()
{
    SqlString mySqlServerName = "UNKNOWN";
    //SET UP
    SqlConnection sqlConn = new SqlConnection();
    sqlConn.ConnectionString = "Context Connection=true";
    SqlCommand sqlCmd = new SqlCommand();
    sqlCmd.CommandText = "SELECT @@SERVERNAME";

    //PREPARE TO OPEN AND RETURN VALUES
    sqlCmd.Connection = sqlConn;
    sqlConn.Open();
    SqlDataReader sqlDr = sqlCmd.ExecuteReader();
```

```
    while (sqlDr.Read())
    {
        mySqlServerName = (SqlString)sqlDr.GetSqlValue(0);
    }
    sqlDr.Close();
    sqlConn.Close();
    //STREAM OUT THE @@SERVERNAME VALUE
    SqlContext.Pipe.Send((string)mySqlServerName);
}
```

That was a lot of work for something you could do in T-SQL by simply refering to the variable. This extra work will be something to consider when coding multistep stored procedures that interact and react heavily with the database, because it goes beyond this silly little example. Using other data-centric functions like UPDATE(column) to determine if a column has been updated or even something like GetDate() or User will require traveling on the context pipeline, and you'll start losing any efficiency you've gained by coding logic in .NET.

Flow of Control

We need some commands to enable a program to behave logically and to control the flow, or the order in which the statements execute. The If and other similar constructs work the same in T-SQL and in .NET. Syntactically, just the way we block the body differs. T-SQL uses a BEGIN..END construct where C# uses braces. One difference in T-SQL is the ability to test for a series of values in the IF statement without restating the comparison. Here's an example of a multi-test IF statement in T-SQL:

```
IF @MYZIP IN('32063', '32055', '32066')
```

And here's the same logic in C#:

```
if(zipcode=="32063"||zipcode=="32055"||zipcode=="32066")
```

Normally, when the conditions of the IF become more involved, you'd shift to using a CASE statement. T-SQL uses the SELECT CASE WHEN ..THEN..END CASE construct, and C# uses a SWITCH statement. The big difference is that the T-SQL CASE statement is not limited to testing a series of values like the C# SWITCH statement. T-SQL can test multiple values within the same CASE statement. The implications are apparent in the implementation of the following business rule:

BUSINESS RULE: If the policy status is pending, and the payment is equal to the billed premium, then use new business account. If the policy status is pending, and the payment is a discrepancy, then use the policy suspense account. If the policy status is active and not suspended, then use the premium account. Otherwise, use a research account.

Here's the T-SQL version:

```
CREATE PROC usp_AccountToApply(
        @PolStatus varchar(25)='UNKNOWN', @PolSuspendCode char(1)='0',
        @AmtBill smallmoney=0.00, @AmtPaid smallmoney=0.00,
        @ReturnAccount varchar(25)='UNKNOWN' OUTPUT)
AS
```

```
SELECT @ReturnAccount = CASE
        When @PolStatus = 'PENDING' AND @AmtBill=@AmtPaid Then 'NEW BUSINESS'
        When @PolStatus = 'PENDING' AND @AmtBill<>@AmtPaid Then 'POLICY SUSPENSE'
        When @PolStatus = 'ACTIVE' AND @PolSuspendCode='0' Then 'PREMIUM ACCOUNT'
        Else 'RESEARCH ACCOUNT' End
```

And this is the C# version:

```
[Microsoft.SqlServer.Server.SqlFunction]
public static string AccountToApply(string PolStatus, string PolSuspendCode, _
                        double AmtBill, double AmtPaid)
        {
        string ReturnAccount = "UNKNOWN";
        switch (PolStatus)
        {
            case ("PENDING"):
                if (AmtBill == AmtPaid){
                    ReturnAccount = "NEW BUSINESS";
                }
                else
                {
                    ReturnAccount = "POLICY SUSPENSE";
                }
                break;
            case ("ACTIVE"):
                if (PolSuspendCode == "0")
                {
                    ReturnAccount = "PREMIUM ACCOUNT";
                    break;
                }
                else
                {
                    goto default;
                }
            default:
                ReturnAccount = "RESEARCH ACCOUNT";
                break;
        }
        return ReturnAccount;
    }
```

The T-SQL version of the function allows for the mixing of conditions at each level of the case statement. This ability to perform complex logic tests is very powerful in T-SQL — you can perform this activity across a selected set, or within an aggregation, instead of at the row level using slower looping techniques. If your task requires performing logic over sets of data, or if you are using any aggregations, perform these logical tasks in T-SQL. A side advantage is that your business analyst can also read this version.

One advantage in the C# implementation of the SWITCH statement is that the developer is immediately confronted with the possibilities of the values of the variable PolStatus in the statement. It is clear when coding the .NET version that each condition must be handled, since we separate the tests of PolStatus, then Amount calculations, and finally the consideration of the suspend code variable.

When developing business requirements like these, set up a grid with all the possibilities and then work together with the business analyst and testers for clear instructions on what to do for each of the possibilities. In T-SQL, a logical possibility resulting from combing multiple value combinations can get overlooked, resulting in dropping into the DEFAULT category — a logic bug that will show up during runtime under conditions that usually were not covered in the testing processes.

Both T-SQL and .NET have looping constructs. T-SQL is limited in range in this regard, because it has only WHILE and GOTO instructions. .NET is more prolific in this area with the addition of DO..WHILE and FOR loop instructions. T-SQL is designed for set-based operations, which generally don't include high-volume looping requirements. T-SQL is also interpreted, unlike .NET, so you would expect .NET to outperform T-SQL in looping type tasks. We've found that looping cycles in T-SQL and .NET will perform differently depending upon what occurs inside the looping body. The speed differences result from the work done within the loop. We created two similar looping functions in both languages to run a demonstrative comparison. In this example, we are just making two looping shells in both languages, with no actions within the loop. The results are shown in Figure 5-1.

T-SQL Looping Stored Procedure Test:

```
CREATE PROC usp_WhileLoop
AS
    DECLARE @i int;
    Set @i=0;
    While @i < 300000
        BEGIN
          Set @i = @i + 1
          --LATER WE'LL PUT SOME LOGIC IN HERE
        END
GO
--SCRIPT TO TEST
DECLARE @STARTDATE datetime, @ENDDATE datetime
SET @STARTDATE = getdate()
EXEC usp_WhileLoop
SET @ENDDATE = getdate()
```

C# Managed Code Looping Stored Procedure Test:

```
public partial class StoredProcedures
{
    [Microsoft.SqlServer.Server.SqlProcedure]
    public static void msp_WhileLoop()
    {
        int i=0;
        while(i<300000){
            i++;
            //LATER WE'LL PUT SOME LOGIC IN HERE
        }
    }
};
```

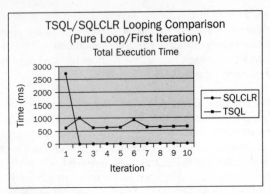
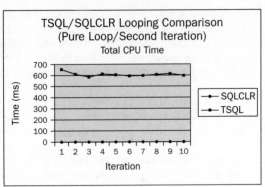

Figure 5-1

From the results in Figure 5-1, it is clear to see why SQL CLR is touted as the computational king. After the first call, in which most of the cost of setting up the assembly is incurred, the time for the execution time for the SQL CLR looping procedure quickly moves down to the submillisecond level and stays there. The T-SQL procedure settles down to slightly over 1/2 a second for 300K loop cycles. This is an impressive example, but a loop by itself is not altogether very useful. Usually we need to do something inside the loop. Add the following lines to the body of the procedures to stream the current date and time at every loop change. These lines simply return the date and time.

Add this to the T-SQL version:

```
PRINT 'CURRENT VALUE ' + Convert(varchar(10), getdate())
```

And add this to the C# version:

```
SqlContext.Pipe.Send("CURRENT DATE: " + onvert.ToString(System.DateTime.Now));
```

The results are shown in Figure 5-2.

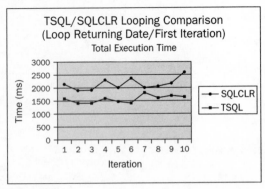
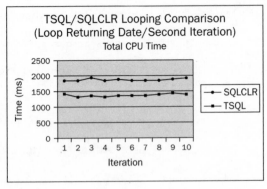

Figure 5-2

The results of the data stream test now show the results turning to favor T-SQL. It is not the action of retrieving the date and time that produces the difference in times. If you want to prove this, go back into the example and store the date, by setting a date type variable, but don't stream it back out. What is most detrimental to .NET-based SQL CLR objects is the extra work required to stream the results back to the database engine. SQL CLR solutions are going to outperform T-SQL-based code on CPU-intensive operations: looping, calculations, and iterations. T-SQL will gain when data needs to be accessed, summarized, or output. The point here is that what you do inside the loop is going to determine the performance of your procedure, regardless of which language you choose. When possible, retrieve all data prior to the loop, use the loops to make needed calculations, and then separate the communication into a separate step outside the loop. Later we'll look at loops like this that involve T-SQL CURSOR objects and computational calculations and build on the points we pointed out in this section.

Syntax Checking

When you are building logic in either language, it would be preferable to catch syntax errors during your build cycle instead of during runtime. If you are building a stored procedure to implement logic in T-SQL, you have the benefits of immediate syntax checking for any keyword within SQL Server Management Studio by selecting the parse button or using the shortcut key of Ctrl-F5. However, be aware of the limitations of this level of syntax checking. SQL Server interprets T-SQL only at runtime and doesn't guarantee resolving database objects during the syntax-checking processes. It is still possible to create a stored procedure that refers to a nonexisting table, like the following statement:

```
CREATE PROC uspMYSyntaxCheckTest
AS
UPDATE [A_NON_EXISTING_TABLE] SET [A_NON_EXISTING_DATE_COLUMN] = getdate()
```

The T-SQL syntax checker will catch incorrect uses of keywords and missing END statements or any fat-finger mistakes such as typing FORM instead of FROM in the next statement.

```
SELECT * FORM [AN_EXISTING_TABLE] /*Intentional misspelling of FROM*/
```

In contrast, SQL CLR access is dynamic — it behaves in many ways to executing a T-SQL statement using the sp_executesql function. That means that as long as the string is valid, you will be able to compile the .NET assembly and load it without ever determining whether the string can execute as a T-SQL statement during runtime. This effectively means there is no syntax checking for T-SQL coded within a .NET assembly until runtime.

Unless you use custom or LINQ database-object-based classes around database objects to abstract the handling of data for the programming environment, you are going to have some issues surrounding improperly created T-SQL. This underscores that there is no promised land of escaping at least a basic understanding of T-SQL to develop SQL CLR objects.

Custom Attributes and Optimizers

When creating stored procedures, user-defined functions, or user-defined types as T-SQL objects in SQL Server, you automatically, and perhaps unknowingly, get the advantage of some immediate optimization. SQL Server evaluates several aspects of your object for later optimal use and stores this information in its metadata. For example, it helps that SQL knows ahead of time whether it needs to load the in-process data provider for data access or whether a user-defined function can be used as an index in a computed column. SQL Server does this by examining the keywords and built-in T-SQL functions.

If an object is written in a .NET language, the only part of the SQL CLR object that SQL Server can access is the basic inputs and outputs and definition of the routine. At this time, SQL Server does not have the capability to interrogate the assembly for all the CLR class libraries to determine any optimizations prior to runtime for objects created using SQL CLR. To compensate for this, the CLR integration team exposed several attributes that you can use to decorate the SQL CLR function definitions. If you do not set these attributes, then your routines will be subject to the defaults, which in some instances will result in reduced performance, in others will simply result in a nonfunctioning object. Remember that these suggestions are similar to T-SQL index and table hints. You can provide them to help the optimization process, but if they are set incorrectly then the optimizer may ignore them. For .NET stored procedures it is assumed that they are built for data access and that they are not deterministic or precise. For the other SQL CLR objects you'll see a set of attributes that you can use the help the optimizer.

The attributes listed in Figure 5-3 are examples of those hints that SQL Server uses for SQL CLR Functions. These specific attributes are principally used to determine if SQL Server can index the results of the function in a derived table or view column. You should use these to decorate your functions depending upon their intended use.

Attribute Name	Does routine involve...	Type	Values
IsDeterministic	Returning the same result given the same input and database state?	Boolean	True False (Default)
IsPrecise	Imprecise computations or floating point operations?	Boolean	True False (Default)
DataAccess	Access to user table?	Enum	DataAccessKind.None (Default) DataAccessKind.Read
SystemData Access	Access to system tables or virtual system tables?	Enum	SystemDataAccessKind.None (Default) SystemDataAccessKind.Read

Figure 5-3

So now that we've reviewed some of the syntactical differences, let's look at how you'll be able to organize your logic in both language sets.

Organizational Comparison

The programming paradigm starts with a problem to solve. Your ideas about how to solve the problem are expressed to other people in the language you choose to use, whether it is English or German. Your ideas manifest themselves in routines written in C#, T-SQL, or VB.NET. How you organize those routines depend sometimes upon the capabilities of the language. A program written in VB6 will not look the same organizationally as a program in C#. In this section, we'll look at some of the organizational challenges of expressing your logical solutions in T-SQL and C#.

Structured Programming

Typically, T-SQL programmers write stored procedures in a top-down style to solve the whole programming problem. Tasks are not typically broken down into smaller procedures and then wired together into a larger stored procedure. Occasionally, you may find some procedural calls, generally to user-defined functions, that return calculated scalar results, or uses of table-valued user-defined functions, but mostly you'll find the entire solution confined to one stored procedure. This organizational style is often the result of the limitations of T-SQL. The language is particularly suited to working with sets of data, yet there is no way currently to pass sets of data as parameters around to different procedures. There are ways to create ##TEMP tables that can be persisted globally so that a series of interconnected procedures can access the same work tables, but this solution must be used with care to avoid query collisions, and it is obviously not scalable.

One of the downsides of the current organizational limitations of T-SQL is that stored procedures can become long, wieldy, and difficult to debug. If something goes wrong with a large stored procedure, rewinding the data and isolating the procedure to the point that is generating the error has not been easy to do.

SQL CLR routines can easily implement a procedural programming style by breaking the task into several smaller tasks. If you need to pass data in sets to sub procedures or functions, you can do this within the .NET environment by retrieving data into a ADO.NET data table or dataset and passing it around to subfunctions. Organizationally, this is a great boost to being able to isolate portion of the problem to take advantage of abstraction and to allow for code reuse. You do need to be careful with your context connection though — you can only perform one action at a time through this connection. We'll dig into this later.

Consider the requirement of creating a list of SQL CLR routines for a database for display as an HTML page. This could be useful for DBAs to keep track of managed code that is on the various servers. The flowchart of the solution is simple:

1. Retrieve the list of managed routines.

2. Convert the list into an HTML table.

The T-SQL stored procedure approach would start by selecting the data and then iterating through the rows to create the HTML table, like this:

```
CREATE PROCEDURE usp_MakeHTMLListofManagedRoutines
    AS
--Procedure TO generate HTML TABLE OF managed code routines
SET NOCOUNT ON
DECLARE @ROUTINE_CATALOG varchar(100)
DECLARE @ROUTINE_SCHEMA varchar(100)
DECLARE @ROUTINE_NAME varchar(100)
DECLARE @html AS varchar(MAX);
SET @html = '';

DECLARE routine_cursor CURSOR FOR
SELECT ROUTINE_CATALOG, ROUTINE_SCHEMA, ROUTINE_NAME
FROM INFORMATION_SCHEMA.ROUTINES
WHERE ROUTINE_BODY = 'EXTERNAL'
AND ROUTINE_CATALOG IS NOT NULL AND ROUTINE_SCHEMA IS NOT null
AND ROUTINE_NAME IS NOT NULL
ORDER BY ROUTINE_CATALOG

OPEN routine_cursor

-- Perform the first fetch.
FETCH NEXT FROM routine_cursor
INTO @ROUTINE_CATALOG, @ROUTINE_SCHEMA, @ROUTINE_NAME
```

```
-- Check @@FETCH_STATUS to see if there are any more rows to fetch.

WHILE @@FETCH_STATUS = 0
BEGIN
    SET @html = @html + '<tr>'
    SET @html = @html + '<td>' + @ROUTINE_CATALOG + '</td>'
    SET @html = @html + '<td>' + @ROUTINE_SCHEMA + '</td>'
    SET @html = @html + '<td>' + @ROUTINE_NAME + '</td>'
    SET @html = @html + '</tr>'
    -- This is executed as long as the previous fetch succeeds.
    FETCH NEXT FROM routine_cursor
    INTO @ROUTINE_CATALOG, @ROUTINE_SCHEMA, @ROUTINE_NAME
END
SET @html = '<table cellspacing=1 class=''data'' width=90%>' + @html
SET @html = @html + '</table>'

CLOSE routine_cursor
DEALLOCATE routine_cursor
SELECT @html AS Managed_Code_Routines_Html_Table
SET NOCOUNT OFF
```

The main organizational issue with T-SQL is that you can't break this into two tasks. Because of T-SQL language constraints, you can't create a general factory-like method to return just any CURSOR because the DECLARE CURSOR operation does not support a variable-based T-SQL statement. The statement DECLARE MyCursor CURSOR FOR @MYSQL is not a valid statement. Even though you can create the cursor in one procedure and then pass the cursor around, the receiver of that cursor is going to need to know how to fetch that information into variables, so you can't just pass any cursor around. You also don't have the rich functionality of the ADO datasets to iterate by column. This means that you would have to create a T-SQL stored procedure to retrieve each cursor and another stored procedure to parse each cursor into HTML. This extra work provides no added benefit for future code use and is why you will see top-down approaches to cursor-based problem solving in T-SQL.

In .NET, you have access to cursors through the ADO.NET libraries, and you can more easily break down the problem into repeatable tasks that you can use later. The following code is the same problem resolved using SQL CLR. First, create a regular C# class named CursorUtilities in a project. Add a GetDataSetWithSQL method to return a general DataSet when provided a SQL string. Then add a method to accept an DataSet to return an HTML-based table.

```
using System;
using System.Data;
using System.Data.SqlClient;
using System.Data.SqlTypes;
using Microsoft.SqlServer.Server;

namespace DatabaseUtilities
{
    public partial class CursorUtilities
    {
        public static DataSet GetDataSetWithSQL(string mySQL)
        {
            SqlDataAdapter sqlDa = new SqlDataAdapter();
            DataSet sqlDs = new DataSet();
            using (SqlConnection sqlConn =
```

```
            new SqlConnection("Context Connection=True"))
        {
            SqlCommand sqlCmd = new SqlCommand(mySQL, sqlConn);
            sqlCmd.CommandType = CommandType.Text;
            sqlDa.SelectCommand = sqlCmd;
            sqlDa.Fill(sqlDs, "TABLE");
            sqlConn.Close();
        }
        return sqlDs;
    }
    public static string CreateHtmlTableWithDataSet(DataSet myDs)
    {
        string html;
        int i = 0;
        int fldCnt = 0;
        // display dataset contents into html table
        // first open the table and set up the table headers
        html = "<table cellspacing=1 class='data' width=90%>";
        fldCnt = myDs.Tables[0].Columns.Count;
        for (int x = 0; x <= fldCnt - 1; x++)
        {
            html += "<TH>" + myDs.Tables[0].Columns[x].ColumnName + "</TH>";
        }

        //Then gather row information into an HTML string
        for (int x = 0; x <= myDs.Tables["TABLE"].Rows.Count - 1; x++)
        {
            html += "<tr>";
            while (i < fldCnt)
            {
                html += string.Concat("<td>",
                    Convert.ToString(myDs.Tables["TABLE"].Rows[x][i]),
                    "</td>");
                i++;
            }
            html += "</tr>";
            i = 0;

        }
        html += "</table>";
        return html;
    }
  }
}
```

To use these utilities add a Stored Procedure class to the project and create the following SQL CLR stored procedure:

```
[Microsoft.SqlServer.Server.SqlProcedure]
public static void msp_MakeHTMLListofManagedRoutines()
{
    string mySQL;
    mySQL = "SELECT ROUTINE_CATALOG, ROUTINE_SCHEMA, ROUTINE_NAME, CREATED ";
    mySQL = string.Concat(mySQL, " FROM INFORMATION_SCHEMA.ROUTINES ");
```

```
        mySQL = string.Concat(mySQL, "WHERE ROUTINE_BODY = 'EXTERNAL'");

        DataSet myDs;
        myDs = CursorUtilities.GetDataSetWithSQL(mySQL);
        SqlContext.Pipe.Send(CursorUtilities.CreateHtmlTableWithDataSet(myDs));
    }
```

This code is a more modular than the T-SQL version. The SQL CLR method msp_MakeHTMLListof
ManagedRoutines uses the DatabaseUtilities namespace to access the static methods to retrieve a
Dataset. Once it has the dataset, it sends it to a method to parse into an HTML table and then streams
those results out to the caller.

The difference between using T-SQL and SQL CLR is that you were able to break down the task into
smaller subtasks. This enables the ability to build a generic set of libraries that you can easily use for
future CLR-based objects. To use the same code to produce a similar result streaming out the total memory used by CLR processes will be easy using your libraries and one of the new views provided for you,
named dm_os_memory_clerks. All you have to do now is add the following method to your existing
stored procedure class:

```
[Microsoft.SqlServer.Server.SqlProcedure]
    public static void msp_MakeHtmlListofCLRMemoryCommitted()
    {
        string mySQL;
        mySQL = "Select Type, Name, virtual_memory_committed_kb " +
                "shared_memory_committed_kb AS Total__Memory_Committed ";
        mySQL = string.Concat(mySQL, "from sys.dm_os_memory_clerks ");
        mySQL = string.Concat(mySQL, "where type = 'MEMORYCLERK_SQLCLR' ");

        SqlDataReader sqlRoutineDr;
        sqlRoutineDr = CursorUtilities.GetDataReaderWithSQL(mySQL);
        SqlContext.Pipe.Send(CursorUtilities._
            CreateHtmlTableWithDataReader(sqlRoutineDr));
    }
(results)..
<table cellspacing=1 class='data'
width=90%><tr><td>MEMORYCLERK_SQLCLR</td><td>Default</td><td>7912</td></tr></table>
```

The major point here is that the SQL CLR code starts to deliver on reusability and potential reliability as
you begin to build on libraries more robust than these simple examples. The things you choose to build
in SQL CLR will benefit from this type of code organization and can make SQL CLR a more organized
coding option than T-SQL.

Object-Oriented Programming?

How far can you take this organizational approach? Should we dare mention object-oriented program-
ming? Well, yes and no. For now, and as far as we know in the immediate future, T-SQL does not have
the capabilities of inheritance and polymorphism—at least in terms of internal object development in
SQL Server. T-SQL is procedural and anything built on top of it will be restricted by these limitations.
T-SQL will not be able to inherit from a SQL CLR user-defined type or even its own T-SQL types. Since
T-SQL can't use inheritance, it is also not going to be able to take advantage of polymorphism—even if

it is possible to coerce an example to work by recoding the inherited methods in the inheriting type. Perhaps the "inability" is really not such a big deal in the larger context of using T-SQL. Perhaps the value of being able to code object-oriented user-defined types in a database is not high on most developer wish lists anyway. Does the revelation that T-SQL doesn't follow all OO tenets turn you away from programming in T-SQL?

The relevant point is that that as long as you stay in the arena of the SQL CLR, you *do* have access to all the four pillars of OO via the underlying .NET Framework. T-SQL is quite capable of calling a user-defined function built upon base classes. That fact alone is an advantage of monumental organizational proportions. Now you have the ability to generate factory methods for your CLR routines that return disconnected datasets or SQL context connections, and these capabilities can enable you to create your own base stored procedure, UDF, or aggregate classes. When you create new SQL CLR procedures, you can then inherit from the base classes and have access to best-practice methods and code. Contrast this with T-SQL development, where "inheritance" is enabled through using cut-and-paste. This provides an organizational advantage that can be leveraged for building things like CLR-based calculation engines that use the power of .NET for CPU processing.

Earlier in the structured programming topic, we discussed the advantages of being able to abstract tasks into procedures. You built a class called `CursorUtilities` that could return a dataset when passed a SQL statement, and another method that could convert a dataset into HTML table output. You can use this same class to demonstrate that SQL CLR allows the use of inheritance and polymorphism. To do this, make sure you have completed the previous cursor utility example and have deployed it into your SQL Server instance. In a new project, add a reference to the `CursorUtilities` class that you just created by right-clicking on the References node in the project explorer and browsing to the assembly that contains the cursor utilities. (Usually, the assembly references in SQLServer use the solution name if you are using the Visual Studio IDE to deploy). Once the reference is added, add a new `StoredProcedures` class, insert the namespace of `DatabaseUtilities,` and have the stored procedures class inherit from the `CursorUtilities` class. Now you have access to the two methods: `GetDataSetWithSQL` and `CreateHtmlTableWithDataSet`.

```
using System;
using System.Data;
using System.Data.SqlClient;
using System.Data.SqlTypes;
using Microsoft.SqlServer.Server;
using DatabaseUtilities;

public partial class StoredProcedures : CursorUtilities
{
    [Microsoft.SqlServer.Server.SqlProcedure]
    public static void msp_BaseStoredProcedureTest()
    {
        string HTML;
        string SQL="SELECT sa.[name], ad.[appdomain_name], clr.[load_time] " +
        "FROM sys.dm_clr_loaded_assemblies AS clr ";
        "INNER JOIN sys.assemblies AS sa ";
        "ON clr.assembly_id = sa.assembly_id ";
        "INNER JOIN sys.dm_clr_appdomains AS ad ";
        "ON clr.appdomain_address = ad.appdomain_address ";
        DataSet myDs;
```

```
        myDs = GetDataSetWithSQL(SQL);
        HTML = CreateHtmlTableWithDataSet(myDs);
        SqlContext.Pipe.Send(HTML);
    }
};
```

Now generating an HTML table to show the assemblies that are currently loaded is trivial. Notice that you have abstracted the tasks of creating a context connection and issuing the command text to retrieve the dataset. This may not be fully object-oriented, but in terms of getting at the purpose of creating and organizing code, this accomplishes the goals of encapsulating best practices and code reuse. If you execute the msp_BaseStoredProcedureTest, you'll see that it successfully generates an HTML table with the contents of your loaded assemblies. Using SQL CLR, future coders can take advantage of proven frameworks to establish reliability and consistency. Best of all, you can maintain a consistent approach that attempts to reduce and factor out details so that you can better focus on solving domain-specific puzzles.

Error Handling

For any logic solution, you need to consider how to organize the handling of unexpected errors. Before SQL Server 2005, error handling for T-SQL was primitive. The model was a lot like classic ASP where you set error handling to Resume Next and catch the error after the fact. Stored procedures everywhere are littered with code checking the @@Error variable after issuing any database command. Now T-SQL includes a TRY...CATCH block that is very similar to the error-handling method that developers use in the .NET environment.

Syntactically, the T-SQL TRY...CATCH block looks just like the C# version, except that the BEGIN and END blocks moved up with the TRY keyword to confuse the T-SQL folks. Just remember that you'll be coding BEGIN TRY and END TRY, not TRY BEGIN..END like all the other T-SQL code blocks that use BEGIN and END. Another difference is that T-SQL doesn't have a FINALLY block. However, you can accomplish the same thing by coding the actions you want to always occur after the TRY block right after the END CATCH block. T-SQL also does not use the Throw keyword, but again can accomplish the same thing using the legacy T-SQL RAISEERROR command. There are also some new functions like ERROR_LINE() that allow you to get to line in the T-SQL batch where the error was thrown and ERROR_MESSAGE() that allow you to examine the message. There is no argument that the new error handling model is more robust and useful in coding context.

The problem organizationally is where do you handle the exception that you catch? In most cases, we've always been in this same scenario. If a client calls a stored procedure expecting a return value of 0 or 1, what do you do with the extra information you have detailing the error? If you return this information in a set of columns, the client may throw it away. If you agree to send the client the error information, what do you do with a stored procedure that normally returns a rowset?

Our experience is that objects located in the database should log detailed error information to the database and raise errors to the calling client. This methodology creates software with consistent error handling that should continue to push the error back to the original calling routine. This is commonly referred to as allowing the error to "unwind up the stack." It will also not be easy for the client to ignore the error using this methodology like it would be if each client had to look for return codes or special rowsets. One thing to remember when using SQL CLR is that the code is hosted, so your SQL CLR code is also a client. If your SQL CLR code is commingled with T-SQL objects, you'll need to be prepared for some errors that will not be detectable during the caching and loading of the assembly during runtime, particularly T-SQL compilation errors. This can produce some unexpected troubleshooting challenges. For detailed information about how to handle errors and troubleshooting SQL CLR routines, refer to Chapter 9.

Capability Comparison

If syntactic and organizational differences aren't differentiating a choice of technology for you, perhaps you are more interested in a comparison of the capabilities of T-SQL and SQL CLR. SQL CLR can be let out of the cage, and we can demonstrate the many things that CLR allows you to do outside of the confines of SQL Server, but to keep the comparison fair, this section will focus on the capabilities of SQL CLR and T-SQL within SQL Server. You will see that SQL CLR fills in nicely where T-SQL falters. String handling, for example, is not really a strong suit of T-SQL, but a .NET managed code routine can really make these tasks trivial by leveraging the rich Base Class Library. You know that if SQL CLR can handle strings, there are better ways of dealing with data in arrays, so we'll take a look at how T-SQL stacks up in that regard. We'll also examine how you'll approach the need to use cursor approaches in both methods to solve a business problem, which is critical to developers. Finally, we'll get down to the nitty-gritty and find out which technique wins the battle of accessing and updating data. There's been a lot of discourse on this topic lately, and we'll show you how both SQL CLR and T-SQL routines stack up. In that regard take a look at some of the differences between how you'll be dealing with the built-in data-centric functions of T-SQL if you move to SQL CLR.

T-SQL Data-Centric Built-Ins

One of the most powerful aspects of T-SQL is the ability to use data-centric built-in functions for set-based calculations that determine averages, standard deviations, max, min, and sum values. These functions work efficiently by design with set based-data, so you can be sure that rewriting them in SQL CLR is not going to improve your performance. You can write your own SUMAMT aggregate to compete with the T-SQL SUM function to get an idea about what you are up against.

If you've done any report programming, SQL CLR user-defined aggregates are just like the running total formulas in Crystal Reports. You define an initializing formula that occurs on the start of a grouping, an accumulator to accumulate new values within the grouping, and a terminator to report the result. The only complication is that UDAs have a merge method that SQL may use when the optimizer chooses to implement the UDA with multiple threads. The merge method merges the results of multiple instances of your UDA back into the parent thread to return a unified result. If you were to rewrite your own version of the T-SQL SUM aggregate function in SQL CLR, it would look something like this:

```
using System;
using System.Data;
using System.Data.SqlClient;
using System.Data.SqlTypes;
using Microsoft.SqlServer.Server;

[Serializable]
[Microsoft.SqlServer.Server.SqlUserDefinedAggregate(Format.Native,
IsInvariantToDuplicates=false, IsInvariantToNulls=true, IsNullIfEmpty=true)]
public struct SumAmt
```

```
{
    private SqlMoney myTotalAmt;
    //This is called once per use of aggregate
    public void Init()
    {
        myTotalAmt = 0;
    }
    //This is called once per value input
    public void Accumulate(SqlMoney myAmt)
    {
        if (!(myAmt.IsNull)){
            myTotalAmt += myAmt;
        }
    }
    //This is used if SQL spawns multithreaded processes and needs to
    //combine results
    public void Merge(SumAmt ThreadedTotalAmt)
    {
        if (!(ThreadedTotalAmt.myTotalAmt.IsNull))
        {
            myTotalAmt += ThreadedTotalAmt.myTotalAmt;
        }
    }
    //return results
    public SqlMoney Terminate()
    {
        if (myTotalAmt.IsNull)
        {
            return SqlMoney.Null;
        }
        else
        {
            return myTotalAmt;
        }
    }
}
```

You'll notice that creating a SQL CLR summation contains a little more code to worry about than just issuing a SELECT SUM() statement, but all this code will be forgotten once you deploy the UDA. Once deployed, the UDA will be available with approximately the same syntax: SELECT dbo.SUMAMT([COLUMN NAME]). In a way, this gives you the ability to pseudo-override default T-SQL functions. How is the performance? If you study this aggregate, you'll realize that you are asking the SQL engine to run each row one at a time through this SQL CLR code. Even though the T-SQL SUM() also has to read each row, it has less distance to travel, fewer layers, and optimized access to index pages. You can't see exactly what the T-SQL version does in the profiler, but if you run the profiler while you summarize a column using the T-SQL SUM(), you'll see only one statement prepared and executed for the T-SQL version for all the rows. In the SQL CLR version, you will see a statement prepared and completed for each row that SQL CLR summarizes. We ran a simulation against the AdventureWorks SalesOrderDetail and TransactionHistory tables using 1,000 iterations to measure the average time per transaction and average CPU time. The results demonstrate that T-SQL was the clear winner at an average of four times faster than the CLR version.

However, the purpose of UDAs is not to replace existing aggregates. You could just have easily issued a SELECT summation query from SQL CLR to use the power of the built-in SQL aggregates. The power of the UDA is in the idea that you can now create your own aggregates. Let's alter this example to summarize only evenly divisible money amounts. Change the test condition in the UDA Accumulate method and T-SQL to the following:

Make this change to the C# code:

```
if (!(myAmt.IsNull) && ((int)(myAmt * 100) % 2 == 0))
```

Make this change to the T-SQL:

```
sum(case WHEN actualcost % 2 = 0 THEN actualcost ELSE 0 end)
```

You can run the test against the order and transaction tables in the AdventureWorks database and compare the results of the original SumAmt and evenly divisible SumAmt execution times. Figure 5-4 graphically demonstrates that the average processing times show T-SQL clearly executing faster by a factor of four.

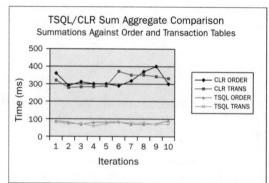 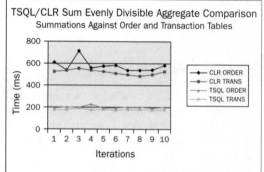

Figure 5-4

Still, since you are still only dealing with subsecond response times, speed may not be the deciding factor when you weigh the possibilities of creating domain-specific aggregations. UDAs have practical uses for domain-specific or advanced statistical calculations that are not available in T-SQL and as overloaded operations for user-defined types.

One of the limitations is that the Accumulate method only allows one input parameter. If you need the ability to summarize and convert a currency amount stored as the native currency amount in one field and the currency type in another to a common currency, you won't be able to use the UDA with both the amount and current type columns. One alternative is to go back to using established methods of creating a cursor-based calculation that pulls back the data and summarizes each row storing and incrementing global variables. However, with SQL CLR you can currently get around this single column limitation of UDAs by creating a user-defined type that stores both the native amount and the currency type. Then create an aggregate called SumUSAmt with an Accumulate method that would accept the user-defined type and apply logic to convert native amounts and summarize to a new currency like the U.S. dollar. The CLR Integration team at SQL Server is aware of this limitation and are working on this feature for a possible future release.

Data aggregated using native SQL data types can be calculated more easily using T-SQL. The following T-SQL script is a solution to the native currency conversion aggregation.

```
DECLARE @AMT AS TABLE(Currency_Type varchar(15), Currency_Amount money)
INSERT INTO @AMT VALUES ('Euro', 10.00)
INSERT INTO @AMT VALUES ('USDollar', 10.00)

DECLARE @CURRRATE AS TABLE(Currency_Type varchar(15),
        USDollarExchangeRate decimal(9,8))
INSERT INTO @CURRRATE VALUES ('Euro', 1.2125)
INSERT INTO @CURRRATE VALUES ('USDollar', 1)

SELECT SumUSAmt=SUM(Amt.Currency_Amount * Rate.USDollarExchangeRate)
FROM @AMT Amt
INNER JOIN @CURRRATE Rate
ON Amt.Currency_Type = Rate.Currency_Type
```

T-SQL is most likely the best choice when the programming problem involves data aggregation or statistical functions—as long as T-SQL can easily make the calculation. If the calculation is float-based and the digits are significant, SQL CLR will produce the more accurate result. If the aggregation is domain-specific, SQL CLR is the best choice over a similar function in T-SQL based on performance, accuracy, and ease of programming.

Handling NULL Values

T-SQL and SQL CLR handle NULL values in a database differently. It is important that you understand the capabilities and limitations of both because a T-SQL object with parameters can handle a NULL value. SQL CLR objects with improperly defined parameters will result in errors if you are feeding a set of rows into the parameters and one of the parameters evaluates to a NULL value. To the T-SQL and database programmers, NULL values are significant. A NULL indicates a missing or undefined value. For a nullable amount field, the value could provide a distinction between a loan balance paid off to $0.00, or an account that has never had a loan balance (NULL). Primitive typed languages like .NET or Java generally don't support null values for value types, so much time is spent attempting to avoid them or code around them. Since we are literally standing in the gap between the UI and the database, we are going to be dealing with NULLs, so we need to understand the differences in using NULL in T-SQL and in the .NET languages.

In T-SQL, you have a NULL keyword, you can test for NULL with IsNull, you can automatically convert NULLs to a default value with the IsNull() function, and you can create parameters for stored procedures and UDFs that use variables that can accept NULL values, or even be specifically assigned default NULL values.

When you're building a SQL CLR object in a database with a potential of NULL values, use the native data types available in the System.Data.SqlTypes namespace. A SQL CLR UDF with a simple String parameter that works on your database (because your DBA bans NULLABLE fields) will suddenly generate NullReferenceException errors if it is moved to, or uses data from, another less restrictive database. The NULL exception occurs in this example during the assignment of the Input parameter, and you can't trap the error within the SQL CLR object.

The good news is that if you use the SQL data types, you inherit, through the INullable interface, the ability to check for NULL by using the .IsNull method on the variable. The bad news is that you have to make sure you add this checking process in all your code. Another downside to using the SQL data types is that you lose some of the rich functionality available in the String classes unless you convert it to a String data type. A method as simple as .Length is not available in a SqlData variable. This unfortunately means casting the value to a CLR data type to calculate the string length.

Programmers coming from the T-SQL environments need to pay more attention to the use of NULLs when building or troubleshooting SQL CLR objects and be aware of the bias towards the way T-SQL manages NULLs and the restrictions within SQL CLR. One of the good things that we see coming out of CLR is that database developers will get some insight into the issues that developers encounter when using NULLs, and together they can agree on some approaches that will make life easier for both sides.

String Parsing

T-SQL is powerful in delivering and updating data, so it is easy to forget that it has capabilities of string manipulation. These capabilities have steadily improved since the removal of the 255-character varchar limitation in version 7.0, but string manipulations still remain CPU-intensive. Since T-SQL is specifically designed for data management functions, it is not natural to expect processing string- or memory-based data to be efficient. Yet it is common to encounter tasks of parsing out information from fields that hardly seem atomic, much less relational. Examples include parsing out ZIP codes from address data, e-mail addresses, and comparing potential name matches by parsing out special characters and spaces. The question up to now has been whether we should do this parsing activity in the database or simply retrieve the data and manipulate it after retrieval in a client application. Because of the higher CPU costs incurred by parsing in T-SQL, most come down on the side of leaving parsing activity with the client. With SQL CLR, you now have a third option to consider. Should you manipulate the string on the server using .NET code on the database prior to sending the data down the network?

Consider a problem where a mainframe sporadically creates a special character in a column of data that was outside the normal alphanumeric ASCII character ranges. The character is not consistent, so it isn't easily solved using the REPLACE() T-SQL function. The solution to this problem will help you examine the question about where the parsing activity should occur and look back at the previous section and examine the concerns about NULL values when working with strings. One way to solve this is with a T-SQL user-defined function to strip out the bad characters that could exist in this data during the ETL process. The T-SQL function body would look like the following:

```
CREATE FUNCTION dbo.ufn_ReplaceNonAscIIChar(
  @MyColumnData as varchar(50)
  )

RETURNS varchar(50)
AS
BEGIN
  /*=================================================
      PROCEDURE:   [ufn_ReplaceNonAscIIChar]
      PURPOSE: Clean up non ascii character data in a
               column
      HISTORY: Created 3/27/2006 5:12:31 PM
    =================================================*/
  DECLARE @i as integer
  DECLARE @lLen as integer
  DECLARE @Char as char(1)
  DECLARE @MyNewColumnData as varchar(50)
```

```
    SET @lLen = LEN(@MyColumnData)
    SET @i = 1

WHILE @i <= @lLen
    BEGIN
      SET @CHAR = SUBSTRING(@MyColumnData, @i, 1)
      IF ASCII(@CHAR) BETWEEN 32 and 126
         SET @MyNewColumnData = isnull(@MyNewColumnData, '') + @CHAR

         SET @i = @i + 1
    END

Return @MyNewColumnData

END
```

There are several ways to perform the same function in SQL CLR. The following code attempts to mimic the T-SQL for comparison purposes. (See section on new BCL capabilities for a faster way to perform this action using regular expressions).

```
[Microsoft.SqlServer.Server.SqlFunction]
public static SqlString mfn_ReplaceNonAscChar(SqlString MySQLColumnData)
{
    string NewColumnData = string.Empty;
    string MyColumnData;
    char OneChar;

    MyColumnData = Convert.ToString(MySQLColumnData);

    //NOTE: We have to check for NULL Here or incur
    //      a NullReferenceException later.
    if (MySQLColumnData.IsNull)
    {
        MyColumnData = string.Empty;
    }
    else
    {
        MyColumnData = (String)Convert.ToString(MySQLColumnData);
    }

    if (MyColumnData.Length <= 1){
        NewColumnData = MyColumnData;
    }
    else{
    for (int i=0; i < MyColumnData.Length; i++){
        OneChar = MyColumnData[i];
        if (OneChar >= 32 && OneChar <= 126)
        {
            NewColumnData += OneChar;
        }
    }
    }
    return (SqlString)NewColumnData;
}
```

Note that in the T-SQL version, you didn't have to concern yourself with NULL values. An incoming NULL value passes through the parameter and evaluates to NULL when the length is checked. In the SQL CLR function, you can't check the length of the SqlString data type without converting to a string class. You also can't convert to the string class until you've validated that the type is not a NULL. If you forget the step of checking for NULLs, you'll end up with a NULL exception error.

Even with all the string conversions in the SQL CLR version, it is faster in execution time than the T-SQL version, as shown in Figure 5-5. You should expect CLR to be faster because of the looping structure implemented in the solution and the performance differences related to looping that we discussed earlier in this chapter. It may be surprising to see that the CPU time involved in the SQL CLR version is much less than the T-SQL version. This is because T-SQL code is interpreted and string functions executed within SQL Server are going to be CPU-intensive.

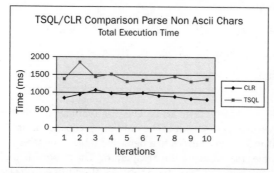 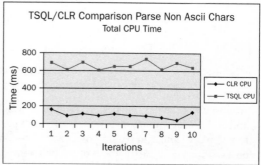

Figure 5-5

So, which option should you use? It depends upon what you are ultimately doing. We chose to implement the T-SQL version because the client is not yet using SQL Server 2005, and SQL CLR is not yet possible for them. Even so, since the process that uses this function runs on off-hours, the CPU intensity is not an issue, so T-SQL may still be the preferred solution. This is just an example of how making decisions about when and where to use SQL CLR are not one-dimensional decisions that can be based solely on performance.

Array Handling

Arrays are convenient temporary structures that organize same-type data to be easily accessible programmatically. Typically, you use arrays in programmatic contexts when you need a fast, convenient, organized work area to store and retrieve data. Arrays use memory and are fast, so most languages have a specification for them. In the database world, the structural paradigm revolves around tables. Tables are similar in structure to arrays, so it is understandable that T-SQL doesn't support a built-in array type, opting instead for temporary table structures. With the addition of table variables in T-SQL, you even have the option to store the table structure in memory, which is recommended for small volumes of data. The following statement creates a nonpersisted table to simulate an array. The advantage to table variables is that they are disposed of automatically once the scope of the batch is completed.

```
DECLARE @MYARRAY AS TABLE(MYID INT IDENTITY(1,1), MYDATA varchar(MAX))
```

If you have large data volumes to manipulate, you should use temporary tables that are persisted in `tempdb`. Temp tables have the advantage of using indexing and constraints such as Identify fields. To create an as a temp table, use a T-SQL statement similar to the following:

```
CREATE TABLE #MYARRAY (MYID INT IDENTITY(1, 1), MYDATA varchar(MAX))
```

Once you have a defined structure, you can perform actions similar to methods available for arrays in .NET 2.0 by using T-SQL. The following table lists some the similar methods.

.NET	T-SQL
.Length	SELECT COUNT(*) FROM @MYARRAY
.Clear	DELETE FROM @MYARRAY
.Find	SELECT * FROM @MYARRAY WHERE MYDATA = '<VALUE>'
.Sort	SELECT * FROM @MYARRAY ORDER BY MYDATA
.Reverse	SELECT * FROM @MYARRAY ORDER BY MYDATA DESC

At the end of the day, the best you can do in T-SQL is to simulate an array. The disadvantage in this T-SQL and SQL CLR comparison is that T-SQL can't pass array types around. The only thing you can do that is functionally similar to passing the array is to store and make changes to a persisted table. This table can be a work table in the database or a global temp table created using the ## operator. The downside to this approach is that it is not a scalable solution, and the danger exists of two processes attempting to access the same table. The inconvenience is that you are constrained into a procedural programming model, because you can't build an array in one function and then process it in another. This makes your solutions lengthy and hard to troubleshoot. The advantage to using T-SQL temp tables is you can perform work into temp locations and then JOIN these results to your real persisted tables and update in a set-based action. This is faster then having to iterate over each item in an array and sending separate UPDATE statements. Later in this chapter you'll see two examples using temp tables in SQL CLR.

Computations and Calculations

If you've been following the rollout of SQL CLR, you'll have noticed that math-intensive or computation-intensive calculations are often cited as a reason to use SQL CLR routines. The consensus is that if you are performing a task that involves extensive computation, number crunching, or custom algorithms, you should begin looking at .NET code and SQL CLR. You might be wondering, then, what constitutes an extensive computation. Adding two numbers together or recreating current T-SQL functions is not an ideal use of SQL CLR, mainly because of the tradeoff between the loss of developer productivity over using a function that is trivial or already exists. Generally, you want to develop calculations in .NET that involve more than one math or logical operation to run through the CPU's ALU. This is because you expect that .NET code, by nature of being compiled, will run very efficiently—at least more efficiently than T-SQL.

So, how computation-intensive does a calculation needs to be to use SQL CLR? You can start with evaluating a simple function like ufn_Add that adds two decimal types together. Running an UPDATE statement using the UDF to update 1,000 rows in 1,000 iterations will generate results similar to Figure 5-6. The SQL CLR function performs the same updates in about one third of the total time taken for a T-SQL addition calculation. You can see in the CPU statistics that almost all the difference between the two methods is taken up in the CPU. The remainder of the time is spent accessing the data. If SQL CLR can get the data, calculate it, and respond faster than T-SQL on a simple add, it should be able to blow by T-SQL on calculations that are more complicated. In fact, you'll find that using SQL CLR on most math calculations will result in some reduced CPU time and total processing time.

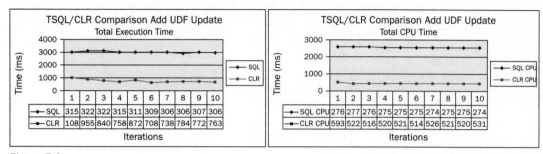

Figure 5-6

If CLR-based calculations are faster, should you use CLR data types as well? Is there a performance advantage in using SQL data types versus native CLR types? Notice in Figure 5-7 that there is a slight edge in total time taken in the simple Add function for the CLR version using SqlTypes over native CLR types. Statistically, this is a slight difference, but there is an edge in the CPU to using the SqlTypes over the CLR types. The benefit in the SqlTypes is that they don't need to be converted, because rows are bound to the function parameters. Earlier, we discussed the danger of not using SQL data types because of the need to handle NULL values in data. There is also another good reason to use SQL data types when working with SQL data — memory. The next example will demonstrate this effect.

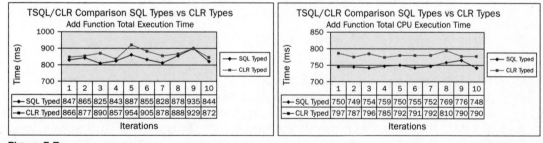

Figure 5-7

As you begin to develop computations in managed code, you'll find that although you can accept data through SQL data type parameters, when you need to perform calculations using the Math class, or anything not typically overridden, you have to perform some conversion into a native CLR type. The more you do this, the less efficient it is to keep the variables throughout your code body as SqlTypes. To examine this, we took a standard financial calculation that calculates a fixed payment for a loan, wrote it first using SqlTypes, and then with native CLR types. The two functions look similar, but notice in the second SqlTypes-based function we have to perform an explicit cast to be able to use the Math.Pow function. The more complicated the formula, the more we are going to encounter the need to cast the SqlTypes. This example shows two ways to code the same SQL CLR function using both data types.

The first example uses unnecessary casting for equal comparison purposes, but you'll notice that you can do almost the same thing with the `SqlTyped` example until you hit the `Math.Pow` function. Then you have to cast the `SqlType` to a standard type.

```
//Loan Payment Example: CLR Typed
[Microsoft.SqlServer.Server.SqlFunction]
 public static double mfn_calcPayment(double presentValue,
                                      double financingPeriod,
                                      double interestRatePerYear)

{
     double a, b, x;
     double monthlyPayment;
     a = ((double)1.000 + (interestRatePerYear / (double)12.000));
     b = ((double)(-1.000) * financingPeriod);
     x = Math.Pow(a, b);
     monthlyPayment = (presentValue * interestRatePerYear)/
                      ((double)12.00 * ((double)1.00 - x));
     return (monthlyPayment);
}

//Loan Payment Example: SqlTyped
[Microsoft.SqlServer.Server.SqlFunction]
 public static SqlDouble mfn_calcPaymentSqlTyped(SqlDouble presentValue,
                                      SqlDouble financingPeriod,
                                      SqlDouble interestRatePerYear)

{
     SqlDouble a, b, x, monthlyPayment;
     a = ((SqlDouble)1.000 + (interestRatePerYear / (SqlDouble)12.000));
     b = ((SqlDouble)( - 1.000) * financingPeriod);
     x = Math.Pow((double)a, (double)b);
     monthlyPayment = (presentValue * interestRatePerYear) /
                      ((SqlDouble)12.00 * ((SqlDouble)1.00 - x));
     return (monthlyPayment);
}
```

The following function is an example of a preferred use of both `SqlTypes` and CLR built-in types in a UDF. Using the `SqlTypes` as parameters, you get the ability to create NULL-safe functions. Converting to CLR types, you get access to the `Math` class and similar functionality. By converting the values twice, once upon entry and once again upon exit, you eliminate unnecessary conversions. It is also noteworthy to mention that the behavior of over- and underflow calculations for CLR types may not generate errors, but instead create "wrap around" logic errors that convert to negative values. SqlTypes throw exceptions for all over- and underflow conditions as well as divide-by-zero errors. So, watch for these issues during conversions.

```
//Loan Payment Example: Preferred use of SqlTypes and CLR Types
[Microsoft.SqlServer.Server.SqlFunction]
 public static SqlDouble mfn_calcPaymentSqlParm(SqlDouble presentValue,
                                      SqlDouble financingPeriod,
                                      SqlDouble interestRatePerYear)
{
     double a, b, x, monthlyPayment, one, twelve;
     double dpresentValue, dfinancingPeriod, dinterestRatePerYear;
     one = 1.000;
```

```
        twelve = 12.000;
        if (presentValue.IsNull || presentValue == 0.00
                || financingPeriod.IsNull || financingPeriod == 0.00
                || interestRatePerYear.IsNull || interestRatePerYear == 0.00)
        {
            return (new SqlDouble(0.00));
        }
        else
        {
            dpresentValue = (double)presentValue;
            dfinancingPeriod = (double)financingPeriod;
            dinterestRatePerYear = (double)interestRatePerYear;
            a = (one + (dinterestRatePerYear / twelve));
            b = ((-1 * one) * (dfinancingPeriod));
            x = Math.Pow(a, b);
            monthlyPayment = (dpresentValue * dinterestRatePerYear)
                                    / (twelve * (one - x));
            return (SqlDouble)(monthlyPayment);
        }
    }
```

How does this improved loan payment calculation stack up to T-SQL? In the T-SQL version that follows, you'll see that the code is very similar in structure to the C# version. In terms of programming time, there is probably no significant difference here in coding one over the other.

```
CREATE FUNCTION [dbo].[ufn_CalcPayment](
                @presentValue money,
                @financingPeriod float,
                @interestRatePerYear float)
RETURNS float
AS
BEGIN

    DECLARE @a float, @b float, @x float
    DECLARE @One float, @Twelve float
    DECLARE @monthlyPayment as float

    If (@presentValue is Null or @presentValue = 0.00
                or @financingPeriod Is Null or @financingPeriod = 0.00
                or @interestRatePerYear Is Null or @interestRatePerYear = 0.00)
        BEGIN
            Set @monthlypayment = 0.00
        END
    Else
        BEGIN
            Set @One = 1.00000;
            Set @Twelve = 12.000;
            Set @a = (@One + (@interestRatePerYear/@Twelve));
            Set @b = (-1.000 * @financingPeriod);
            Set @x = POWER(@a, @b)
            Set @monthlyPayment = (@presentValue * @interestRatePerYear)
                                        /(@Twelve * (@One - @x))

        END
    Return @monthlypayment
END
```

In terms of performance, you can run a simple test for each loan calculation method using 1,000 loan calculations in 10 iterations and get a result similar to Figure 5-8. In the result you'll find two stories. The first is a comparison between SQL CLR and T-SQL. You'll find that the CLR version is running in less time and using less CPU resources than the T-SQL version. The average time for the CLR version to make the calculations regardless of data types is around 27.1 ms versus the T-SQL time of 59.4 ms. The difference in CPU usage is an over 50% advantage of SQL CLR to T-SQL, where T-SQL taking an average of 49.2 ms in the CPU versus CLR taking only 17.6 ms.

The other story is related to the data types in the SQL CLR versions. The difference in this example also insignificantly, but slightly favors the SqlTypes. This is even with the casting to CLR type `double` that must occur to use the `Math.Pow` function. This small advantage combined with the larger `Nullable` abilities are why it is a good idea to use `SqlTypes` as your parameters and types when possible, but then convert to CLR native types within your managed code as needed.

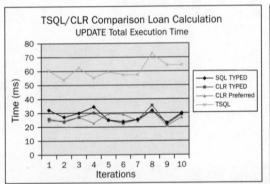 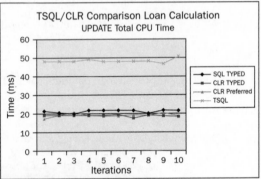

Iteration	SQL Typed	CLR Typed	CLR Preferred	TSQL	SQL Typed	CLR Typed	CLR Preferred	TSQL
1	32	26	25	59	19	17	16	49
2	27	24	25	53	18	17	17	49
3	30	27	27	61	18	17	18	49
4	34	30	23	54	19	17	17	50
5	25	25	30	58	19	17	17	49
6	24	23	29	56	19	17	17	49
7	26	25	24	56	19	16	17	49
8	32	35	32	71	18	17	17	49
9	23	22	22	63	19	17	18	48
10	30	29	27	63	19	17	17	51
Average	28.3	26.6	26.4	59.4	18.7	16.9	17.1	49.2
StdDev	3.8	3.9	3.2	5.4	0.5	0.3	0.6	0.8
StdErr	1.2	1.2	1.0	1.7	0.2	0.1	0.2	0.2

Figure 5-8

It's clear to see that even in these simple examples SQL CLR has better overall performance than T-SQL for computations. This shouldn't be too much of a surprise, since the SQL Server query engine is optimized for data operations, not to deliver computational instructions to a CPU like CLR. However, before you go out and rewrite all your math and computational formulas in SQL CLR, experiment with and compare the performance of your current T-SQL and some new SQL CLR code. For this chapter, we ran many more calculations than we discussed here, some of which only showed marginal improvement when rewritten in SQL CLR. As a general rule, the more complicated the calculation that can be made in memory, the better SQL CLR performs. Make your choices based on the performance of your function in your environment.

Cursor Processing

Cursor processing is an activity of pulling back data rows and moving through them directionally one at a time to perform some action. Typically, you can find a set-based solution to supplant a cursor, but there are times when a cursor-based solution is completely appropriate. Let's take a requirement right from an everyday situation and look at the solution from a T-SQL and a CLR perspective.

Stocks belong to industry groups that move up and down in a ranking system. Group rankings on a daily basis are stored in a table that contains dimensions of the industry group name, the date, and the ranking. From these data, we need to look at industry groups that are in the Top 30 rankings list for the most recent date, and then examine the last 30 days history of the rankings of those industry groups. To better visualize this information, we'd like to be able to cut and paste it into Microsoft Excel and immediately draw a graph of the progression of the industry groups over the last 30 days into the top 30 industry groups.

Create the table you'll need for this example in the CLRTESTDB database by running the following T-SQL script.

```
CREATE TABLE [dbo].[IndustryGroupRankings](
   [PaperDate] [datetime] NULL,
   [RankThisWeek] [int] NULL,
   [RankLastFri] [int] NULL,
   [RankLastMonth] [int] NULL,
   [IndustryGroupName] [varchar](50) NULL,
   [NbrStocksInGroup] [int] NULL,
   [PctChangeSinceJan1] [numeric](18, 2) NULL,
   [PctChangeDaily] [numeric](18, 2) NULL,
   [ProcessedDate] [datetime] NULL
) ON [PRIMARY]
GO
```

The following is an abbreviated sample of rows to insert into the table. To fully experience this example, download the script for all the data and the code from this book's web site at www.wrox.com.

```
INSERT INTO industrygrouprankings
Select 'Feb 21 2006 12:00AM', '194', '194', '67', 'Bldg-Resident/Comml', '23',
'-0.10', '-0.10', 'Feb 19 2006 11:32PM'
INSERT INTO industrygrouprankings
Select 'Feb 21 2006 12:00AM', '195', '195', '171', 'Retail/Whlsle-Jewelry', '12',
'-4.40', '-0.10', 'Feb 19 2006 11:32PM'
INSERT INTO industrygrouprankings
Select 'Feb 21 2006 12:00AM', '196', '193', '190', 'Media-Newspapers', '15',
'-1.40', '-0.30', 'Feb 19 2006 11:32PM'
INSERT INTO industrygrouprankings
Select 'Feb 21 2006 12:00AM', '197', '197', '155', 'Food-Confectionery', '6',
'-4.60', '-0.40', 'Feb 19 2006 11:32PM'
INSERT INTO industrygrouprankings
Select 'Feb 21 2006 12:00AM', '0', '0', '0', 'S&PMidcap400Ind', '0', '5.00',
'0.00', 'Feb 19 2006 11:32PM'
INSERT INTO industrygrouprankings
Select 'Feb 21 2006 12:00AM', '0', '0', '0', 'S&P500Index', '0', '3.10', '-0.20',
'Feb 19 2006 11:32PM'
```

To do this, you need to output each industry group in one row with columns that represent each of the possible trading days for the last 30 days. You'll generate the columns from your data using a cursor to create a dynamic cross-tab query by date using SQL2005's new PIVOT statement. For the purpose of having an example that demonstrates using a temp table in CLR, we'll pull the sample of data we need into a temp table and the report the results. The T-SQL stored procedure to PIVOT New Top 30 Industry groups by the last historical 30-day rankings looks like the following:

```
CREATE PROC [dbo].[usp_IndustryGroupsNewToTop30_ShowLast30DaysRankings]
AS
SET NOCOUNT ON
DECLARE @CURRDATE as datetime
DECLARE @PIVOTSQL as varchar(3040)
DECLARE @DATE As varchar(10)
DECLARE @DATES as varchar(1000)
DECLARE @CRLF As char(2)

SET @DATES = ''
SET @CURRDATE = '02/28/06' --<<SET TO GETDATE() WITH LIVE DATA. (SAMPLE DATA FIXED)
SET @CRLF = char(13) + char(10)

--BUILD TEMP STORAGE FOR
--INDUSTRY GROUPS OF CONCERN
SELECT industrygroupname, RankThisWeek, PaperDate
INTO #tmpRankings
FROM industrygrouprankings
WHERE industrygroupname
  --IS IN THE LATEST TOP 30 RANKING...
  IN (
    SELECT top 30 industrygroupname
    FROM industrygrouprankings
      WHERE paperdate =
        (SELECT max(paperdate)
          FROM industrygrouprankings)
      and rankthisweek <> 0
    ORDER BY rankthisweek
  )
AND industrygroupname
--BUT WAS NOT IN TOP 30 THIRTY DAYS AGO..
NOT IN (
    SELECT top 30 industrygroupname
    FROM industrygrouprankings
      WHERE paperdate =
        (SELECT max(paperdate)
          FROM industrygrouprankings
          WHERE paperdate <= dateadd(day, -30, @CURRDATE))
    and rankthisweek <> 0
    ORDER BY rankthisweek
  )
  AND paperdate >= dateadd(day, -30, @CURRDATE)
ORDER BY industrygroupname, paperdate

--USE CURSOR TO CREATE A LISTING
--OF DATES FOR DYNAMIC PIVOT COLUMNS IN SQL
```

```
DECLARE oRSDates CURSOR FORWARD_ONLY
FOR
   SELECT PaperDate=Convert(varchar(10), paperdate, 101)
   FROM #tmpRankings
   GROUP BY paperdate

OPEN oRSDates;
FETCH NEXT FROM oRSDates INTO @DATE;

WHILE (@@FETCH_STATUS <> -1)
BEGIN
   IF (@@FETCH_STATUS <> -2)
   BEGIN
      SET @Dates = @Dates + ' [' + RTRIM(@Date) + '],';
   END;
   FETCH NEXT FROM oRSDates INTO @Date;
END;
CLOSE oRSDates;
DEALLOCATE oRSDates;

IF right(@DATES, 1) = ','
   SET @DATES = left(@DATES, len(@Dates)-1)

--BUILD PIVOT DYNAMIC SQL STATEMENT
SET @PIVOTSQL =
   'SELECT industrygroupname, ' + @Dates + @CRLF +
   'FROM  (SELECT industrygroupname, paperdate, rankthisweek ' + @CRLF +
   '          FROM #tmpRankings ' + @CRLF +
   '          WHERE paperdate >= dateadd(day, -30, ' +
               convert(varchar(10), @CURRDATE, 101) +
      ')) p ' + @CRLF +
      'PIVOT ' + @CRLF +
   '(MAX(RankThisWeek) ' + @CRLF +
   '  For PaperDate IN ' + @CRLF +
   '  (' + @Dates + ') ' + @CRLF +
   '  ) pvt ORDER BY industrygroupname'

EXEC(@PIVOTSQL)

--CLEAN UP
DROP TABLE #tmpRankings
SET NOCOUNT OFF
```

This example demonstrates how programming in T-SQL stored procedures usually results in a top-down script instead an approach that breaks the job into several tasks. The tasks are simply:

1. Generate a temp table of industry groups new to the Top 30 list.

2. Create a dynamic SQL statement to represent the columns.

3. Create a PIVOT statement.

4. Return the results.

Breaking up the T-SQL into tasks is not practical. Creating T-SQL stored procedures or functions to return strings is not a good use of a T-SQL object. There is no performance gain, and your database becomes cluttered with objects returning strings. Passing a temp table, or any table, around as a function parameter is not possible, and creating in-memory tables can create collisions if they're not properly disposed. While this is fairly simple to create, it is more difficult to troubleshoot because of the inability to isolate and troubleshoot small segments of code. This essentially has been one of the major barriers for developers in using T-SQL for business logic.

From a programming perspective, SQL CLR data readers will seem more native and easier to handle. If you rebuild the same example in SQL CLR, you can isolate the problem down to the tasks defined previously, and define a function to perform each task. The biggest organizational improvement is being able to create a temp table in one function and access it in another. Since the temp table is created using a context connection, you can able to access it using the same connection. It remains available until you kill that connection. The rewritten SQL CLR stored procedure looks like this:

```
using System;
using System.Data;
using System.Data.SqlClient;
using System.Data.SqlTypes;
using Microsoft.SqlServer.Server;

public partial class StoredProcedures
{
    [Microsoft.SqlServer.Server.SqlProcedure]
    public static void msp_IndustryGroupsNewToTop30_ShowLast30DaysRankings()
    {
        string pivotTableSQL;
        pivotTableSQL = CreatePivotTableSql();

        using (SqlConnection sqlConn = new SqlConnection
                ("Context Connection=True"))
        {
            SqlCommand sqlCmd = sqlConn.CreateCommand();
            sqlCmd.CommandText = pivotTableSQL;
            sqlConn.Open();
            SqlContext.Pipe.ExecuteAndSend(sqlCmd);
        }
    }

    public static void CreateTempTable()
    {
        string tempTableSQL;

        //--BUILD TEMP STORAGE FOR
        //--INDUSTRY GROUPS OF CONCERN
        tempTableSQL = "SELECT industrygroupname, RankThisWeek, PaperDate " +
                        "INTO #tmpRankings FROM industrygrouprankings " +
                        "WHERE industrygroupname " +
                        "    IN (SELECT top 30 industrygroupname " +
                        "        FROM industrygrouprankings " +
                        "        WHERE paperdate = (SELECT max(paperdate) " +
                        "        FROM industrygrouprankings) " +
                        "            and rankthisweek <> 0 " +
```

```
"                ORDER BY rankthisweek) " +
"AND industrygroupname " +
"NOT IN (SELECT top 30 industrygroupname " +
"            FROM industrygrouprankings " +
"            WHERE paperdate = " +
"                (SELECT max(paperdate) " +
"                FROM industrygrouprankings " +
"                WHERE paperdate <= " +
"                    dateadd(day, -30, '02/28/06')) " +
"                    and rankthisweek <> 0 " +
"            ORDER BY rankthisweek) " +
"AND paperdate >= dateadd(day, -30, '02/28/06') " +
"ORDER BY industrygroupname, paperdate ";

    using (SqlConnection sqlConn = new SqlConnection
                ("Context Connection=True"))
    {
        SqlCommand sqlCmd = sqlConn.CreateCommand();
        sqlCmd.CommandText = tempTableSQL;
        sqlConn.Open();
        sqlCmd.ExecuteNonQuery();
    }
}

public static string CreateDateColumnDynamicSql()
{
    string selectSQL;
    string columnSQL = string.Empty;
    selectSQL = "SELECT PaperDate=Convert(varchar(10), paperdate, 101) \n" +
                "FROM #tmpRankings GROUP BY paperdate";
    //Make sure the temp table is created
    CreateTempTable();
    using (SqlConnection sqlConn = new SqlConnection
                ("Context Connection=True"))
    {
        SqlCommand sqlCmd = sqlConn.CreateCommand();
        sqlCmd.CommandText = selectSQL;
        sqlConn.Open();
        using (SqlDataReader dr = sqlCmd.ExecuteReader())
        {
            while (dr.Read())
                columnSQL += "[" + dr.GetString(0) + "],";
        }
    }
    return columnSQL.Remove(columnSQL.Length - 1);
}

public static string CreatePivotTableSql()
{
    string pivotTableSQL;
    string columnSQL;
    columnSQL = CreateDateColumnDynamicSql();
    pivotTableSQL =
            "SELECT industrygroupname, " + columnSQL + "\n" +
```

```
                    "FROM   (SELECT industrygroupname, paperdate, rankthisweek " +
                    "          FROM #tmpRankings \n" +
                    "WHERE paperdate >= dateadd(day, -30, '02/28/06')) p \n" +
                    "PIVOT \n" +
                    "(MAX(RankThisWeek) \n" +
                    "FOR PaperDate IN \n" +
                    "(" + columnSQL + ") \n" +
                    ") pvt ORDER BY industrygroupname";
              return pivotTableSQL;
         }

    };
```

The partial results using the full data file look like this:

```
Industry Group Name      02/10/2006  02/14/2006  02/16/2006  02/21/2006
-----------------------  ----------  ----------  ----------  ----------
Bldg-Cement/Concrt/Ag        35          29          24          29
Computer-DataStorage         16          18          15          13
Food-Flour&Grain              8           9          12          15
Medical-Biomed/Biotech       22          26          23          16
Medical-Genetics             46          36          25          26
Retail-Clothing/Shoe         30          24          20          28
Transportation-Svcs          24          21          21          19
```

From a coding experience, this is what we wish T-SQL could do. The code is better organized, easier to read, and faster to troubleshoot. If there is an issue with the PIVOT string, you can isolate the CreatePivotTableSql method and get it corrected without disturbing the rest of the code. Dealing with the cursor is also now a trivial task. Solving the problem with SQL CLR means no more looking up the unfamiliar syntax of CURSOR manipulation, trying to remember how to fetch into variables, and guessing at how to use the @@Fetch_Status codes. To .NET programmers, using the data reader will make building stored procedures like this seem as native as working in the middle tier.

Your potential performance improvement is going to depend upon what you are doing within the dataset. In this example, the use of the cursor demonstrates no advantage in SQL CLR over T-SQL, as you can see in Figure 5-9. Generally, if you are performing some calculation or string-building operations on data in the dataset, then SQL CLR will be faster. If you need to update data in dataset rows though the in-proc ADO.NET provider, you'll need to use T-SQL updateable cursors, since this functionality is not supported currently in SQL CLR.

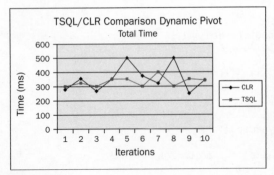
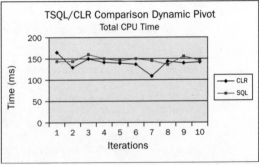

Figure 5-9

New .NET Base Class Library (BCL) Capabilities

With the introduction of SQL CLR, you are no longer limited to T-SQL-based functions when working with data. Many times, the functionality that you need, and would have to code in T-SQL, or send to a client app for validation, already exists in the CLR base class library. You only need to expose this functionality for use in your T-SQL programming tasks. This is a whole lot easier than using extended stored procedures to expose operating system functionality. A simple example, repeated in almost every primer of SQL CLR, is the use of a regular expression. We suspect this is because regular expressions are perfect as content validators, and it probably doesn't hurt that Oracle didn't fully support use of regular expressions until version 10g. So, we'll follow this bandwagon, except instead of first building a SQL CLR function that performs specific validation, we'll simply wrap the existing functionality in our own base class to demonstrate the ability to access BCL capabilities easily.

The regular expression functions are located in the namespace System.Text.RegularExpressions. Add a reference to this namespace to a new SQL CLR user-defined function. The parameters of the function are simple. Since you are just wrapping the IsMatch function in the RegEx class, you need an expression to validate and a regular expression to use for the validation. These will be the function parameters. Within the body of the function, you'll add some minimal handling for Null inputs, but otherwise you'll simply feed the parameters into the IsMatch function. The final SQL CLR wrapper will look like this:

```
using System.Data.SqlTypes;
using Microsoft.SqlServer.Server;
using System.Text.RegularExpressions;

public partial class UserDefinedFunctions
{
    [Microsoft.SqlServer.Server.SqlFunction]
    public static SqlBoolean mfn_RegExValidate(SqlString expressionToValidate,
                                               SqlString regularExpression)
    {
        if (expressionToValidate.IsNull)
        {
            return new SqlBoolean(false);
        }
        else
        {
            Regex expression = new Regex(regularExpression.Value);
            return expression.IsMatch(expressionToValidate.Value);
        }
    }
};
```

Compile and deploy this SQL CLR function into the CLRTESTDB database. To use the SQL CLR function run a SQL statement similar to the following example:

```
DECLARE @regex NVARCHAR(100)
SET @regex = N'^([\w-\.]+)@((\[[0-9]{1,3}\.[0-9]{1,3}\.[0-9]{1,3}\.)|' +
                '(([\w-]+\.)+))([a-zA-Z]{2,4}|[0-9]{1,3})(\]?)$'

SELECT firstname, middlename, lastname, emailaddress,
  dbo.mfn_RegExValidate(emailaddress, @regex ) AS validemail
FROM AdventureWorks.Person.contact
...
```

The results should look like this:

```
firstname  middlename lastname    emailaddress                    validemail
---------- ---------- ---------   ------------------------------  ----------
Gustavo    NULL       Achong      gustavo0@adventure-works.com        1
Catherine  R.         Abel        catherine0@adventure-works.com      1
Kim        NULL       Abercrombie kim2@adventure-works.com            1
```

This is possible to code in T-SQL, but as your expressions get more complicated to validate, using the regular expression version will be much easier. Take the example back in the "String Parsing" section earlier in the chapter. Remember that your mission was to evaluate whether you had valid ASCII characters in a string. Now to identify the bad data, you can use your SQL CLR regular expression function mfn_RegExValidate to find any bad columns in a fictional table with a T-SQL statement like this:

```
DECLARE @regex NVARCHAR(100)
SET @regex = N'[^a-zA-Z0-9]'
SELECT policy
FROM [fictionaltable]
WHERE dbo.mfn_RegExValidate([column], @regex) <> 1
```

This ability to tap into the BCL is enormous to T-SQL developers. However, this ability may lead to situations where you exceed even the boundries of common sense. I'm not so sure there is a great amount of benefit in allowing us to have access to the Threading namespace, but luckily at least some namespaces are off-limits, like System.Windows.Forms, and others require specific security context permissions. One thing to put the DBA minds at ease: You can't access capabilities of the CLR through your database unless an assembly has been loaded with a method that provides the capability. So, you are the gatekeepers to what capabilities of the CLR you choose to expose on SQL Server. Monitor the using statements when assemblies are provided to you to add to SQL Server, and limit the security rights for folks to create and alter assemblies so that you are completely aware of the capabilities that are exposed on the server at all times.

Commingling SQL CLR and T-SQL

What you'll find very quickly is that once a SQL CLR object is hosted in SQL Server, you will start interacting with it as if it were native T-SQL. This is by design, and mainly because of the T-SQL DDL function prototype that wraps all assembly access. It feels like T-SQL. The next thing you know, you'll be trying to commingle SQL CLR and T-SQL objects. The good news is that not only is this possible, it makes a lot of sense in many instances. Just be aware of the limitations of T-SQL and SQL CLR that do exist. Some we've already covered, some we have not.

❑ ByVal is the same as an Input parameter in T-SQL. ByRef is the same as an input output parameter. <Out()> has no T-SQL equivalent.

❑ .NET can't handle NULL values very well if you are using value data types and will throw exceptions.

❑ Data types used as input, output, or return values must be supportable by T-SQL. This means no arrays, or widget objects, or non-UDT objects.

Not *all* CLR types can be converted exactly to T-SQL types. Pay attention to the conversions in the following table.

CLR Data Type (SQL Server Based)	T-SQL Data Type
Decimal	smallmoney
SqlMoney	smallmoney
Decimal	money
DateTime	smalldatetime
SQLDateTime	smalldatetime
Decimal	Decimal (results not the same)

In the last section, we wrapped the regular expression IsMatch method from the BCL as a SQL CLR object. However, this form is not very efficient. To use it, you have to pass in the regular expression to perform a validation. This leads to some messy T-SQL code. How does this look deployed in a column constraint?

```
CREATE TABLE dbo.EMAILADDRESS (
   EmailAddress NVARCHAR(255) NOT NULL
, CONSTRAINT EMAILADDRESS_ck_validemailaddress CHECK ( dbo. mfn_RegExValidate (
EmailAddress, N'^([\w-\.]+)@((\[[0-9]{1,3}\.[0-9]{1,3}\.[0-9]{1,3}\.)|((
[\w-]+\.)+))([a-zA-Z]{2,4}|[0-9]{1,3})(\]?)$' ) = 1 )
)
```

What you'd really like to do is create some abstraction from the base wrapper function to a specific function. Instead of creating a new CLR UDF, just create a new T-SQL UDF that uses the existing function mfn_RegExValidate. The new function will look like this:

```
CREATE   FUNCTION [dbo].[mfn_IsValidEmail](
   @ColumnData nvarchar(max)
)
RETURNS bit
AS
BEGIN
  DECLARE @isValidEmail bit
  DECLARE @regex NVARCHAR(100)

  SET @regex = N'^([\w-\.]+)@((\[[0-9]{1,3}\.[0-9]{1,3}\.[0-9]{1,3}\.)' +
               '|(([\w-]+\.)+))([a-zA-Z]{2,4}|[0-9]{1,3})(\]?)$'

  SELECT @isValidEmail = dbo.mfn_RegExValidate(@ColumnData, @regex )

    RETURN @isValidEmail
END
GO
```

You can now recreate the DDL, and you'll know what the constraint is doing.

```
CREATE TABLE dbo.EMAILADDRESS (
   EmailAddress NVARCHAR(255) NOT NULL
, CONSTRAINT EMAILADDRESS_ck_validemailaddress CHECK ( dbo.mfn_IsValidEmail(
                                                EmailAddress) = 1 )
)
```

Before you commingle T-SQL with SQL CLR, make sure that you are aware of how the object you are wrapping handles errors. This can get confusing because the lowest unhandled error will bleed up into the calling object, and the error message will reference an object that you may not be aware you were dependent upon. You can see this if you create a quick addition function that accepts two CLR `Int` value types as parameters and name it `mfn_AddNonSQLTyped`. The function should look like this:

```
[Microsoft.SqlServer.Server.SqlFunction]
public static int mfnAddNonSQLTyped(int x, int y)
{
    try
    {
        return x + y;
    }
    catch(Exception ex)
    {
        throw new Exception("Caught Error", ex);
    }
}
```

This function will generate an error if it is called with Null parameters. To see how it interacts with T-SQL, wrap the function with a T-SQL function that accepts Nulls, and name it `ufn_ComingledTest`:

```
CREATE    FUNCTION [dbo].[ufn_ComingledTest](
  @X INT=NULL,
  @Y INT=NULL
)
RETURNS INT
AS
BEGIN
  DECLARE @RETURN INT
  SET @RETURN=dbo.mfn_AddNonSQLTyped(@X, @Y)
    RETURN @RETURN
END
```

Running the commingled test function with two NULLS as parameters like this

```
SELECT [dbo].[ufn_ComingledTest](NULL, NULL)
```

generates the following error:

```
Msg 6569, Level 16, State 1, Line 1
'mfn_AddNonSQLTyped' failed because parameter 1 is not allowed to be null and is
not an output parameter.
```

Simple to see, but add one more layer and you get the picture. The good news is that SQL Server will keep track of all your dependencies, even commingled dependencies. This is important because even though SQL CLR is not a panacea, being able to leverage functionality from the CLR can provide a real productivity and capability boost to the T-SQL programmer. It is nice to know that all these bits that we are creating are still catalogued, traced, and treated as if they were native to SQL server.

Submitting Data to Database

Getting data into the database on the server involves changing or adding data by executing a SQL statement in a database. There are three main methods to do this:

- ❑ Issue a SQL statement to the database. This includes building T-SQL statements with or without parameters for submission.

- ❑ Provide parameters to database objects like T-SQL or SQL CLR stored procedures, which defer execution of T-SQL statements.

- ❑ Pull data into DataAdapters, change the data in the adapter dataset or table structures, and update the original source data. (This uses a command object as well that could be either a T-SQL statement or a stored procedure.)

If you have removed all other layers and technologies, the bottom line is that a T-SQL statement must execute within the database. It stands to reason that T-SQL should be able to perform the statement with the most efficiency since the trip from accepting the command to executing the command in the database is very short. Every step you take moving away from executing that T-SQL statement is going to cost something. If your .NET application uses the technique of building a T-SQL statement in code, whether that statement is built with parameters or without, you move at least one layer or more away from the advantage of executing T-SQL on the server. To benchmark database updates, we'll use an existing T-SQL stored procedure in the AdventureWorks database for comparison named uspUpdateEmployeePersonalInfo. This procedure updates the Birthdate, NationalIDNumber, Marital Status, and Gender attributes of an employee.

To start, we'll pull out just the UPDATE statement from the procedure and compare the execution of a T-SQL statement to the execution of similar statement in SQL CLR. As you can see in Figure 5-10, the CLR version never overtakes the T-SQL version. Even if you give the SQL CLR version a handicap for the overhead of calling the CLR the first time, the SQL CLR executes in an average of 35 ms to execute the statement and T-SQL is taking 20% less time at 20 ms. In Figure 5-10 you'll notice that we've got almost the reverse affect on the CPU as we did in the computational examples. This time T-SQL is running better in the CPU because this is what T-SQL is optimized to do.

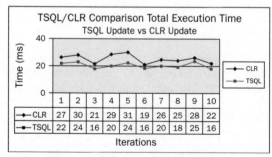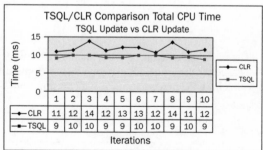

Figure 5-10

However, this comparison is not fair to SQL CLR. In an application, you'll never be able to achieve a zero-layer T-SQL execution. You have to add in a small connection time for moving through the ADO.NET connection layers to get to the database. Since it can only go downhill from here, it is clear that CLR is not going to be a match to simply issuing the T-SQL statement, from a performance perspective. This comparison is also not practical. No one would create UPDATE T-SQL statements embedded in code without passing any parameters to the statement. We need to build a stored-procedure-like CLR routine that accepts parameters to use in the T-SQL statement. This will be a SQL CLR stored procedure that loads the assembly (and CLR, if it is not loaded) to accept the parameters to send to the database. We'll try first just wrapping the same T-SQL stored procedure we are benchmarking against. This not a practical example, because if you already have a T-SQL stored procedure, then you should code your application code to it, not add a superfluous layer in between. The code will look just like it would look in your data layer. The following is a stripped down essentials-only version to keep this sample short.

```
[Microsoft.SqlServer.Server.SqlProcedure]
public static void mspUpdateEmployeePersonalInfo_ExecSP(
                            SqlInt32 EmployeeID,
                            SqlString NationalIDNumber,
                            SqlDateTime BirthDate,
                            SqlString MaritalStatus,
                            SqlString Gender)
{
    using (SqlConnection sqlConn = new
            SqlConnection("Context Connection=True"))
    {
        SqlCommand sqlCmd = sqlConn.CreateCommand();
        sqlCmd.CommandText = "HumanResources.uspupdateemployeepersonalinfo";
        sqlCmd.CommandType = CommandType.StoredProcedure;
        sqlCmd.Parameters.Add("@EmployeeID", SqlDbType.Int, 8);
        sqlCmd.Parameters["@EmployeeID"].Value = EmployeeID;
        sqlCmd.Parameters.Add("@NationalIDNumber", SqlDbType.NVarChar, 15);
        sqlCmd.Parameters["@NationalIDNumber"].Value = NationalIDNumber;
        sqlCmd.Parameters.Add("@BirthDate", SqlDbType.DateTime, 8);
        sqlCmd.Parameters["@BirthDate"].Value = BirthDate.Value;
        sqlCmd.Parameters.Add("@MaritalStatus", SqlDbType.NVarChar, 1);
        sqlCmd.Parameters["@MaritalStatus"].Value = MaritalStatus;
        sqlCmd.Parameters.Add("@Gender", SqlDbType.NVarChar, 1);
        sqlCmd.Parameters["@Gender"].Value = Gender;
        sqlConn.Open();
        SqlContext.Pipe.ExecuteAndSend(sqlCmd);
    }

}
```

The perfomance aspect has declined a bit as we expected. The total execution time for T-SQL is now almost 24% better than the CLR version when the only difference is the CLR housing around the stored procedure call. Our CPU percentage is also increasing from 24% in the UPDATE statement to 30% using the procedure.

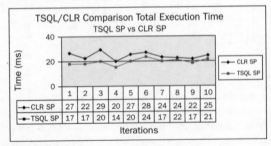

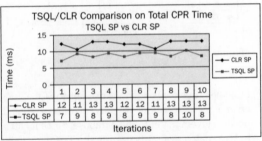

Figure 5-11

If we pull data into a `DataAdapter` to perform an UPDATE in a SQL CLR routine, we are talking about creating a very "chatty" architecture. A solution like this requires the following steps: calling a T-SQL entry point, instantiating an assembly, pulling down data to update, making the changes to the dataset by applying the variables, and sending the updates to the database via the `DataAdapter update` method. Updating through a `DataAdapter` stripped down to the essentials would look like this:

```
[Microsoft.SqlServer.Server.SqlProcedure]
public static void mspUpdateEmployeePersonalInfoRS(
                            SqlInt32 EmployeeID,
                            SqlString NationalIDNumber,
                            SqlDateTime BirthDate,
                            SqlString MaritalStatus,
                            SqlString Gender)
{
    using (SqlConnection sqlConn =
                new SqlConnection("Context Connection=True"))
    {
        string selectSQL;
        DataSet EmployeeDS = new DataSet();

        DataRow EmployeeRow;
        selectSQL = "SELECT * FROM [HumanResources].[Employee]" +
                    "WHERE EmployeeID = " + Convert.ToString(EmployeeID);
        sqlConn.Open();

        // Assumes connection is a valid SqlConnection.
        SqlDataAdapter dataAdapter = new SqlDataAdapter(selectSQL, sqlConn);

        dataAdapter.UpdateCommand = new SqlCommand(
            "UPDATE [HumanResources].[Employee] SET " +
            "[NationalIDNumber] = @NationalIDNumber " +
            ",[BirthDate] = @BirthDate " +
            ",[MaritalStatus] = @MaritalStatus " +
            ",[Gender] = @Gender " +
            "WHERE [EmployeeID] = @EmployeeID", sqlConn);

        dataAdapter.SelectCommand = new SqlCommand(
             "SELECT * FROM [HumanResources].[Employee]" +
                            "WHERE EmployeeID = " +
             Convert.ToString(EmployeeID), sqlConn);

        dataAdapter.UpdateCommand.Parameters.Add(
            "@NationalIDNumber", SqlDbType.NVarChar, 15, "NationalIDNumber");
        dataAdapter.UpdateCommand.Parameters.Add(
            "@BirthDate", SqlDbType.DateTime, 8, "BirthDate");
        dataAdapter.UpdateCommand.Parameters.Add(
            "@MaritalStatus", SqlDbType.NVarChar, 1, "MaritalStatus");
        dataAdapter.UpdateCommand.Parameters.Add(
             "@Gender", SqlDbType.NVarChar, 1, "Gender");
        dataAdapter.UpdateCommand.Parameters.Add(
             "@EmployeeID", SqlDbType.Int, 8, "EmployeeID");

        dataAdapter.Fill(EmployeeDS, "Employee");
        EmployeeRow = EmployeeDS.Tables["Employee"].Rows[0];
        EmployeeRow["NationalIDNumber"] = NationalIDNumber;
        EmployeeRow["BirthDate"] = BirthDate.Value;
```

```
          EmployeeRow["MaritalStatus"] = MaritalStatus;
          EmployeeRow["Gender"] = Gender;
          //EmployeeRow["EmployeeID", DataRowVersion.Original]=EmployeeID;
          dataAdapter.Update(EmployeeDS, "Employee");
      }
  }
```

An advantage to updating data through a `DataAdapter` like this is that the knowledge of T-SQL needed is minimal. You just need a basic understanding of the `UPDATE` and `SELECT` DDL statements. From the standpoint of developer productivity, this approach may seem attractive. When we compare the execution of this CLR code to using the T-SQL stored procedure, the performance comparisons of this test look familiar, as shown in Figure 5-12. The total execution of SQL CLR is taking about 28 to 30% longer than T-SQL to run. At an average of 39 ms, this is the slowest update method yet. We would expect this because of the round trip of retrieving and then updating that is involved in this solution.

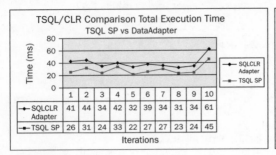
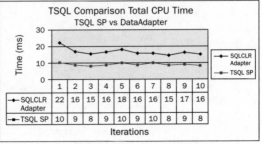

Figure 5-12

The important thing to note here is that you can't get around coding the `UPDATE` T-SQL statement. You either have to place it within a T-SQL stored procedure or embed it into the .NET project. The slower performance of the SQL CLR approach is due to the layers of code and infrastructure between the entry point and submitting native SQL to the SQL engine. In this section, we explored the different methods of submitting data and found that T-SQL is consistently faster, as shown in Figure 5-13, than any of the other methods using the `In-Proc` provider. The consensus is that you should not use the SQL CLR for updating data because of these performance concerns. However, the method you choose for updating data will be dependent on how that difference (20 ms in our tests) in total time and increase in CPU time balances against what it is worth to you to use the SQL CLR object.

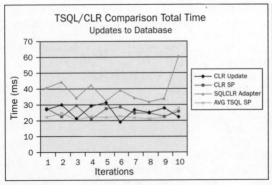
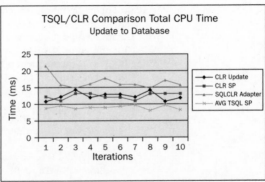

Figure 5-13

Retrieve Data from Database

The other side to the data-access coin is the need to retrieve data from a database. You are going to have the same performance issues competing with SQL Server returning data as you did sending data for updates. At the end of the line, you must execute the T-SQL statement to retrieve the data. You can't get any faster than executing the T-SQL statement in SQL Server. Once the statement executes, retrieving the data means gathering up a set of rows and simply pushing them down to a client. Inside of T-SQL-based-objects, like stored procedures and in-line T-SQL UDFs, rows are sent by executing the T-SQL statement. In SQL CLR you'll have to send the T-SQL statement, then manually connect the results to a special stream object called a SqlPipe. Think of the SqlPipe as a new standard output (STDIO) or an ASP.NET response object. One major advantage is that using the SqlPipe object transfers data without first copying it into a memory object. Figure 5-14 shows the results of a demonstration between a T-SQL statement and a SQL CLR stored procedure that is executing a SQL statement with one parameter to query the Employee table in the AdventureWorks database. The T-SQL version is about 25% more efficient than the CLR version in total execution time, 30% more efficient in CPU time.

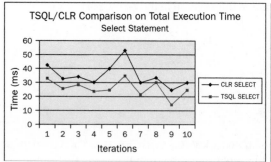
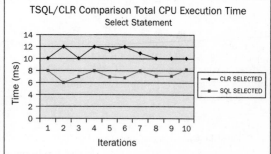

Figure 5-14

A portion of the SQL CLR stored procedure code in the example above is shown here:

```
sqlCmd.CommandText = "SELECT * FROM HumanResources.Employee " +
                     "WHERE BirthDate >= @BirthDate";
sqlCmd.Parameters.AddWithValue("@BirthDate", BirthDate.Value);
SqlContext.Pipe.ExecuteAndSend(sqlCmd);
```

In T-SQL, you can also send results out using an in-line table or table-valued UDF. In SQL CLR, this is a little more involved. First you need to build a T-SQL table-valued UDF to return this employee data. In the T-SQL UDF we define the function prototype and return a TABLE type that is resolved by the SELECT statement. The whole T-SQL TVF looks like this:

```
CREATE FUNCTION [dbo].[ufnGetEmployeesGT1980](@BirthDate [datetime])
RETURNS   TABLE
AS
RETURN(
  SELECT EmployeeID, NationalIDNumber, BirthDate
  FROM HumanResources.Employee
  WHERE BIRTHDATE >= @BirthDate
  )
```

To build a table-valued UDF in SQL CLR, we have to do at least three things:

1. Create a method to retrieve the data. The method has to return a collection that implements an `IEnumerable` interface.

2. Create a method to be used as a callback method to process each enumerated item in the collection and return values as out parameters.

3. Annotate the function with the `FillRowMethodName` attribute to point to the callback method. If you are developing in the Visual Studio 2005 IDE and you want to autodeploy, you are going to need to provide the actual T-SQL string to define the T-SQL Table to be returned in the `TableDefinition` function attribute.

In T-SQL, you don't have to provide the actual table definition, because that would be redundant. When the syntax of the DDL is checked, this can be determined by stripping the SELECT statement from the body of the function. In SQL CLR, the SELECT statement can't be determined by the SQL syntax checker, so you have to provide this in a format that can be plugged into the UDF prototype. A completed TVF for the SQL CLR function will have this table definition information in the T-SQL portion of return clause:

```
RETURNS  TABLE (
  [EmployeeID] [int] NULL,
  [NationalIDNumber] [nvarchar](15) COLLATE SQL_Latin1_General_CP1_CI_AS NULL,
  [BirthDate] [datetime] NULL
)
```

This table definition is generated in T-SQL when the IDE deploys the SQL CLR TVF. The Visual Studio Deployment Wizard gets the information to build this table definition from the function attribute `TableDefinition`, which looks like this:

```
[Microsoft.SqlServer.Server.SqlFunction(
      DataAccess=DataAccessKind.Read,
      FillRowMethodName = "ReturnARow",
      TableDefinition="EmployeeID int, " +
      "NationalIDNumber NVarchar(15), BirthDate Datetime"
  )]
```

You may notice that you are basically defining the T-SQL as metadata in the SQL CLR function decorations. If you don't maintain the integrity of a single unbroken string in the definition, it will be caught immediately by the compiler. However, If you misspell a column in the `TableDefinition` attribute, it will not get caught during the .NET build process. As long as the column is the right type, your UDF will simply return the new column name. If you use the wrong data type, you'll get an error during deployment that you've got a bad column, like this:

```
Error   1   Function signature of "FillRow" method (as designated by
SqlFunctionAttribute.FillRowMethodName) does not match SQL declaration for table
valued CLR function'mfnGetEmployeesGT1980' due to column 1.   SELECTINGDATA
```

If you use the wrong size, you will not get an error during compile or deployment time. An error like this will occur during execution time:

```
Msg 6260, Level 16, State 1, Line 1
An error occurred while getting new row from user defined Table Valued Function :
System.Data.SqlServer.TruncationException: Trying to convert return value or output
parameter of size 16 bytes to a T-SQL type with a smaller size limit of 10 bytes.
```

The reason to point these errors out is that these are new issues to creating table-valued UDFs in SQL CLR that you don't have to worry about with the T-SQL UDF version. Watch for them. The completed SQL CLR version of the UDF is:

```csharp
using System;
using System.Data;
using System.Data.SqlClient;
using System.Data.SqlTypes;
using Microsoft.SqlServer.Server;
using System.Collections;
public partial class UserDefinedFunctions
{
    [Microsoft.SqlServer.Server.SqlFunction(
            DataAccess=DataAccessKind.Read,
            FillRowMethodName = "ReturnARow",
            TableDefinition="EmployeeIDNbr datetime, " +
                    "NationalIDNumber NVarchar(15), BirthDate Datetime"
        )]
    public static IEnumerable mfnGetEmployeesGT1980(SqlDateTime BirthDate)
    {
        String sqlSelect;
        sqlSelect = "SELECT EmployeeID, NationalIDNumber, BirthDate " +
                    "FROM HumanResources.Employee WHERE BirthDate >= @BirthDate";

        using (SqlConnection sqlConn =
                        new SqlConnection("Context Connection = true"))
        {
            sqlConn.Open();
            SqlCommand sqlCmd = sqlConn.CreateCommand();
            sqlCmd.CommandType = CommandType.Text;
            sqlCmd.CommandText = sqlSelect;
            sqlCmd.Parameters.AddWithValue("@BirthDate", BirthDate.Value);

            using (SqlDataAdapter da = new SqlDataAdapter(sqlCmd))
            {
                DataTable dt = new DataTable();
                da.Fill(dt);
                return dt.Rows;    // Rows collection implements IEnumerable
            }
        }
    }
    public static void ReturnARow(Object item, out SqlInt32 EmployeeID,
                                    out SqlString NationalIDNumber,
                                    out SqlDateTime BirthDate)
    {
        DataRow aRow = (DataRow)item;
        EmployeeID = Convert.ToInt32(aRow["EmployeeID"]);
```

```
            NationalIDNumber = Convert.ToString(aRow["NationalIDNumber"]);
            BirthDate = Convert.ToDateTime(aRow["BirthDate"]);
        }
    };
```

That is a little more involved than creating the UDF in T-SQL, and if you notice we moved from a set-based `select` statement into a row-by-row data delivery method. From a performance perspective, you should expect to take a hit here, as shown in the charts in Figure 5-15.

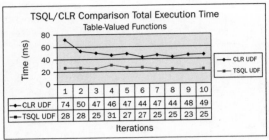
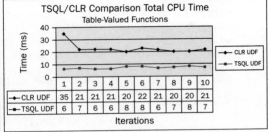

Figure 5-15

In total time, T-SQL beats SQL CLR by almost 50% (47% to be precise). In total CPU time, T-SQL outperforms SQL CLR by 65%. It is clear to see why you don't hear folks recommending using SQL CLR for retrieving data from the database. T-SQL is clearly optimized to deliver sets of data more efficiently. But if you've got the CPU bandwidth, is there ever a reason to use a SQL CLR table-valued UDF? Absolutely. One use is to generate a streaming table-valued SQL CLR UDF to deliver contents of a log file, or a web service method. These things aren't even possible with T-SQL. The best use for a table-valued UDF that compares to T-SQL directly is for applications that need a parameterized view where you can benefit from streaming that information. In T-SQL TVFs, the whole contents have to be queried before the results are sent back to the caller. In SQL CLR, you have control over the contents and can begin streaming with the first row. This enhances the experience of your application over using T-SQL TVFs, especially with large datasets. The key to what differentiates SQL CLR table-valued functions is the ability to turn anything that can implement an `IEnumerable` interface into a table—that can be queried or joined. This means you can write functions that return rows of files in a directory, from an array, from stock prices from a web service, or even from RSS feed information. By embedding these rows into a TVF, you also get the best practice of being able to use joins and parameters. See Chapter 6 for some examples of using TVFs with these capabilities.

Set-Based Operations

Set-based operations are updates to blocks of rows that comprise a set of data. T-SQL is going to be the better choice for declarative set-based operations—unless there is some sort of calculation or computation involved. We have already experimented with updating or submitting data to the database using T-SQL and CLR and witnessed a slightly better performance with pure updating speed and ease of programming with T-SQL. We've also seen the significantly better performance of SQL CLR in the calculation and computational competitions. We suggest for set based operations that you either:

❑ Build the computation in SQL CLR and use T-SQL to build the set and invoke the computation across the set.

❑ Call the T-SQL set-based operation from within SQL CLR. This can be a set-based T-SQL statement or a call to a T-SQL object to do the bulk work.

Use T-SQL by itself for set-based operations.

Forward-Only, Read-Only Row Navigation Example

There are situations that cause one to pause to decide whether the logic should occur on the client or in the server. One of these situations is the need to iterate over a rowset of nonrelational data to examine or process items in series to get the data in a relational state. The solutions to these problems depend on whether the programmer is comfortable in programming T-SQL and using cursors, or if they prefer to pull the data down to the client and perform the activity in datasets. This is the Promised Land that many developers have in mind when thinking about using SQL CLR. I don't think most developers are thinking they can replace the read-write-and-delete or CRUD part of their applications with SQL CLR, but how many have wondered if SQL CLR can make it possible to code complicated logic to run on the server? Just think, no more needing to dig out the T-SQL book to code complicated, involved database logic to run in the database. It's important to spend a little time comparing a T-SQL and a SQL CLR approach to solving a problem like this.

One such example presented itself recently. We'll use a simplified example to demonstrate solving the problem in T-SQL and in SQL CLR. A bank sends a lockbox file that contains three type of flat-file entries: a header containing the batch balance and date, then a series of invoice lines and check lines. There can be many invoice lines to many check lines and the task is to put them together and attempt to make payments. In this example, other prelogic has pulled out invoice (I) and check (C) amounts that exactly match. The remaining items are usually multiple check items that need to be combined, or payment amounts that don't match exactly to the invoiced amounts but are close enough to match acceptably for payment. The last bit of information is that the customer number is embedded in the invoice number at position 4-5. This will allow matching of separate invoices belonging to one customer together. If you want to create this example and follow along, the full script to create and populate the tables and a copy of each iteration of the code are available for download from this book's web site at www.wrox.com. A set of this data to process (without the header data) looks like Figure 5-16.

	LockBoxSubID	SubType	InvoiceNbr	PaidAmt
1	1	I	Z0181844972	0.00
2	2	C	X	287.44
3	3	I	Z0181844944	0.00
4	4	C	X	1016.94
5	5	I	M0169223112	0.00
6	6	C	X	1287.44
7	7	I	ZNONE	0.00
8	8	C	X	1287.44
9	9	I	Z0185836083	0.00
10	10	I	Z0185836084	0.00
11	11	C	X	2517.89
12	12	C	X	1258.60
13	13	C	X	1287.44

Figure 5-16

The invoice data we'll represent for simplicity as Figure 5-17.

	INVOICENBR	BILLAMOUNT
1	Z0181844972	2008.00
2	Z0181844944	600.76
3	M0169223112	2574.88
4	Z0185836083	2531.97
5	Z0185836084	2531.97

Figure 5-17

You can see that the first two checks total $1,304.38, and they are for invoices that total $2,608.76. This amount seems odd, but a quick calculation shows that it is exactly one half the expected payment. Business rules allow us to accept this payment. This is the type of logic that you need to implement. Read rows until the customer changes, and then attempt to make sense of the payment.

This involves navigating the rows produced by a SQL statement one at a time in a forward-only, read-only fashion. In T-SQL, this is implemented through a forward-only, read-only cursor. In CLR, it is implemented through a `SqlDataReader` object. Typically, there is some processing involved for each statement. If you ignore the processing associated with each row, then the navigation of rows in CLR is slightly slower than in T-SQL cursors. If you factor in the processing that is performed for every row, however, the advantage tilts more towards CLR since the CLR significantly outperforms T-SQL on such processing. In this example, the basic steps are to:

1. Create a set of the items to match so you can move through the list to determine what items belong together in the series.

2. Store the invoice items in one structure. Store the check items in another structure. You need to be able to account for handling each line.

3. Process the transactions when the customer number changes for potential payment matches. Invoices designated as "ZNONE" are considered to belong to the previous customer.

4. Look up invoice amounts by invoice number.

5. Evaluate whether the expected billing amounts and payment amounts belong together. In the real world, these calculations involve multiple lookups on invoices by invoice and customer number to establish a statistical confidence in the payment belonging to the customer. This example will just allow payments that are in half-billed payment increments or within $0.99.

6. If the grouped transactions belong together, you need to annotate them as processed. In the real world, you'd link these together and create new rows in a paid lockbox table. For this example, you'll just mark each with a status of "M-matched."

If you're coding the solution in T-SQL, you can encapsulate very little logic to keep the procedure more maintainable. One thing you can do is to move the decision about whether the payment and billed amounts are within standard into a UDF scalar function. You can't modularize the code much further without using global tables for our processing structures or passing complicated strings that can be broken out into arrays. Finally, the logic of updating billing amounts, determining how much is billed and paid, sending the information to the UDF, and then all the housekeeping work has to not only reside in the main body of the procedure but also be repeated at the end of the loop. The T-SQL version is:

```
CREATE PROC [dbo].[usp_ProcessLockboxUnMatched]
AS
DECLARE @SUBID INT
DECLARE @SUBTYPE CHAR(1)
DECLARE @LASTSUBTYPE CHAR(1)
DECLARE @INVOICENBR VARCHAR(50)
DECLARE @CUSTOMER CHAR(5)
DECLARE @LASTCUSTOMER CHAR(5)
DECLARE @PAIDAMT MONEY
DECLARE @CANPAYIT BIT

DECLARE @TOTALPAID MONEY
DECLARE @TOTALBILLED MONEY

SET @CANPAYIT = 0
SET @SUBTYPE = 'X'
SET @LASTSUBTYPE = 'X'

CREATE TABLE #TMPI(LOCKBOXSUBID INT, INVOICENBR VARCHAR(50), BILLEDAMT MONEY)
CREATE TABLE #TMPC(LOCKBOXSUBID INT, PAIDAMT MONEY)

DECLARE oRS CURSOR FOR
SELECT [LockBoxSubID], [SubType], [InvoiceNbr], [PaidAmt]
FROM LOCKBOXSUBDTL WHERE STATUS IS NULL
ORDER BY LOCKBOXSUBID

OPEN oRS

-- Perform the first fetch.
FETCH NEXT FROM oRS
INTO @SUBID, @SUBTYPE, @INVOICENBR, @PAIDAMT

WHILE @@FETCH_STATUS = 0
BEGIN
  IF @SUBTYPE = 'I'
    BEGIN
      IF LEN(@INVOICENBR) > 8
        SET @CUSTOMER = substring(@INVOICENBR, 4, 5)
      ELSE
        SET @CUSTOMER = @INVOICENBR

      IF @INVOICENBR = 'ZNONE'
        SET @CUSTOMER = @LASTCUSTOMER

      If @LASTCUSTOMER = 'XXXXX'
        SET @LASTCUSTOMER = @CUSTOMER

      IF @LASTSUBTYPE = 'C'
        BEGIN
        IF @CUSTOMER <> @LASTCUSTOMER
          BEGIN
            --FIND TOTAL PAID
            SELECT @TOTALPAID = SUM(ISNULL(PAIDAMT, 0))
            FROM #TMPC
```

```
            --UPDATE INVOICE AMOUNTS (IF FIND)
            UPDATE I
            SET BILLEDAMT = INV.BILLAMOUNT
            FROM #TMPI I INNER JOIN Invoice INV
            ON I.InvoiceNbr = INV.InvoiceNbr

            --FIND TOTAL BILLED
            SELECT @TOTALBILLED = SUM(BILLEDAMT)
            FROM #TMPI

            --SEE IF YOU CAN PAY IT
            SELECT @CANPAYIT =dbo.usp_AcceptPaymentAmount(@TOTALBILLED,
                                                          @TOTALPAID)

            --IF SO UPDATE STATUS
            IF @CANPAYIT = 1
              BEGIN
                UPDATE LB
                SET STATUS = 'M'
                FROM LockboxSubDtl LB
                INNER JOIN #TMPC CHK
                ON LB.LockBoxSubID =
                CHK.LockBoxSubID

                UPDATE LB
                SET STATUS = 'M'
                FROM LockboxSubDtl LB
                INNER JOIN #TMPI INV
                ON LB.LockBoxSubID=
                INV.LockBoxSubID
              END

          --CLEAR OUT TEMP TABLE
          DELETE FROM #TMPI
          DELETE FROM #TMPC
          --RESET VARS
          SET @TOTALBILLED = 0
          SET @TOTALPAID = 0
          SET @CANPAYIT = 0
        END
      END

    --THEN BOOK THE INVOICE IN CURRENT LOOP INTO TEMP
    INSERT INTO #TMPI
    SELECT @SUBID, @INVOICENBR, 0

    SET @LASTSUBTYPE = 'I'

    SET @LASTCUSTOMER = @CUSTOMER
  END

IF @SUBTYPE = 'C'
  BEGIN
    INSERT INTO #TMPC
    SELECT @SUBID, @PAIDAMT
```

```
        SET @LASTSUBTYPE = 'C'
    END

  -- Perform the first fetch.
  FETCH NEXT FROM oRS
    INTO @SUBID, @SUBTYPE, @INVOICENBR, @PAIDAMT
END

CLOSE oRS
DEALLOCATE oRS

--AN ADDITIONAL PAYMENT ROUTINE
--FOR ITEM FOUND IN LAST LOOP
--FIND TOTAL PAID
SELECT @TOTALPAID = SUM(ISNULL(PAIDAMT, 0))
FROM #TMPC

--UPDATE INVOICE AMOUNTS (IF FIND)
UPDATE I
SET BILLEDAMT = INV.BILLAMOUNT
FROM #TMPI I INNER JOIN Invoice INV
ON I.InvoiceNbr = INV.InvoiceNbr

--FIND TOTAL BILLED
SELECT @TOTALBILLED = SUM(BILLEDAMT)
FROM #TMPI

--SEE IF YOU CAN PAY IT
SELECT @CANPAYIT = dbo.usp_AcceptPaymentAmount(@TOTALBILLED, @TOTALPAID)

--IF SO UPDATE STATUS
IF @CANPAYIT = 1
  BEGIN
    UPDATE LB
    SET STATUS = 'M'
    FROM LockboxSubDtl LB
    INNER JOIN #TMPC CHK
    ON LB.LockBoxSubID = CHK.LockBoxSubID

    UPDATE LB
    SET STATUS = 'M'
    FROM LockboxSubDtl LB
    INNER JOIN #TMPI INV
    ON LB.LockBoxSubID = INV.LockBoxSubID
  END

  DROP TABLE #TMPI
  DROP TABLE #TMPC
```

When approaching the development of a SQL CLR version, we are going to make use of several techniques that we've discussed in this chapter. You'll see temp tables within the same context connection — but using different `sqlConnections`. You'll use factory code in other namespaces to show the ability of .NET code reuse. We'll demonstrate using the same T-SQL UDF within your SQL CLR code to show some T-SQL code reuse as well.

One of the big differences between coding in SQL CLR and .NET or T-SQL is that you have to pay close attention to your Context connection. Within the execution scope of any SQL CLR method, you can only have one sqlConnection with a state of ConnectionState.Open at a time. This means that you can't open up DataReader and iterate through it while firing UPDATE statements through the Context connection. You can either use a disconnected dataset or fill an ArrayList as we did here. In T-SQL, you can have a cursor open and issue statements at the same time without restriction.

To simplify the UPDATE statements, the example uses a call to ExecuteNonQueryFactory. This method is built in a separate namespace called SqlClrHelperUtilities in a static class SqlClrHelper. Building helper classes like this makes the future development of SQL CLR objects quicker and more robust. Notice that the SqlConnection is closed before leaving the method.

```
using System;
using System.Data;
using System.Data.SqlClient;
using System.Data.SqlTypes;
using Microsoft.SqlServer.Server;

namespace SqlClrHelperUtilities
{
    public partial class SqlClrHelper
    {
        public static void ExecuteNonQueryFactory(string sqlStatement)
        {
            using (SqlConnection sqlConn =
                    new SqlConnection("Context Connection=true"))
            {
                sqlConn.Open();
                SqlCommand sqlCmd = sqlConn.CreateCommand();
                sqlCmd.CommandType = CommandType.Text;
                sqlCmd.CommandText = sqlStatement;
                sqlCmd.ExecuteNonQuery();
                sqlConn.Close();
            }
        }
    }
}
```

The ability to isolate each step makes the programming task easier to team develop and to troubleshoot. In the real world, you would have a more computative calculation process that involves looking at customer past due and past paid invoice activity instead of the simplistic calculation in the IsMatched() method. Separating this logic would make it easy to test the basic procedure and then add the proprietary logic in later iterations. To use this code later, deploy this assembly into SQL Server. Notice as well that you can create and use #temp tables through the context of the SQL CLR execution scope (except for the T-SQL UDF). One thing you want to be careful of here though is using T-SQL approaches when developing solutions in SQL CLR. Modeling a T-SQL approach won't allow you to capitalize on the advantages of the .NET architecture for performance reasons. To demonstrate, bear with a few lenghtly iterations of creating and then tuning a SQL CLR by copying a version of the T-SQL procedure using the same approach first. Note that you are also using the namespace for the ExecuteNonQueryFactory method that you just created. To do this, make sure you add a reference to the project for the SQL Server hosted assembly that contains this function before adding the namespace to this project.

```csharp
using System;
using System.Data;
using System.Data.SqlClient;
using System.Data.SqlTypes;
using Microsoft.SqlServer.Server;
using SqlClrHelperUtilities;
using System.Collections;

public static class StoredProcedures
{
    [Microsoft.SqlServer.Server.SqlProcedure]
    public static void mfnProcessLockboxUnmatched()
    {
        //PURPOSE: TO PROCESS UNMATCHED LOCKBOX ITEMS
        SqlInt32 subId = 0;
        SqlString subType = string.Empty;
        SqlString lastSubType = "X";
        SqlString invoiceNbr = string.Empty;
        SqlString customer = string.Empty;
        SqlString lastCustomer = "XXXXX";
        SqlMoney paidAmt = new SqlMoney(0.00);
        ArrayList lbItems;
        CreateTempWorkTables();
        {
            lbItems = GetLockboxItems();
            foreach (LockboxSubItem lbItem in lbItems)
            {
                subId = lbItem.SubId;
                subType = lbItem.SubType;
                invoiceNbr = lbItem.InvoiceNbr;
                paidAmt = lbItem.PaidAmt;
                if (subType == "I")
                {
                    //PARSE CUSTOMER FROM INVOICE
                    if (Convert.ToString(invoiceNbr).Length > 8)
                        customer = Convert.ToString(invoiceNbr).Substring(3, 5);
                    else
                        customer = Convert.ToString(invoiceNbr);

                    if (customer == "ZNONE")
                        customer = lastCustomer;

                    //FIRST TIME CASE
                    if (lastCustomer == "XXXXX")
                        lastCustomer = customer;

                    if (lastSubType == "C")
                    {
                        if (customer != lastCustomer)
                            TryToMatchAndPay();
                    }
                    AddInvoice(subId, invoiceNbr);
                    lastSubType = "I";
                }
```

```
                else if (subType == "C")
                {
                    AddCheck(subId, paidAmt);
                    lastSubType = "C";
                }
            }
            TryToMatchAndPay();
        }
        RemoveTempWorkTables();
    }
    public static ArrayList GetLockboxItems()
    {
        //PURPOSE: TO RETRIEVE LOCKBOX ITEMS TODO
        //          INTO AN ARRAYLIST STRUCTURE OF TYPE LOCKBOXSUBITEM
        ArrayList lbItems = new ArrayList();
        using (SqlConnection sqlConn =
                new SqlConnection("Context Connection=True"))
        {
            sqlConn.Open();
            SqlCommand sqlCmd = sqlConn.CreateCommand();
            sqlCmd.CommandText = "SELECT [LockBoxSubID], [SubType],  " +
                        "  [InvoiceNbr], [PaidAmt] " +
                        "FROM LOCKBOXSUBDTL " +
                        "WHERE STATUS IS NULL " +
                        "ORDER BY LOCKBOXSUBID ";
            SqlDataReader LockboxItemsDr = sqlCmd.ExecuteReader();
            while (LockboxItemsDr.Read())
            {
                lbItems.Add(new LockboxSubItem(
                        LockboxItemsDr.GetSqlInt32(0),
                        LockboxItemsDr.GetSqlString(1),
                        LockboxItemsDr.GetSqlString(2),
                        LockboxItemsDr.GetSqlMoney(3)));
            }
            LockboxItemsDr.Close();
            sqlConn.Close();
        }
        return lbItems;
    }
    public static void TryToMatchAndPay()
    {
        //PURPOSE: DRIVER METHOD TO PULL MATCHING AND
        //          PAYMENT OPERATIONS TOGETHER
        LookupInvoiceBillAmts();
        if (IsMatched()){
            SqlClrHelper.ExecuteNonQueryFactory("UPDATE LB " +
                        "SET STATUS = 'M' " +
                        "FROM LockboxSubDtl LB " +
                        "INNER JOIN #TMPC CHK " +
                        "ON LB.LockBoxSubID = CHK.LockBoxSubID ");

            SqlClrHelper.ExecuteNonQueryFactory("UPDATE LB " +
                        "SET STATUS = 'M' " +
                        "FROM LockboxSubDtl LB " +
                        "INNER JOIN #TMPI INV " +
```

```
                              "ON LB.LockBoxSubID = INV.LockBoxSubID ");
        }
        ClearTempWorkTables();
    }
    public static void LookupInvoiceBillAmts()
    {
        //PURPOSE: TO USE DATABASE LOOKUPS TO FIND THE BILLING AMOUNTS
        SqlClrHelper.ExecuteNonQueryFactory("UPDATE I " +
                "SET BILLEDAMT = INV.BILLAMOUNT " +
                "FROM #TMPI I INNER JOIN Invoice INV " +
                "ON I.InvoiceNbr = INV.InvoiceNbr ");
    }
    public static bool IsMatched()
    {
        //PURPOSE: TO DETERMINE IF THE INVOICES AND CHECKS CAPTURED
        //             MEET QUALIFICATIONS TO BE MATCHED TOGETHER
        //             (MORE SOPHISTICATED LOGIC WOULD BE HERE)
        SqlMoney paidAmt = new SqlMoney(0.00);
        SqlMoney billedAmt = new SqlMoney(0.00);
        SqlBoolean isMatched = false;
        SqlConnection sqlConn = new SqlConnection("Context Connection=True");
        SqlCommand sqlCmd = new SqlCommand();
        SqlDataReader sqlWorkDr;
        sqlConn.Open();
        sqlCmd.Connection = sqlConn;
        sqlCmd.CommandText = "SELECT sum(isnull(PAIDAMT, 0)) FROM #TMPC ";
        //GET PAID TOTAL
        sqlWorkDr = sqlCmd.ExecuteReader();
        while (sqlWorkDr.Read()){
            paidAmt = sqlWorkDr.GetSqlMoney(0);
        }
        sqlWorkDr.Close();
        //GET BILLED TOTAL
        sqlCmd.CommandText = "Select sum(BILLEDAMT) FROM #TMPI";
        sqlWorkDr = sqlCmd.ExecuteReader();
        while (sqlWorkDr.Read()){
            billedAmt = sqlWorkDr.GetSqlMoney(0);
        }
        sqlWorkDr.Close();
        //SEE IF WE CAN ACCEPT PAYMENT USING AN EXTERNAL TSQL UDF
        sqlCmd.CommandText = "select dbo.usp_AcceptPaymentAmount(" +
            Convert.ToString(billedAmt) +
            ", " + Convert.ToString(paidAmt) + ")";
        sqlWorkDr = sqlCmd.ExecuteReader();
        while (sqlWorkDr.Read()){
            isMatched = sqlWorkDr.GetBoolean(0);
            }
        sqlWorkDr.Close();
        sqlConn.Close();
        return (bool)isMatched;
    }
    public static void AddInvoice(SqlInt32 LockboxSubID, SqlString InvoiceNbr)
    {
        //PURPOSE: TO ADD A INVOICE DIMENSION TO THE INVOICE TEMP TABLE
        SqlClrHelper.ExecuteNonQueryFactory("INSERT INTO #TMPI SELECT " +
```

```
                                          Convert.ToString(LockboxSubID) + ", '" +
                                          Convert.ToString(InvoiceNbr) + "', 0");
    }
    public static void AddCheck(SqlInt32 LockboxSubID, SqlMoney PaidAmt)
    {
        //PURPOSE: TO ADD A CHECK DIMENSION TO THE CHECK TEMP TABLE
        SqlClrHelper.ExecuteNonQueryFactory("INSERT INTO #TMPC SELECT " +
                                          Convert.ToString(LockboxSubID) + ", '" +
                                          Convert.ToString(PaidAmt) + "'");
    }
    public static void CreateTempWorkTables()
    {
        //PURPOSE: TO CREATE #TMP TABLES TO WORK IN
        SqlClrHelper.ExecuteNonQueryFactory("CREATE TABLE #TMPI(" +
                "LOCKBOXSUBID INT, INVOICENBR VARCHAR(50), BILLEDAMT MONEY)");
        SqlClrHelper.ExecuteNonQueryFactory("CREATE TABLE #TMPC(" +
                "LOCKBOXSUBID INT, PAIDAMT MONEY)");
    }
    public static void ClearTempWorkTables()
    {
        //PURPOSE: TO CLEAR OUT #TMP TABLES USED FOR CALCULATIONS
        SqlClrHelper.ExecuteNonQueryFactory("DELETE #TMPI; DELETE #TMPC");
    }
    public static void RemoveTempWorkTables()
    {
        //PURPOSE: TO REMOVE #TMP TABLES USED FOR CALCULATIONS
        SqlClrHelper.ExecuteNonQueryFactory("IF EXISTS " +
            "(SELECT * FROM sysobjects where name = '#TMPI') DROP TABLE #TMPI");
        SqlClrHelper.ExecuteNonQueryFactory("IF EXISTS " +
            "(SELECT * FROM sysobjects where name = '#TMPC') DROP TABLE #TMPC");
    }
}


class LockboxSubItem
{
    //CLASS TO PROVIDE STRUCTURE TO STORE IN AN ARRAYLIST
    public SqlInt32 subId;
    public SqlString subType;
    public SqlString invoiceNbr;
    public SqlMoney paidAmt;

    public LockboxSubItem(SqlInt32 subId, SqlString subType,
                    SqlString invoiceNbr, SqlMoney paidAmt)
    {
        this.subId = subId;
        this.subType = subType;
        this.invoiceNbr = invoiceNbr;
        this.paidAmt = paidAmt;
    }
}
;
```

Because we didn't fully reengineer the SQL CLR version to use more efficient storage structures like arrays or collections, we don't expect to gain much in terms of processing time. We are still doing a lot of database work. All we've done is move it inside the context of the SQL CLR object. This is why the performance in Figure 5-18 doesn't show any benefit in moving that T-SQL approach methodology into SQL CLR.

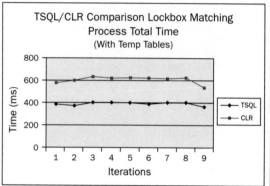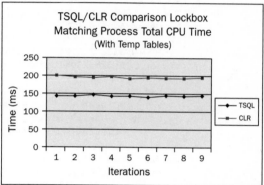

Figure 5-18

There may be an advantage here on the programming side based on the ease of programming or the better maintainability of modular versus procedural code. To achieve any performance benefits of CLR, you need to program using .NET-based programming techniques. One of the first changes you can make to your program is to remove the use of the temp tables and replace them with in-memory structures. The code now looks more like a .NET program. Here are two of the methods that have changed:

```
public static void TryToMatchAndPay(ArrayList matchedItems)
{
    //PURPOSE: DRIVER METHOD TO PULL MATCHING AND
    //         PAYMENT OPERATIONS TOGETHER
    string inClause=string.Empty;
    if (IsMatched(matchedItems))
    {
        foreach (LockboxSubItem lbItem in matchedItems)
        {
            if (inClause.Length > 0)
                inClause += "," + Convert.ToString(lbItem.subId);
            else
                inClause += Convert.ToString(lbItem.subId);
        }

        SqlClrHelper.ExecuteNonQueryFactory("UPDATE LB " +
                "SET STATUS = 'M' " +
                "FROM LockboxSubDtl LB " +
                "WHERE LockboxSubID IN (" + inClause + ")");
    }
    ClearTempWorkArray(matchedItems);
}

public static bool IsMatched(ArrayList matchedItems)
{
    //PURPOSE: TO DETERMINE IF THE INVOICES AND CHECKS CAPTURED
```

```
//          MEET QUALIFICATIONS TO BE MATCHED TOGETHER
//            (MORE SOPHISTICATED LOGIC WOULD BE HERE)
SqlMoney paidAmt = new SqlMoney(0.00);
SqlMoney billedAmt = new SqlMoney(0.00);
SqlBoolean isMatched = false;
string inClause=string.Empty;
SqlDataReader sqlDr;

//GET INVOICE INSTRING TO PULL BILLED AMOUNT
foreach (LockboxSubItem lbItem in matchedItems)
{
    if (inClause.Length > 0)
        inClause += ",'" + Convert.ToString(lbItem.invoiceNbr) + "'";
    else
        inClause += "'" + Convert.ToString(lbItem.invoiceNbr) + "'";
}
if (inClause.Length > 0){
    using (SqlConnection sqlConn =
            new SqlConnection("Context Connection=True"))
    {
        SqlCommand sqlCmd = sqlConn.CreateCommand();
        sqlCmd.CommandText = "SELECT SUM(BILLAMOUNT) FROM INVOICE " +
                    "WHERE INVOICENBR IN (" + inClause + ")";

        sqlConn.Open();
        sqlDr = sqlCmd.ExecuteReader();
         while (sqlDr.Read())
        {
            billedAmt = sqlDr.GetSqlMoney(0);
        }
        sqlDr.Close();
        sqlConn.Close();
    }
}
//GET PAID AMOUNT
foreach (LockboxSubItem lbItem in matchedItems)
{
    paidAmt += lbItem.paidAmt;
}

//SEE IF WE CAN ACCEPT PAYMENT USING AN EXTERNAL TSQL UDF
using (SqlConnection sqlConn =
        new SqlConnection("Context Connection=True"))
{
    SqlCommand sqlCmd = sqlConn.CreateCommand();
    sqlCmd.CommandText = "select dbo.usp_AcceptPaymentAmount(" +
        Convert.ToString(billedAmt) +
        ", " + Convert.ToString(paidAmt) + ")";
    sqlConn.Open();
    sqlDr = sqlCmd.ExecuteReader();
    while (sqlDr.Read())
    {
        isMatched = sqlDr.GetBoolean(0);
    }
```

```
            sqlDr.Close();
            sqlConn.Close();
    }
    return (bool)isMatched;
}
```

You can take this even further by converting the call to the external T-SQL UDF and processing that logic in the CLR routine, but already we've gained and surpassed the performance of the T-SQL approach. Figure 5-19 shows all three methods with the performance metric comparisons.

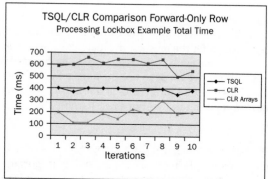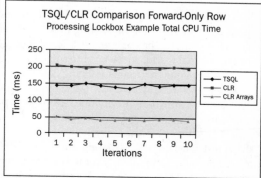

Figure 5-19

The key here is to demonstrate that SQL CLR can be used to solve complicated data-based tasks involving iteration over data with forward-only row navigation. The counterpoint is just because it is written in CLR doesn't mean there is going to be any advantage in performance unless you consider the medium you are working in. A T-SQL solution operates on a different set of constraints and optimizations then a .NET SQL CLR solution, so code accordingly. The technology doesn't replace the need for good common sense in applying and engineering code solutions to each language's strengths.

Performance and Other Comparisons

How did we go about measuring all the performance metrics for this comparison? We started with knowing that we wanted to look at things like total execution time, memory usage, disk usage, and CPU usage. We had several options to use for this information. The first option was to set up a counter log in the performance monitor. There is a ton of information available from the performance monitor that will help you in the day-to-day monitoring of a server. However, the performance monitor polls this information on intervals, so we couldn't accurately predict when the monitor will poll. We'd either be too early or too late to have information timely enough for us to perform direct comparisons.

The second option was to use some of the data available within SQL through some of the system views. Along with the old standbys of Sys.Processes are a slew of new dynamic management views like sys.dm_os_memory_objects that gives specific information relative to the use of CLR by SQL Server. We could retrieve this information in a more timely fashion and in the same environment that we were performing our comparisons. This option provides more than enough data for us to evaluate the two approaches side by side.

We then came up with a methodology of comparison that we used as we evaluated SQL CLR and T-SQL in a variety of tests. That methodology is detailed in the next section.

Note that performance benchmarking has a lot to do with machine configuration. Before you accept anyone's benchmarking, make sure you've tried the examples in the environment where you are considering deploying them. Feel free to use and build on what we've started here to decide whether using SQL CLR based routines is appropriate for your solutions.

Methodology of Comparison

Isolating the performance of server-based products is extremely difficult. Our method was based on running two processes and measuring them relatively. Run a T-SQL process and gather metrics. Reset the environment, run the comparable SQL CLR process, and gather the metrics. Evaluate. We are developers out in the real world, so we tried to come up with a way to measure performance that you could easily replicate in your environment. Being database programmers, we chose to use the data available within SQL Server via the system views and dynamic management views for metrics gathering. This is because we could capture that information before and after running each test within a test-harness-like stored procedure.

Each test consisted of alternating calling one T-SQL object and then a SQL CLR object in a set of 10 trials of 100 iterations and taking average measurements. The multiple iterations are incredibly important. All sorts of things are going on in the server environment — garbage collection, tempdb transaction logging, and competing operating system resources — that can affect your results. You need to run several iterations and average out the results to minimize the things that don't happen consistently. Otherwise, you won't get a clear picture of the trends, and these are what we are most interested in. In some instances, we compared the performance of like objects, for example two SQL CLR objects, to compare coding differences between things like SqlTypes and CLR types. This is the final protocol used to benchmark each example in this chapter:

1. Reset caching in the server using DBCC commands:

   ```
   DBCC DROPCLEANBUFFERS
   DBCC FREEPROCCACHE
   ```

2. Capture starting server conditions using the Sys.Processes and sys.dm_os_memory_objects views.

3. Run one version of a solution.

4. Capture the final server conditions using the same methods.

5. Store the results, including the test name and iteration, in a temp table.

6. Reset caching on the server.

7. Capture starting server conditions using the same methods.

8. Run second version of a solution in the alternate technology.

9. Capture final server conditions using the same methods.

10. Store the results, including the test name and iteration in a temp table.

11. After all iterations were complete, the results were pivoted into a table that could be easily turned into graphs within Microsoft Excel.

As you can imagine, performing these tasks over and over again becomes tedious, so we created several stored procedures to run single, comparative, fixed interval, and variable interval tests. These procedures accept one or two test descriptions, one or two SQL-based test scripts represented by strings that can be executed, and the number of iterations we wished to perform. To run the parallel test for a T-SQL and SQL CLR version of the function that adds two numbers together, build a script like the following:

```
DECLARE @TESTSQL1 NVARCHAR(3000)
DECLARE @TESTSQL2 NVARCHAR(3000)

SET @TESTSQL1 = 'SELECT dbo.usp_ADD(COLX, COLY) ' +
                        'FROM MYTESTDATA '
SET @TESTSQL2 = 'SELECT dbo.msp_ADD(COLX, COLY) ' +
                        'FROM MYTESTDATA '

EXEC usp_ParallelTestingPerfMon 'TSQL', @TESTSQL1, 'SQLCLR', @TESTSQL2, 3
```

To get consistent results we averaged the times across the runs into 10 iterations. The procs all have a dynamic pivot statement that pivots this data, as shown in Figure 5-20. It is then an easy process to cut and paste the grid data into a Microsoft Excel spreadsheet to display the results in a graph, as shown in Figure 5-21. Select the columns you want to graph in Excel. Select the line graph and choose the series-in-columns option. The result should like similar to what you've been seeing throughout this chapter.

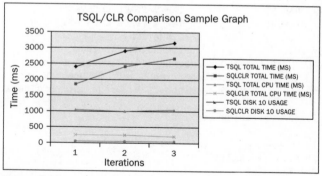

Figure 5-20

Figure 5-21

The metrics we captured are by no means exhaustive. For this chapter, we stuck to some of the basics. If there are metrics that you'd like to benchmark, here's the entire testing procedure for usp_Parallel TestingPerfMon_1000INT that we used for this chapter. The other test procs are available for download from this book's web site at www.wrox.com.

```
CREATE PROC [dbo].[usp_ParallelTestingPerfMon_1000INT] (
      @TESTDESC1 NVARCHAR(50),
      @TESTSQL1  NVARCHAR(3000),
      @TESTDESC2 NVARCHAR(50),
      @TESTSQL2  NVARCHAR(3000)
      )

AS
SET NOCOUNT ON

--EXAMPLE OF HOW TO POPULATE VARIABLES
--@TESTDESC1 = 'MSP FN'
--@TESTSQL1 = 'select
CLRTESTDB.dbo.msp_ReplaceNonAscIIChar(Purchaseordernumber)
from sales.salesorderheader'
--@TESTDESC2 = 'USP FN'
--@TESTSQL2 = 'select
CLRTESTDB.dbo.usp_ReplaceNonAscIIChar(Purchaseordernumber)
from sales.salesorderheader'
--1000 = 1

--===== Variables Section
DECLARE @TestStartTime DATETIME
DECLARE @TestEndTime DATETIME
DECLARE @CpuUsageStart INT
DECLARE @CpuUsageEnd INT
DECLARE @DiskIOStart INT
DECLARE @DiskIOEnd INT
DECLARE @MemUsageStart INT
DECLARE @MemUsageEnd INT
DECLARE @CLRMemUsageStart INT
DECLARE @CLRMemUsageEnd INT
DECLARE @RESHAPEDSQL VARCHAR(MAX)
DECLARE @CRLF CHAR(2)              --CRLF CONSTANT
DECLARE @TAB9 CHAR(9)             --TAB 9 SPACE CONSTANT
DECLARE @TAB4 CHAR(4)             --TAB 4 SPACE CONSTANT
DECLARE @i INT                   --ITERATION
DECLARE @Bigi INT                --ITERATION MOD 100
DECLARE @RESULTS TABLE(TestDesc varchar(50), Iteration int,
                   TestElapsedTimeMS int, CPUUsageMS int, DiskIOUsage int,
                   MemUsage int, CLRMemUsage int, BigIteration int)

--===== Initialize Variables Section
SET @i = 1
SET @Bigi = 1
SET @CRLF = CHAR(13) + CHAR(10)
SET @TAB9 = SPACE(9)
SET @TAB4 = SPACE(4)

WHILE @i <= 1000
   BEGIN
      --Drop all caching so we can get a
      --base-lined measure for performance tests
      DBCC DROPCLEANBUFFERS
```

```
DBCC FREEPROCCACHE

--Capture starting conditions
SELECT @TestStartTime = GETDATE(),
@CpuUsageStart = SUM(CPU),
@DiskIOStart = SUM(Physical_IO),
@MemUsageStart = SUM(MemUsage)
FROM Master.dbo.SysProcesses
WHERE SPID = 'ID

--CLR Specific conditions
SELECT @CLRMemUsageStart =
  sum(pages_allocated_count * page_size_in_bytes/1024)
FROM sys.dm_os_memory_objects
WHERE [type] LIKE '%clr%'

--Run Test Number 1
exec sp_executesql @TESTSQL1

--Capture the end-of-test conditions
SELECT @TestEndTime = GETDATE(),
@CpuUsageEnd = SUM(CPU),
@DiskIOEnd = SUM(Physical_IO),
@MemUsageEnd = SUM(MemUsage)
FROM Master.dbo.SysProcesses
WHERE SPID = 'ID

--CLR Specific conditions
SELECT @CLRMemUsageEnd =
  sum(pages_allocated_count * page_size_in_bytes/1024)
FROM sys.dm_os_memory_objects
WHERE [type] LIKE '%clr%'

--Save Conditions into temp table
INSERT INTO @RESULTS(TestDesc, Iteration, TestElapsedTimeMS,
                     CPUUsageMS, DiskIOUsage, MemUsage, BigIteration)
SELECT @TESTDESC1, @i, DATEDIFF(ms,@TestStartTime,@TestEndTime),
                   (@CpuUsageEnd-@CpuUsageStart), (@DiskIOEnd-@DiskIOStart),
                   (@MemUsageEnd-@MemUsageStart), @Bigi
--Drop all caching so we can get a
--base-lined measure for performance tests
DBCC DROPCLEANBUFFERS
DBCC FREEPROCCACHE

--Capture starting conditions
SELECT @TestStartTime = GETDATE(),
@CpuUsageStart = SUM(CPU),
@DiskIOStart = SUM(Physical_IO),
@MemUsageStart = SUM(MemUsage)
FROM Master.dbo.SysProcesses
WHERE SPID = 'ID

--CLR Specific conditions
```

```
SELECT @CLRMemUsageStart =
    sum(pages_allocated_count * page_size_in_bytes/1024)
FROM sys.dm_os_memory_objects
WHERE [type] LIKE '%clr%'

--Run Test Number 2
exec sp_executesql @TESTSQL2

--Capture the end condition of the resources used so far
-- as an ending point.
SELECT @TestEndTime = GETDATE(),
@CpuUsageEnd = SUM(CPU),
@DiskIOEnd = SUM(Physical_IO),
@MemUsageEnd = SUM(MemUsage)
FROM Master.dbo.SysProcesses
WHERE SPID = 'ID

--CLR Specific conditions
SELECT @CLRMemUsageEnd =
    sum(pages_allocated_count * page_size_in_bytes/1024)
FROM sys.dm_os_memory_objects
WHERE [type] LIKE '%clr%'

--Capture the end-of-test conditions
INSERT INTO @RESULTS(TestDesc, Iteration, TestElapsedTimeMS,
    CPUUsageMS, DiskIOUsage, MemUsage, CLRMemUsage, BigIteration)
SELECT @TESTDESC2, @i, DATEDIFF(ms,@TestStartTime,@TestEndTime),
(@CpuUsageEnd-@CpuUsageStart), (@DiskIOEnd-@DiskIOStart),
(@MemUsageEnd-@MemUsageStart), (@CLRMemUsageEnd-@CLRMemUsageStart), @Bigi

IF @i % 100 = 0
    SET @Bigi = @Bigi + 1

--Increment iteration
SET @i=@i + 1

END

SET @RESHAPEDSQL = 'SELECT    [ITERATION], ' + @CRLF + @TAB9 +
'[' + @TESTDESC1 + ' TOTAL TIME (MS)] = MAX(CASE WHEN TESTDESC = ''' +
@TESTDESC1 + ''' THEN [TestElapsedTimeMS] ELSE 0 END), ' + @CRLF + @TAB9 +
'[' + @TESTDESC2 + ' TOTAL TIME (MS)] = MAX(CASE WHEN TESTDESC = ''' +
@TESTDESC2 + ''' THEN [TestElapsedTimeMS] ELSE 0 END), ' + @CRLF + @TAB9 +
'[' + @TESTDESC1 + ' TOTAL CPU TIME (MS)] = MAX(CASE WHEN TESTDESC = ''' +
@TESTDESC1 + ''' THEN [CPUUsageMS] ELSE 0 END), ' + @CRLF + @TAB9 +
'[' + @TESTDESC2 + ' TOTAL CPU TIME (MS)] = MAX(CASE WHEN TESTDESC = ''' +
@TESTDESC2 + ''' THEN [CPUUsageMS] ELSE 0 END), ' + @CRLF + @TAB9 +
'[' + @TESTDESC1 + ' DISK IO USAGE] = MAX(CASE WHEN TESTDESC = ''' +
@TESTDESC1 + ''' THEN [DiskIOUsage] ELSE 0 END), ' + @CRLF + @TAB9 +
'[' + @TESTDESC2 + ' DISK IO USAGE] = MAX(CASE WHEN TESTDESC = ''' +
@TESTDESC2 + ''' THEN [DiskIOUsage] ELSE 0 END), ' + @CRLF + @TAB9 +
'[' + @TESTDESC1 + ' MEM USAGE] = MAX(CASE WHEN TESTDESC = ''' +
@TESTDESC1 + ''' THEN [MemUsage] ELSE 0 END), ' + @CRLF + @TAB9 +
```

```
'[' + @TESTDESC2 + ' MEM USAGE] = MAX(CASE WHEN TESTDESC = ''' +
@TESTDESC2 + ''' THEN [MemUsage] ELSE 0 END), ' + @CRLF + @TAB9 +
'[' + @TESTDESC1 + ' CLR MEM USAGE] = MAX(CASE WHEN TESTDESC = ''' +
@TESTDESC1 + ''' THEN [CLRMemUsage] ELSE 0 END), ' + @CRLF + @TAB9 +
'[' + @TESTDESC2 + ' CLR MEM USAGE] = MAX(CASE WHEN TESTDESC = ''' +
@TESTDESC2 + ''' THEN [CLRMemUsage] ELSE 0 END) ' + @CRLF +
'FROM ##Results ' + @CRLF + 'GROUP BY ITERATION '

IF EXISTS(SELECT * FROM TEMPDB.dbo.SYSOBJECTS
    WHERE TYPE = 'U' and NAME='##RESULTS')
  DROP TABLE ##RESULTS

SELECT * INTO ##RESULTS
FROM (
  SELECT TestDesc, Iteration=BigIteration,
    TestElapsedTimeMS=AVG(TestElapsedTimeMS),
    CPUUsageMS=AVG(CPUUsageMS), DiskIOUsage=AVG(DiskIOUsage),
    MemUsage=AVG(MemUsage), CLRMEMUSAGE=AVG(CLRMEMUSAGE)
  FROM @RESULTS
  GROUP BY TestDesc, BigIteration) A

EXEC(@RESHAPEDSQL)

DROP TABLE ##RESULTS
```

To capture additional metrics, add columns for them to the table variable definition, and then capture the settings at each of the capture points. Then update the reshaping SQL or alternatively just remove these lines and simply select the contents of the @Results table.

A Final Word on Performance

Performance seems to be the biggest benchmark of comparison between the T-SQL and SQL CLR approaches. There is no denying that SQL CLR can earn a place at the table in SQL Server-based development. In the examples where we compared T-SQL and SQL CLR on string parsing and computations, we saw that SQL CLR is a clear winner, measured in terms of performance by execution time, CPU cycles, and disk IO.

As it relates to a performance comparison between SQL CLR and T-SQL, we have shown in this chapter that:

❑ String parsing and processing perform better with less CPU resources using CLR base classes.

❑ Computation of even simple proportions performs better in SQL CLR.

❑ SQL CLR table-valued functions can stream results faster to client than T-SQL

❑ T-SQL is still the king of data manipulation, extraction, and updating.

However, performance will most likely not be the deciding factor in whether SQL CLR proliferates into development shops. Development projects are still largely conceived and executed on the time-honored constraints of time, functionalities, budget, and a sprinkling of politics. Performance is important, but look at our comparisons in the light of these constraints. If implementing a SQL CLR routine reduces the total time of a T-SQL-based transaction by half, first put that reduction in context. Reducing a routine from eight minutes to four minutes is outstanding. However, if the routine runs once a day during off-hours, what is the real benefit? If the routine runs all during the day, then you have something to talk about. If you can wrap an existing .NET library to leverage some code reuse and can reduce the CPU cycles for a set of T-SQL routines, find out the impact to your shop in total terms. When you present SQL CLR in terms of improvements in time and budget savings, or the ability to add new functionality, this technology will have a better chance of getting to the table.

Maintainability

How many folks are there who are just not going to turn on CLR integration because they've read a little something about the technology and have made a decision that it will be too difficult to maintain? In comparing SQL CLR to T-SQL, this is an aspect that we have to consider. How much does it cost to have a DBA maintain hosted SQL CLR objects that contain code they may not understand?

First, SQL Server has always had "unmaintainable" code in the form of extended and encrypted stored procedures. DBAs can't maintain this code today — even if they wanted to. There also haven't been too many complaints (if you don't count those about xp_Sendmail). There have been no movements to shut down extended stored procedures. This even when extended stored procedures have more destructive access to the operating system and contain unmanaged code. If you require that the assemblies be loaded into the meta-tables, DBAs can extract the code in precompiled format. This ensures that you can at least examine what the code is doing and even maintain the code if the need arises. Functionally, what's the difference between extracting a stored procedure from the syscomments table? It's code stored in a meta-table. The only difference really is that assemblies can't be written in T-SQL.

Second, DBAs are not helpless to the power of the CLR. From the perspective of working within SQL Server, the hosted assembly and the dependent SQL CLR objects look and act like T-SQL objects. The DBA is going to have a lot of the same information as if the object were native to SQL Server. One of the few differences is that the DBA can't see inside the activity of a stored procedure like you can with T-SQL objects. In Figure 5-22, you can see the profiler activity for two procedures; one, usp_Add, is a T-SQL stored procedure. The other, msp_Add, is a C# CLR procedure. For the T-SQL procedure, you can get procedure-level trace information using the T-SQL_SPs trace. You can see the starting time and contents of each internal statement. For the SQL CLR version, you get only information about the loading of the assembly, and the access of the entry point, then the unloading of the assembly. There is less information available to the DBA, because SQL Server can't look inside the assembly. Therefore, in this one instance, troubleshooting from SQL Server is going to harder. Otherwise, all your existing troubleshooting logs, warnings, and supporting systems will work the same.

EventClass	TextData	Databa...	DatabaseName	Objec...	ObjectName		StartTime
SQL:BatchStarting	select usp_Add(1000, 1000)	6	CLRTESTDB				2006-04-19 01:24:00...
SQL:BatchStarting	select dbo.usp_Add(1000, 1000)	6	CLRTESTDB				2006-04-19 01:24:06...
SP:Starting	select dbo.usp_Add(1000, 1000)	6	CLRTESTDB	9941...	usp_ADD		2006-04-19 01:24:06...
SP:StmtStarting	SET @Return = @x + @y	6	CLRTESTDB	9941...	usp_ADD		2006-04-19 01:24:06...
SP:StmtStarting	Return @Return	6	CLRTESTDB	9941...	usp_ADD		2006-04-19 01:24:06...
SP:Completed	select dbo.usp_Add(1000, 1000)	6	CLRTESTDB	9941...	usp_ADD		2006-04-19 01:24:06...
SQL:BatchStarting	select dbo.msp_Add(1000, 1000)	6	CLRTESTDB				2006-04-19 01:24:33...
SP:Starting	select dbo.msp_Add(1000, 1000)	6	CLRTESTDB	1858...	msp_Add		2006-04-19 01:24:33...
SP:Completed	select dbo.msp_Add(1000, 1000)	6	CLRTESTDB	1858...	msp_Add		2006-04-19 01:24:33...

Figure 5-22

If the DBA finds a problem with a procedure, how easy is it to troubleshoot the code within the procedure? How easy is it now with T-SQL? With SQL CLR, you have all the benefits of using the Visual Studio IDE along with the ability to attach debug processes to walk through your code. It's hard to argue with the advantages that SQL CLR gives you in code organizational capabilities.

The only unknown thing to worry about is what happens when the CLR itself is updated. Just as with any service path or update, you'll need to be aware of any CLR changes and the impact this may have on your existing SQL CLR basic objects. We will be addressing a code-based solution for this in Chapter 6.

If you are introducing SQL CLR to your shop, do yourself a favor and pick just one .NET language to implement at first. Pick a language that your development staff has experience with. Developers and DBAs will benefit from the cross-learning experiences. Add a few simple objects to your development cycles now and start getting used to the advantages of SQL CLR. You'll see that from a maintainability standpoint they are no different from T-SQL based objects.

Portability

If one your development requirements is that your software project be portable, then code T-SQL for your database logic as close to ANSI SQL standards as possible. Coding in SQL CLR will require your customers to have at least one version of SQL Server 2005 to host the CLR code. If they are willing to buy SQL Server then you don't have a portability constraint.

SQL CLR objects can connect to external database tables from linked servers like Microsoft Access, Excel, and Paradox or through regular ADO.NET providers. As long as there is a SQL Server to host the assembly, you can use it to connect to any ADO-based data source either as a linked server or with an appropriate connection string to the source. To the SQL CLR object, the linked server looks just like another database and outside the change in the connection object the development process is the same.

Summary

We have spent some time looking at some of the basic comparisons between solving problems in T-SQL and SQL CLR and have found a little of what we expected to find and some things we didn't. We expected to see better overall performance in the computational problems, and we did. You may not have expected to see such a tight race between the two technologies in the areas of data access. Sure, the CPU utilization numbers are coming in higher on some of the tests, but these results are more favorable than what we were looking at with the initial integration of Java in Oracle a few years back.

So, how does SQL CLR stack up T-SQL? Is performance your guiding principle? If so, you'll want to use SQL CLR when you need to perform computational scalar functions, custom aggregations, or to access capabilities that don't currently exist in the T-SQL language set. You'll want to use T-SQL when your solution involves set-based logic and process that perform heavy database update activity. Is making database programming easier to use what matters to you? Then you may find that coding in .NET against the database makes sense now because you can use the programming paradigm of which you are familiar. You may now see possibilities that have not existed before because .NET allows you to more easily manage and troubleshoot complicated, multistep backend processes. There are clear advantages to code organization, reuse, and encapsulation when using the SQL CLR methods. There are clear advantages to managing relational data using T-SQL.

Chapter 5

Appropriate application of technology is the key. Spending a day to improve a few milliseconds may not be worth your time. It may mean your business. If you are a T-SQL programmer, add this new capability to your toolkit. If you are coding in .NET today, running through some of these examples to have an idea of the capabilities may open some doors to the possibilities. Writing queries against files in folders? Joining relational data to data in web service methods? Can this be useful? Is it even possible? In the next chapter we'll explore some of the new capabilities that have up to now only been possible by using binary code exposed through extended stored procedures.

6

Replacing Extended Stored Procedures, Functions, and Other T-SQL Objects

If you're wondering whether Microsoft is serious about its commitment to CLR integration, you only need to look up the topic of extended stored procedures (XPs) in Books Online. On top of every page is this ominous warning: "This feature [extended stored procedures] will be removed in a future version of SQL Server. . . . Use CLR integration instead." Enough said. Prior to SQL Server 2005, extended procedures provided the main mechanism to tinker around in operating system resources. The question is, how many folks actually used extended procedures by the time SQL Server 2000 rolled around? The xp_SendMail procedure was popular, but because of the need to load a mail client and the difficulties associated with keeping it working, most administrators have pulled its use and a few hairs along with it. Most likely the remaining extended procedures have been quarantined behind sysadmin-only access because of security issues and susceptibly to buffer overruns.

It is a shame that extended stored procedures were difficult to develop and control. There are many little niches of problem solving where T-SQL capabilities leave us at the edge of a cliff and we have to build either external applications or use something like SSIS to accomplish a task that could otherwise be completely handled with logic inside of the database. The good news is that everything you could do in extended procedures, you can accomplish in SQL CLR. Even better, the xp_SendMail procedure has been replaced in SQL 2005 with a more reliable and secure Simple Mail Transfer Protocol (SMTP) based e-mail mechanism. In this chapter, we'll look at replacing existing reliance on extended stored procedures and Component Object Model (COM) automation stored procedure with SQL CLR.

Historical Perspective on Extended Stored Procedures

Extended stored procedures extend the capabilities of SQL Server by exposing functions within a special type of dynamic link library (DLL). These functions mostly involved interactions with the operating system, such as reading the registry, checking if a file exists, or writing to logs. SQL Server ships with many extended procedures using DLLs, loaded either externally in the \BIN directory or internally in the resource database exposed with the dynamic view sys.dm_os_loaded_modules. You could write your own functionality in a DLL, but you'd have to use the Open Data Services (ODS) API and a set of C header files, which usually meant that you would need to write the DLL in C or C++. If you were really adventurous and were willing to translate the ODS header files, you could write them in other languages. As long as the language supports function export — not VB.NET or C#, by the way — SQL Server can host the extended procedure DLL. There is nothing special about SQL Server that forces the DLL to be written in C, C++, or any Microsoft-centric language. The reality though is that most of us fall into the category of mere mortals, and writing DLLs of this type is beyond our ability to justify the amount of time we'd spend on it.

To register an ODS-based DLL to SQL Server, you'd supply the entry point, or function name, and the DLL name. The system procedure sp_addextendedproc would call a DBCC addextendedproc command that registered the exported function in the DLL and created the T-SQL DDL needed to call the procedure, to handle the parameters, and to retrieve return values. An extended stored procedure could return resultsets, output parameters, error messages, or return values. They could also be used to update data within the SQL Server environment as well as the operating system environment. If you're overly concerned with security of SQL CLR routines, do you know how often extended procedures are being used in your databases? Are extended procedures locked down in your current databases? You might not be aware that SQL Server 2000 granted EXECUTE permissions automatically to the public database role. If you are concerned about SQL CLR objects wreaking havoc on your machines, you might want to make sure that execute permissions are revoked from the public database role for all your extended stored procedures. At least SQL Server 2005 out-of-the-box limits the public role rights to execute extended stored procedures that can do the least amount of damage like reading registry settings (xp_regread) but denies the right to write into registry settings (xp_regwrite). You can easily revoke these permissions to the public role using a T-SQL statement like this for each extended stored procedure:

```
REVOKE EXECUTE ON master.dbo.xp_regwrite FROM public
```

Extended procedures can be dangerous because, as DLLs, they are loaded in the address space of the calling process. The calling process is SQL Server itself. That means that if the DLL is not using memory or threads safely (and how do you know?), then SQL Server itself can be adversely affected. As bad as that sounds, the worst scenario is that SQL Server may *keep* running while something in memory has been stomped on and random things would start happening. Troubleshooting scenarios like this would be a nightmare.

Why Replace XPs with SQL CLR?

So, what are the situations that might drive you to want to develop a replacement for an extended stored procedure? Here are a few of the most common reasons:

- ❑ To perform tasks that are central to operating systems and are not exposed via the T-SQL constructs

- ❑ To hide proprietary business logic

- ❑ To use external APIs

- ❑ To supplant existing extended procedures like xp_CMDShell with a more secure, specific purpose

These reasons sound remarkably similar to the reasons that we and others are recommending SQL CLR. If you are going to do anything outside of the SQL Server in the realm inhabited by extended stored procedures, SQL CLR gives you the best of all worlds, because they are now so simple to develop and you are using managed code.

Faster and Easier to Code

To mimic extended procedure behavior in SQL CLR, you don't need to learn the ODS API, C++, or C. There is no need to deal with header files, or with a complicated compilation and loading process. If you are even somewhat proficient in .NET, you'll be able to quickly duplicate an existing extended procedure. Using Visual Studio's SQL Server database project allows you to start with a programming shell that is already integrated with SQL Server. If you've walked through some of the examples in this book, you'll realize that compiling and deploying using Visual Studio is a no-brainer compared to what you have to do with extended stored procedures.

Plays Nice with SQL Server

Working in SQL CLR provides performance advantages of running within the SQL Server engine but the protection of type safety during compilation. SQL Server provides a runtime sandbox to protect its own internal memory buffers and data structures. The CLR requests memory from SQL Server, so the engine can keep track of total memory used, stay within configured limits, and coordinate data access and CPU processing activities. This is completely different from traditional extended stored procedures that can retrieve memory directly from SQL Server's address space, creating a potentially unstable environment. Memory leaks are also contained. If an assembly is not cleaning up behind itself, SQL Server can force garbage collection operations in the hosted CLR when under memory pressure.

Although both extended and SQL CLR procedures can present a challenge to SQL Server in the use of unsafe threading, SQL CLR requests these resources from SQL Server, so all tasks are at least known to the internal scheduler. Although SQL CLR code runs in a multi-threaded mode, SQL Server has the ability, through the shared thread objects, to monitor deadlocking and resource hogging threads and to adjust priorities.

Not Restricted to the Master Database

A secondary advantage to SQL CLR routines is that they can be deployed in any database, as opposed to XPs, which can only be deployed in the master database. Although SQL Server 2005 provides a more granular security model, and you can restrict access within the master database, routines that are specifically built for a database make sense when they are co-located in that database. For vendors, this makes security setup, and backup and recovery, a lot easier. There is no longer the need to coordinate security access within your own database and the master database. For SQL CLR routines that are truly global in nature, they can still be deployed in the master database and can even be exposed as system-stored procedures that can be called from any database. This multi-scoping capability provides the best of both worlds and at least for convenience sake helps explain why SQL CLR will ultimately replace extended stored procedures.

SQL CLR Replacements for XPs

Building replacements for existing extended procedures has many benefits, but reaching outside of SQL Server to do things in the operating system requires some setup considerations in your development environment and some security related tasks to watch out for in your production environments. Visual Studio projects need to be set up to use the EXTERNAL_ACCESS permission set, which can allow the SQL CLR objects a lot of leeway in the operating system. Expect that if you create a SQL CLR routine using this permission set, DBAs and system administrators will want a full accounting of what is going on inside these routines. The database also has to be set up to allow the loading and execution of assemblies with EXTERNAL_ACCESS permission sets. SQL Server 2005 doesn't allow just anyone to load assemblies with this permission set unless that access is specifically granted. The restrictions in SQL Server get even tighter when you move into the realm of the UNSAFE permission set (more about that later). In this section, we'll go over what you'll need to do to replace existing extended stored procedures with custom-built SQL CLR procedures.

Preparing SQL Server for External-Access Assemblies

Since extended procedures are by definition stored procedures that perform tasks outside of SQL Server the permission set on SQL CLR objects built to replace them must be set to EXTERNAL_ACCESS. This is easy enough to do. In the project properties, find the database tab. Set the Permission Level combo box to External. To be able to load an assembly with these access permissions, you are also going to need specific server access permissions that can be set using this T-SQL:

```
USE MASTER
GRANT EXTERNAL ACCESS ASSEMBLY to <USER>
```

The rights to even load an assembly are set at the server level. The user can be a specific user, an Active Directory group, or even a database role. Typically, you'll give your developer groups access to load these assemblies in the development servers and only allow trusted users to perform this task in QC or production environments. This way you know what is loaded on your production servers.

In this 2005 version, SQL Server introduces the use of a database TRUSTWORTHY flag. This flag indicates that the database was deemed trustworthy by an administrator or similar role. This flag does not have to be set to load the assembly but is required before the assembly can actually be used. The idea is that a database could be backed up and an unsavory character could restore the backup and add a rogue assembly to it. Anytime a database is backed up, the TRUSTWORTHY flag in the backup (not the live database) will be set to OFF. So, now if you restore a backup the database is also going to have to be re-prepared to allow the running of the assembly by setting a trustworthy flag in the database to true. Do this by running this T-SQL:

```
ALTER DATABASE clrtestdb SET TRUSTWORTHY ON
```

This seems like a lot of work just to prepare SQL Server to allow an extended SQL CLR procedure to run, but these barriers are essential to creating a secure environment for the SQL Server host. Yet this is not the end to the barriers. You can still apply code access security to limit the reach of EXTERNAL_ACCESS assemblies to specific directories, URLs, or even registry keys. You can see that the requirements of just getting the assemblies to work are high, and this design will make it more difficult to deploy harmful assemblies. Once the environment is prepared and your Visual Studio project properties are set, you are ready to begin replacing some external procedures.

Determining If a File Exists

SQL Server has included an extended stored procedure to check to see if a file exists for a while now, but you won't find xp_fileexist by searching in the Books Online, because it's undocumented. Usually that's all a DBA needs to restrict its use in production, but this functionality is crucial when you have something like a bulk load operation or any task-based job that is dependent upon a file being in a certain place before starting and you aren't in control of when that file is put in that certain place. In this section, we'll build a replacement for xp_fileexist using SQL CLR.

The current xp_fileexist function accepts a full file path and an optional output parameter to store either a one (1) if the file provided exists, or a zero (0) if the file doesn't exist. If you run this procedure, you'll need to explicitly reference the master database and have rights to run the procedure. An example of testing for the existence of a paging file (pagefile.sys) is this:

```
exec master..xp_fileexist 'c:\pagefile.sys'
```

The results are not true/false as you might expect. Instead, you get information about whether the file provided exists, is a directory, or if the parent directory exists:

```
File Exists File is a Directory Parent Directory Exists
----------- ------------------- -----------------------
1           0                   1
```

This is not as useful as a true/false answer, but you can use the secondary output parameter to retrieve this result. First, create a variable to store the results of the output parameter, then call the extended procedure and allow it to set the output parameter for display with an additional SELECT.

```
declare @FileExists int
exec master..xp_fileexist 'c:\pagefile.sys', @FileExists OUTPUT
Select @FileExists
```

The result now returns the value of 1 to indicate that the file is located in the parent path c:\.

```
-----------
1
```

To recreate this functionality in SQL CLR, add a stored procedure class to a new database project. In the System.IO namespace, you can access a static class called File that has a method called Exists that will check the full file path and return a true or false. This sounds just like what you are looking for. How do you find pre-built functionality in the BCL like this? Easy. First, open the Object Browser in Visual Studio using View ➪ Object Browser or use the hot keys Ctrl-Alt-J. Then put a one-word search criterion into the Object Browser Search combo. Searching for "file" brings up many entries. Searching by "exists" brings up fewer, and you'll see the class and method `File.Exists` in the `System.IO` namespace. Add this namespace into your class like this:

```
Using System.IO;
```

The parameters for the stored procedure must be a full file path and an integer output parameter. Since this procedure may be mapped to nullable columns in a database, use `SqlTyped` parameters. The output parameter must be proceeded by the `out` attribute to send back this value as a result.

```
[Microsoft.SqlServer.Server.SqlProcedure]
public static void xmsp_FileExists(SqlString FileName, out SqlInt32 FileExists)
```

The main task of checking to see if the file exists is done by the `File.Exists` method of the `File` class. The method needs a full file path as a string, so convert the `FileName` parameter to a string using the built-in `ToString` method. The output parameter must be set to a value regardless of the logic path in the code, so set this value early to a default of zero (0). If you fail to do this, the compiler will catch it and generate an error. The finished basic procedure looks like this:

```
Using System.IO;
[Microsoft.SqlServer.Server.SqlProcedure]
public static void xmsp_FileExist(SqlString FileName, out SqlInt32 FileExists)
{
    FileExists = 0;

    //Determine if fullfilepath is a file and if exists
    if (File.Exists(FileName.ToString()))
        FileExists = 1;
}
```

When you compile and deploy a SQL CLR procedure, you have the option of changing the database connection to control the database in which the procedure will be ultimately reside. You are not constrained to deploying these procedures to the master database as you would be with an extended procedure, even though you are performing an extended procedure-like task.

Call the procedure using the following T-SQL code:

```
DECLARE @FileExists INT
EXEC xmsp_FileExist 'c:\pagefile.sys', @FileExists OUTPUT
SELECT @FileExists
```

The expected result of 1 indicates that the file exists:

```
-----------
1
```

Notice that you can call the managed code version `xmsp_FileExists` without referring to the master database, because it was deployed into the CLRTESTDB database we've been using throughout this book. The results provide the functionality that we were looking for, but don't quite match the resultset that the `xp_FileExist` produces. The `xp_FileExist` extended procedure also has a provision for returning a usage statement if the `FileName` parameter is not provided. Change the procedure to implement this functionality, so that the SQL CLR version `xmsp_FileExist` matches the replaced `xp_FileExist` procedure.

Since the procedure parameters use `SqlTypes`, it is easy to test for NULL using the built-in methods of the typed variable. If the `FileName` variable is NULL, then we will just stream out a message using the `Pipe` method of the `SqlContext` object. If not, then you want to produce the recordset that contains the information about the file, the directory, and parent directory. This is a little more work, but when finished, it should look something like this:

```
[Microsoft.SqlServer.Server.SqlProcedure]
public static void xmsp_FileExist(SqlString FileName, out SqlInt32 FileExists)
{
    string[] szfile;
    string parentdir = "";
    string FullFilePath = "";
    string sqlSelect = "";
    SqlInt32 isparentdir = 0;
    SqlInt32 isfiledir = 0;
    FileExists = 0;
    string usagemsg = "Usage:  EXECUTE xp_fileexist <filename> " +
                      "[, <file_exists INT> OUTPUT]";

    if (FileName.IsNull)
    {
        SqlContext.Pipe.Send(usagemsg);
    }
    else
    {
        FullFilePath = FileName.ToString();

        //Determine if fullfilepath is a file and if exists
        if (File.Exists(FullFilePath))
            FileExists = 1;

        //Determine if fullfilepath is a directory instead of a file
        if (Directory.Exists(FullFilePath))
            isfiledir = 1;

        //parse the parent directory
        szfile = FullFilePath.Split("\\".ToCharArray());
        for (int i = 0; i < szfile.GetUpperBound(0); i++)
        {
            parentdir = parentdir + szfile[i].ToString() + "\\";
        }
        //Determine if parent directory exists
        if (Directory.Exists(parentdir))
            isparentdir = 1;

        sqlSelect = "Select " + FileExists.ToString() +
          " as [File Exists], " + isfiledir.ToString() +
          " as [File is a Directory], " + isparentdir.ToString() +
          " as [Parent Directory Exists] ";
        using (SqlConnection sqlConn =
                new SqlConnection("Context Connection=True")){
            sqlConn.Open();
            SqlCommand sqlCmd = sqlConn.CreateCommand();
            sqlCmd.CommandText = sqlSelect;
```

```
            SqlContext.Pipe.ExecuteAndSend(sqlCmd);
      }
   }
}
```

Now when you run the same T-SQL code, you get the expected result of 1 for the output parameter, but you can also run it using a NULL value for the output parameter to see the resultset, like this:

```
EXEC xmsp_FileExist 'c:\pagefile.sys', NULL
```

You'll get these results:

```
File Exists File is a Directory Parent Directory Exists
----------- ------------------- -----------------------
1           0                   1
```

This looks just like the results you got from the extended stored procedure. To see the usage message, change the `FileName` parameter to NULL as well. Then the usage statement that rounds out the full functionality is printed in the message output.

```
Usage:  EXECUTE xp_fileexist <filename> [, <file_exists INT> OUTPUT]
```

The one thing we glossed over is that the output parameter must always be provided when you run the SQL CLR version of the `fileexist` procedure. In other words, you couldn't just run the procedure like the original `xp_fileexist` without the output parameter, like this:

```
EXEC xmsp_FileExist 'c:\pagefile.sys'
```

If you did, you'd get this error:

```
Msg 201, Level 16, State 4, Procedure xmsp_FileExists, Line 0
Procedure or Function 'xmsp_FileExists' expects parameter '@FileExists',
which was not supplied.
```

That's not exactly what you want. So, how do you make the output parameter optional? That's a subject of great debate. Normally, this can be accomplished by overloading the function with a prototype that doesn't include the output parameter, and calling the existing function with a dummy parameter. This overloaded stored procedure in your class would look like this:

```
//INTENDED TO BE USED AS AN OVERLOAD TO XMSP_FILEEXIST WITH
//OUTPUT PARAMETER
//NOTE: DOESN'T WORK: OVERLOADING NOT ALLOWED IN SQL CLR...
   [Microsoft.SqlServer.Server.SqlProcedure]
   public static void xmsp_FileExist(SqlString FileName)
   {
        SqlInt32 FileExists=0;
        xmsp_FileExist(FileName, out FileExists);
   }
```

The problem is that this doesn't work. The code compiles because overloading is an allowed syntactical construction of the .NET languages. However, during deployment, the assembly is rejected with the following message:

```
More than one method, property or field was found with name 'xmsp_FileExist' in
class 'StoredProcedures' in assembly 'XPReplacements'. Overloaded methods,
properties or fields are not supported.   XPReplacements
```

When you think about it, it makes perfect sense. T-SQL is the limiting factor. Each method in the class designated with the `SqlProcedure` attribute is converted into a T-SQL stored procedure prototype. You can't create two T-SQL entry point objects with the same name and two different parameter lists using Visual Studio to deploy the assembly. The CLR in SQL Server rightly rejects this construction. One way to reproduce this function is to create a new method in your class with a slightly different name. The following would compile and deploy to allow the use of the function without the second output parameter:

```
[Microsoft.SqlServer.Server.SqlProcedure]
public static void xmsp_FileExist_NoOutputParm(SqlString FileName)
{
    SqlInt32 FileExists=0;
    xmsp_FileExist(FileName, out FileExists);
}
```

Another way to reproduce the function with the optional parameter is to deploy the assembly, but hand-code the T-SQL wrapper with a default value on the `@FileExists` parameter set to 0, like this:

```
ALTER PROCEDURE [dbo].[xmsp_FileExist]
  @FileName [nvarchar](4000),
  @FileExists [int] OUTPUT=0
WITH EXECUTE AS CALLER
AS
EXTERNAL NAME [XPReplacements].[StoredProcedures].[xmsp_FileExist]
GO
```

The point here is to demonstrate how easily you are able to duplicate the existing extended stored procedure `xp_fileexist`. You can extend this example easily and create other procedures that delete files, create directories, or enumerate file folders using the same file class in the `System.IO` namespace. File-system-based activities are just one type of extension to the normal, expected capabilities of T-SQL. We'll expand this a bit by looking at replacing the extended stored procedures that read information from the registry.

Reading from the Registry

This example is a start for replacing the `xp_regread` extended procedure that allows for reading specific keys in the registry. The advantage of using SQL CLR over extended stored procedures is that you can restrict access by machine to the registry keys allowed to be updated, accessed, or removed in the code access security (CAS) policy.

The `xp_regread` extended procedure allows for the reading of registry keys. The parameters are broken up into four parts of a registry entry:

❑ **The root:** The root should be one of the following strings representing a subtree in the registry: `HKEY_CLASSES_ROOT`, `HKEY_CURRENT_USER`, `HKEY_LOCAL_MACHINE`, or `HKEY_USERS`.

You may not access `HKEY_DYN_DATA`, `HKEY_PERFORMANCE_DATA`, *or* `HKEY_CURRENT_CONFIG`
using the extended procedure `xp_regread`.

❏   **The key:** This is a string representing the path to the value pair from the root. The key can end with a backslash but may not start with one.

❏   **The value name:** This is the name part of the value pair. This is expected to be written without backslashes.

❏   **The value (as output parameter):** If this value is supplied, then the value is provided as an input/output parameter. If the parameter is not provided, xp_regread produces a rowset with one column representing the value name and the other for the value data.

The last parameter results in something new that we haven't encountered so far. This parameter needs to be accessible from the calling T-SQL as an output parameter, but you also need the ability to read from this parameter to use as a default if something is provided in the parameter. In SQL CLR, you can accomplish this by annotating the parameter with the ref attribute. This sets up a parameter in C# that is *passed by reference*, meaning that it can be read from within and outside the function.

To build a replacement SQL CLR stored procedure for this extended procedure, add a new stored procedure class to your existing or new database project. You now need to find a class to use to edit the registry. If you search in the Object Browser, you'll find a class called Registry in the Microsoft.Win32 namespace. Add this namespace into your project. Then create a function prototype that looks like this:

```
[Microsoft.SqlServer.Server.SqlProcedure]
public static void xmsp_regread(SqlString rootKey,
    SqlString pathKey, SqlString valueKey, ref SqlString defaultValue)
```

Notice that the last parameter is defined using the ref attribute to allow this parameter to function like a T-SQL IN/OUT parameter.

The Registry class has a method GetValue that retrieves value pairs from the registry. To use it, you need the full path to the key instead of the root and the path. The first task in your SQL CLR procedure will be to validate the rootkey and the pathkey and put them together to make the full key path. Check to make sure backslashes are added into the right spots as well. When you are working with C#, you'll find that the backslash in a string "\" is the start of an escape sequence. To use a backslash for comparison, either prefix the string with an @ sign or use a double backslash ("\\"). An example of this comparison code is:

```
if (rootKey.ToString().StartsWith(@"\"))
    pathKey = rootKey.ToString().Substring(2);
```

Once you build a proper path, using the Registry.GetValue method is simple. The result variable will store the value of the registry key even if it is NULL since it is a SqlString nullable data type.

```
myKey = (string)(rootKey + "\\" + pathKey);
result = Registry.GetValue(myKey, (string)valueKey, defaultValue).ToString();
```

In the xmsp_fileexist SQL CLR extended procedure replacement, you used the command object to issue a select statement through a connection to build a resultset using the SQL engine. In this example, you will create the resultset-like structure within the managed code to avoid the extra overhead of using the SQL engine. The SqlDataRecord object can be used to define such a custom structure for the registry value pairs since we will only be returning one row per call. The code that does this is here:

```
//Create a data record structure to use to send back to simulate rowset
SqlDataRecord valuepair = new SqlDataRecord(
                new SqlMetaData("Value", SqlDbType.VarChar, 1040),
                new SqlMetaData("Data", SqlDbType.VarChar, 1040));
//This sets the first column to the value key text
valuepair.SetSqlString(0, valueKey);
```

The remaining tasks involve determining whether to return a resultset or an output parameter. If the value provided as a default is not NULL, an output parameter will be returned. If the output parameter is NULL, the resultset will be returned. The final code for the xmsp_regread SQL CLR procedure looks like this:

```
[Microsoft.SqlServer.Server.SqlProcedure]
public static void xmsp_regread(SqlString rootKey, SqlString pathKey,
                                SqlString valueKey, ref SqlString defaultValue)
{
    string myKey;
    SqlString result;

    if (defaultValue.IsNull)
        defaultValue = null;

    if (!rootKey.IsNull && !pathKey.IsNull)
    {
        //Fix root key if not proper format
        if(rootKey.ToString().EndsWith(@"\"))
          rootKey = rootKey.ToString().Substring(1, rootKey.ToString().Length - 1);
        if (rootKey.ToString().StartsWith(@"\"))
          pathKey = rootKey.ToString().Substring(2);

        //Make sure pathKey is in proper format
        if (pathKey.ToString().StartsWith(@"\"))
            pathKey = pathKey.ToString().Substring(2);

        myKey = (string)(rootKey + "\\" + pathKey);
        result = Registry.GetValue(myKey,
                (string)valueKey, defaultValue).ToString();

        //Create a data record structure to use to send back to simulate rowset
        SqlDataRecord valuepair = new SqlDataRecord(
                new SqlMetaData("Value", SqlDbType.VarChar, 1040),
                new SqlMetaData("Data", SqlDbType.VarChar, 1040));
        valuepair.SetSqlString(0, valueKey);

        //if no result is found and we have a default use it
        if (result.IsNull && !defaultValue.IsNull)
        {
            result = defaultValue;
        }
        //Decide whether to return a rowset or an output parameter
        if (defaultValue.IsNull)
        {
            defaultValue = result;
            valuepair.SetSqlString(1, (string)result);
```

```
            SqlContext.Pipe.Send(valuepair);
        }
        else
        {
            defaultValue = result;
        }
    }
}
```

To use this procedure, deploy it to the CLRTESTDB database and run the following T-SQL statement:

```
--To retrieve just the key value in an output parameter
Declare @DefaultVal as varchar(1040)
Set @DefaultVal = 'default'
exec xmsp_regread 'HKEY_LOCAL_MACHINE',
    'SOFTWARE\Microsoft\Microsoft Sql Server\90\', 'VerSpecificRootDir',
        @DefaultVal output
select @DefaultVal

--To view the key value pair
exec xmsp_regread 'HKEY_LOCAL_MACHINE',
    'SOFTWARE\Microsoft\Microsoft Sql Server\90\', 'VerSpecificRootDir',
    Null
```

This statement produces these results on our test machine:

```
----------------------------------------
C:\Program Files\Microsoft SQL Server\90\

Value                   Data
-------------------     ----------------------------------------
VerSpecificRootDir      C:\Program Files\Microsoft SQL Server\90\
```

Using the exact same project and class, you could easily add a method to recreate the xp_regwrite extended stored procedure in SQL CLR. Obviously, coding an extended stored procedure that can alter registry settings is more dangerous than reading the same settings. You can restrict the damage that this extended stored procedure could cause by using the CAS model on your server to restrict the registry settings that can be altered. See Chapter 10 for an example of implementing the CAS with SQL CLR.

Replacing xp_CmdShell

The extended procedure xp_cmdshell is probably one of the main Swiss army knives in a SQL developer's toolkit. We've seen some pretty creative uses of this extended proc, from enabling T-SQL to do things like FTP files, zip up import files, and run SSIS packages, to starting and stopping custom middle-tier Windows services. While these capabilities can be useful, the other side to this double-edged knife is that it is extremely dangerous to have it running in a production environment. Because of its versatility, this extended procedure can be easily hijacked and used for evil purposes. One of the advantages of SQL CLR is that you can duplicate the capabilities of the xp_cmdshell procedure in a narrower, more specific way to reduce its misuse, but still be able have the functionality it provides by building your own specific versions of this procedure.

Preparing SQL Server for Unsafe Assemblies

As evidence of the respect xp_cmdshell should demand, SQL Server 2005 ships with it turned off. It is one of the features in the surface area configuration that must specifically be turned on using sp_configure. If you are curious, and try to execute the xp_cmdshell extended stored procedure without turning it on, you'll be greeted with this error message:

```
Msg 15281, Level 16, State 1, Procedure xp_cmdshell, Line 1
SQL Server blocked access to procedure 'sys.xp_cmdshell' of component 'xp_cmdshell'
because this component is turned off as part of the security configuration for this
server. A system administrator can enable the use of 'xp_cmdshell' by using
sp_configure. For more information about enabling 'xp_cmdshell', see "Surface Area
Configuration" in SQL Server Books Online.
```

The question is should you ever turn it on? Obviously, the answer depends upon what you are doing, but we think that you'd be better off leaving xp_cmdshell disabled and only use very specific SQL CLR routines to perform tasks formally performed by this procedure.

Just because you can start processes in SQL CLR, don't think that this will get you around the barriers in the surface area configuration. The Base Class Library exposes a class called Process that is in the namespace System.Diagnostics. You can use this class to turn system processes off and on, using SQL CLR routines. However, just using this namespace escalates the need of your assembly to use the Unsafe permission setting for SQL CLR assemblies. The problem here is that you may have a hard time convincing a DBA to remove one of the security barriers by even loading the unsafe assembly permissions. There are several barriers to allowing an assembly marked as unsafe or even using what SQL Server considers unsafe namespaces.

An assembly that uses namespaces that could potentially do harm, like System.Diagnostics, must be marked with the UNSAFE permission setting. Set this in the project property settings before compiling and deploying the assembly. Even if you follow the rest of these instructions, but fail to set the permissions correctly, the assembly may load, but SQL Server will not allow the procedure to execute. The inconsistency is the SQL Server will allow you to load an assembly using an unsafe namespace if you don't set this permission setting, but doesn't allow you to run it. In other words, SQL Server doesn't interrogate the assembly during load time to determine whether you have rights to load the assembly. However, if the assembly is marked with the unsafe assembly permissions, it cannot be loaded unless the loading user has been granted the right to do so. To remove this security barrier, run the follow T-SQL with your login user context to allow loading and running of assemblies marked with unsafe permission sets:

```
USE MASTER
GRANT UNSAFE ASSEMBLY to <USER>
```

Optimally, the user granted this right should only be the DBA responsible for the SQL Server. However, if you do grant this right to a user, be reassured that after he or she has loaded the unsafe assembly, this right can be immediately revoked and the unsafe assembly can still be executed.

If you haven't deployed an assembly with External_Access or UNSAFE to your database, you'll also need to prepare by setting a trustworthy flag in the database to true. Do this by running this T-SQL:

```
ALTER DATABASE clrtestdb SET TRUSTWORTHY ON
```

Now, you can continue with developing your own flavor of the xp_cmdShell extended procedure. You'll can probably ascertain at this point that mimicking the xp_cmdShell identically is not going to be a good strategy. If you need the functionality of the xp_cmdShell, you'll need to narrow down the functionality and create a SQL CLR stored procedure that the DBA will have some confidence deploying into production servers.

Running a Windows Service or Executable

To build a replacement SQL CLR procedure for xp_cmdShell-like functionality to start and stop Windows processes, start with a new assembly. This means open up a new project. Go ahead and set the permission set on this project to UNSAFE. It's easy to forget to do this and find later that you have permission issues postdeployment. A best practice is to not mix procedures that are not in the same permission sets, because if this assembly needs to be isolated, you don't want to lose other, more secure functionality. You'll need to add a reference to the System.Diagnostics namespace to gain control over an external program. In this namespace is a class called Process that will need to be instantiated. It is not a static class. Using the process class is simple. The start method on the class accepts the full path of a window process or executable to be started. The kill method on the class terminates a process by process ID (PID). We'll get to how you determine that later.

Building a generic SQL CLR procedure that could start and stop any process is possible, but not advisable, since you will not be able to easily monitor what processes are being stopped and started using the SQL CLR procedure. A better and safer design is to code SQL CLR procedures to control specific known processes. Do this by embedding even the name of the process into the procedure. This way, calling the procedure simply calls the one specific process and nothing else. You'll have to decide if it is an acceptable risk to create a SQL CLR stored procedure that is generalized, for example, to call any SSIS package, or if you should create and limit each SQL CLR procedure to one package. A sample that starts a windows service named pam.exe, for example, should look like this:

```
[Microsoft.SqlServer.Server.SqlProcedure]
public static void xmsp_cmdShell_StartPamExe()
```

Notice that it is clear what this SQL CLR procedure is doing. It simply starts the pam.exe Windows service. The stored procedure also allows no input parameters that can be used to start any other executable. Internally, you can specifically name the process that you want to start by hard-coding the path and executable into the Start method of the Process class. The whole thing would look like this:

```
[Microsoft.SqlServer.Server.SqlProcedure]
public static void xmsp_cmdShell_StartPamExe()
{
    //specifically starts and runs pam using default parms
    Process mycmd = Process.Start("c:\\windows\\system32\\pam.exe");
}
```

You'd start the pam executable by running this T-SQL statement:

```
EXEC xmsp_cmdShell_StartPamExe
```

If you want to test this procedure, copy an executable like winword.exe, *rename it as* pam.exe, *and move it to the* windows\system32\ *directory. SQL CLR will not allow the Windows components to activate and will run the executable as a service. Stop the process in the Task Manager if you run this example before creating the* xmsp_cmdShell_StopPamExe *procedure.*

If you have a permission issue running this first unsafe permission set SQL CLR object, make sure that your project permissions are set to UNSAFE. One thing that would improve this procedure is a parameter or a registry setting that could be used to limit the number of pam.exe instances that could be running concurrently. (What a good use for the xmsp_regread and xmsp_regwrite procedures!)

The Process class also has a method that we referred to earlier that allows the retrieval and iteration of all the processes on a machine. We'll use this to develop a procedure to stop or kill a process. In SQL 2005, the extended stored procedure xp_terminate_process was dropped. This procedure could kill a running process if you knew PID for it. This procedure wasn't documented, so you can't say you weren't warned if you were using it. Use what you learned about the Process class to create your own SQL CLR procedure to terminate the pam.exe process. Start by adding a new procedure definition in your current class named xmsp_cmdShell_StopPamExe. In this procedure, you'll cycle through a collection of processes to find the ones named "pam." You can do this a couple of ways, either by requesting an array of all the current processes or by requesting only the processes with a name matching "pam." With an array, it will be easy to grab a reference to the process and then call the Kill method on the process object to terminate the process. The procedure is:

```
[Microsoft.SqlServer.Server.SqlProcedure]
public static void xmsp_cmdShell_StopPamExe()
{
    string processmsg="";
    //Retrieve all processes on the current machine with name "pam"
    Process[] myprocesses = Process.GetProcessesByName("pam");
    for (int i = 0; i <= myprocesses.GetUpperBound(0); i++)
    {
        //Make sure the process is "pam"
        if (myprocesses[i].ProcessName.ToString().StartsWith("pam"))
        {
            //Create a message to stream to results
            processmsg = "Terminated " +
                        myprocesses[i].ProcessName.ToString() +
                        " PID: " + myprocesses[i].Id;

            //Kill the process
            myprocesses[i].Kill();
            SqlContext.Pipe.Send(processmsg);
        }
    }
}
```

Notice that the process method GetProcessesByName allows you to load an array with all processes with the name "pam." The array contains the PID that you need to kill the process. The procedure then creates a message to stream out to the message output using the pipe method of the sqlContext class. This is mainly for your benefit so that you get some interaction to report that the process has been terminated. Deploy this class and then call the procedure using T-SQL:

```
xmsp_cmdShell_StopPamExe
```

This results in a message that enumerates the processes and the associated PIDs terminated as a result:

```
Terminated pam PID: 5040
```

You can see that if you have to go about starting and stopping processes, you can easily perform these activities within SQL CLR without creating the larger exposure of allowing any executable to run.

Executing a Command-Line Program into a Resultset

The other great power of the xp_cmdshell procedure was the ability to run batch files and command-line utilities. You can still perform the same tasks using the Process class. For this example, you can just add a new stored procedure to an existing project with unsafe permissions, or start a new project. Just don't forget to set the project permission settings to unsafe with a new project. You are going to create a procedure to allow you to read in the contents of a directory into a resultset. Logic like this is often used to determine if there are any files in a directory or to enumerate and store the names of files to be loaded for the day. The basic command line to generate such a list is dir *.<file ext>. But because you'll be running a command window, you need to first open up a command-line interface and then send the command to it. To do that, you'll have to preface the command line with "/c", which tells the command window to interpret the input as a command.

```
//Create a process start info object
ProcessStartInfo myprocinfo = new ProcessStartInfo();
myprocinfo.FileName = "cmd";
myprocinfo.WorkingDirectory = dir.ToString();
myprocinfo.Arguments = "/c dir *.txt";
```

You want to be able to intercept the standard output of the command window in order to send it to the results output. To do that, you'll need to use the ProcessStartInfo class. This class contains all the settings for a process that we can preset before sending the class to the process.start method to run. In this class, you can set the standard output to redirect, and you'll be able to capture the stream in a streamreader object. Using a stream object means adding a reference to the System.IO namespaces to the stored procedure class.

The more interesting part of this example involves streaming the results back as a resultset. To do this, you create a DataRecord with one column named output with this statement:

```
SqlDataRecord diroutput = new SqlDataRecord(
    new SqlMetaData("output", SqlDbType.VarChar, 1040));
```

As you loop through the steam, you are basically going to put data into this column and send it to the pipe as a result. The loop is wrapped with calls to start and end the sending of the results to allow for continuous streaming of results instead of waiting for all the results to be built into a SqlDataReader before sending. The completed code for this procedure is here for closer examination:

```
[Microsoft.SqlServer.Server.SqlProcedure]
public static void xmsp_cmdShell_ListFiles(SqlString dir, SqlString ext)
{
    //set defaults
    if (dir.IsNull)
        dir = "c:\\";
    if (ext.IsNull)
        ext = "txt";

    //Create a process start info object
    ProcessStartInfo myprocinfo = new ProcessStartInfo();
```

```
myprocinfo.FileName = "cmd";
myprocinfo.WorkingDirectory = dir.ToString();
myprocinfo.Arguments = "/c dir *." + ext.ToString();
myprocinfo.UseShellExecute = false;
myprocinfo.CreateNoWindow = true;
myprocinfo.WindowStyle = ProcessWindowStyle.Hidden;
myprocinfo.RedirectStandardOutput = true;
Process mycmd = Process.Start(myprocinfo);
StreamReader stdio = mycmd.StandardOutput;
mycmd.WaitForExit(1000);
string results = "";

SqlDataRecord diroutput = new SqlDataRecord(
        new SqlMetaData("output", SqlDbType.VarChar, 1040));
SqlContext.Pipe.SendResultsStart(diroutput);
while ((results = stdio.ReadLine()) != null)
{
    diroutput.SetSqlString(0, results.ToString());
    SqlContext.Pipe.SendResultsRow(diroutput);
}
SqlContext.Pipe.SendResultsEnd();
}
```

The parameters allow this procedure to be used in any directory to retrieve a listing of files with a provided extension. Run the procedure with T-SQL like this:

```
xmsp_cmdShell_ListFiles "c:\windows", "log"
```

You'll see results like these:

```
output
----------------------------------------
 Volume in drive C is Local Disk
 Volume Serial Number is 9999-9999

 Directory of c:\

01/25/2006  10:43 PM                 38 AUTOEXEC.BAT
              1 File(s)             38 bytes
              0 Dir(s)  10,127,691,776 bytes free
```

You can further refine this procedure by parsing the lines coming from the stream to only fill rows with information about the files. The row could also be separated into columns to report the date, size, and name of the file separately. We'll do something similar to this in the next section. The point here is that you can easily reproduce the capabilities of the xp_cmdShell extended stored procedures by using SQL CLR. The advantage to the DBAs is that they can examine the code to see exactly what is happening and what is allowed to happen instead of exposing unexpected functionality in your SQL Server. This narrowing of the scope of the procedure may convince the DBA to allow you to deploy this assembly on a production machine.

Using these similar techniques, you could create SQL CLR extended stored procedures to use FTP to transfer files or to use WinZIP command-line utilities to zip up files in a directory or even read log file contents and use BCP operations. Not to discourage you from attempting to build this type of functionality, but you should attempt to use xp_cmdShell-like techniques only as a last resort. This next section will attempt to encourage you to look at some of the features available in the BCL of the CLR before resorting to these methods.

Extended Stored Procedures for Mere Mortals

If you walked through the previous section and built the example procedures, you literally replaced four or more extended stored procedures. We are talking about fire-breathing, ODS-header-file, built-by-giants-before-us, DLL-based stored procedures that interact with the operating system. From a programming perspective, it wasn't that bad. In fact, it was rather easy. Well, that's the point isn't it? SQL CLR provides a launch pad for some amazing extensions to add to the traditional reach of T-SQL. That's what this section is about. Extended stored procedures are now for the mere mortals, and you are going to build a few of them.

Writing Data to a CSV File

The first extended procedure you'll build is something that you probably need from time to time—the ability to execute a SELECT statement from within SQL Server and have the results dumped into a comma-delimited format in a file. As soon as we start mentioning files, you should be thinking System.IO. Add that namespace to the stored procedures class and make sure that the project is using the EXTERNAL_ACCESS permission set. To approach this problem, think of it as three subtasks: a driver task, a task to take an SQL statement and return a dataset, and a task to turn a dataset into a file. The driver task is the only C# function in your SQL CLR stored procedure class that will have a T-SQL interface, so it is the only one with the SqlProcedure decoration attribute. For parameters, you'll allow a SQL SELECT statement, a full file path, and a flag to designate where the output should allow overwriting if a file already exists in the full file path. Like all our extended procedure examples, use SqlTypes for input parameters so that if the required parameters aren't provided, a usage message will appear in the output to warn that all the information wasn't provided properly. The first section that serves as the driver and interface looks like this:

```
[Microsoft.SqlServer.Server.SqlProcedure]
public static void xmsp_writecsvfile(SqlString sqlSelect,
                    SqlString fullFilePath, SqlBoolean sqlOverwrite)
{
    if (sqlSelect.IsNull || fullFilePath.IsNull)
    {
        SqlContext.Pipe.Send("Usage xmsp_WriteCsvFile <Select Statement>,
                        <fullFilePath>, [Overwrite?]");
    }
    else
    {
        string select = sqlSelect.ToString();
        Boolean overwrite = (Boolean)sqlOverwrite;
        DataSet sqlDs = GetDataSetWithSQL(select);
        overwrite = !(overwrite);
        CreateCSVFile(sqlDs, fullFilePath.ToString(), overwrite);
```

```
                    SqlContext.Pipe.Send("File " + fullFilePath.ToString() +
                                " was created successfully \n" +
                            "(" + sqlDs.Tables[0].Rows.Count.ToString() +
                            " row(s) affected)");
                sqlDs.Dispose();
            }
        }
```

The next section retrieves and returns a dataset object when provided a raw SQL SELECT statement. Anytime you see a SELECT statement being accepted as an input parameter, it warrants a close inspection to eliminate the possibility of SQL injection. This extended procedure would need to be hardened and code added to insure that SQL injection is minimized and should not be exposed to an external connection as written. Notice that this function is not decorated with the SqlProcedure attribute. It is a helper function that will not be implemented as a T-SQL object. You may not have noticed before, but the SqlProcedure attribute is used the function is deployed with a same-named T-SQL stored procedure prototype. The code for this utility function will look like this:

```
        public static DataSet GetDataSetWithSQL(String mySQL)
        {
            SqlDataAdapter sqlDa = new SqlDataAdapter();
            DataSet sqlDs = new DataSet();
            using (SqlConnection sqlConn =
            new SqlConnection("Context Connection=True"))
            {
                SqlCommand sqlCmd = new SqlCommand(mySQL, sqlConn);
                sqlCmd.CommandType = CommandType.Text;
                sqlDa.SelectCommand = sqlCmd;
                sqlDa.Fill(sqlDs, "TABLE");
                sqlConn.Close();
            }
            return sqlDs;
        }
```

The last section of the code contains the work of parsing the rows from the dataset into a file stream using a comma delimiter. By loading the data into a dataset, you have access to metadata for the columns. You can retrieve the column name from the metadata when building the row headers for your export file. If the Overwrite parameter is true, then the file will be recreated: otherwise, the data will be appended to the existing file.

```
        public static void CreateCSVFile(DataSet myDs,
                                    String FullFilePath, Boolean Overwrite)
        {
            int i = 0;
            int fldCnt = 0;

            StreamWriter sw = new StreamWriter(FullFilePath, Overwrite);

            fldCnt = myDs.Tables[0].Columns.Count;
            //Gather and create csv line for columns
            for (int x = 0; x <= fldCnt - 1; x++)
            {
```

```
            sw.Write("[" + myDs.Tables[0].Columns[x].ColumnName + "]");
        if (x < fldCnt - 1)
            sw.Write(",");
    }
    sw.Write(sw.NewLine);

    //Then gather row information into an HTML string
    for (int x = 0; x <= myDs.Tables["TABLE"].Rows.Count - 1; x++)
    {
        while (i < fldCnt)
        {
            if (!Convert.IsDBNull(myDs.Tables["TABLE"].Rows[x][i]))
            {
                sw.Write(Convert.ToString(myDs.Tables["TABLE"].Rows[x][i]));
            }
            if (i < fldCnt - 1)
                sw.Write(",");

            i++;
        }
        i = 0;
        sw.Write(sw.NewLine);
    }
    sw.Close();
}
```

Once the assembly and T-SQL prototype are deployed, you can use this SQL CLR procedure to generate a listing of your assemblies in a database that allows UNSAFE_ACCESS or EXTERNAL_ACCESS permission sets. Verify that you have the directory c:\prosqlclr\ on your machine before running this example.

```
DECLARE @SQL AS VARCHAR(300)
SET @SQL = 'select name as Assembly_Name,
                Permission_set_desc
            from sys.assemblies
            where permission_set_Desc IN
            (''UNSAFE_ACCESS'', ''EXTERNAL_ACCESS'')'
EXEC xmsp_writecsvfile @SQL, 'c:\prosqlclr\assembly_catalogue.csv', true
```

This produces a file named assembly_catalogue in a CSV format, with contents that look like this:

```
[Assembly_Name],[Permission_set_desc]
WriteDateFile,EXTERNAL_ACCESS
XPReplacements_Unsafe,UNSAFE_ACCESS
XPReplacements,EXTERNAL_ACCESS
```

Even though you are able to create a file on the c:\ drive of the current SQL Server machine, this capability can be reigned in using the CAS model. If you want to see an example of how to restrict the writing of files to a specific directory on a machine, turn to Chapter 10 of this book. The point of this example is to show how easy it is to work with file IO using SQL CLR instead of extended stored procedures. You could use the same stream-based IO to write custom log files or to even read files from the operating system around SQL Server in much less time, with a safer piece of managed code.

Retrieving HttpWebRequest Content

As a further demonstration of the capabilities that you could expose in an extended stored procedure, consider retrieving content from the web in a resultset. These capabilities could help mine data directly from the Internet for things like stock quotes or book listings. Many sites participate in providing stream-based information, uncluttered to make a developer's life easier, although you could retrieve any stream and scrub the text. Yahoo! has a stock retrieval service that is easy to use and provides a lot of information about the day's activity for a series of provided stock symbols. The Yahoo! URL accepts a series of stock symbols separated by a + symbol. The URL requires a specific format string to define the columns that can be retrieved from the service. In the following URL the symbols "snohg" translate by character as "symbol," "name," "open," "high," and "low."

```
http://finance.yahoo.uicom/d/quotes.csv?s=" + symbol + "&f=snohg"
```

The resulting stream from this `HttpWebRequest` in a browser using the symbols "MSFT+IBM+DELL" looks like this:

```
"MSFT","MICROSOFT CP",21.58,21.94,21.55
"IBM","INTL BUSINESS MAC",76.93,77.85,76.93
"DELL","DELL INC",25.20,25.33,24.71
```

Once you have captured a stream like this, it is just as easy to turn this into a resultset as it was to turn the directory file listing into a recordset, as you did earlier. To build this SQL CLR stored procedure, add the `System.Net`, `System.IO` and `System.Text` namespaces to a new stored procedure class named `xmsp_GetYahooQuote`. You set up the connection to the HyperText Transfer Protocol (HTTP) URL using the `HttpWebRequest` class like this:

```
HttpWebRequest webreq = (HttpWebRequest)WebRequest.Create(serverURL);
```

You can then capture the resulting stream by making a web request and then diverting the web response into a `StreamReader` class. The completed procedure should look like this:

```
[Microsoft.SqlServer.Server.SqlProcedure]
public static void xmsp_GetYahooQuote(string symbol)
{
    string serverURL =
      @"http://finance.yahoo.com/d/quotes.csv?s=" + symbol + "&f=snohg";
    string results = "";
    string[] szresults;
    string[] separator ={ "," };
    HttpWebRequest webreq = (HttpWebRequest)WebRequest.Create(serverURL);
    webreq.MaximumAutomaticRedirections = 60;

    //Retrieve  HttpWebResponse object from the Search server URL
    HttpWebResponse webresp = (HttpWebResponse)webreq.GetResponse();
    StreamReader strm =
        new StreamReader(webresp.GetResponseStream(), Encoding.ASCII);

    SqlDataRecord stockoutput = new SqlDataRecord(
        new SqlMetaData("symbol", SqlDbType.VarChar, 15),
        new SqlMetaData("stockname", SqlDbType.VarChar, 25),
        new SqlMetaData("open", SqlDbType.Money),
```

```
                new SqlMetaData("high", SqlDbType.Money),
                new SqlMetaData("low", SqlDbType.Money));

        //Start sending the stream
        SqlContext.Pipe.SendResultsStart(stockoutput);
        while ((results = strm.ReadLine()) != null)
        {
            //Parse each line into the columns
            szresults = results.Split
                    (separator, StringSplitOptions.RemoveEmptyEntries);
            for (int i = 0; i <= szresults.GetUpperBound(0); i++)
            {
                if (i <= 1)
                {
                    stockoutput.SetSqlString(i,
                            (SqlString)szresults[i].Replace("\"", string.Empty));
                }
                else
                {
                    stockoutput.SetSqlMoney(i,
                            (SqlMoney)Convert.ToDecimal(szresults[i]));
                }
            }
            SqlContext.Pipe.SendResultsRow(stockoutput);
        }
        SqlContext.Pipe.SendResultsEnd();

        strm.Close();
    }
```

As you loop through the stream results, you have to break each line into columns and clean the content for the quotes that are in the data. The `SqlRecord` structure is used to create the metadata for the columns that you will be filling row by row and streaming into the `SqlContext.Pipe` object. Compile this assembly and deploy it. To simulate storing the results of this HTTP stream, create a temp table to store the results and insert the results of the proc using T-SQL similar to this:

```
CREATE table #myStocks(symbol varchar(15), stockname varchar(25), [open] money,
[high] money, [low] money)
go
INSERT INTO #myStocks
EXEC xmsp_GetYahooQuote 'MSFT+IBM+DELL'
go
SELECT * FROM #MyStocks
```

You'll retrieve data in a resultset that looks like this:

```
symbol    stockname          open      high      low
--------  ----------------   --------  --------  ---------
MSFT      MICROSOFT CP       21.58     21.94     21.55
IBM       INTL BUSINESS MAC  76.93     77.85     76.93
DELL      DELL INC           25.20     25.33     24.71
```

In some ways this is really interesting, and in some ways this is really bizarre. Think about it for a minute. You are issuing a T-SQL command and in turn are accessing the Internet, calling a web page, retrieving the results, and storing the content into a temporary table. We sometimes wonder how this will get put to use, but it's pretty amazing stuff for such a little amount of work.

Calling Unmanaged Code API Functions

Our last mere-mortal extended stored procedure example involves calling a function in a dynamic DLL written in unmanaged code. The Windows APIs are examples of these DLLs. The managed-to-unmanaged-code interaction is made possible by a service in the CLR called Platform Invoke. The Platform Invoke service, or PInvoke, as it is commonly called, allows the CLR to locate the DLL, load it into memory, locate the function address, and begin marshaling data using COM interop as needed. For this reason, any SQL CLR routine that uses PInvoke will need the System.Runtime.InteropServices namespace. This namespaces will require that your SQL CLR assembly be marked with the UNSAFE permission set. For this reason, keep like stored procedures using PInvoke together and don't mix them with other procedures that use the SAFE permission set.

As a developer, you won't really be aware of PInvoke; it just happens behind the scenes. To use a dynamic DLL or API, you are going to need to follow some housekeeping rules. Follow along and build a SQL CLR stored procedure using the kernel32.dll to read ini file settings:

1. First, you need to know at least the name of the DLL. Add a DLLImportAttribute to the StoredProcedures class: [DllImport("kernel32")].

2. The function to read ini file settings is GetPrivateProfileString. In an API viewer, you can find the function prototype by reading in the win32api.txt file. The function prototype looks like this:

   ```
   Public Declare Function GetPrivateProfileString Lib "kernel32" Alias
   "GetPrivateProfileStringA" (ByVal lpApplicationName As String, ByVal lpKeyName As
   Any, ByVal lpDefault As String, ByVal lpReturnedString As String, ByVal nSize As
   Long, ByVal lpFileName As String) As Long
   ```

3. To plug this definition into your SQL CLR project, you need to rearrange some things .NET-style. You'll need to do this for any conversion of an API function. Replace the keywords Declare Function with the keywords static extern. Remember from Chapter 2 that SQL CLR needs static entry points. Then convert the Long to an Int32 and move the return value to match a C#-style function.

4. Remove the string Lib "kernel32" Alias "GetPrivateProfileStringA. This is handled for you in the DllImportAttribute.

5. Convert the parameters from unmanaged data types into managed data types. For this declaration, some conversions are obvious. However, note that parameter strings passed by reference must be represented with the StringBuilder class because of a .NET requirement that the string must be mutable. See the Books Online topic "Platform Invoke Data Types" for all conversions.

The result is a function prototype that you can use in your SQL CLR assembly. With some of the parameters renamed, it should look something like this:

```
[DllImport("kernel32")]
private static extern Int32 GetPrivateProfileString(String section,
         String key, String def, StringBuilder retVal, Int32 size,
         String filePath);
```

Now with a working prototype, you can build a SQL CLR stored procedure with the same parameters. Since this procedure is not likely to be executed in T-SQL against a set of mapped-to-data columns, it is safe to use normal .NET string data types. In this example only the last parameter could use a nullable `SqlString` parameter, since it is an optional placeholder for a default value. If a default was provided it will be used; otherwise, we can handle the NULL situation. The rest of the code simply maps the parameters, calls the external function using PInvoke, and supplies the result through the `ByReference` parameter. Along with the default namespaces, the completed code looks like this:

```
using System;
using System.Data;
using System.Data.SqlClient;
using System.Data.SqlTypes;
using Microsoft.SqlServer.Server;
using System.Text;
using System.IO;
using System.Runtime.InteropServices;

public partial class StoredProcedures
{
    //IMPORT DLL PROTOTYPE FOR PINVOKE
    [DllImport("kernel32")]
    private static extern Int32 GetPrivateProfileString(String section,
            String key, String def, StringBuilder retVal, Int32 size,
            String filePath);

    //SQLCLR DEFINITION -- NOTE IN/OUT PARM DefaultValue
    [Microsoft.SqlServer.Server.SqlProcedure]
    public static void xmsp_readini(String FullINIFileName, String Section,
        String Key, ref SqlString DefaultValue)
    {
        string mdefault = "";
        if (!DefaultValue.IsNull)
            mdefault = DefaultValue.ToString();

        StringBuilder retValue = new StringBuilder(1000);
        GetPrivateProfileString(Section, Key, "", retValue, 1000, FullINIFileName);

        if (retValue.Length != 0)
            mdefault = retValue.ToString();

        //SET OUTPUT PARAMETER
        DefaultValue = (SqlString)mdefault;
    }

};
```

If you use an INI file named TEST.INI in the directory c:\proSQL CLR\ that looks like this:

```
[heading]
mykey=1
```

calling T-SQL code to execute the SQL CLR stored procedure and retrieve the value of the `mykey` setting in the `ini` file would look like this:

```
DECLARE @INIVALUE AS VARCHAR(1040)
SET @INIVALUE = 'mydefault'
exec xmsp_readini 'C:\prosqlclr\test.ini', 'heading', 'mykey', @INIVALUE OUTPUT
SELECT @INIVALUE as myKeyValue
```

The results, of course, are:

```
myKeyValue
----------
1
```

These are just some short examples to demonstrate the power and range of programming tasks that CLR integration in SQL Server can perform. As you can see, it is not really difficult to get some powerful functionality up and running very quickly. It is easy to predict how the SQL CLR is going to replace extended stored procedures. The harder part is going to be convincing DBAs and system administrators to allow the deployment of assemblies that are specifically marked as UNSAFE. How much work ends up getting done using SQL CLR outside of the SQL Server boundries remain to be seen, but the possibilities have now been exposed.

Replacing OLE Automation

For anyone who's ever been brave enough to tackle wrapping OLE, COM-based function calls in SQL Server, you'll be glad to know that this task has been made much easier. Although arguably it would be preferable to port old ActiveX, COM-based DLLs into .NET, if you have a significant investment and a shortage of time, you can use .NET and COM interop to access these business rules and expose them as SQL CLR objects quickly. Previously, using the OLE automation family of procedures like sp_OACreate, and sp_OAMethod, it was an alphabet soup of procedures to instantiate and then call methods on the DLL, which made the development process intimidating. The issues related to reference counting and proper disposal of objects often left the SQL Server with memory leaks and instability. In .NET, you can also use the PInvoke services to access your legacy COM-based business rules.

For an example, we'll take a business rule for payments that takes billed and paid amounts and provides commentary on whether the transaction was paid-as-billed, not paid, added, or paid in an odd amount, better known as a discrepancy. To start, you'll wrap a simple `ActiveX.dll` project in Visual Basic 6.0 into a SQL CLR routine. The project is named `VendorComLogic`, and it contains one class module named `Payment` that looks like this:

```
'VB CODE TO BE COMPILED INTO VENDORCOMLOGIC.DLL
Option Explicit
Option Compare Text

Private mvarBaseBilledAmt As Currency
Private mvarPaidAmt As Currency
Private mvarPayrollFactor As Double

Public Property Let BaseBilledAmt(cData As Currency)
    mvarBaseBilledAmt = cData
End Property
```

```
Public Property Let PaidAmt(cData As Currency)
    mvarPaidAmt = cData
End Property

'ACCEPTS FACTOR OF BASE BILL AMOUNT
Public Property Let PayrollFactor(dblData As Double)
    mvarPayrollFactor = dblData
End Property

'FUNCTION TO GENERATE A COMMENTARY ON PAYMENT AS DISCREPANCY
Public Function GetDiscrepancyType() As String
    Dim TotalBilled As Currency
    TotalBilled = (mvarBaseBilledAmt * mvarPayrollFactor)

    If TotalBilled = mvarPaidAmt And TotalBilled <> 0 Then
        GetDiscrepancyType = "PAID AS BILLED"
    ElseIf TotalBilled <> mvarPaidAmt And TotalBilled = 0 Then
        GetDiscrepancyType = "ADDED ITEM"
    ElseIf TotalBilled <> mvarPaidAmt And TotalBilled <> 0 And _
                mvarPaidAmt <> 0 Then
        GetDiscrepancyType = "PAID DISCREPANCY"
    ElseIf mvarPaidAmt <> mvarPaidAmt And TotalBilled <> 0 And _
                mvarPaidAmt = 0 Then
        GetDiscrepancyType = "NO PAY"
    End If
End Function
```

We don't want to make this too complicated, but we do want to demonstrate how to interact with methods and public properties on COM objects that are typical of the type of COM libraries that you can encounter. To create a version to use in this example, compile this project into an ActiveX DLL. The problem now is how to call this logic from a SQL CLR routine. The first thing is to get this into a .NET assembly, because you can't load and expose a COM object for use in SQL Server.

There are several methods for wrapping COM DLLs into .NET assemblies. In this example, we'll use the command-line tool TLBIMP.EXE, which comes in the .NET Software Development Kit (SDK). It is as simple as opening up the Visual Studio command line and firing off the command with the path of the COM DLL and the resulting assembly file path.

An example of how to use TLBIMP.EXE to convert VendorComLogic.DLL into VendorNetLogic.DLL is shown in Figure 6-1.

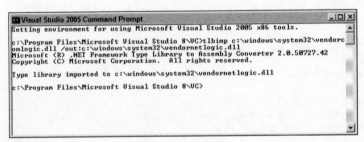

Figure 6-1

Now that you have a .NET assembly, you need to make it available to SQL CLR. You do this by loading the assembly into SQL Server by manually executing the CREATE ASSEMBLY TSQL DDL.

```
CREATE ASSEMBLY vendornetlogic
FROM 'c:\windows\system32\vendornetlogic.dll'
WITH PERMISSION_SET = UNSAFE
```

By the way, since you have to use the interop namespace, this assembly will be considered unsafe. So, make sure you mark the assembly with the UNSAFE permission set and that you've prepared the server and database for unsafe assemblies. Once an assembly is in SQL Server, you'll be able to select a reference to it from within any .NET SQL CLR project. Open up a project explorer, and on the reference node right-click to add a reference. You should see the new vendornetlogic assembly as in Figure 6-2.

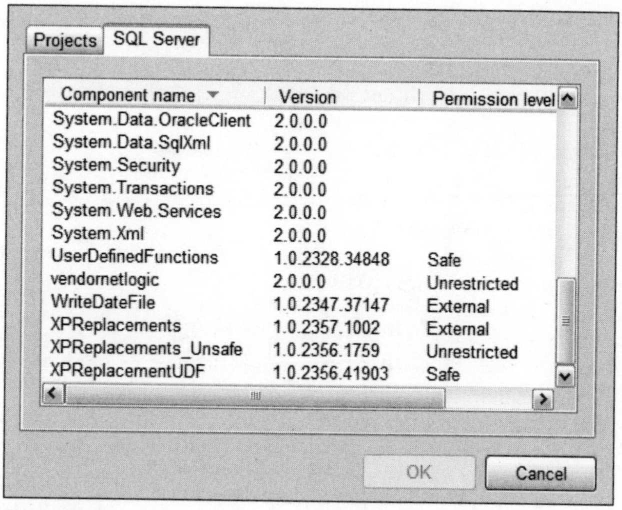

Figure 6-2

Add this vendornetlogic reference to your SQL CLR project. Then add the vendornetlogic namespace to a User-Defined Function class. The equivalent of calling SP_OACREATE is instantiating the payment class from the assembly. It is done like this:

```
//instantiate OA Payment Class (SP_OACREATE)
PaymentClass mypayment = new PaymentClass();
```

The properties are exposed as methods with the SET keywords attached to the property name. For example, the property PaidAmt is exposed as Set_PaidAmt. In VB6, parameters to functions, subroutines, or properties were passed by reference unless specifically prefaced with ByVal. This is why all the properties import to .NET passed by reference. Calling the function in the COM component is straightforward and replaces the old method of calling SP_OAMethod. All you really have to do to complete the SQL CLR user-defined function (UDF) is handle situations where you might get NULL inputs. You do this by coding SqlDataTypes into the function parameters and mapping them to .NET data types internally to map to the COM data types. The finished SQL CLR UDF is:

```
using System;
using System.Data;
```

```csharp
using System.Data.SqlClient;
using System.Data.SqlTypes;
using Microsoft.SqlServer.Server;
using vendornetlogic;

public partial class UserDefinedFunctions
{
    [Microsoft.SqlServer.Server.SqlFunction]
    public static string xmfn_SPOA_Sample(SqlDecimal baseBilledAmt,
                    SqlDecimal paidAmt, SqlDouble payFactor)
    {
        //THESE INTERNAL REPRESENTATIONS OF FUNCTION PARMS
        //ALLOW THE FUNCTION TO DEAL WITH NULL COLUMN VALUES
        decimal mbasebilledamt, mpaidamt;
        double mpayfactor;

        if (baseBilledAmt.IsNull)
            mbasebilledamt = (decimal)0;
        else
            mbasebilledamt = (decimal)baseBilledAmt;

        if (paidAmt.IsNull)
            mpaidamt = (decimal)0;
        else
            mpaidamt = (decimal)paidAmt;

        if (payFactor.IsNull || payFactor < 0)
            mpayfactor = (double)1;
        else
            mpayfactor = (double)payFactor;

        //instantiate OA Payment Class (SP_OACREATE)
        PaymentClass mypayment = new PaymentClass();
        mypayment.set_PaidAmt(ref mpaidamt);
        mypayment.set_PayrollFactor(ref mpayfactor);
        mypayment.set_BaseBilledAmt(ref mbasebilledamt);
        return mypayment.GetDiscrepancyType().ToString();
    }
};
```

To see the UDF in action, compile and deploy the code to the test database for this book, CLRTESTDB. Then run the following T-SQL to build a test table for the function:

```sql
CREATE TABLE tblAmt(myPaid smallmoney, myBilled smallmoney)
GO
INSERT INTO tblAmt
SELECT '3.00', '12.00'
INSERT INTO tblAmt
SELECT '16.16', '32.32'
INSERT INTO tblAmt
SELECT '54.54', '72.72'
INSERT INTO tblAmt
SELECT '33.33', '66.66'
```

```
INSERT INTO tblAmt
SELECT '100.00' , NULL
INSERT INTO tblAmt
SELECT '55.55', '75.33'
INSERT INTO tblAmt
SELECT '140.24', '100.00'
INSERT INTO tblAmt
SELECT '25.00', '99.99'
```

When you're building SQL CLR UDFs, you need to pay attention to data that could be NULL. If you do not, you'll get a nice transaction abort in the middle of running the function across the table that looks like this:

```
Msg 6569, Level 16, State 1, Line 1
'xmfn_SPOA_Sample' failed because parameter 1 is not allowed to be null and is not
an output parameter.
```

To test the UDF, run this T-SQL:

```
select myPaid, MyBilled,
       discrepancytype=dbo.xmfn_SPOA_Sample(mybilled, myPaid, .25)
from tblamt
```

You should get these results:

myPaid	MyBilled	discrepancytype
3.00	12.00	PAID AS BILLED
16.16	32.32	PAID DISCREPANCY
54.54	72.72	PAID DISCREPANCY
33.33	66.66	PAID DISCREPANCY
100.00	NULL	ADDED ITEM
55.55	75.33	PAID DISCREPANCY
140.24	100.00	PAID DISCREPANCY
25.00	99.99	PAID AS BILLED

Not only did you replace the OLE extended stored procedures, but you were also able to integrate your business logic into a UDF. We think you'll agree that if you have to automate your COM ActiveX DLLs, that this method is a lot easier, and more controlled than using the old OLE extended procedures.

Creating System SPs and UDFs

System stored procedures are useful when you want to create some functionality with SQL CLR that is intended to be global in nature. System stored procedures are not limited to SQL CLR procedures; they've always been available for T-SQL procedures. System stored procedures reside in the master database, but they can be called in any database, and they run as in the context of the current database. This can be a timesaver for utility-type procedures. As you may recall, SQL CLR objects are deployed via assemblies to local databases. To be able to call a procedure in all databases, you'd have to deploy that assembly to each database that needed to use it.

The magic to creating a system stored procedure is to name the T-SQL or SQL CLR procedure with a SP_prefix. This is a special prefix to the SQL Server engine. When this stored procedure prefix is used in a T-SQL batch, SQL Server automatically looks in the master database first for the prototype. If the procedure is found in the master database, it is loaded and run using the current database context.

Summary

In the past, functionality lay untapped within SQL Server, available only to extended stored procedures because of the difficulties of programming in a C++ environment and of security concerns. CLR integration into SQL Server changes all of that. In this chapter, we looked at how SQL CLR objects will become the next extended stored procedures by creating replacements for some of them. We examined replacements for file IO, reading the registry, even tackled creating safer objects to implement the functionality of the xp_CmdShell procedure. In the process, you discovered that mere mortals could perform things in SQL CLR that only the giants before us would dare tackle. We proved this by jumping into some assemblies that demonstrate more of the breadth and capabilities of the CLR in SQL Server. We even examined how SQL CLR can replace the whole family of OLE extended stored procedures by implementing a UDF using business logic embedded in an COM-based ActiveX DLL. Replacing the extended procedures is where we began, but after this chapter, you should see that extending SQL Server will not stop at these small borders. Next we'll dive into the Base Class Library and push SQL CLR routines into consuming XML, web services, and dealing with more detailed and complex uses of these ready-made code bases.

7

The .NET Framework's Base Class Library

Chapter 6 was all about using the SQL CLR technology in applications. In this chapter, we'll show you how to leverage the .NET Framework's Base Class Library (BCL), where the intended consumer is SQL Server itself. In addition, this chapter will follow the popular Problem/Design/Solution paradigm. This paradigm can be an effective learning tool because it shows how to bridge business requirements to a particular technology. The BCL is at the very heart of Microsoft's .NET Framework, providing developers with reusable routines for performing common tasks on the Windows platform. Like any consumer of the .NET Framework, SQL CLR routines can instantiate these base classes and use them to provide powerful capabilities that are hosted within SQL Server. We will be using the AdventureWorks sample database for the examples in this chapter.

Accessing External Data Sources

One of the first benefits you can reap from the SQL CLR technology is the ability to access external data sources that were previously both difficult and unstable to access. Practically any data source that can be accessed by using a class in the BCL is a candidate. A few of the more popular data sources are traditional flat files, XML documents, and web services. In this section, we will show working examples of accessing each of these popular data sources.

Performing File IO

.NET has supported programmatic access to the file system via the `System.IO` namespace since its inception. A developer can use the classes found in `System.IO` to manipulate both files and directories. One of the most useful classes found in the `System.IO` namespace is the `FileSystemWatcher` class, which provides the developer with raised events when a file or directory change has occurred in the file system.

Problem

Adventure Works wants a routine that will copy a new employee's data to an external file. This file will be used by the company's interns to fill out the paperwork required to obtain the new employee's parking badge without giving the interns database access. In addition, if the employee's last name changes, a new parking badge must be issued. Finally, when the employee is terminated or resigns, the parking badge file must be removed and the badge itself will expire, since the interns only renew those badges for the flat files that are present.

Design

To solve these problems, you'll need to create a total of three managed triggers. The first is the managed DML trigger that will fire after INSERT statements occurring on the HumanResources.Employee table. This DML trigger will create a new text file populated with the new employee's information. A second trigger will be created for detecting UPDATE statements occurring on the HumanResources.Employee table. This DML trigger will monitor for an UPDATE that has occurred on the CurrentFlag column. If an update to the CurrentFlag column does occur, and it has been set to false, delete the employee's corresponding file.

A third trigger will monitor the Person.Contact table for UPDATE. If the trigger determines that an employee's last name has been changed, then it will first remove the original file and replace it using the employee's new last name.

Solution

Since we have two triggers that need to run off of the HumanResources.Employee, table, we have physically combined their logic into one DML trigger. The following code implements our design's logic for the HumanResources.Employee table triggers. The goal for this trigger is to create and delete an employee's file.

Both UDTs_ins_upd_HumanResourcesEmployees *and* udt_upd_PersonContact *require the EXTERNAL ACCESS permission set.*

```
public partial class Triggers
{
    //[Microsoft.SqlServer.Server.SqlTrigger
    //(Name="udt_ins_upd_HumanResourcesEmployees",
    //Target="HumanResources.Employee", Event="FOR INSERT")]
    public static void udt_ins_upd_HumanResourcesEmployees()
    {
        using (SqlConnection oInProcessConn = new SqlConnection("context connection
                = true"))
        {
            //get trig context
            SqlTriggerContext oTrigContext = SqlContext.TriggerContext;

            try
            {
                //which action did the trigger fire after?
                if (oTrigContext.TriggerAction == TriggerAction.Insert)
                {
                    //open db connection
                    oInProcessConn.Open();
```

```
//create command & reader objects
SqlCommand oCmd = oInProcessConn.CreateCommand();
SqlDataReader oRead;

//get the new employee record from the pseudo table
oCmd.CommandText = "SELECT I.NationalIDNumber, C.LastName" +
',' + "C.FirstName AS [Name], I.Title FROM " +
"inserted I INNER JOIN Person.Contact C ON (I.ContactID =
    C.ContactID)";

//populate the reader
oRead = oCmd.ExecuteReader(CommandBehavior.CloseConnection);

while (oRead.Read())
{
    //create text file for employee's badge
    StreamWriter oSW = File.CreateText("C:\\AW_Employee_Badges\\" +
        oRead["Name"].ToString() + ".txt");

    //create file' content
    oSW.WriteLine(oRead["Name"].ToString());
    oSW.WriteLine(oRead["NationalIDNumber"].ToString());
    oSW.WriteLine(oRead["Title"].ToString());

    //close file
    oSW.Close();
}

//close reader
oRead.Close();
}
else if (oTrigContext.TriggerAction == TriggerAction.Update &&
    oTrigContext.IsUpdatedColumn(13) == true)
{
    //Employee's Current Flag Has Been Updated

    //open db connection
    oInProcessConn.Open();

    //create command & reader objects
    SqlCommand oCmd = oInProcessConn.CreateCommand();
    SqlDataReader oRead;

    //get the employee's new current flag value with his/her
    //original Name
    oCmd.CommandText = "SELECT I.CurrentFlag, C.LastName" + ',' +
    "C.FirstName As [OrigName] FROM inserted I INNER JOIN deleted D " +
    "ON (I.EmployeeID = D.EmployeeID) INNER JOIN Person.Contact C ON " +
    "(D.ContactID = C.ContactID)";

    //populate the reader
    oRead = oCmd.ExecuteReader(CommandBehavior.CloseConnection);

    while (oRead.Read())
    {
```

```
                            //debug
                            SqlContext.Pipe.Send(oRead[0].ToString());

                            //is the employee's Current flag set to off?
                            if (oRead[0].ToString() == "False")
                            {
                                //remove text file for employee's badge renewal
                                File.Delete("C:\\AW_Employee_Badges\\" +
                                    oRead["OrigName"].ToString() + ".txt");
                            }
                        }

                        //close reader
                        oRead.Close();
                    }
                }
                catch (Exception ex)
                {
                    //log failure to local machine's event log
                    EventLog oLog = new EventLog("Application");
                    oLog.Source = "udt_ins_upd_HumanResourcesEmployees";
                    oLog.WriteEntry("udt_ins_upd_HumanResourcesEmployees failed to execute
                        on " + System.DateTime.Now.ToString() + " The error message was:" +
                        ex.Message.ToString(), EventLogEntryType.Error);

                    //return error message to client
                    SqlContext.Pipe.Send(ex.Message.ToString());
                }
                finally
                {
                    //ensure database connection is closed
                    oInProcessConn.Close();
                }
            }
        }
    }
};
```

This next trigger implements our design logic for the Person.Contact table. Again, the goal here is to detect when a person's last name has changed and update the corresponding file.

```
public partial class Triggers
{
    //[Microsoft.SqlServer.Server.SqlTrigger (Name="udt_upd_PersonContact",
Target="Person.Contact", Event="FOR UPDATE")]
    public static void udt_upd_PersonContact()
    {
        using (SqlConnection oInProcessConn = new SqlConnection("context connection
            = true"))
        {
            try
            {
                //open db connection
                oInProcessConn.Open();

                //get trig context
```

```csharp
SqlTriggerContext oTrigContext = SqlContext.TriggerContext;

//did a contact's last name get updated?
if (oTrigContext.IsUpdatedColumn(5) == true)
{
    //create command & reader objects
    SqlCommand oCmd = oInProcessConn.CreateCommand();
    SqlDataReader oRead;

    //get the updated employee record from the pseudo table
    oCmd.CommandText = "SELECT E.NationalIDNumber, D.LastName " +
        ',' + "D.FirstName As [OldName], I.LastName " +
        ',' + "I.FirstName As [NewName], E.Title FROM " +
        "inserted I INNER JOIN deleted D ON (I.ContactID =
            D.ContactID) " +
        "INNER JOIN HumanResources.Employee E ON (I.ContactID =
            E.ContactID)";

    //populate the reader
    oRead = oCmd.ExecuteReader(CommandBehavior.CloseConnection);

    while (oRead.Read())
    {
        //remove pre-xisitng file first
        File.Delete("C:\\AW_Employee_Badges\\" +
            oRead["OldName"].ToString() + ".txt");

        //create new version of the file
        StreamWriter oSW =
            File.CreateText("C:\\AW_Employee_Badges\\" +
                oRead["NewName"].ToString() + ".txt");

        //recreate file's content
        oSW.WriteLine(oRead["NewName"].ToString());
        oSW.WriteLine(oRead["NationalIDNumber"].ToString());
        oSW.WriteLine(oRead["Title"].ToString());

        //close file
        oSW.Close();
    }

    //close reader
    oRead.Close();
}
}
catch (Exception ex)
{
    //log failure to local machine's event log
    EventLog oLog = new EventLog("Application");
    oLog.Source = "udt_upd_PersonContact";
    oLog.WriteEntry("udt_upd_PersonContact failed to execute on " +
        System.DateTime.Now.ToString() + " The error message was:" +
        ex.Message.ToString(), EventLogEntryType.Error);

    //return error message to client
    SqlContext.Pipe.Send(ex.Message.ToString());
```

```
        }
        finally
        {
            //ensure database connection is closed
            oInProcessConn.Close();
        }
    }
}
};
```

You can copy and paste these routines (excluding changing your connection strings) and deploy them to the AdventureWorks database. You may have noticed that we left the `SqlTrigger` attribute(s) commented out in these two DML triggers. We did this on purpose because it relates to a bug that currently exists (2047/sp1 is the latest build at the time of this writing), when you wish to autodeploya managed DML trigger that targets a schema other than dbo. No matter what we tried, our triggers above just would not find the target table. The common workaround to this bug is to use pre/postdeployment `.sql` scripts in your database projects (see Chapter 10 for more information on the pre/post-`.sql` scripts).

In Figure 7-1, we have created a new employee and verified that the corresponding file has been created.

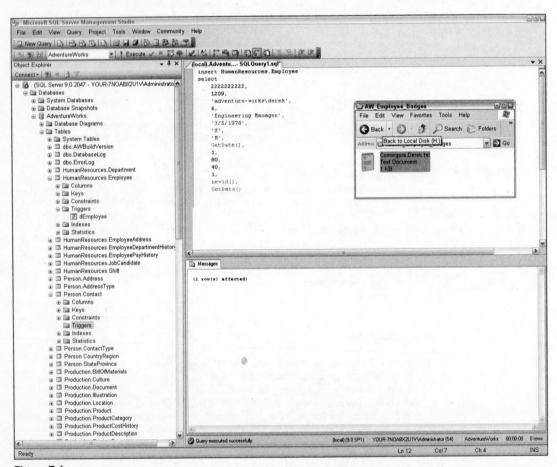

Figure 7-1

Conclusion

Certainly, the solution here does not cover all scenarios that you would be required to address in the real implementation of this solution. For one thing, if an employee can have his or her current flag set back to 1, you would need to recreate their file. There is also the case of whether an employee record can be created with a current flag value of 1. But our goal here is not to cover every related scenario; rather it is to show how powerful managed triggers can be in linking your SQL Server logic with the underlying file system. And we accomplished all of this through the CLR as opposed to native code, so you can feel comfortable knowing that your code is not going to harm the hosting SQL Server with its EXTERNAL ACCESS permission set.

Creating and Consuming XML Documents

Like performing File IO, Extensible Markup Language (XML) manipulation has been a part of the .NET Framework since it initially shipped with the 1.0 build. XML has become so prevalent in the software industry because it solves one of the oldest and most common problems, sharing data among heterogeneous systems. SQL Server 2005 provides native support for storing XML in the database.

There are XML-related technologies for performing validation of a document's content, the most common being the Extensible Schema Definition (XSD). XML validation is important and required because without validation you have no guarantee that your documents conform to a particular specification. For example, if you wish to accept all XML documents that adhere to `<employee><FirstName></FirstName/><Lastname></LastName></employee>`, then you need some entity to ensure this, thus the existence of XSDs. SQL Server 2005 natively supports XSDs via the CREATE/ALTER/DROP XML SCHEMA COLLECTION statements. SQL Server uses the term *collection*, because you can optionally define more than one schema in a collection.

> *If you would like to learn more about SQL Server 2005's native XML support, check out Professional SQL Server 2005 XML by Scott Klein (Wiley, 2006).*

Problem

When a person applies for a position with Adventure Works, there is a workflow that the candidate's résumé progresses through. First, the candidate e-mails his or her résumé to a particular e-mail address. At this point an Adventure Works HR employee will review the submitted résumé for completeness. If the résumé is found to not be complete, the candidate is contacted for more information. Once the résumé is complete, it is transformed into an XML document that is placed inside a directory for the Adventure Works system to then validate and store. Once the candidate's résumé is in the Adventure Works system, it can then be considered for the opportunity it was originally submitted for, as well as others. There is also the case when an existing candidate sends an updated résumé; for these cases, HR needs to detect that the candidate has an existing résumé in the system and then "refresh" its content.

Design

To fulfill these requirements, we will create a managed stored procedure that gets executed on a recurring basis by SQL Server Agent. This procedure will poll a predefined directory for the existence of any XML documents. If an XML document is found, the procedure will parse and store the document's content in the `HumanResources.JobCandidate` table. In addition, if a candidate submits a new résumé when there is already an existing one in the Adventure Works system, we update the candidate's résumé in the `HumanResources.JobCandidate table`.

Solution

First, you need to create a traditional T-SQL-based procedure for returning the existing candidates' names from the `HumanResources.JobCandidate` table. This procedure will be called from our managed stored procedure so that it can be aware of any existing résumés in the system.

```
USE [AdventureWorks]
GO
/****** Object:  StoredProcedure [dbo].[usp_ReturnResumeCandidates]
Script Date: 07/04/2006 14:46:00 ******/
SET ANSI_NULLS ON
GO
SET QUOTED_IDENTIFIER ON
GO
CREATE PROCEDURE [dbo].[usp_ReturnResumeCandidates]
AS
BEGIN
  SET NOCOUNT ON
  SELECT
   JobCandidateID,
    Resume.value('declare namespace
     ns="http://schemas.microsoft.com/sqlserver/2004/07/adventure-works/Resume";
    (/ns:Resume/ns:Name/ns:Name.Last)[1]', 'nvarchar(100)')
    + ',' +
    Resume.value('declare namespace
     ns="http://schemas.microsoft.com/sqlserver/2004/07/adventure-works/Resume";
    (/ns:Resume/ns:Name/ns:Name.First)[1]', 'nvarchar(100)') AS [CandidateName]
  FROM
    HumanResources.JobCandidate

  SET NOCOUNT OFF
END
```

With that procedure created, we can now focus on the managed code that will fulfill our design's logic. First, the code gets all of the existing résumés in the system. Next, it loops through any XML documents found in a predefined directory. Finally, it performs either an INSERT or UPDATE with the new résumé's content, depending upon whether the candidate was already in the system or not.

```
public partial class StoredProcedures
{
    [Microsoft.SqlServer.Server.SqlProcedure]
    public static void usp_ProcessResumes()
    {
        using (SqlConnection oInProcessConn =
            new SqlConnection("context connection=true"))
        {
            try
            {
                //local vars
                Boolean bFound = false;
                Int32 iCandID = 0;
                SqlCommand oCmd = oInProcessConn.CreateCommand();
                String sFileName = "";
```

```
//open db connection
oInProcessConn.Open();

//get existing resume names
DataSet oDS = new DataSet();
SqlDataAdapter oDA =
    new SqlDataAdapter("dbo.usp_ReturnResumeCandidates",
                       oInProcessConn);
oDA.Fill(oDS);
DataRowCollection oRows = oDS.Tables[0].Rows;

//loop through xml docs
String[] arrFiles =
    System.IO.Directory.GetFiles("C:\\AW_Resumes", "*.xml");

foreach (String sFile in arrFiles)
{
    //open the xml doc as a stream
    StreamReader oStream = new System.IO.StreamReader(sFile);

    //get file name
    sFileName = System.IO.Path.GetFileName(sFile);

    //compare file name to candidates allready in DB
    foreach (DataRow oRow in oRows)
    {
        if (oRow["CandidateName"].ToString() ==
            sFileName.Substring(0, (sFileName.Length - 4)))
        {
            bFound = true;
            iCandID = Convert.ToInt32(oRow["JobCandidateID"]);
        }
    }

    if (bFound == false)
    {
        //insert new resume
        oCmd.CommandText = "INSERT HumanResources.JobCandidate
            SELECT Null,@Resume,GetDate()";
        oCmd.Parameters.Add("@Resume", SqlDbType.Xml).Value =
            oStream.ReadToEnd().ToString();
        oCmd.ExecuteNonQuery();
    }
    else
    {
        //update resume
        oCmd.CommandText =
"UPDATE HumanResources.JobCandidate SET Resume = @Resume WHERE JobCandidateID = " +
iCandID.ToString();
        oCmd.Parameters.Add("@Resume", SqlDbType.Xml).Value =
            oStream.ReadToEnd().ToString();
        oCmd.ExecuteNonQuery();
    }
```

```
                        //close xml reader
                        oStream.Close();

                        //reset flag
                        bFound = false;
                    }
                }
                catch (Exception ex)
                {
                    //log failure to local machine's event log
                    EventLog oLog = new EventLog("Application");
                    oLog.Source = "usp_ProcessResumes";
                    oLog.WriteEntry("usp_ProcessResumes failed to execute on " +
                        System.DateTime.Now.ToString() + " The error message was:" +
                        ex.Message.ToString(), EventLogEntryType.Error);

                    //return error message to client
                    SqlContext.Pipe.Send(ex.Message.ToString());
                }
                finally
                {
                    //ensure database connection is closed
                    oInProcessConn.Close();
                }
            }
        }
};
```

Now, let's test our new solution. Create a new XML document based on the Adventure Works résumé XSD, and place it in a directory that matches what the literal you have used in your version of the above code (we are using c:\AW_Resumes). Name the file after a person's name (we are using Comingore,Derek.xml). The following xml is the content of Comingore,Derek.xml.

```
<ns:Resume xmlns:ns="http://schemas.microsoft.com/sqlserver/2004/07/adventure-
works/Resume">
  <ns:Name>
    <ns:Name.Prefix>Mr.</ns:Name.Prefix>
    <ns:Name.First>Derek</ns:Name.First>
    <ns:Name.Middle></ns:Name.Middle>
    <ns:Name.Last>Comingore</ns:Name.Last>
    <ns:Name.Suffix></ns:Name.Suffix>
  </ns:Name>
  <ns:Skills> Considerable expertise in all areas of the sales cycle. 13 years of
achievement in increasing organization revenue.
  Experience in sales planning and forecasting, customer development, and multiple
selling techniques. 5 years of experience in sales management, including lead
generation, sales force leadership, and territory management. Leverage management
style and technical ability to effectively manage and communicate with a
distributed sales force composed of field representatives, product demonstrators,
and vendors.
  Excellent communication and presentation skills.
    </ns:Skills>
  <ns:Employment>
    <ns:Emp.StartDate>1998-03-01Z</ns:Emp.StartDate>
```

```
        <ns:Emp.EndDate>2000-12-30Z</ns:Emp.EndDate>
        <ns:Emp.OrgName>Wide World Imports</ns:Emp.OrgName>
        <ns:Emp.JobTitle>Sales Manager</ns:Emp.JobTitle>
        <ns:Emp.Responsibility> Managed a sales force of 20 sales representatives and 5
support staff distributed across 5 states. Also managed relationships with vendors
for lead generation. Lead the effort to leverage IT capabilities to improve
communication with the field. Improved lead-to-contact turnaround by 15 percent.
Did all sales planning and forecasting. Re-mapped territory assignments for maximum
sales force productivity. Worked with marketing to map product placement to sales
strategy and goals.
   Under my management, sales increased 10% per year at a minimum.
        </ns:Emp.Responsibility>
        <ns:Emp.FunctionCategory>Sales</ns:Emp.FunctionCategory>
        <ns:Emp.IndustryCategory>Import/Export</ns:Emp.IndustryCategory>
        <ns:Emp.Location>
          <ns:Location>
            <ns:Loc.CountryRegion>US </ns:Loc.CountryRegion>
            <ns:Loc.State>WA </ns:Loc.State>
            <ns:Loc.City>Renton</ns:Loc.City>
          </ns:Location>
        </ns:Emp.Location>
      </ns:Employment>
      <ns:Employment>
        <ns:Emp.StartDate>1992-06-14Z</ns:Emp.StartDate>
        <ns:Emp.EndDate>1998-06-01Z</ns:Emp.EndDate>
        <ns:Emp.OrgName>Fourth Coffee</ns:Emp.OrgName>
        <ns:Emp.JobTitle>Sales Associater</ns:Emp.JobTitle>
        <ns:Emp.Responsibility>Selling product to supermarkets and cafes. Worked
heavily with value-add techniques to increase sales volume, provide exposure to
secondary products. Skilled at order development.
   Observed and built relationships with buyers that allowed me to identify
opportunities for increased traffic.
        </ns:Emp.Responsibility>
        <ns:Emp.FunctionCategory>Sales</ns:Emp.FunctionCategory>
        <ns:Emp.IndustryCategory>Food and Beverage</ns:Emp.IndustryCategory>
        <ns:Emp.Location>
          <ns:Location>
            <ns:Loc.CountryRegion>US </ns:Loc.CountryRegion>
            <ns:Loc.State>WA </ns:Loc.State>
            <ns:Loc.City>Spokane</ns:Loc.City>
          </ns:Location>
        </ns:Emp.Location>
      </ns:Employment>
      <ns:Education>
        <ns:Edu.Level>Bachelor</ns:Edu.Level>
        <ns:Edu.StartDate>1986-09-15Z</ns:Edu.StartDate>
        <ns:Edu.EndDate>1990-05-20Z</ns:Edu.EndDate>
        <ns:Edu.Degree>Bachelor of Arts and Science</ns:Edu.Degree>
        <ns:Edu.Major>Business</ns:Edu.Major>
        <ns:Edu.Minor></ns:Edu.Minor>
        <ns:Edu.GPA>3.3</ns:Edu.GPA>
        <ns:Edu.GPAScale>4</ns:Edu.GPAScale>
        <ns:Edu.School>Louisiana Business College of New Orleans</ns:Edu.School>
        <ns:Edu.Location>
```

```
          <ns:Location>
            <ns:Loc.CountryRegion>US </ns:Loc.CountryRegion>
            <ns:Loc.State>LA</ns:Loc.State>
            <ns:Loc.City>New Orleans</ns:Loc.City>
          </ns:Location>
        </ns:Edu.Location>
      </ns:Education>
      <ns:Address>
        <ns:Addr.Type>Home</ns:Addr.Type>
        <ns:Addr.Street>30 151st Place SE</ns:Addr.Street>
        <ns:Addr.Location>
          <ns:Location>
            <ns:Loc.CountryRegion>US </ns:Loc.CountryRegion>
            <ns:Loc.State>WA </ns:Loc.State>
            <ns:Loc.City>Redmond</ns:Loc.City>
          </ns:Location>
        </ns:Addr.Location>
        <ns:Addr.PostalCode>98052</ns:Addr.PostalCode>
        <ns:Addr.Telephone>
          <ns:Telephone>
            <ns:Tel.Type>Voice</ns:Tel.Type>
            <ns:Tel.IntlCode>1</ns:Tel.IntlCode>
            <ns:Tel.AreaCode>425</ns:Tel.AreaCode>
            <ns:Tel.Number>555-1119</ns:Tel.Number>
          </ns:Telephone>
          <ns:Telephone>
            <ns:Tel.Type>Voice</ns:Tel.Type>
            <ns:Tel.IntlCode>1</ns:Tel.IntlCode>
            <ns:Tel.AreaCode>425</ns:Tel.AreaCode>
            <ns:Tel.Number>555-1981</ns:Tel.Number>
          </ns:Telephone>
        </ns:Addr.Telephone>
      </ns:Address>
      <ns:EMail>Stephen@example.com</ns:EMail>
      <ns:WebSite></ns:WebSite>
    </ns:Resume>
```

Now, deploy the new managed procedure to your target SQL Server instance, and call EXEC dbo.usp_ ProcessResumes from a T-SQL editor in Management Studio. Open the HumanResources.JobCandidate table, and you should now see a new record with the above XML stored in the Resume column. In the real-world application of this solution, you would also create a SQL AGENT job that would periodically fire off usp_ProcessResumes procedure. We are going to use the following T-SQL to query the HumanResources.JobCandidate table to see if the new résumé was inserted into the table (if you are using a different name, just replace "Comingore" with the last name you used).

usp_ProcessResumes *requires the EXTERNAL ACCESS permission set.*

```
SELECT
   [JobCandidateID]
     , [EmployeeID]
     , [Resume]
     , [ModifiedDate]
FROM
```

```
    [AdventureWorks].[HumanResources].[JobCandidate]
WHERE
    Resume.value('declare namespace
ns="http://schemas.microsoft.com/sqlserver/2004/07/adventure-works/Resume";
        (/ns:Resume/ns:Name/ns:Name.Last)[1]', 'nvarchar(100)') = 'Comingore'
```

Figure 7-2 shows the results of this query.

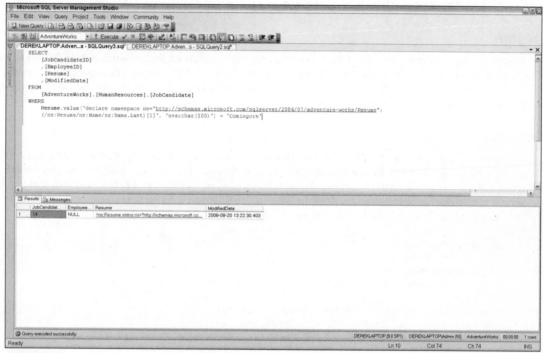

Figure 7-2

Conclusion

As with the other examples in the chapter, we could extend this solution for real-world applications. Both SQL Server 2005 and the .NET 2.0 Framework offer considerable XML functionality, including the passing of XML between one another. SQL CLR provides us with another mechanism to import and export XML to and from the database.

Consuming Web Services

Web services are one of the most successful demonstrations of the XML technology. Web services are all about distributed computing; that is, performing a task using more than one machine. Not only do web services facilitate distributed computing, but they also support distributed computing in heterogeneous environments. Web services are enabled by a suite of protocols and technologies all based upon XML and HTTP.

Problem

Adventure Works has an HR system that is used for storing performance reviews of employees. If a particular review recommends (and is approved) that the employee receive an adjustment of his or her salary, the AdventureWorks database must be updated to reflect this change in employee compensation. The HR system does not allow direct access except for HR staff and in general it is a locked-down system. To facilitate the needs of the Adventure Works system, a developer (who does have HR system access) has created a web service that exposes the compensation adjustments. The web service has been implemented in .NET and is only consumable by certain parties via its security restrictions.

Design

Every Sunday evening, a managed stored procedure will be executed that consumes the HR web service. If any new pay adjustments have been found, the procedure will then update the HumanResources .EmployeePayHistory table in the AdventureWorks database. The SQL Server Agent's logon account will be assigned the required permission to access the web service.

Solution

To begin, we need to review the HR Performance Reviews web service. We are going to use a very simplistic web service because the goal here is not to teach you web services, but how to consume them from SQL CLR. The following is our sample web service, which represents a real-world web service that would return this same information from an HR system. This web service is residing on a local test machine at http://localhost/wsPerformanceReviews/Service.asmx.

```
using System;
using System.Web;
using System.Web.Services;
using System.Web.Services.Protocols;

[WebService(Namespace = "http://tempuri.org/")]
[WebServiceBinding(ConformsTo = WsiProfiles.BasicProfile1_1)]
public class Service : System.Web.Services.WebService
{
    public Service () {

        //Uncomment the following line if using designed components
        //InitializeComponent();
    }

    [WebMethod]
    public string GetPerformanceReviews() {
        return "Kevin,Brown,8/20/2006,85.0000,1";
    }

}
```

If you wish to build this sample, your local machine will require Internet Information Services (IIS).

With you new web service code complete, you need to publish it to a location where your SQL CLR routines can find and consume it. Select Build ⇨ Publish from Visual Studio's main menu. With the publish web site dialog now being shown, click the ellipses in the top-right corner. Select Local IIS on the left-hand side of the dialog. Expand Default Web Site, and click on the Create New Web Application icon on the right-hand side above the Explorer pane. Type in a name for your new local web application (we are using wsPerformanceReviews), ensure the new application is highlighted, and click the Open button. Select the OK button in the previous dialog that is still being shown. Your new web service has now been successfully published.

Now, examine the consumer of this web service, a managed stored procedure. After you add a new stored procedure to a SQL Server project we need to add a web reference to our web service. In Solution Explorer, by default, you will not see a Web References listing. To add a web reference in a SQL Server project, right-click on the References listing and select Add Web Reference. This will then display the Add Web Reference dialog, as shown in Figure 7-3.

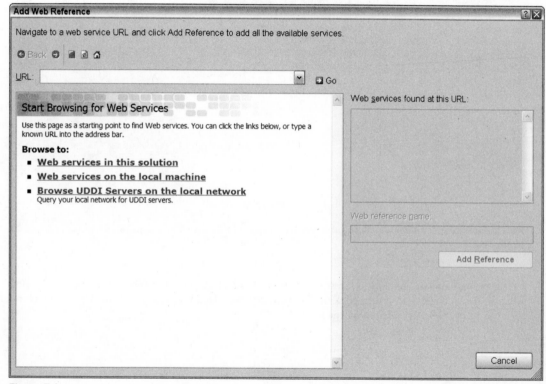

Figure 7-3

For our environment, we will use the web services on the local machine link, but you can type in the direct address in the URL text box and click the Go button regardless of where the service resides. After you click on the local machine link, you can see the sample service listed with a name of Service, as shown in Figure 7-4.

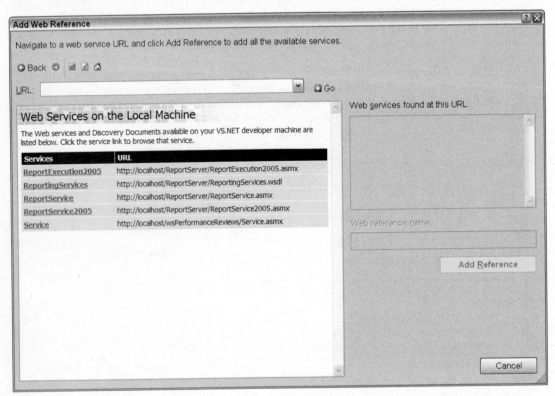

Figure 7-4

At this point, you can add your reference via the Add Reference button, as shown in Figure 7-5. After you add the web reference, right-click on the web reference itself and select rename. Give the web reference the name `wsPerformanceReviews`.

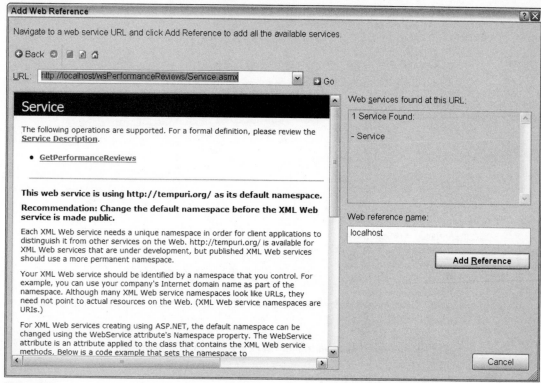

Figure 7-5

With the web reference added, you now need to create the procedure's code to implement the design. In this solution, you are going to create a traditional T-SQL based procedure that the managed procedure will call for data access. The following T-SQL creates your stored procedure for creating a new employee pay history record; again, the managed procedure will call this, passing in the values it has obtained from the web service. Open up a new query window in Management Studio and execute the following code:

```
USE [AdventureWorks]
GO
CREATE PROCEDURE usp_CreatePayRecord
   @FirstName        NVARCHAR(50)
  ,@LastName         NVARCHAR(50)
  ,@RateChangeDate   DATETIME
  ,@Rate             sMONEY
  ,@PayFreq          TINYINT
AS
BEGIN
   SET NOCOUNT ON
```

```
INSERT
   HumanResources.EmployeePayHistory
SELECT
   Z.EmployeeID
   ,@RateChangeDate
   ,@Rate
   ,@PayFreq
   ,GETDATE()
FROM
(
SELECT
   EmployeeID
FROM
   HumanResources.Employee E
INNER JOIN
   Person.Contact C ON (E.ContactID = C.ContactID)
WHERE
   C.LastName = @LastName
   And C.FirstName = @FirstName
) Z
END
```

You can now create the managed procedures code to call the web services and then pass its data into our T-SQL procedure.

usp_GetPerformanceReviews *requires the EXTERNAL ACCESS permission set.*

```
public partial class StoredProcedures
{
    [Microsoft.SqlServer.Server.SqlProcedure]
    public static void usp_GetPerformanceReviews()
    {
        using (SqlConnection oRemoteConn =
            new SqlConnection("Data Source=.\\sqlexpress;Initial
Catalog=AdventureWorks;Integrated Security=true;"))
        {
            try
            {
                //Create WSProxy
                Chapter7.wsPerformanceReviews.Service oWS =
                    new Chapter7.wsPerformanceReviews.Service();

                //Get New Performance Reviews
                string sWSReturn = oWS.GetPerformanceReviews();
                string[] arrReturn = sWSReturn.Split(",".ToCharArray());

                SqlCommand oCmd = new SqlCommand();
                oCmd.Connection = oRemoteConn;
                oCmd.CommandType = CommandType.StoredProcedure;

                //pass in procedure name and inputs
                oCmd.CommandText = "usp_CreatePayRecord";

                // Add the input parameter and set its properties.
```

```csharp
SqlParameter oParmFirstName = new SqlParameter();
oParmFirstName.ParameterName = "@FirstName";
oParmFirstName.SqlDbType = SqlDbType.NVarChar;
oParmFirstName.Direction = ParameterDirection.Input;
oParmFirstName.Value = arrReturn[0];
// Add the parameter to the Parameters collection.
oCmd.Parameters.Add(oParmFirstName);

SqlParameter oParmLastName = new SqlParameter();
oParmLastName.ParameterName = "@LastName";
oParmLastName.SqlDbType = SqlDbType.NVarChar;
oParmLastName.Direction = ParameterDirection.Input;
oParmLastName.Value = arrReturn[1];
// Add the parameter to the Parameters collection.
oCmd.Parameters.Add(oParmLastName);

SqlParameter oParmRateChangeDate = new SqlParameter();
oParmRateChangeDate.ParameterName = "@RateChangeDate";
oParmRateChangeDate.SqlDbType = SqlDbType.DateTime;
oParmRateChangeDate.Direction = ParameterDirection.Input;
oParmRateChangeDate.Value = Convert.ToDateTime(arrReturn[2]);
// Add the parameter to the Parameters collection.
oCmd.Parameters.Add(oParmRateChangeDate);

SqlParameter oParmRate = new SqlParameter();
oParmRate.ParameterName = "@Rate";
oParmRate.SqlDbType = SqlDbType.Money;
oParmRate.Direction = ParameterDirection.Input;
oParmRate.Value = Convert.ToDouble(arrReturn[3]);
// Add the parameter to the Parameters collection.
oCmd.Parameters.Add(oParmRate);

SqlParameter oParmPayFreq = new SqlParameter();
oParmPayFreq.ParameterName = "@PayFreq";
oParmPayFreq.SqlDbType = SqlDbType.TinyInt;
oParmPayFreq.Direction = ParameterDirection.Input;
oParmPayFreq.Value = Convert.ToInt16(arrReturn[4]);
// Add the parameter to the Parameters collection.
oCmd.Parameters.Add(oParmPayFreq);

//fire off command
oRemoteConn.Open();
oCmd.ExecuteNonQuery();

//return success message for adhoc callers
SqlContext.Pipe.Send("SUCCESS");
}
catch (System.Exception ex)
{
//log failure to local machine's event log
EventLog oLog = new EventLog("Application");
oLog.Source = "usp_WhatsRunning";
oLog.WriteEntry("usp_WhatsRunning failed to execute on " +
    System.DateTime.Now.ToString() + " The error message was:" +
```

```
                    ex.Message.ToString(), EventLogEntryType.Error);

                //return error message to client
                SqlContext.Pipe.Send(ex.Message.ToString());
            }
            finally
            {
                //ensure database connection is closed
                oRemoteConn.Close();
            }
        }
    }
};
```

With the new managed procedure created, you can now test it. Execute the following T-SQL in a new query window. You should see a result similar to that in Figure 7-6.

```
EXECUTE [AdventureWorks].[dbo].[usp_GetPerformanceReviews]
```

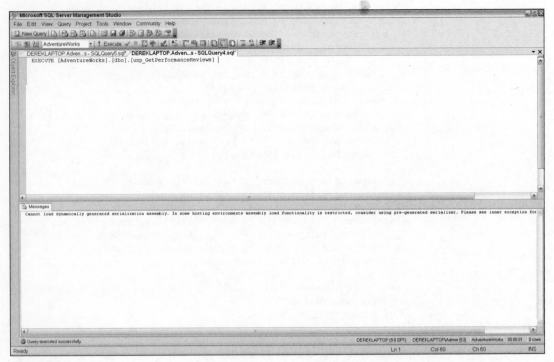

Figure 7-6

So what happened? In order to consume web services, you must serialize all types to XML, and SQL Server does not allow this to occur. To get around this problem, add two new items using Solution Explorer, with the names predeployscript.sql and postdeployscript.sql, in the root of your solution. Now, populate the predeployscript.sql file with the following T-SQL.

```
IF EXISTS (SELECT [name] FROM sys.assemblies WHERE [name] =
N'Chapter7.XmlSerializers.dll')
DROP ASSEMBLY myAsmXML with NO DEPENDENTS;
```

And add this SQL to the `postdeployscript.sql` file:

```
CREATE ASSEMBLY myAsmXML
FROM 'C:\Documents and Settings\Admin\My Documents\Visual Studio
2005\Projects\Chapter7\Chapter7\bin\Release\Chapter7.XmlSerializers.dll'
```

Before you attempt to run this code via another Deploy command in Visual Studio, you need to create the serialization assembly manually. To do this, you need to use the `sgen.exe` .NET SDK tool, which creates serialization assemblies. To make calling the executeable with the assembly easier, we recommend using the .NET Framework SDK command prompt, which can be accessed via Start ➪ Programs ➪ Microsoft .NET Framework SDK v2.0 ➪ SDK Command Prompt. You need to pass in the SQL Server Project's assembly to the `sgen.exe` utility, like this:

```
sgen.exe Chapter7.dll
```

Finally, issue a Deploy command in Visual Studio. Now, try calling our managed procedure again as shown in the following code. You should get a "SUCCESS" message returned, as shown in Figure 7-7.

```
EXECUTE [AdventureWorks].[dbo].[usp_GetPerformanceReviews]
```

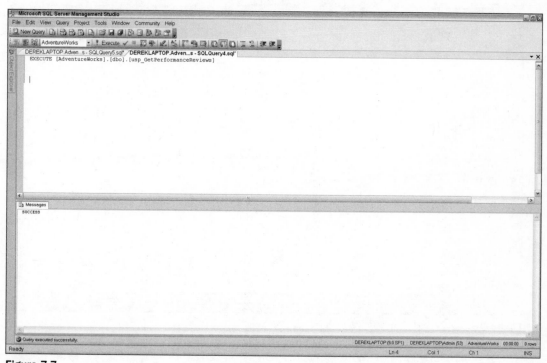

Figure 7-7

Now, run one more query to confirm the new record was pulled from the web services and inserted into the `HumanResources.EmployeePayHistory` table. Run the following T-SQL in a query window using Management Studio. You should see results similar to those in Figure 7-8.

```
SELECT
  *
FROM
  HumanResources.EmployeePayHistory
WHERE
  EmployeeID IN
  (
  SELECT
    EmployeeID
  FROM
    HumanResources.Employee E
  INNER JOIN
    Person.Contact C ON (E.ContactID = C.ContactID)
  WHERE
    C.LastName = 'Brown'
    And C.FirstName = 'Kevin'
  )
```

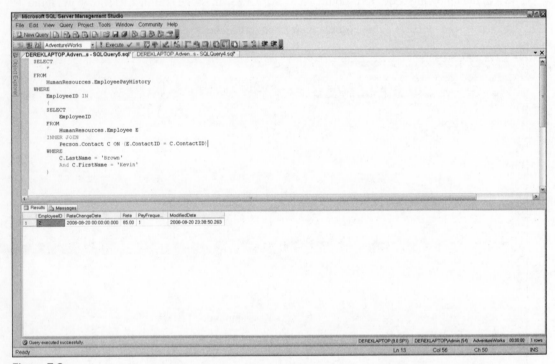

Figure 7-8

Conclusion

With the prevalence of web services, it is quite common to need SQL CLR routines calling them. In regard to the real-world application of this solution, we would first need to implement the actual HR web services as opposed to it just returning sample data. You would also need to create a SQL Agent job to execute the managed procedure on a scheduled basis and ensure that the account SQL Agent is running under has access to both the web services and the remote SQL Server instance.

Building Effective Monitoring Tools

In today's world, security can never be emphasized enough. Worms, Trojans, and viruses all scour the Internet looking for susceptible victims. SQL Server is increasingly becoming the database powering public websites, especially the Express edition of SQL Server 2005. SQL Server 2005 Express Edition has been a highly successful release of the SQL Server engine, targeting the free database market that has been dominated by MySQL. By using the classes found in the System.Diagnostics namespace you can create effective monitoring utilities to help detect if a server becomes targeted by such malicious software. In this section, we will create several of these monitoring utilities.

Auditing Server Processes

Processes are an important entity of a machine to monitor. Without regularly monitoring your server's processes, a new process can begin running and you might never know it. Such processes are usually malicious in nature, and this is why monitoring what processes are running on your server is a good security measure. A *process* is a running instance of a program; thus, you could have multiple processes based on the same base program. Processes are allocated resources such as CPU execution time and memory, and an operating system component known as the process scheduler will coordinate the machine's processing of the processes and their associated threads.

Problem

As of late the Adventure Works DBA team has noticed that a variety of worms have been infecting their production SQL servers. Thus far the team's most used solution is to simply rebuild the servers once a worm has been detected, but this is a costly decision as it requires a member of the DBA team to rebuild an entire server. In addition to the team keeping patches up to date and locking down ports, they also wish to audit all running processes on their production SQL Servers using a recurring schedule. The DBA team will persist this information into table(s) and then produce several interfaces that hook into the data for auditing and reporting purposes.

Design

To accomplish the DBA team's wishes, we will create a managed stored procedure that collects all of the running processes and their associated attributes on the host machine. The procedure will then pass this information to a remote SQL server for storage. SQL Server Agent will execute this procedure on a daily basis. If any new processes are detected, an SMTP e-mail will be sent to the DBA team.

Solution

To begin, create your destination table for the procedure. Here is the T-SQL you can use to create the sample table, dbo.WhatsRunning:

```
USE [AdventureWorks]
GO
/****** Object:  Table [dbo].[WhatsRunning]    Script Date: 07/02/2006 10:09:32
******/
SET ANSI_NULLS ON
GO
SET QUOTED_IDENTIFIER ON
GO
SET ANSI_PADDING ON
GO
CREATE TABLE [dbo].[WhatsRunning](
  [ID] [int] IDENTITY(1,1) NOT NULL,
  [Machine] [varchar](50) COLLATE SQL_Latin1_General_CP1_CI_AS NOT NULL,
  [TimeStamp] [datetime] NOT NULL CONSTRAINT [DF_RunningProcesses_TimeStamp]
    DEFAULT (getdate()),
  [ProcessID] [int] NOT NULL,
  [ProcessName] [varchar](200) COLLATE SQL_Latin1_General_CP1_CI_AS NOT NULL,
  [Threads] [int] NOT NULL,
  [NonpagedSystemMemorySize64] [int] NOT NULL,
  [PagedMemorySize64] [int] NOT NULL,
  [VirtualMemorySize64] [int] NOT NULL,
  [PriorityClass] [varchar](50) COLLATE SQL_Latin1_General_CP1_CI_AS NOT NULL,
  [PriorityBoostEnabled] [bit] NOT NULL,
  [Responding] [bit] NOT NULL,
 CONSTRAINT [PK_RunningProcesses] PRIMARY KEY CLUSTERED
(
  [ID] ASC
)WITH (PAD_INDEX  = OFF, IGNORE_DUP_KEY = OFF) ON [PRIMARY]
) ON [PRIMARY]

GO
SET ANSI_PADDING OFF
```

With the table in place, it's now time to build the managed procedure that will monitor the server's processes.

usp_WhatsRunning *requires the UNSAFE permission set.*

```
public partial class StoredProcedures
{
    [Microsoft.SqlServer.Server.SqlProcedure]
    public static void usp_WhatsRunning()
    {
        using (SqlConnection oRemoteConn =
            new SqlConnection("Data Source=.\\sqlexpress;Initial
Catalog=AdventureWorks;Integrated Security=true;"))
        {
```

```
try
{
    SqlCommand oCmd = new SqlCommand();
    oCmd.Connection = oRemoteConn;

    //get all local processes
    Process[] arrProcesses = Process.GetProcesses();

    //open db connection
    oRemoteConn.Open();

    //loop through processes
    foreach (Process oProcess in arrProcesses)
    {
        if (oProcess.ProcessName.ToString() != "Idle")
        {
            //build command text
            oCmd.CommandText = "INSERT dbo.WhatsRunning SELECT " +
                "'" + System.Environment.MachineName.ToString() + "',"
                +
                "GetDate()," +
                "'" + oProcess.Id.ToString() + "'," +
                "'" + oProcess.ProcessName.ToString() + "'," +
                "'" + oProcess.Threads.Count.ToString() + "'," +
                "'" + oProcess.NonpagedSystemMemorySize64.ToString() +
                    "'," +
                "'" + oProcess.PagedMemorySize64.ToString() + "'," +
                "'" + oProcess.VirtualMemorySize64.ToString() + "'," +
                "'" + oProcess.PriorityClass.ToString() + "'," +
                "'" + oProcess.PriorityBoostEnabled.ToString() + "'," +
                "'" + oProcess.Responding.ToString() + "'";

            //fire off command
            oCmd.ExecuteNonQuery();
        }
    }

    //return success message to client
    SqlContext.Pipe.Send("Success");
}
catch (Exception ex)
{
    //log failure to local machine's event log
    EventLog oLog = new EventLog("Application");
    oLog.Source = "usp_WhatsRunning";
    oLog.WriteEntry("usp_WhatsRunning failed to execute on " +
        System.DateTime.Now.ToString() + " The error message was:" +
        ex.Message.ToString(), EventLogEntryType.Error);

    //return error message to client
    SqlContext.Pipe.Send(ex.Message.ToString());
}
finally
```

```
        {
            //ensure database connection is closed
            oRemoteConn.Close();
        }

    }
  }
};
```

Build and deploy your SQL Server project after you have created our new managed procedure. If you wish to stay inside of the Visual Studio environment to test your code simply insert EXEC usp_WhatsRunning into the Test.sql file and run the project as opposed to deploying it. If all goes well there should be a "Success" message displayed in the output window. Open the dbo.WhatsRunning table on your remote SQL instance; the results should look similar to Figure 7-9.

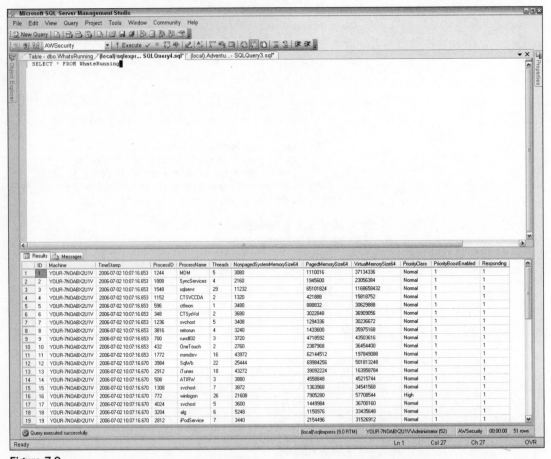

Figure 7-9

Conclusion

For real-world applications using this solution, we would need to create a SQL Agent job to execute the procedure on a scheduled basis. Monitoring processes are key for security because one of the first signs of a server being attacked is an unrecognized process running on the server.

Auditing Installed Software

The registry in a nutshell is a centralized database that stores settings for all of a machine's hardware, software, users, and preferences. Today, when an application gets installed on a Windows machine, the installer will perform several tasks, including making entries in the registry. The registry is another very import entity of a machine to monitor because almost any software that "touches" a machine will affect the registry. One such location is SOFTWARE\\Microsoft\\Windows\\CurrentVersion\\Uninstall, where all installed programs have entries for performing an uninstall at a later time.

Problem

Due to the security issues described in the previous section that Adventure Works has been suffering from, the DBA team also wants to audit all installed software on their production SQL servers. The data collection should be on a recurring basis, and the results should be sent to a remote SQL server. The hope is that the servers are locked down enough to prevent future intrusions, but in the event that security has failed the DBA team can become aware of any newly installed applications (another common symptom of attacks).

Design

We will be creating a managed stored procedure that again gets scheduled by SQL Server Agent on a scheduled basis. The procedure will query the local server's registry for installed programs and then send the results to a remote SQL server.

Solution

Before we create our managed procedure, we need a table to store its results in. Below is the T-SQL you can use to create the sample table, dbo.SoftwareInstalled. Remember this is the table that is going to be on our remote SQL server:

```
USE [AdventureWorks]
GO
/****** Object:  Table [dbo].[InstalledSoftware]
    Script Date: 07/02/2006 00:43:00 ******/
SET ANSI_NULLS ON
GO
SET QUOTED_IDENTIFIER ON
GO
SET ANSI_PADDING ON
GO
CREATE TABLE [dbo].[InstalledSoftware](
  [ID] [int] IDENTITY(1,1) NOT NULL,
  [Machine] [varchar](50) COLLATE SQL_Latin1_General_CP1_CI_AS NOT NULL,
  [TimeStamp] [datetime] NOT NULL
```

```
  CONSTRAINT [DF_InstalledSoftware_TimeStamp]  DEFAULT (getdate()),
   [Software] [varchar](200) COLLATE SQL_Latin1_General_CP1_CI_AS NOT NULL,
 CONSTRAINT [PK_InstalledSoftware] PRIMARY KEY CLUSTERED
(
  [ID] ASC
)WITH (PAD_INDEX  = OFF, IGNORE_DUP_KEY = OFF) ON [PRIMARY]
) ON [PRIMARY]

GO
SET ANSI_PADDING OFF
```

Now that you have the table created, you need to create the new managed procedure. Again, this managed procedure needs to access the server's registry to determine if any new programs were installed.

usp_InstalledSoftware *requires the EXTERNAL ACCESS permission set.*

```
 public partial class StoredProcedures
 {
     [Microsoft.SqlServer.Server.SqlProcedure]
     public static void usp_InstalledSoftware()
     {
         using (SqlConnection oRemoteConn =
             new SqlConnection("Data Source=.\\sqlexpress;Initial
                 Catalog=AdventureWorks;Integrated Security=true;"))
         {
             try
             {
                 SqlCommand oCmd = new SqlCommand();
                 oCmd.Connection = oRemoteConn;
                 RegistryKey oRootKey =
                     Registry.LocalMachine.OpenSubKey("SOFTWARE\\Microsoft\\Windows
                         \\CurrentVersion\\Uninstall", false);
                 String[] sKeyNames = oRootKey.GetSubKeyNames();
                 Int32 i;
                 RegistryKey oKey;

                 //open db connection
                 oRemoteConn.Open();

                 for (i = 0; i <= oRootKey.SubKeyCount - 1; i++)
                 {
                     //get next key
                     oKey =
                         Registry.LocalMachine.OpenSubKey("SOFTWARE\\Microsoft\\
                             Windows\\CurrentVersion\\Uninstall\\" +
                             sKeyNames[i], false);

                     if (oKey.GetValue("DisplayName", "").ToString() != "")
                     {
                         //build command text
                         oCmd.CommandText = "INSERT dbo.InstalledSoftware SELECT '" +
```

```
                                    System.Environment.MachineName.ToString() +
                                    "', GetDate(), '" + oKey.GetValue("Displayname",
                                    "").ToString() + "'";

                                //fire off command
                                oCmd.ExecuteNonQuery();
                            }
                    }

                    //return success message to client
                    SqlContext.Pipe.Send("SUCCESS");
                }
                catch (Exception ex)
                {
                    //log failure to local machine's event log
                    EventLog oLog = new EventLog("Application");
                    oLog.Source = "usp_InstalledSoftware";
                    oLog.WriteEntry("usp_InstalledSoftware failed to execute on " +
                        System.DateTime.Now.ToString() + " The error message was:" +
                        ex.Message.ToString(), EventLogEntryType.Error);

                    //return error message to client
                    SqlContext.Pipe.Send(ex.Message.ToString());
                }
                finally
                {
                    //ensure database connection is closed
                    oRemoteConn.Close();
                }
            }
        }
    };
```

Now, build your database project with the above procedure (don't forget to change connection string values first) and then deploy it to your target SQL Server. If you place the T-SQL EXEC usp_InstalledSoftware into your Test.sql file, and you elect to run (F5) the project as opposed to deploying it, you will notice a "SUCCESS" message in the output window if all goes well.

Because of the previous example's requirements you should not receive any errors, but if you are just trying this one example out you may receive the common "Database requires trustworthy . . ." error in Visual Studio upon deploying the project. See Chapter 10 for more information on the database-level TRUSTWORTHY setting. Finally, open the dbo.InstalledSoftware table on your remote SQL instance; the results should look similar to Figure 7-10.

Conclusion

In the real world, you would create a SQL Agent job that would periodically fire off usp_Installed Software to collect the data on a recurring basis. Monitoring installed software is another key aspect for security; malicious software quite frequently will attempt to install unauthorized once it has permissions to do so.

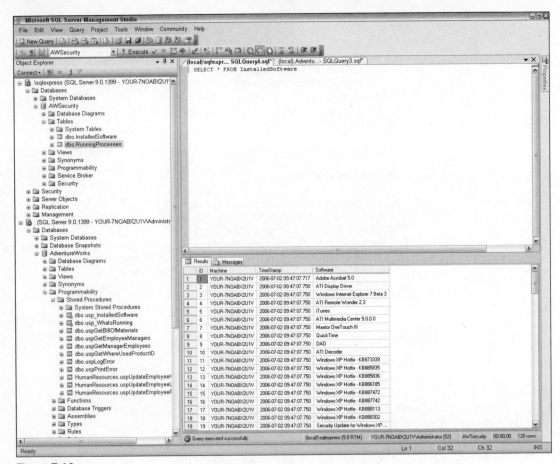

Figure 7-10

Summary

In this chapter, we demonstrated concrete examples of using the BCL in your SQL CLR routines, and we did so in a manner that maps the technical solutions to the business requirements. The majority of these code samples could be altered slightly for your specific environment and deployed to production. We have covered several areas of functionality that can benefit from the SQL CLR technology. Overall, the lasting impression we want to leave you with is that there is a lot of functionality the BCL offers your SQL CLR routines.

In the next chapter, we will be applying the same real-world examples concept to that of applications consuming your SQL CLR routines. Leveraging the SQL CLR technology in SQL Server Integration Services (SSIS) can be beneficial for custom transformations. And using SQL CLR routines in SQL Server Reporting Services (SSRS) can provide your reports with atypical data sources.

Using SQL CLR Stored Procedures in Your Applications

In this book, we've covered the development processes of each SQL CLR routine and have demonstrated from a nuts-and-bolts perspective how to code and host them in SQL Server 2005. However, as we put these routines to work, we've used a T-SQL-based test harness — essentially calling the routines from within the SQL Server environment. Out in the real world, these routines are going to be used by applications, and you'll need to know how developers will be interacting with objects that we create and host in SQL Server.

This chapter tackles the integration of SQL CLR routines into your development processes. We'll show you how to access the SQL CLR objects and demonstrate that this is no different than using T-SQL objects. We'll also demonstrate the use of programming to the new SQL CLR user-defined types and how to display and save user-input information to database structures that use these types. Finally, we'll get to create some atypical data sources using SQL CLR user-defined table-valued functions and show how these can be easily created and plugged into SSIS ETL processes or Reporting Services.

SQL CLR Application Usage Architecture

One of the more frequent questions that we get from first-timers to SQL CLR is how to connect applications to managed code in SQL Server. It seems that there is some initial confusion between the .NET parts and the T-SQL parts of the SQL CLR routines, and to which parts you should connect. This confusion is undoubtedly the result of building the routines in a .NET language and the familiarity with other middle-tier or data access layers. The developers in us see CLR and instinctually want to connect to the code. It seems like we should be able to import a reference to the class and start coding, but the trick is to remember the "SQL" in front of the CLR. This should remind that you even though you are using the CLR, it is not the same CLR hosted on your machine; rather it is hosted within SQL Server. The only way to access this version of the CLR is through SQL Server. Another way of looking at it is that SQL CLR routines are simply T-SQL objects with .NET implementations. Looked at this way, it may be more obvious that you need to connect to SQL Server to access the T-SQL-based objects.

Connecting to SQL Server is the easy part. You do this as you have always done. Use an abstracted data access provider like ADO.NET to connect to and use SQL CLR objects. If you are capable of doing so, you can code to the data access APIs. As long as you can connect to the database, you will be able to use the managed-code-based procedures, functions, and aggregations. You can also indirectly reach the triggers, but because applications normally do not interact with triggers, these will be ignored in this chapter. The important point is that the interaction with SQL CLR routines is just like interacting with T-SQL objects. This is by design. The .NET code in the modules simply exposes entry points that are wrapped in T-SQL DDL. Once you realize this, integrating SQL CLR objects into applications becomes trivial. Even old code bases can take advantage of new SQL CLR routines. Since SQL CLR routine are exposed as T-SQL objects, you can call these even using classic ADO or even Open DataBase Connectivity (ODBC) (for basic tasks). Figure 8-1 shows an overall view of how these pieces and parts work together.

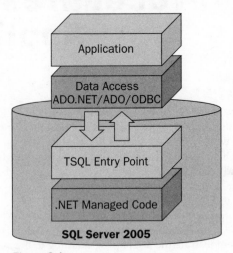

Figure 8-1

SQL Server Connections and SQL CLR Stored Procedures

During the chapters on SQL CLR development, you will have noticed that the connections are generally made using a Context Connection method. This special type of connection method uses the context of the connection that calls the SQL CLR routine instead of requiring a separate connection string. This also allows you to develop SQL CLR routines and defer the details of making the SQL Server connection. Even though you could still build your own connection strings and reconnect within the SQL CLR objects, most of the time, it is more appropriate to use the connection that the caller had to use to get to the SQL CLR object. The exception would be if you were building an integration SQL CLR object that needed to connect to another data stores and combine the results within SQL Server. The other 99% of the time, the SQL CLR routines need to access the SQL Server in which they reside. To connect to them, you need a method of connecting to the database. Most applications will use one of the data providers from ADO.NET, based on ODBC, OLE DB, or the new SQL Client APIs. To get an idea of what this will look like for a SQL CLR stored procedure, we'll use each of the different access methods from a client perspective to update columns in a test table with the current date and a calculated Julian date. For these examples, you'll need to create a test table using this T-SQL code:

```
USING CLRTESTDB
GO
CREATE TABLE DateValues(CurrDate smalldatetime, JulianDate smallint)
```

You'll also need to build a SQL CLR stored procedure that we can connect to with a client using different connection methods. Create a new .NET SQL Server project and add a new stored procedure class to the project. The SQL CLR stored procedure you'll use for comparison will look like this:

```csharp
using System;
using System.Data;
using System.Data.SqlClient;
using System.Data.SqlTypes;
using Microsoft.SqlServer.Server;

public partial class StoredProcedures
{
    [Microsoft.SqlServer.Server.SqlProcedure]
    public static void mspCalcJulianDateFromCurrentDate()
    {
        using (SqlConnection sqlConn =
                    new SqlConnection("Context Connection=true"))
        {
            sqlConn.Open();
            SqlCommand sqlCmd = sqlConn.CreateCommand();
            //Adds current date and julian date to datevalues table
            sqlCmd.CommandText = "INSERT INTO DateValues(CurrDate, JulianDate) " +
                        "SELECT '" + DateTime.Now.ToString() + "', " +
                        "'" + DateTime.Now.DayOfYear.ToString() + "'";
            SqlContext.Pipe.ExecuteAndSend(sqlCmd);
        }
    }
};
```

This procedure basically just inserts the current date and Julian date into a table. Build your project and deploy the assembly into the CLRTESTDB database. Notice that some date calculations are much easier using the classes in .NET instead of coding in T-SQL. The DayofYear property encapsulates the following equivalent T-SQL code to calculate the current day or the year:

```
DECLARE @StartDate as smalldatetime
SET @StartDate = convert(smalldatetime, '01/01/' +
                    convert(varchar, year(getdate()))), 101)
SELECT DATEDIFF (day, @StartDate, getdate()) + 1
```

Once you've run the script to create the table and have loaded the assembly for the SQL CLR stored procedure mspCalcJulianDateFromCurrentDate, you are ready to build a test harness graphical user interface (GUI) app. Create a new Windows application project with three buttons on a default Windows form. Name the buttons ODBC, OLE DB, and SQL CLIENT, for each of the connections that we'll create to SQL Server to execute this stored procedure using a command object. Your form will look similar to Figure 8-2.

Figure 8-2

This connection just assumed all the rights and roles of the ODBC connection string that was used to access the SQL CLR procedure.

Using SQL CLR with ODBC

To access SQL Server with ODBC, import the reference to the ODBC namespace into your form:

```
using System.Data.Odbc;
```

Connect the Windows form to your database by creating an ODBC connection object using an ODBC connection string. In each of the following examples, we put a few items in the connection string that you'll have to configure:

1. Replace <<YOURSERVER>>\\SQLEXPRESS with your server name and SQL Express instance.

2. Add a test user to access the database using SQL Authentication. These examples use a TestUser, but you can create your own user and substitute that user name.

3. Replace the password or PWD setting to the password of your TestUser account.

4. Replace the CLRTESTDB database name if you are using a difference database.

With the connection strings properly formatted, you'll be able to connect using the special odbcConn class. This is different from the old ADO which didn't use strongly typed connection objects in favor of one generic connection object.

```
using (OdbcConnection odbcConn = new OdbcConnection(connectionString))
...
odbcConn.Open();
```

Then create an ODBC brand of a command object to connect and execute the SQL CLR stored procedure. This is done by instantiating an OdbcCommand object, passing it the connection string and the connection object:

```
OdbcCommand odbcCmd = new OdbcCommand(mySQL, odbcConn);
```

The final code below should be pasted behind a click event for the ODBC button.

```
using System.Data.Odbc;
private void ODBC_Click(object sender, EventArgs e)
{
    string mySQL = "mspCalcJulianDateFromCurrentDate";
    string connectionString = "Driver={SQL Server};" +
            "Server=<<YOURSERVER>>\\SQLEXPRESS;UID=TestUser; " +
            "PWD=testuser;Database=CLRTESTDB;";
    using (OdbcConnection odbcConn = new OdbcConnection(connectionString))
    {
        odbcConn.Open();

        OdbcCommand odbcCmd = new OdbcCommand(mySQL, odbcConn);
        odbcCmd.CommandType = CommandType.StoredProcedure;

        odbcCmd.ExecuteNonQuery();
        MessageBox.Show("Updated", "Updated", MessageBoxButtons.OK,
                        MessageBoxIcon.Information);
    }
}
```

Now that you got some data access code, you can connect to the database and execute the SQL CLR stored procedure from within the Windows application using the ODBC connection. Click the ODBC button on the window to get the "Updated" message, which you can see in Figure 8-3. Run a query in your database to select rows from the test DateValue table to see that a row was entered.

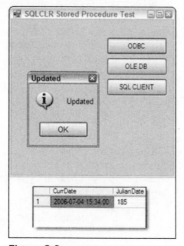

Figure 8-3

Although updating a database table is not a recommended use for SQL CLR, you can see what it takes to connect to the hosted .NET object—and it's not any different from calling a normal T-SQL stored procedure.

What's important to understand is that even though you connected to the database using an ODBC connection string, you connect to SQL Server within the SQL CLR stored procedure using the `SqlClient` version of the connection object.

```
using (SqlConnection sqlConn =
            new SqlConnection("Context Connection=true"))
```

This difference is that the SQL CLR connection just assumed all the rights and roles of the ODBC connection string that was used to access the stored procedure. You'll see, as we work through each method of connecting to the database, you'll see that the connection from within the SQL CLR stored procedure remains the same.

Using SQL CLR with OLE DB

Using the SQL CLR stored procedure with an OLE DB data access method is similar to the ODBC method, except that we are using the OLE DB APIs. Notice the change in the connection string and the use of a strongly typed `OleDbConnection` class.

```
using (OleDbConnection oledbConn = new
        OleDbConnection(connectionString))
```

Cut and paste this code behind the OLE DB button, so you can continue to call your SQL CLR procedure:

```
using System.Data.OleDb;
private void OLEDB_Click(object sender, EventArgs e)
{
    string mySQL = "mspCalcJulianDateFromCurrentDate";
    string connectionString = "Provider=sqloledb;" +
                "Data Source=<<YOURSERVER>>\\SQLEXPRESS;" +
                "Initial Catalog=CLRTESTDB;" +
                "User Id=TestUser;" +
                "Password=testuser";

    using (OleDbConnection oledbConn = new
        OleDbConnection(connectionString))
    {
        oledbConn.Open();
        OleDbCommand oledbCmd = new
            OleDbCommand(mySQL, oledbConn);
        oledbCmd.CommandType = CommandType.StoredProcedure;
        oledbCmd.ExecuteNonQuery();
        MessageBox.Show("Updated", "Updated", MessageBoxButtons.OK,
                            MessageBoxIcon.Information);
    }
}
```

Again you'll see that the `DateValue` table has a new entry in it.

Using SQL CLR with SQL Client

Using the SQL Client APIs should be really familiar to you, since these are the classes that you normally use to build SQL CLR stored procedures. Here's where some confusion may originate. Because you are rebuilding a connection and a command object just like in the SQL CLR stored procedure, it seems redundant that you are doing this all over again. It is important to note that this time, although you are coding data-access-type code again, it is only to gain access to the CLR stored procedure, not to update the data in the table. Unlike before, you can use the same connection string that you used for the OLE DB connection. However, you will need to add a `SqlConn` connection and a `SqlCommand` object from the `System.Data.SqlClient` namespace.

```
using (SqlConnection sqlConn = new SqlConnection(connectionString))
```

Otherwise, the client code looks the same:

```
using System.Data.SqlClient;
private void SQLCLIENT_Click(object sender, EventArgs e)
{
    string mySQL = "mspCalcJulianDateFromCurrentDate";
    string connectionString = "Data Source=<<YOURSERVER>>\\SQLEXPRESS;" +
                "Initial Catalog=CLRTESTDB;" +
                "User Id=TestUser;" +
                "Password=testuser";
    using (SqlConnection sqlConn = new SqlConnection(connectionString))
    {
        sqlConn.Open();
        SqlCommand sqlCmd = new
            SqlCommand(mySQL, sqlConn);
        sqlCmd.CommandType = CommandType.StoredProcedure;
        sqlCmd.ExecuteNonQuery();
        MessageBox.Show("Updated", "Updated", MessageBoxButtons.OK,
                            MessageBoxIcon.Information);
    }
}
```

Hopefully, you've been able to see that using a SQL CLR stored procedure is the same as connecting to any T-SQL stored procedure. You need to connect to the database to access the stored procedure. If the stored procedure is based on the CLR, you'll be able to assume the security and the context of the connection and perform the action inside the .NET method. Once the method is complete, it can stream out information to the `SqlContext.Pipe` class which uses the tabular data stream to send back results that can be interpreted by ODBC, OLE DB, SQL Client, or any other SQL Server 2005–compliant data access technology.

Using SQL CLR with ADO for Legacy Applications

Since your applications only need to interface with SQL Server T-SQL object definitions, you can even call your .NET-based SQL CLR stored procedure from VB6 or classic ASP without any COM interop or special coding. The only requirement is a connection to a SQL Server 2005 instance. To prove this point we'll execute the same SQL CLR stored procedure `mspCalcJulianDateFromCurrentDate` from a VB6 application using classic ADO. The connection string is not remarkable, but the connection is a little different. In classic ADO the connection object was generic and didn't require a specific typing.

```
Set oConn = New Connection
oConn.connectionString = connectionString
oConn.Open
```

The remainder of the code can be cut and pasted behind a button with the name ADO in a VB6.0 form:

```
Private Sub ADO_Click()
    Dim oConn As ADODB.Connection
    Dim oCmd As ADODB.Command

    Dim mySQL As String
    Dim connectionString As String

    mySQL = "mspCalcJulianDateFromCurrentDate"
    connectionString = "Provider=SQLOLEDB.1;Integrated Security=" & _
        "SSPI;Persist Security Info=False;Initial Catalog=CLRTESTDB;Data" & _
        "Source=<<YOURSERVER>>\SQLExpress"

    Set oConn = New Connection
    oConn.connectionString = connectionString
    oConn.Open

    Set oCmd = New ADODB.Command
    oCmd.ActiveConnection = oConn
    oCmd.CommandText = mySQL
    oCmd.CommandType = adCmdStoredProc
    oCmd.Execute
    MsgBox "Updated", vbInformation, "Updated"
End Sub
```

Connection Conclusions

You'll notice that even though we are executing a SQL CLR stored procedure in each example, the data access code is the same as it would be for a T-SQL-based stored procedure. This is the greatest part of the SQL CLR architecture. This ease of integration means that outside of the development of the SQL CLR object themselves, using SQL CLR stored procedures, user-defined functions, types, and aggregates is seamless to the developers. It also means that existing T-SQL stored procedures can be reimplemented as SQL CLR stored procedures when there is a benefit without any impact to the existing code.

Console Apps and SQL CLR Extended Procs

Console applications are often used to jump-start the learning of a new language because you can isolate the language from the more complicated aspects of Windows management. There are also perfect application templates for command-line-based utilities. In Chapter 6, you learned how to use SQL CLR routines to develop some replacements for extended stored procedures. One of the procedures, named xmsp_writecsvfile, enabled the ability to pass in a T-SQL statement, a file name, and an overwrite-file flag. This procedure evaluates the T-SQL statement and produces a CSV file using the file name provided. Although this procedure can be useful from the SSMS environment to retrieve quick file exports, it could be useful as a command-line utility for simple SELECT statements. We'll build a command-line shell around the procedure to show how to integrate SQL CLR stored procedures into your console-based applications.

1. First, open a console application project in Visual Studio by selecting the Console Application template. If you haven't worked with Console applications before, you'll notice a default class with a `Main` function already defined. You'll also notice that the main function accepts a series of arguments into a string array called `args`. Use this string array to pass in the three arguments that you need to pass through to the SQL CLR stored procedure. You could pass in two additional arguments for the server and database names, but we'll hard code this connection for now and leave this enhancement up to you.

2. Within the `Main` function, you'll need to code the SQL Client objects to execute the stored procedure. In this example, we used parameters instead of building a T-SQL string like we did earlier in the "Using SQL CLR with SQL Client" section. To avoid repeating the same information, you can view the full code at the end of these steps.

3. Finally, we wrap the setting of the parameters and the execution of the stored procedure with a `Try...Catch` block that results in the streaming out of a usage message if any of the parameters can't be set or the stored procedure incurs an error during execution.

The final code looks like this:

```
using System;
using System.Collections.Generic;
using System.Text;
using System.Data.SqlClient;

namespace CSVFileGen
{
    class Program
    {
        static void Main(string[] args)
        {
            string connectionString = "Persist Security Info=False;" +
                    "Integrated Security=true;Initial Catalog=CLRTESTDB;" +
                    "server=<<PUT YOUR SERVER HERE>>\\SQLEXPRESS";

            using (SqlConnection sqlConn = new SqlConnection(connectionString))
            {
                sqlConn.Open();
                SqlCommand sqlCmd = sqlConn.CreateCommand();
                sqlCmd.CommandText = "xmsp_writecsvfile";
                sqlCmd.CommandType = System.Data.CommandType.StoredProcedure;
                try
                {
                    sqlCmd.Parameters.Add("@sqlSelect",
                            System.Data.SqlDbType.VarChar);
                    sqlCmd.Parameters["@sqlSelect"].Value = args[0].ToString();
                    sqlCmd.Parameters.Add("@fullFilePath",
                            System.Data.SqlDbType.VarChar);
                    sqlCmd.Parameters["@fullFilePath"].Value =
                            args[1].ToString();
                    sqlCmd.Parameters.Add("@sqlOverwrite",
                            System.Data.SqlDbType.Bit, 8);
                    sqlCmd.Parameters["@sqlOverwrite"].Value =
```

```
                        Convert.ToBoolean(args[2]);
            sqlCmd.ExecuteNonQuery();
        }
        catch (Exception)
        {
            Console.WriteLine("Usage: CSVFILEGEN " +
                "<SELECT STATEMENT>, <FULLFILEPATH>, <OVERWRITE>");
        }
    }
}
}
}
```

To run the console application, copy the `csvfilegen.exe` file into a directory like `c:\prosqlclr\chapter8\csvfilegen\`, and then call the program, passing in arguments for a T-SQL statement, output file, and overwrite flag. Figure 8-4 shows an example of using the console application once using the proper settings and then the second time what the results would be if the arguments are omitted. You can see that the Usage statement prints into the standard-out stream and the command window.

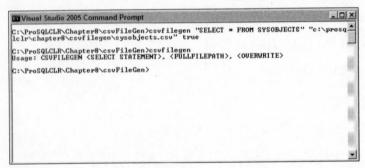

Figure 8-4

You should also find a CSV-formatted file in the directory named `sysobjects.csv` that looks something like this:

```
[name],[id],[xtype],[uid],[info],[status],[base_schema_ver],[replinfo],[parent_obj]
,[crdate],[ftcatid],[schema_ver],[stats_schema_ver],[type],[userstat],[sysstat],[in
dexdel],[refdate],[version],[deltrig],[instrig],[updtrig],[seltrig],[category],[cac
he]
sysrowsetcolumns,4,S ,4,0,0,0,0,0,10/14/2005 1:36:15 AM,0,0,0,S ,1,1,0,10/14/2005
1:36:15 AM,0,0,0,0,0,2,0
sysrowsets,5,S ,4,0,0,0,0,0,10/14/2005 1:36:15 AM,0,0,0,S ,1,1,0,10/14/2005 1:36:15
AM,0,0,0,0,0,2,0
...
```

Console applications that use SQL CLR stored procedures are probably a stretch, but we've shown in this section that it is possible to create a useful command-line utility out of one.

WinForms and SQL CLR UDTs

One of the least discussed (and perhaps rightly so) SQL CLR objects is user-defined types (UDTs). Even less apparent is how you would actually use them in an application. You may be surprised to find that you can't bind SQL Server UDTs to typed datasets or `TableAdapters`, or basically any designer for that matter. If you do, you'll see an error message that looks like Figure 8-5.

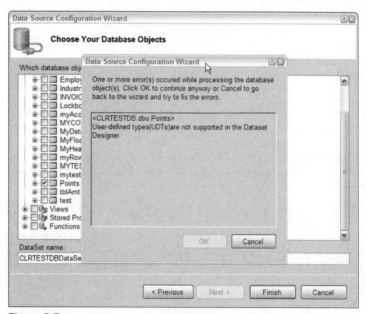

Figure 8-5

Fortunately, this is just a temporary issue that should be resolved when the next major version of SQL Server is released. This feature was removed from the CTP release because the SQL team just ran out of time while dealing with the complexities of implementing the binding of the UDT. However, this doesn't mean that it is not possible to load UDT values into a grid. You just have to do it the old-fashioned way. To get a taste of what this would involve, we'll create a Windows forms example that allows you to display some UDT values in a grid and add new values. For simplicity, we'll use the UDT for an (X,Y) point from the Books Online, so we can focus on the integration into the Windows form instead of the development of the UDT.

Creating the Point SQL CLR UDT

In the C# filtered section of the Books Online, look for the keywords "user-defined types [ADO.NET]." Under the subheading titled "creating," you'll find the complete code listings of VB.NET and C# versions of a point UDT. It is also listed later in this section, or you can download it from www.wrox.com. We'll use this code to quickly create a point UDT and populate a table with this new data type for our windows application.

1. First open a new SQL Server Database project template and connect to the CLRTESTDB database. Add a new User-Defined Type class to the project named point. Cut and paste the code listing from the Books Online completely over the code in the point UDT class in the project.

2. Save the project, so you know where it is located. Then compile and deploy the UDT.

3. Create a table named points that contains a UDT of type point and load it with some initial data. The T-SQL script to do this is:

```
Use CLRTESTDB
GO
--CREATES TABLE
CREATE TABLE dbo.Points
(ID int IDENTITY(1,1) PRIMARY KEY, PointValue Point)
GO
--INSERTS TWO TEST POINTS
INSERT INTO dbo.Points (PointValue) VALUES (CONVERT(Point, '3,4'));
INSERT INTO dbo.Points (PointValue) VALUES (CONVERT(Point, '1,5'));
```

Keep track of where you compiled the UDT into a DLL — it should be in the project directory under a subdirectory called \bin. You'll need this in the next step of building the Windows form.

Creating a Windows Form to Display a SQL CLR UDT

To view and add new points to your points table, you'll want to build a quick interface using the Windows application template. Create a new Windows application project. Add a dataviewgrid, two text boxes, and a button on a form. The look we are going for is shown in Figure 8-6.

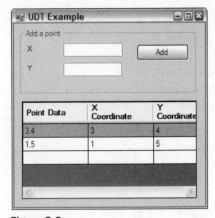

Figure 8-6

To load the dataviewgrid, you'll need to select the values from the points table. If you were to issue a SELECT statement directly on the points table and look at the raw contents of the fields, it might not look promising for the two default records that are already loaded.

```
SELECT * FROM POINTS
GO
```

The results would be:

```
ID          PointValue
-----------  --------------------
1           0x008000000380000004
2           0x008000000180000005
```

To get the point value to match the human-readable values of (3,4) and (1,5), you just need to cast the columns of the point UDT to a string value like this:

```
SELECT ID, CONVERT(Varchar, PointValue) as PointValue FROM points
```

This statement casts the points value to a string to look like this:

```
ID          PointValue
-----------  -----------------
1           3,4
2           1,5
```

What the Convert function does is use the ToString() method of the Point structure to convert the point value into a Varchar data type. SQL Server can do this because the structure definition for the Point UDT is loaded into SQL Server via the assembly. You have to decide whether you want to perform the casting in your application or in SQL Server. If you use the SELECT statement here, you will not need to perform casting in the application, but you'll need to prepare your SELECT statement to parse out the X and Y coordinates as well.

To be able to perform casting in your applications, you need to link to the Points SQL CLR assembly by browsing to the UDT point assembly and adding a reference to your application project. Note here that you aren't linking to a reference to the assembly that is loaded and hosted in SQL Server. You are actually referencing the file-based assembly in the debug\bin directory of your solution. Another thing that may be confusion is that you don't add the namespace to the code using the Point data type. This is because it isn't a class. It is a type. When the reference is added, the type is available for use. If you try to convert the PointValue column to a Point type within your application without a reference to the UDT definition, you'll get an error similar to this:

```
Could not load file or assembly 'PointUDT, Version=1.0.2378.42574, Culture=neutral,
PublicKeyToken=null' or one of its dependencies. The system cannot find the file
specified.
```

This is unusual because for all other SQL CLR objects, SQL Server completely wraps the assemblies and you do not have to be aware of implementation details. It is only because of the casting that your current project has to be aware of the type definitions and therefore you must include the reference in your project.

The other surprise that we mentioned earlier in this section is that you can't use the designers to snap the recordset with a SQL CLR UDT definition together with a GUI grid. This just means that you'll have to code this interaction the old-school way. For this sample project, we separated the construction of the DataViewGrid from the loading of the grid with two methods: SetUpDataGridView() and PopulateDataGridView(). The SetUpDataGridView() subrenders three columns in the grid to hold the point value represented by the X and Y coordinate pair, and separate columns for each X and Y value. Leaving all the formatting in the grid control at default values, the code to set up the `DataViewGrid` looks like this:

```
private void SetupDataGridView()
{
     pointsDataGridView.ColumnCount = 3;
     pointsDataGridView.Columns[0].Name = "Point Data";
     pointsDataGridView.Columns[1].Name = "X Coordinate";
     pointsDataGridView.Columns[2].Name = "Y Coordinate";
}
```

To populate the `DataGridView` with the `Point` UDT data, you'll build a `DataReader` and iterate through the reader to add each row. The columns will be populated by calling the `ToString()` methods for the UDT itself and the individual values of X and Y which are exposed as properties in the UDT. If you look back at the definition of the UDT, you'll see the properties exposed like this:

```
// X and Y coordinates exposed as properties.
// in Point UDT in Books Online
public Int32 X
{
     get
     {
          return this._x;
     }
     // Call ValidatePoint to ensure valid range of Point values.
     set
     {
          Int32 temp = _x;
          _x = value;
          if (!ValidatePoint())
          {
               _x = temp;
               throw new ArgumentException("Invalid X coordinate value.");
          }
     }
}
```

The code to populate the rows in the `DataViewGrid` looks like this:

```
private void PopulateDataGridView()
{
     using (SqlConnection sqlConn = new SqlConnection(connectionString))
     {
          sqlConn.Open();
          SqlCommand sqlCmd = sqlConn.CreateCommand();
          sqlCmd.CommandText = "SELECT PointValue FROM Points";
          sqlCmd.CommandType = CommandType.Text;
          SqlDataReader sqlDr = sqlCmd.ExecuteReader();
          pointsDataGridView.Rows.Clear();
          while (sqlDr.Read())
          {
               Point pnt = (Point)sqlDr[0];
```

```
            string[] row =
                    {pnt.ToString(), pnt.X.ToString(), pnt.Y.ToString() };
            pointsDataGridView.Rows.Add(row);
        }
    }
}
```

The code of interest occurs in the `while` loop of the `SqlDataReader`. Because you have the reference to the point UDT, it become a data type in .NET that is fully eligible for casting. The casting of the column to a `Point` SQL CLR UDT structure couples the data coming from SQL Server to the proper interpretation of an X and Y coordinate. It is then easy to access the point as a string or to separate the X and Y values of the coordinate using the SQL CLR UDT properties of X and Y. You can see that the building of the row only involves casting each value to a string for display purposes. You would use the same technique to push the values of X an Y into the text boxes for editing purposes. Let's look now at how you would save information from a Windows Form back into the SQL CLR UDT.

Accepting WinForm Input to Save a SQL CLR UDT

Since the `Point` SQL CLR UDT is defined as an X and a Y coordinate, you need to be able to accept both values to store them in SQL Server. Assuming that you've already created two text boxes to accept user input for the X and Y values, you'll just work backwards to cast these values as a `Point` SQL CLR UDT. Push them back into the database using an `INSERT` statement that looks like this:

```
INSERT INTO dbo.Points (PointValue) VALUES (CONVERT(Point, @newPoint))
```

Although we've used some examples where we build the string with input values, it is safer to use named parameters to reduce the chance of SQL injection. To look at how you can push the casting back into SQL Server, we are casting the value of the user input in the X and Y text boxes with a T-SQL `Convert` function. Load the parameter like this:

```
sqlCmd.Parameters["@newPoint"].Value = x.ToString() + "," + y.ToString();
```

The entire function to perform the task of adding a SQL CLR UDT `Point` would then load the parameter with the user input and build the `INSERT` statement to defer the `Point` casting like this:

```
        private void AddPoint(Int32 x, Int32 y)
        {
            string insertSQL = "INSERT INTO dbo.Points (PointValue) " +
                               "VALUES (CONVERT(Point, @newPoint))";

            using (SqlConnection sqlConn = new SqlConnection(connectionString))
            {
                sqlConn.Open();
                SqlCommand sqlCmd = sqlConn.CreateCommand();
                sqlCmd.CommandText = insertSQL;
                sqlCmd.CommandType = CommandType.Text;
                sqlCmd.Parameters.Add("@newPoint",SqlDbType.VarChar);
                sqlCmd.Parameters["@newPoint"].Value =
                                   x.ToString() + "," + y.ToString();
                sqlCmd.ExecuteNonQuery();
            }
        }
```

To wire the `AddPoint()` sub to the Add Button, you'd need to add code to the button to validate the user input and then pass the values to the sub, like this:

```
private void btnAdd_Click(object sender, EventArgs e)
{
    AddPoint(Convert.ToInt32(txtX.Text), Convert.ToInt32(txtY.Text));
    PopulateDataGridView();
}
```

A call to the `PopulateDataGridView()` method completes the add by refreshing the `DataGridView` with the newly added SQL CLR `Point` entry. This example shows that even though Visual Studio does not yet support the integration of SQL CLR UDTs through the designers, it is not too difficult to plug them into your development processes.

Web Forms and SQL CLR Aggregates

In Chapter 5, we compared T-SQL and SQL CLR capabilities, and you worked through a SQL CLR aggregate function that summarized only evenly divisible amounts in a column. If you haven't completed that example, see the section "T-SQL Data-Centric Built-Ins" in Chapter 5. SQL CLR UDF aggregates are more difficult to create than they are to use. Using a SQL CLR UDF aggregate is as simple as any other T-SQL-based aggregate. To put this aggregate to use, we'll use a common medium of a web form or web page to select data from a table for summarization and web presentation. Prepare the CLRTESTDB by adding a table to store some money and customer data by running this SQL Script:

```
create table Amounts(myAmt money, custname varchar(15))
insert into Amounts Select 10.12, 'CUST1'
insert into Amounts Select 5.59, 'CUST1'
insert into Amounts Select 3.33, 'CUST2'
insert into Amounts Select 6.06, 'CUST2'
```

What we'd like to do is show a summary of the evenly divisible amounts by customer. The SQL is trivial. We simply use the SQL CLR aggregate in the same way we would use a T-SQL data-centric function except that like all other user-defined functions, we have to specify the role along with the function name. The SQL summary query would look like this:

```
select custname, dbo.mfnSumEvenAmt(myAmt) as SumEvenAmounts
from Amounts
group by custname
```

To plug these results into a web form, you'll need to start a new web site project using an ASP.NET project template. A default ASPX page is built and opened for you. Drag and drop a `GridView` from the toolbox onto the `default.aspx` design surface. You'll be prompted to define a data source for the grid. Give it the name CLRTESTDB and then create or select a connection to the CLRTEST DB. The Configure Data Source Wizard will give you the option to select from an existing table or view or a custom SQL statement. Choose the custom SQL statement option. Then provide the SQL statement using the SQL CLR aggregate above so that the wizard looks like Figure 8-7.

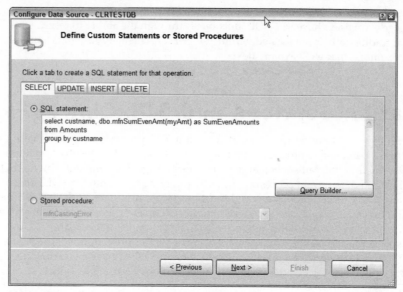

Figure 8-7

Walk through the rest of the wizard to complete the data source for the web form `datagrid`. The result is a web page named `default.aspx` with a `datagrid` where the source has been defined using a summary query with your SQL CLR user-defined aggregate. The page is ready to run and review. The easiest way to view the results immediately is to press the green arrow in the toolbar or use the menu option Debug ⇨ Start Debugging. The page will be compiled and then displayed to show the final results, as shown in Figure 8-8.

Figure 8-8

As you may realize, from an application standpoint, using SQL CLR functions and stored procedures is not much different from using T-SQL functions and stored procedures. You could use this aggregation in a web page, or just as easily in a reporting service. This is powerful, because now you have a way to have logic that can be used in a single value calculation and across sets. You can have logic that applies to reports and can be used within applications. One of the ways SQL CLR functions can really open up possibilities that we don't have in T-SQL functions is through the ability to return table-like structures for data that traditionally is not located within SQL Server. These atypical data sources provide some interesting examples that we'll explore next.

Integration Services and SQL CLR TVFs

SQL Server Integration Services (SSIS) are great for any ETL processes, and come with a robust data flow environment for parsing and processing text file information. Add to this the combination of the capabilities of SQL CLR, and you can supercharge your SSIS package development. You use SQL CLR objects to perform advanced parsing and processing tasks by plugging them into the SQL Execute tasks. This is just like using T-SQL stored procedures and functions to perform parts of the ETL processes. You could use SQL CLR functions to calculate and store complicated business hour calculations on time-sheet-based granular data or even to parse data pumped into single column storage locations. However, the real paradigm shift comes when you use SQL CLR to create new sources from unstructured data. To demonstrate, we'll take a real-world example of some data to import that was generated in a third-party application by exporting a PDF-formatted report file out to an unstructured text file.

A page of the text data contains some newly enrolled employee benefit information that looks like Figure 8-9.

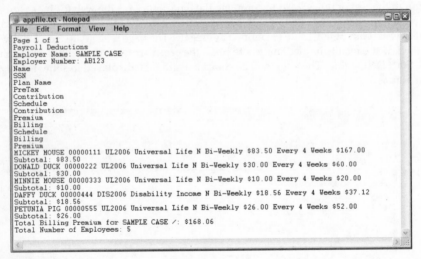

Figure 8-9

Above and below the data that we are interested in are column report headers and footers with subtotals that are not necessary. What we really want to extract is around the middle of the page. We want to pull out the employee name and benefit information to store in our database. It's obvious that the source data in its current form is unstructured in a way that will make it difficult to import straight into a database using SSIS. One way to approach this problem is to use the Flat File Source with the Ragged Right format to import the whole row as one column and then use the transform tasks to manipulate the file in memory until you end up with only the rows containing the benefit information. This technique is fine on a small file like this sample.

Another way to approach this problem is to use the powerful string-handling functions in the .NET BCL to consume the text file and produce parsed rows. Even better, produce only the rows that have value. SQL CLR provides a ready-made solution to requirements to consume data and parse out a set of rows in a table-valued SQL CLR function. A table-valued function is not only a construct that can produce a set of rows like a stored procedure, but it can also function as a data source that can be used in subsequent queries.

Building the SQL CLR TVF

SQL CLR TVFs have an advantage over the similar T-SQL construct in that the whole resultset doesn't have to be persisted into a table before results are returned to the caller. Conversely, SQL CLR TVFs are a streaming construct that uses an IEnumerable interface in conjunction with the SQL Query plan to pull rows as they are parsed instead of waiting until all rows are parsed. From the perspective of the application, data is available almost instantly, even with large files. To build a SQL CLR TVF, you need two things: an IEnumerable interface to iterate through the rows, and a parsing function to parse rows into meaningful attributes.

To start, you'll need to create a new SQL Server project and add a user-defined function class. Since you'll be accessing a file, you'll need to set the project permission set to External in the project property pages. (This may also mean that you'll need to set the database trustworthy level and the server-level security access to load and administer External Access assemblies. See Chapter 10 for more information.) Create a class within the UserDefinedFunction class that will handle reading the file line by line, called AppFileReader, which looks like this:

```
// This internal class reads an unstructured text file
// created from dumping pdf report contents and
// enumerates its contents using stream reader
public class AppFileReader : IEnumerable, IDisposable
{
    StreamReader appSr;

    //Constructor expects a file path reachable on
    //same machine as SQL Server
    public AppFileReader(string fullfilepath)
    {
        appSr = new StreamReader(fullfilepath);
    }

    public void Dispose()
    {
        if (appSr != null)
            appSr.Close();
    }

    //This enumerator provides the interface that the
    //TVF needs to return rows for parsing
    public IEnumerator GetEnumerator()
    {
        while (appSr.Peek() != -1)
        {
            string line = appSr.ReadLine();
            yield return line;
```

```
            }
        Dispose();
    }


}
```

The important thing to notice in this class is that it implements the IEnumerable interface through inheritance. If you were using a class like the EventLog class in the Books Online, the class already implements an IEnumerable contract, so there is no need to go through the trouble we have in this example. This is an area ripe for examples, since there are not many in the Book Online, so contribute your own when you get a handle on how this works. The actual implementation of the IEnumerable interface is the GetEnumerator function. This is the function called by the query plan the same way that each loop would be executed in a for...each loop in your application. In the GetEnumerator function, the Peek method reads forward to the next character to insure that you haven't read an EOF marker. If not, then the next whole line is copied into a string variable. This is not necessary normally, but we will later come back and alter this function to throw away lines that don't parse into high-value targets.

The actual TVF definition starts out with the SqlFunction decoration that names the function that will parse out the rows and a table definition that can be pasted by the deployment wizard into the T-SQL function definition. The function name will also be used by the Deployment Wizard, so we name it using a prefix that indicates that this is a managed-code-based function. Add the top part of the SQL CLR TVF so that it looks like this:

```
[Microsoft.SqlServer.Server.SqlFunction(FillRowMethodName = "ParseRow",
    TableDefinition="fullName NVARCHAR(MAX), empID NVARCHAR(MAX), " +
                    "billfreq NVARCHAR(MAX), basebillamt MONEY")]
public static IEnumerable mfnReadAppSourceData(string AppFilePath)
{
    return new AppFileReader(AppFilePath);
}
```

For this example, you may notice that only four of the attributes of the text file are being parsed. You can determine this because the table definition only contains information about the fullname, empid, billfreq, and basebillamt. This information comes from paring each text row in the function ParseRow. This function accepts a line and breaks it into tokens to determine if the row is one of the highly valued employee benefit records. The target rows look like this:

```
MICKEY MOUSE 00000111 UL2006 Universal Life N Bi-Weekly $83.50 Every 4 Weeks$167.00
```

The ParseRow function will be fed each line in the input stream. It will first break this line up into tokens by looking for spaces using the Split() method:

```
string[] tokens = line.Trim().ToLower().Split(' ');
```

Then because you have so many rows that are of no interest, you'll have to iterate through the text to find high-value target rows that match what you're looking for. Since all the rows that are of no interest have a limited subset of labels, the ParseRow function will ignore these known labels and rows if the label is the first token: tokens[0].

The `ParseRow` method needs to be added to the `UserDefinedFunctions` class as well. It should look like this:

```csharp
public static void ParseRow(object fileLine, out SqlString fullName,
        out SqlString empID, out SqlString billfreq, out SqlMoney basebillamt)
{
    string line = (string)fileLine;
    string[] tokens = line.Trim().ToLower().Split(' ');
    switch (tokens[0])
    {
        case "page":
        case "payroll":
        case "employer":
        case "name":
        case "ssn":
        case "plan":
        case "pretax":
        case "contribution":
        case "schedule":
        case "billing":
        case "premium":
        case "subtotal:":
        case "total":
            fullName = null;
            empID = null;
            billfreq = null;
            basebillamt = (SqlMoney)0.00;
            break;
        default:
            fullName = (SqlString)(tokens[1] + ", " + tokens[0]);
            empID = (SqlString)tokens[2];
            billfreq = (SqlString)tokens[7];
            basebillamt =
                    (SqlMoney)Convert.ToDecimal(tokens[8].TrimStart('$'));
            break;
    }
}
```

When the solution is built and deployed to the CLRTESTDB database, you can test the SQL CLR function by calling it directly using the SSMS query window. Provide the file location as a parameter. The T-SQL to test the SQL CLR TVF should look like this:

```sql
select *
from dbo.mfnReadAppSourceData('c:\prosqlclr\chapter6\appfile.txt')
```

A sample of the results (pulled down to show significant results) shows that we are getting a line back for every line in the text file, as shown in Figure 8-10.

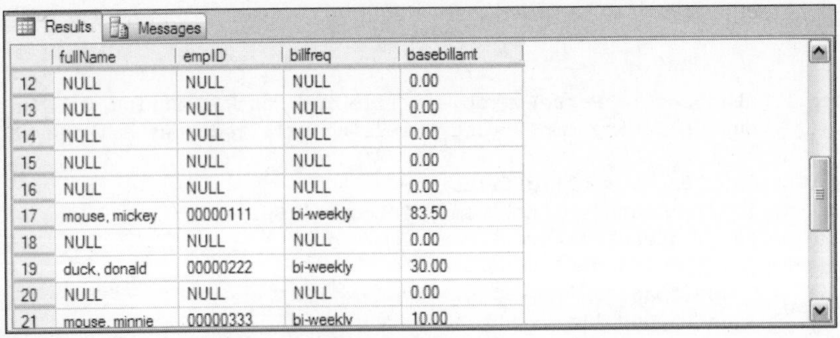

	fullName	empID	billfreq	basebillamt
12	NULL	NULL	NULL	0.00
13	NULL	NULL	NULL	0.00
14	NULL	NULL	NULL	0.00
15	NULL	NULL	NULL	0.00
16	NULL	NULL	NULL	0.00
17	mouse, mickey	00000111	bi-weekly	83.50
18	NULL	NULL	NULL	0.00
19	duck, donald	00000222	bi-weekly	30.00
20	NULL	NULL	NULL	0.00
21	mouse, minnie	00000333	bi-weekly	10.00

Figure 8-10

You could reduce this output by adding a T-SQL `WHERE` clause to only return rows where the value for an attribute like `EmpID` is not null, but this will require that all consumers of this SQL CLR function know to use the `WHERE` clause. However, it is worth looking at, because it is so unusual. Add the following `WHERE` clause to the T-SQL to test the SQL CLR TVF:

```
select *
from dbo.mfnReadAppSourceData('c:\prosqlclr\chapter6\appfile.txt')
Where empID is Not NULL
```

It is strange to see that you can query a text file and not only get results but also filter the results using SQL commands, as shown in Figure 8-11.

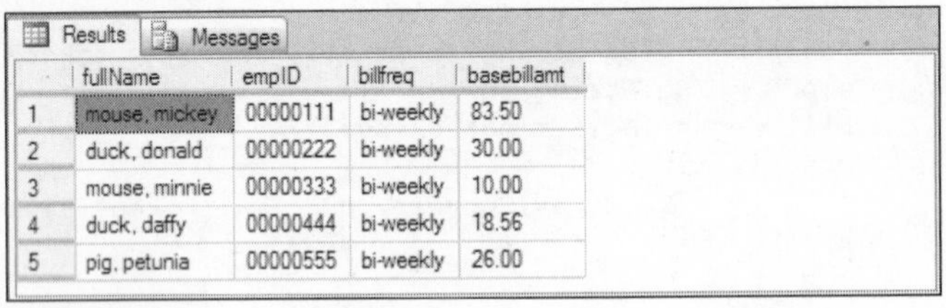

	fullName	empID	billfreq	basebillamt
1	mouse, mickey	00000111	bi-weekly	83.50
2	duck, donald	00000222	bi-weekly	30.00
3	mouse, minnie	00000333	bi-weekly	10.00
4	duck, daffy	00000444	bi-weekly	18.56
5	pig, petunia	00000555	bi-weekly	26.00

Figure 8-11

Again this is not the optimal solution, since it requires special knowledge to use the WHERE clause when using the SQL CLR TVF. What we really want to do is only show the high-value target rows, so it would be a better design to filter these rows out as we consume the text file. This can be done by moving some of the parsing logic from the parse function into the `AppFileReader` class. The resulting `AppFileReader` final `GetEnumerator` method will look like this:

```
//This enumerator provides the interface that the
//TVF needs to return rows for parsing
public IEnumerator GetEnumerator()
{
    while (appSr.Peek() != -1)
    {
        string line = appSr.ReadLine();
        string[] tokens = line.Trim().ToLower().Split(' ');
```

```
        switch (tokens[0])
        {
            case "page":
            case "payroll":
            case "employer":
            case "name":
            case "ssn":
            case "plan":
            case "pretax":
            case "contribution":
            case "schedule":
            case "billing":
            case "premium":
            case "subtotal:":
            case "total":
                break;
            default:
                yield return line;
                break;
        }
    }
    Dispose();
}
```

By rearranging the parsing and determination of whether the line is a high-value target during the enumeration, you avoid sending rows that are of no interest down to the parsing function. The results of modifying the enumeration function are the same as you achieved earlier by adding the WHERE clause to the test T-SQL statement. However, by rearranging the enumeration function, you don't require the WHERE clause to get the same results. Further, this solution doesn't require any outside knowledge of the application file to use the function and follows good design principles. You can leave the same parsing activity in the ParseRow or streamline the function to only deal only with well-identified rows.

Using the SQL CLR TVF in an SSIS Package

After compiling and redeploying your SQL CLR TVF to parse an unstructured employee benefits text file, you can integrate the data into an SSIS package that will import only the high-value rows. In an SSIS package, create a DataFlow task by dragging and dropping a DataFlow task on the design surface. Double-click the task to drill into the implementation details. What you'd like to do is add a source that can consume the file and produce some rows that you can work with. To plug in your SQL CLR TVF, you need a source that can consume the tabular data stream that is the result of your T-SQL command to SELECT everything from a known text file. The DataReader is a highly efficient consumer of rows, so use this as a data source. Since you need to do something with the data, you should use an OLE DB Destination transform to store the results of our text file parsing activity.

1. Drag and drop a DataReader Source and an OLE DB Destination transform onto the DataFlow design surface.

2. Set up a connection manager to your CLRTESTDB database instance in the Connection Managers tab. Use an ADO.NET connection manager wizard to create a connection.

3. Set the DataReader Source transform Connection Manager to the connection you just created.

4. Set the SQLCommand in the Component Properties tab to the following T-SQL:

```
select * from dbo.mfnReadAppSourceData('c:\prosqlclr\chapter6\appfile.txt')
```

5. Click the Column Mappings tab to have the data queried and mapped into the transform object. Click OK to save the settings in the DataReader source and connect the output to the input of the OLE DB Destination.

6. Set up a connection manager to your CLRTESTDB database using an OLE DB connection.

7. Open the OLE DB Destination transform and set the OLE DB connection to the new connection you created in the previous step. Keep the Data Access Mode to Table or View Fast Load and click the New button to define a Name of the Table or View. The columns should be populated from the DataReader source, but you'll need to give the destination table a name. Change the current table name of [OLE DB Destination] to something like AppData.

8. Click the Mapping property page to have the input and output columns mapped for data transport. Press OK to save your work.

At this point, your SSIS package is completed and is ready to run. When the SSIS package is run, five rows are parsed by the SQL CLR TVF into a set of rows that are consumed by the SSIS DataReader source and input into a table in the CLRTESTDB database, as shown in Figure 8-12. What at first seemed like a complicated task to parse and extract in SSIS is trivial when combined with the power of SQL CLR.

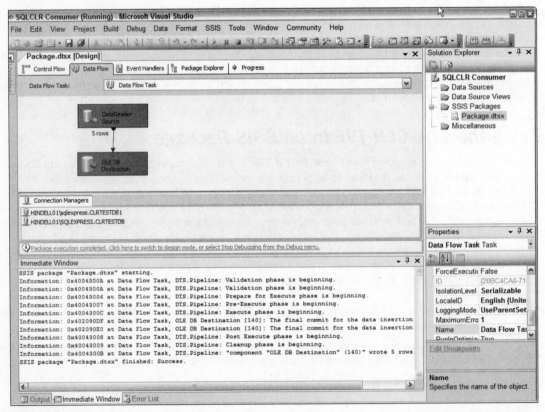

Figure 8-12

Reporting Services and SQL CLR TVFs

When you think of Reporting Services, you expect to be retrieving data to report into a tabular or matrix format. You may not see an immediate fit for SQL CLR as a data retrieval replacement for T-SQL stored procedures, but one way is to use SQL CLR to produce unusual data sources that previously would have been inaccessible from SQL Server. To get some mileage out of the SQL CLR TVF that you created previously with the SSIS package, we'll create a report for the benefits that are above $25.00 in base billing premium. Remember that this TVF is parsing unstructured data from a text file.

The easiest way to create a reporting service with SQL Server Reporting Services is to start a new Visual Studio 2005 project using the Business Intelligence project Report Server Project Wizard. This wizard will walk you through the connection to a SQL Server database, the selection of a data source, and the final formatting of a quick report. If you've worked with Active Data reports, Crystal Reports, or Access Reporting, this wizard will be very familiar.

When the wizard starts, provide a new data source name of "CLRTESTDB" to point to the CLRTESTDB instance. Click the Edit button to define how you expect the report to connect to the database. For this example, choose Windows Authentication. In the second step, set the query string the same as the SSIS example, but with a WHERE clause to filter the results on the basebillamt field to base billing premium greater than $25.00. When completed the results of this step should look like Figure 8-13.

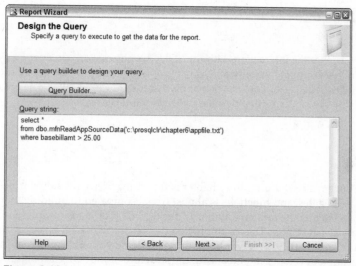

Figure 8-13

Continue through the wizard, allowing the default, a tabular report. Skip the grouping and sorting step. Select the default table style of Slate. Allow the default Report Server and Deployment folder settings. Click Finish to save the settings. A report will be created and loaded into your Visual Studio environment for editing. Without any further changes, you can click onto the preview button to get a preview of the report. It will look like Figure 8-14.

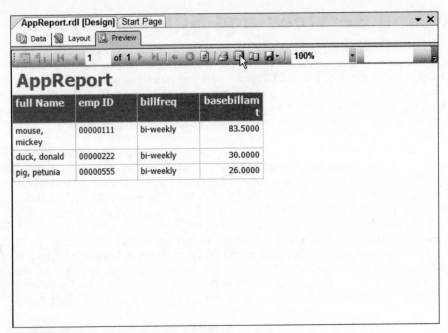

Figure 8-14

Again, you can see that the interaction with the SQL CLR object works in every way like a standard T-SQL object. In this example, not only are you able to easily integrate the SQL CLR object by calling the TVF using standard T-SQL, but you can also apply a standard WHERE filter. The amazing thing is that you can display this using Reporting Services with very little effort.

Summary

What you will have realized during this chapter is that using SQL CLR stored procedures and user-defined types, aggregates, and functions is almost trivial compared to building them. The important thing to remember is that the implementation of the SQL CLR object is completely different from the application that uses the object. The assembly that defines the SQL CLR object is loaded into SQL Server itself, and for the most part, SQL Server hides those implementation details from the application developer. The application developer interacts with the structure of the SQL CLR object using T-SQL so that the SQL CLR objects look and feel just like T-SQL objects. The only exception is when working with SQL CLR User-Defined Type objects, because you need the assembly to resolve type conversions within the application, but we've shown that this too, can be differed to the server. This all sounds well and good, but what happens when things go wrong? Errors can occur in the database, within the SQL CLR component, or in the Windows client. Take a look at Chapter 9 for a discussion of what to expect with error-handling issues in SQL CLR.

Handling Errors in CLR Stored Procedures

An error is an unexpected, unplanned event that occurs in the process of running code. Code in the context of SQL CLR development has us concerned with errors in two locations. First, we are concerned with the code that makes up both the SQL CLR and the T-SQL objects and how we should handle errors that occur within them. Second, we are concerned with how errors will be handled in a client that can be a middle tier, a data layer with no user interface, or a business- or UI-level interface. The issue is whether we should handle the error in the lowest levels of the hierarchy or send them up to the client to handle. It is common in the middle-tier levels to perform only minimal error handling. What do we do with SQL CLR objects? Do they act as a data access layer, or are these objects considered clients? If we do encounter errors in a SQL CLR procedure how do we communicate the details back to the logic that called it in the first place? What if a SQL CLR procedure calls a T-SQL procedure and a batch error occurs in the procedure? These issues are essential to understand if you are going to merge SQL CLR objects into your development architectures.

For a full discussion of error handling, we have to consider not only the error-handling environment of the CLR but also the native error handling of the T-SQL language and the SQL engine. These wide and varying error-handling mechanisms all interact within the context of SQL CLR development, and each handles errors a bit differently. Errors can be categorized into four distinct categories:

- **Design bugs:** These are errors where the code doesn't perform to specifications.

- **User errors:** Users are allowed to produce scenarios that create exceptions.

- **Recoverable exceptions:** An unexpected, temporary condition has occurred, that if resolved, can allow the user to reattempt the action and succeed. These can usually be resolved without the intervention of a DBA.

- **Unrecoverable exceptions:** An unexpected environmental condition has occurred that requires the intervention of a DBA to correct to continue.

If you understand how your SQL CLR objects react to each of these errors, then you can begin to develop a best practice for dealing with them. First, we'll examine the two error-handling mechanisms available in SQL Server 2005 and then the method used in .NET SQL CLR. We'll look at how these interact, since we'll be merging T-SQL objects with SQL CLR objects and calling them using other languages and technologies.

Exception-Handling Mechanisms Used in SQL CLR

An error that occurs within running SQL CLR code creates some unique troubleshooting issues. Because SQL CLR is hosted within SQL Server and can interact directly with the SQL engine, SQL exceptions can be generated as well as CLR-based exceptions. This can be even further complicated when T-SQL and SQL CLR objects are commingled. You may wonder how to determine where the error occurred. Is the error in the CLR-based object or within the depending T-SQL object? Before you get too far into building and deploying SQL CLR-based solutions, you should get a handle on the error-handling issues at each level in your architecture. In this section, we'll examine the exception-handling models for T-SQL, both old and new, and then the SQL CLR model, to give you an idea of the issues associated with each method.

How T-SQL @@Error Exception-Handling Works

If you have some older stored procedures, or other T-SQL objects that don't use the TRY...CATCH method in SQL Server 2005, you will encounter a nonstructured exception-handling method that uses the @@Error system variable. After each T-SQL statement executes, the SQL engine sets the value of this integer variable to 0 if the statement is successful or to an appropriate error code if not. The two biggest problems with this error-handling method are that the errors were too easily ignored and that it just doesn't work as advertised. These unexpected behaviors of how the error can be handled and the inconsistency of the rules of handling are the main focus of this section. If you are planning to integrate a T-SQL object with a CLR stored procedure, aggregate, or UDF, or if you are a developer who hasn't spent much time with T-SQL development, you'll want to review some of the common issues associated with T-SQL nonstructured error handling in this section. This knowledge will ensure that your SQL CLR objects interact the way you intend when an exception occurs.

The @@Error error-handling method is designed to work like a one-level, one-entry error stack. After each significant T-SQL statement, the value of @@Error can be set to a number. (The error number corresponds to a message in the sys.messages table.) This means that the @@Error variable needs to be checked after each T-SQL statement to determine if an error has occurred. Unfortunately, even checking the variable with an IF statement can reset @@Error to 0. This is a common mistake with new T-SQL programmers and can result in an error being mishandled or not handled. A best practice is to create and then set an intermediary variable to the value of @@Error before testing the value. Using this technique after every significant T-SQL statement, you can create effective error-handling strategies, even if they take up a substantial amount of redundant programming.

A close comparison to how we mentally expect this error management method to work can be found in classic ASP web development. In ASP, you could set the ON ERROR statement to RESUME NEXT, and then catch and handle errors after they had occurred. The method catches error and can be effective, but the weakness of this error-handling method in both instances is that it depends upon the developer to check the value of the error after each potential error-generating statement. If the error is not handled, the code simply resumes to the next line and the error is effectively absorbed into never-never land. T-SQL, prior to SQL2005, purports to support error handling in the same way, but doesn't exactly work as expected. To demonstrate this, you can develop a calculation procedure in T-SQL to handle a potential overflow situation like this:

```
CREATE TABLE test(billamount money)
GO
INSERT INTO test values(100)
INSERT INTO test values(200)
GO
CREATE PROC uspOverflowError(
        @MyInt AS tinyInt
        )
AS
    DECLARE @DEFAULTVALUE tinyint
    SET @DEFAULTVALUE=2
    SET @MyInt = @MyInt * 100   --<<generates overflow error
    IF @@Error <> 0
        SET @MyInt = @DEFAULTVALUE

    UPDATE test SET billamount = billamount * @myInt

    SELECT @MyInt as MyInt
GO
EXEC uspOverflowError 5
```

The procedure is set up to purposely generate an overflow error that you'd expect to be able to catch immediately in the following statement. In this example, the error is generated in the statement:

```
Set @myInt = @MyInt * 100
```

The error handling seems like it would catch the error and set the value of @MyInt to the default value in @DEFAULTVALUE. However, when this procedure runs in an SSMS query window the result looks like this:

```
Msg 220, Level 16, State 2, Procedure uspOverflowError, Line 7
Arithmetic overflow error for data type tinyint, value = 300.
(2 row(s) affected)
```

It looks like you've got an error, but two rows (the number of rows in the test table) are updated. The contents of the rows have changed to two times the original values:

```
billamount
--------------------
1000.00
2000.00
```

The error handling worked — well, sort of — but not the way we expected. You get the behavior of the error handling as evidenced by the return of the value 10 for MyInt along with the changes to the test table. The problem is the procedure still returned the SQL error. We did not expect to get an error at all. Client code in C# that calls this T-SQL procedure will also generate the SQL error shown in Figure 9-1.

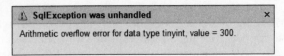

Figure 9-1

We just don't expect a handled error like this one on the server to result in an error propagated to the client. This is one of the reasons that T-SQL error handling has been so dubious. Many developers, upon encountering this behavior, just hope for the best and don't bother to check the value of the @@Error variable. This can create a new set of logical database errors. Consider the following T-SQL code that doesn't bother to handle an error. Here the intent is to make an insert into a header table and use the identity to create an entry in a detail table. It is not a good practice to perform such activity without a transaction, but this demonstrates the dangers of ignoring errors. Between the insertion of the header and the detail record we'll purposely generate an error and see what happens.

```
CREATE PROC uspHeaderDetailError(
      @HeaderAttrib as varchar(50)=NULL,
      @DetailAttrib as varchar(50)=NULL
      )
AS
    DECLARE @MYHEADERID as int
    INSERT INTO myheadertable SELECT @HeaderAttrib
    SET @MYHEADERID = Scope_Identity()
    SELECT @MyHeaderID
    INSERT INTO myDetailTable SELECT @MyHeaderID, @DetailAttrib
go
EXEC uspHeaderDetailError NULL, 'MYDETAILATTRIB'
```

The results look like this:

```
Msg 515, Level 16, State 2, Procedure uspHeaderDetailError, Line 7
Cannot insert the value NULL into column 'MyHeaderAttrib', table
'CLRTESTDB.dbo.MyHeaderTable'; column does not allow nulls. INSERT fails.
The statement has been terminated.
```

If our ASP comparison holds up, and we are in a ON ERROR RESUME NEXT mode, you might expect that during the insert into MyHeaderTable and after encountering the first error, that the T-SQL code would continue to run and insert into MyDetailTable. You would be right. Now there is an orphaned row in the MyDetailTable (see Figure 9-2).

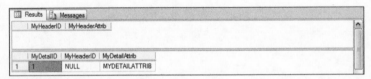

Figure 9-2

The fact that unchecked errors like these can wreck havoc on relational databases is one of the main reasons that the SQL engine does not really follow the method of ON ERROR RESUME NEXT. Upon encountering an error, SQL Server will opt in certain conditions to execute what is called an *abort*. The abort action stops the execution of the T-SQL at some level that depends upon the severity of the error. The SQL engine can generate statement-level aborts, which are the nature of the two examples you've seen so far. In these scenarios, the subsequent statements in a batch are allowed to continue, but the error is propagated regardless of how you attempt to handle the error. This behavior ensures that the calling code is aware that an error occurred during the processing of a multi-statement batch.

The SQL engine can go further than just killing an offending T-SQL statement. SQL has the ability to abort transactions, roll back transactions automatically, kill a connection, or even shut down a server under severe conditions. This type of abort is called a batch-level abort and is perhaps the most common abort type. When you get this type of problem at the batch level, it effectively terminates all further batch activity. This means that you won't have a chance to react to the error at all, regardless of your efforts to use error handling. For those who want to write purposeful code, it is frustrating to try to predetermine which errors do and don't result in batch-level aborts. Books Online states that you should be able to trap and handle errors with severity codes from 11 to 16, but this is not consistent. As you can see in this table, many of the common errors that occur during runtime with levels of severity in these ranges result in batch aborts. What's even more confusing is that some of the same types of errors produce different levels of batch aborts. Look at the two messages for error code 241 and 242. Both are for datetime value conversion errors, but one leads to a statement abort, the other to a batch-level abort.

Abort	Error ID	Severity	Message
Batch*	27	15	A TOP N value may not be negative
Batch*	155	15	'%.*ls' is not a recognized %ls option
Statement*	201	16	Procedure or function '%.*ls' expects parameter
Batch*	206	16	Operand type clash: %ls is incompatible with . . .
Batch*	208	16	Invalid object name '%.*ls'.
Batch*	209	16	Ambiguous column name '%.*ls'.
Batch*	213	16	Insert Error: Column name or number of supplied values does not match table definition.
Statement*	220	16	Arithmetic overflow error for data type %ls, . . .
Statement	229	16	%ls permission denied on object '%' . . .
Batch*	235	16	Cannot convert a char value to money.
Batch*	241	16	Conversion failed when converting datetime from character string.
Statement	242	16	The conversion of a char data type to a datetime data type resulted in an out-of-range datetime
Batch*	245	16	Conversion failed when converting the % value
Batch*	297	16	The user does not have permission to perform this action.

Table continued on following page

Abort	Error ID	Severity	Message
Statement*	313	16	An insufficient number of arguments were supplied for the procedure or function `%.*ls`.
Statement*	8134	16	Divide by zero error encountered.
Batch*	8170	16	Insufficient result space to convert `uniqueidentifier` value to `char`.

* Errors that can be handled either in SQL 2005 during compile, recompile, or in TRY . . . CATCH.

An awareness of this behavior can help you to develop more robust code. For example, you can check the value of a @TOPX variable to ensure that it is not negative to avoid error number 127.

This section demonstrates some of the pitfalls in the error-handling mechanisms that you may encounter when integrating some of your legacy T-SQL code with SQL CLR. This error handling doesn't always work in a way most procedural languages do and is certainly not an elaborate method. Because of the batch-abort and statement-abort mechanisms, the T-SQL objects using this method are not always going to be able to gracefully handle errors. This adds an extra expectation that needs to be built into the calling stack. If you are interacting with legacy T-SQL objects within SQL CLR, your objects will interact as clients, so you'll need to be ready to process errors. If you understand the limitations of how T-SQL deals with errors using the nonstructured error handling, you'll be able to design better SQL CLR objects. We'll get to that interaction later in this chapter.

How T-SQL Try . . . Catch Error-handling Works

SQL 2005 introduced the structured error-handling mechanism of TRY . . . CATCH. Not only is this construct more robust than the older @@Error handling method (which still exists), but it also more closely parallels the same constructs in the CLR-based languages. This structure is more robust because it provides the opportunity to catch most exceptions (but not all) that occur during runtime that before may have resulted in batch aborts. This method is also easier to implement because you don't have to check every T-SQL statement that might generate an error, and you can instead group statements into blocks of code that can be handled for errors. Because TRY . . . CATCH error handling is easier to implement, and it is more likely to be used by T-SQL developers, and T-SQL code will benefit by producing behavior that is more consistent and predictable.

Functionally, there are two logic blocks in this method: a TRY block that wraps code that could potentially produce an exception, and a CATCH block that is only called if an exception occurs within the TRY block. The TRY . . . CATCH block differs from CLR-based constructs in that there is no FINALLY block. The first T-SQL statement after the CATCH block is called by default and performs the same purpose. If the CATCH block is the last statement, then control returns to the calling client. To implement a protected block of T-SQL code, it must be wrapped in BEGIN TRY and END TRY statements. At first, it seems like the block should follow the T-SQL format of the IF statement. For example, you might think the TRY statement should be blocked by a BEGIN . . . END like this:

```
--THIS IS NOT HOW TRY...END STATEMENTS WORK
--BUT IS A COMMON MISPERCEPTION
TRY
BEGIN
```

```
--..DO SOMETHING
END
```

It makes sense when you realize that the BEGIN TRY block is just another flavor of a BEGIN...END block and should look like this:

```
--CORRECT IMPLEMENTATION OF TRY...END
    BEGIN TRY
        --DO SOMETHING...
    END TRY
```

The difference between the two blocks is that you get the additional benefit of error handling with the TRY...END blocks. Just like a BEGIN...END block, you have the ability to execute many T-SQL statements within the block. The same goes for the CATCH block, but the code isn't activated unless a trappable error occurs in the TRY block. So how does it work? Think back to the overflow example. You attempted to catch the error using the @@Error variable, but the error message printed anyway. The following example code is the same stored procedure, rewritten using the BEGIN TRY...END block.

```
CREATE PROC uspOverflowErrorTryCatch(
            @MyInt AS tinyInt
            )
AS
    DECLARE @DEFAULTVALUE tinyint
    SET @DEFAULTVALUE=2
    BEGIN TRY
        SET @MyInt = @MyInt * 100  --<<generates overflow error
    END TRY
    BEGIN CATCH
        SET @MyInt = @DEFAULTVALUE
    END CATCH
    UPDATE test SET billamount = billamount * @myInt
    SELECT @MyInt as MyInt
go
EXEC uspOverflowErrorTryCatch 5
```

The results look like this:

```
MyInt
-----
  2
```

This is the result that you were after in the first place. The TRY block gives you a chance to trap the error, and you can resolve the error in a way that you choose within the CATCH block. In this case, you provided a new value of @MyInt=2 when an overflow error occurred. The value of @MyInt is displayed as proof.

There still are a few situations that will continue to create noncatchable events, or statement aborts, even with the TRY...CATCH method. One situation occurs because the T-SQL compile processes don't perform a deep compile to verify object dependencies. This makes it possible to create a T-SQL object that syntatically compiles but will not execute. This type of error will result in a batch statement abort, and we want this to happen. The following stored procedure written for a table that doesn't exist is an example of this.

```
CREATE PROCEDURE uspNonExistingTableTryCatch
AS
BEGIN TRY
    PRINT 'IN TRY'
    DECLARE @MYDATA as varchar(10)
    SET @MYDATA = 'THIS INFO'
    UPDATE MYNONEXISTINGTABLE
    SET MYNONEXISTINGCOLUMN = 1
END TRY

BEGIN CATCH
    PRINT 'CAUGHT AN ERROR'
END CATCH
GO
EXEC uspNonExistingTableTryCatch
```

The table MYNONEXISTINGTABLE in the update statement portion of the procedure doesn't exist.

```
UPDATE MYNONEXISTINGTABLE
SET MYNONEXISTINGCOLUMN = 1
```

We set up the TRY...END block around this statement to catch the error that should occur when the SQL engine attempts to execute this update statement against a table that is not in the database. When you run this stored procedure, the catch block is never accessed. Look back to the error and abort table cross-reference. As you learned earlier, error number 208 is a batch-level abort error, which results in the termination of the batch. Because the batch terminated, there is no amount of error catching that is going to help you in that situation. To SQL Server, a batch-level abort is the equivalent of a DBA killing your database connection. From this explanation, you can see why SQL Server doesn't allow you to continue regardless of your error-handling coding skills. This is where an understanding of the nonstructured error handling of T-SQL provides the insight you need to prepare for the limitations of TRY...CATCH. The result of running the proc is shown here:

```
IN TRY
Msg 208, Level 16, State 1, Procedure uspNonExistingTableTryCatch, Line 5
Invalid object name 'MYNONEXISTINGTABLE'.
```

Notice that the print statement after the BEGIN TRY block prints. This indicates that the error occurred during the recompilation step of executing the stored procedure. You can easily see where the error occurs by running the SQL profiler to see that the last action taken is SP:Recompile. This shows the limitation of the initial syntax compile process and what can happen in the real world, if a view or table is removed or renamed unexpectantly. Any calling code accessing those objects will have to be able to handle the batch abort error. A strategy to overcome this is to organize your code differently. You can easily handle this type of potential error as long as the calling code is in a separate batch from the code that can incur the batch abort, like this:

```
BEGIN TRY
    EXEC uspNonExistingTableTryCatch
END TRY

BEGIN CATCH
    PRINT 'CAUGHT AN ERROR.  NO BATCH ABORT'
END CATCH
```

The results look like this:

```
IN TRY
CAUGHT AN ERROR.  NO BATCH ABORT
```

Notice that since the error occurs within the `uspNonExistingTableTryCatch` proc, you pass to a separate T-SQL object than the rest of the code. The batch abort then occurs in the called procedure, or batch. The calling code is not aborted and can easily recover and handle the error. Although this is a legitimate strategy for dealing with potential batch abort situations, breaking up code into separate T-SQL objects or batches is not always going to be a practical solution.

The good news is that most of the previous batch abort situatations can be caught in the `CATCH` block. In the previous error table these items are marked with an (*) to denote that they can either be handled in a `TRY...CATCH` method or fall into other situations that can be caught during syntax compiling and initial testing. The remaining errors occur during the recompiling process and are a result of changes to schema or environment or are errors that are currently thought of as unrecoverable and continue to generate aborts. This is perhaps not the best way for SQL to respond, but it is an understandable method. There is a current school of thought that SQL should allow developers to `CATCH` some of these errors, particulary errors that occur during the recompile aborts.

The best thing about the new `TRY...CATCH` method is the new `Error_Number()` function doesn't reset just because a T-SQL statement was run. There is no need to create an additional variable and waste time storing the error code or complicating a stored procedure. The `Error_Number()` function continues to return the last error code until you reach a new `CATCH` block that is either nested within, or outside the scope of the original `CATCH` block. What's even more remarkable for us T-SQL programmers is that the error code is persisted and continues to be so even if you transfer control to a new T-SQL object. The example procedure shown here, called `uspReportErrorInfo`, reports error details that would not be possible using the `@@Error` handling methods.

```
CREATE PROC uspNestedErrorsTryCatch
AS
BEGIN TRY
    DECLARE @MYTOP INT
    SET @MYTOP = -1
    SELECT TOP (@MYTOP)* FROM SYS.MESSAGES --<<Generates Error 127
END TRY
BEGIN CATCH
    BEGIN TRY
        exec uspReportErrorInfo --<<Reports Error 127
        SELECT 1/0 --<<Generates Error
    END TRY
    BEGIN CATCH
        exec uspReportErrorInfo --<<Reports Error 8134
    END CATCH
END CATCH
GO
--SEPARATE PROCEDURE THAT RETURNS DETAILED ERROR INFORMATION
CREATE PROC uspReportErrorInfo
AS
    SELECT
        ERROR_NUMBER() AS ErrorNumber,
        ERROR_SEVERITY() AS ErrorSeverity,
```

```
        ERROR_STATE() AS ErrorState,
        ERROR_PROCEDURE() AS ErrorProcedure,
        ERROR_LINE() AS ErrorLine,
        ERROR_MESSAGE() AS ErrorMessage
GO
EXEC uspNestedErrorsTryCatch
```

If you run the `uspNestedErrorsTryCatch` procedure, you'll see all the error details (shown in Figure 9-3), even though they are being reported in a separate procedure. Notice that not only are the error number and description reported, but also information about the procedure and the line within the procedure is available.

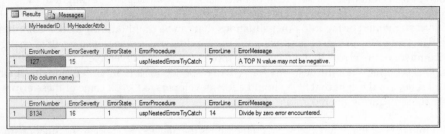

Figure 9-3

This is the real improvement in SQL 2005 error-handling methodology. Not only do you have a better exception-catching mechanism to reduce the number of batch aborts, but you can also reduce the amount of code you previously needed to cut and paste throughout a lengthy stored procedure. These features enable your T-SQL code to become more uniform and robust. We'll use this ability to maintain awareness of error state later as we develop an error-handling strategy for SQL CLR objects. If you are building stored procedures that use T-SQL code with the `TRY...CATCH` error-handling mechanisms, you can expect that the code will be able to handle most exceptions elegantly.

How .NET Structured Error-Handling Works

The method of error handling in SQL CLR is the same as that of .NET CLR. The code is similar syntactically to the T-SQL TRY...CATCH method in SQL Server 2005, and the try and catch blocks function fundamentally the same. You'll also notice an additional finally block, which contains code that always executes regardless of whether an exception is thrown, or even if an exception is thrown in the try that is not caught.

```
try
{
    // Code that may generate an error.
}
catch (SqlException sqlex)
{
    // Code to handle sqlclient-specific exceptions here.
}
catch (System.Exception ex)
{
    // Code to handle general system exceptions here.
```

```
}
finally
{
    // Code to execute after try and/or catch here.
}
```

The biggest difference in this exception-handling model is that .NET throws (or raises) specialized error type structures called *exception classes* rather than relying on setting, retrieving, and responding to a global error code. These exception classes are based on a core exception class called System.Exception. You"ll find exception classes in each .NET assembly that are specific to the assembly. For file-oriented activities, you'll find exceptions classes like DirectoryNotFoundExceptions and EndofStreamExceptions. You'll find exceptions for data access activities depending upon the access method you are using. There are specific exceptions like OleDBExceptions for OLE DB, DataExceptions for ADO.NET, and SqlExceptions for SQL Client. The power of the exception class is that it can contain more than just error information. Error classes can also encapsulate and centralize actions such as logging and other needs of specific frameworks. This means SQL CLR error handling is practically not even the same thing as the TRY...CATCH method of T-SQL. The code below shows that not just an error is raised, but a unique error class of type System.DivideByZeroException.

```
Int32 i, j;
double z;
i = Convert.ToInt32(integer1.Text);
j = Convert.ToInt32(integer2.Text);
try
{
    z = i / j;
    Result.Text = Convert.ToString(z);
}
catch (Exception ex)
{
    Console.WriteLine("Error of type: " + ex.GetType().ToString());
}
```

The results you'd see from this code look like this:

```
Error of type: System.DivideByZeroException
```

This model requires a fundamentally different approach that you may not be familiar with if you are a T-SQL programmer. Your error-handling designs in .NET typically do not look for specific error codes but respond instead to the type of exception that is thrown. You can think of the error-catching mechanism like a T-SQL CASE statement that can evaluate multiple similar, but distinct, error structures. This is why the .NET version of the try...catch can have multiple catch statements that listen for different types of exceptions. Catch statements can catch specific or general exceptions, as opposed to the T-SQL CATCH block, which is activated in response to an error state. The advantage of being able to specifically catch exceptions is that you don't have to turn around and test the error code to determine what action to take. You know by the catch statement what type of exception you are dealing with. Here are a few housekeeping rules to remember when working with catch:

❑   The first applicable catch statement that can handle the exception will be selected by the runtime. So, make sure you code the more specific exceptions first.

❑　　Don't catch an exception that you don't have a reasonable response for, unless you intend to throw a new exception to the next handler.

❑　　Don't catch an exception and do nothing with it.

One of the reasons that .NET error handling is so different from T-SQL error handling has to do with what type of errors you can expect to get in T-SQL versus .NET. Sometimes we forget what error handling means. It doesn't mean we have to handle every error. Instead, it is a facility that we use when there is a possibility of an error occurring to which we have a valid response. An example of responding to an unacceptable condition without relying of an error-handling mechanism is replacing NULL values with zeros, or automatically truncating string that are too long. If you suspect an exception and can plan ahead, these techniques are far preferred over using error-handling techniques to detect the error and then responding to the event. Error handling is an expensive activity and should only be used for unexpected errors. In the database arena, when working within a discrete context of updating and retrieving data, an error should be considered an event considered unrecoverable. This is why the T-SQL CATCH is so generalized. If any error occurs in T-SQL, the idea is to clean up the environment. When you start going beyond basic data access and programming stored procedures and SQL CLR objects, the need to be able to respond to known conditions, even error conditions, becomes more specialized.

In .NET code you should attempt, if at all possible, to catch the most specific error exception possible. Unexpected or specialized exceptions should simply be thrown up to the next error handler. Throwing an error is the same thing as sending the pesky neighborhood kid to the next house. You are not sure what to do with him, so you pass him to the next house on the block. You can pass information about an error in .NET by throwing the exception with the throw command, as in these examples:

```
throw new DivideByZeroException ();
throw new DivideByZeroException ("SOMETHING BAD HAPPENED!");
throw new DivideByZeroException ("SOMETHING BAD HAPPENED!", ex);
```

These exceptions are shown in each of the overloads available for the exception constructor. You have the choice of throwing a brand-new exception, a new exception with a custom exception message, or a combination of your message and the exception that occurred in the first place. When you throw an exception like this, you are adding an error to a stack of errors. This stack is called the *calling stack*, and it will be *unwound*, or interpreted, by the calling code. Typically, the calling code catches the exception as a general exception, because at this level you can't be expected to know the exact type of exceptions that lower-level logic could encounter. You wouldn't want to enumerate all of the possibilities either. If you pass the exception that occurs in the lower levels, like the last throw statement above, you can retrieve the detailed information later for troubleshooting purposes. To see how this works, create a .NET Windows console application and use this code in the main function of the Program class:

```
static void Main(string[] args)
{
    try
    {
        GenError(0);
    }
    catch (Exception ex)
    {
        Console.WriteLine(ex.ToString());
    }
    Console.WriteLine("Press Enter to continue...");
```

```
        Console.Read();

        //Add GenError Method here...
    }
```

Create a function like this and add it to the `Program` class, so you can use it to generate exceptions for a divide-by-zero error.

```
    public static void GenError(int x)
    {
        try{int i = 32/x;}
        catch(DivideByZeroException ex)
        {
            throw new DivideByZeroException();
        }
    }
```

Now, run the console application. The next three exception messages demonstrate the differences in the error messages that the caller retrieves from the call stack if you change the exception handler to use each of the three `throw` methods above.

```
//throw new DivideByZeroException()
"System.DivideByZeroException: Attempted to divide by zero.
at ErrorTest.Program.GenError(Int32 x)
    in C:\\PROSQLCLR\\ErrorTest\\Program.cs:line 32
at ErrorTest.Program.Main(String[] args)
    in C:\\PROSQLCLR\\ErrorTest\\Program.cs:line 14"

//throw new DivideByZeroException("SOMETHING BAD HAPPENED!")
"System.DivideByZeroException: SOMETHING BAD HAPPENED!
at ErrorTest.Program.GenError(Int32 x)
    in C:\\PROSQLCLR\\ErrorTest\\Program.cs:line 32
at ErrorTest.Program.Main(String[] args)
    in C:\\PROSQLCLR\\ErrorTest\\Program.cs:line 14"

//throw new DivideByZeroException("SOMETHING BAD HAPPENED!")
"System.DivideByZeroException: SOMETHING BAD HAPPENED!
---> System.DivideByZeroException: Attempted to divide by zero.
at ErrorTest.Program.GenError(Int32 x)
    in C:\\PROSQLCLR\\ErrorTest\\Program.cs:line 29\r\n
--- End of inner exception stack trace ---
at ErrorTest.Program.GenError(Int32 x)
    in C:\\PROSQLCLR\\ErrorTest\\Program.cs:line 32\r\n
at ErrorTest.Program.Main(String[] args)
    in C:\\PROSQLCLR\\ErrorTest\\Program.cs:line 14"
```

Notice that the exception description is delivered in the order that the exception occurs. The first error on the stack occurs at the top. In each of the first two examples, you don't get any information about the exception that occurred within the `GenError` method. The last example shows details that include the line number of the code that caused the error. You can see that detail because you specifically threw the exception back up to the caller. Another cheaper and common way to send this information to the caller is by sending only the string contents of the exception. This can be done like this:

```
throw new DivideByZeroException(ex.ToString());
```

269

Another difference from T-SQL and .NET that may cause some initial trouble is variable scoping within the `try`, `catch`, and `finally` blocks. Variables created within these blocks are scoped specifically to these blocks. The following code would not compile because the `sqlCmd` object doesn't exist outside the `try` block:

```
try
{
    SqlCommand sqlCmd = sqlConn.CreateCommand();
}
catch (SqlException sqlex)
{
    throw new Exception("out of scope example", sqlex);
}
finally
{
    sqlCmd.Dispose();--<<Doesn't exist/out of scope
}
```

It is evident that these three error-handling methodologies: `@@Error`, `TRY...CATCH`, and `try/catch/finally` vary in complexity and capabilities. When building SQL CLR objects, it will be increasingly common to encounter a interaction with one or more of these methods. As a result of going over each method, this will make more sense as we put together a comprehensive strategy for handling errors within SQL CLR objects.

How SQL CLR Error Handling Works

SQL CLR objects are unique in the type of exceptions that can be generated to software or processes that use them. The error-handling mechanisms are born from the .NET language that you build them in, but hosting the assemblies in SQL Server exposes the code to errors that can occur in dependent T-SQL objects or in the SQL engine itself. Take a simple stored procedure that can generate a divide-by-zero error with no error handler:

```
[Microsoft.SqlServer.Server.SqlProcedure]
public static void msp_DivideByZero(SqlInt32 myNumerator,
                                    SqlInt32 myDenominator)
{
    SqlContext.Pipe.Send(Convert.ToString
            ((SqlDouble)myNumerator /(SqlDouble)myDenominator));
}
```

If you call the stored procedure with the T-SQL EXEC command with invalid arguments, you get a distinctly T-SQL-like error response:

```
EXEC msp_DivideByZero 'ABC', '123'
```

The resulting error response is:

```
Msg 8114, Level 16, State 1, Procedure msp_DivideByZero, Line 0
Error converting data type varchar to int.
```

If you execute the statement to trip the divide by zero exception, you again get a T-SQL-like error response but it reports a general error in the .NET Framework.

```
Msg 6522, Level 16, State 1, Procedure msp_DivideByZero, Line 0
A .NET Framework error occurred during execution of user defined routine or
aggregate 'msp_DivideByZero':
System.DivideByZeroException: Divide by zero error encountered.
System.DivideByZeroException:
    at System.Data.SqlTypes.SqlDouble.op_Division(SqlDouble x, SqlDouble y)
    at StoredProcedures.msp_DivideByZero(SqlInt32 myNumerator, SqlInt32
myDenominator)
```

The first six items in the error message correspond to the new error functions in T-SQL 2005. The last item looks like a stack but is actually the contents of the `Error_Message()` function. In essence, this .NET-built SQL CLR routine is generating a `SqlException`. To prove it, create a quick .NET app to call this procedure and code it to catch a general exception and print to the console the value of ex.GetType().ToString(). It will return the type as `System.Data.SqlClient.SqlException`.

This seems unusual, not only because it returns a `SqlException`, but because it returns a managed exception at all. Nowhere in the .NET implementation did you implement error handling. So, how did you get such a structured error? When you load an assembly into SQL Server the method specifier `"AS EXTERNAL NAME"` marks the procedure as a SQL CLR procedure. A T-SQL prototype is built to provide a T-SQL-based access point to the CLR function. When the T-SQL prototype is executed, the SQL engine wraps the whole call to the CLR function in a T-SQL-based managed error handler. So, if the SQL CLR code generates an exception, it is caught by the server in the auto-provided `TRY...CATCH` block and thrown as a `SqlException`. Even if you attempt to put a `try/catch` block into the SQL CLR procedure to rethrow the `System.DivideByZeroException`, you'll still get a `SqlException`.

```
[Microsoft.SqlServer.Server.SqlProcedure]
public static void msp_DivideByZero
                (SqlInt32 myNumerator, SqlInt32 myDenominator)
{
    try
    {
        SqlContext.Pipe.Send(Convert.ToString
                    ((SqlDouble)myNumerator / (SqlDouble)myDenominator));
    }
    catch (System.DivideByZeroException ex)
    {
        throw new System.DivideByZeroException("Denominator", ex);
    }
}
```

No matter what you do inside of the SQL CLR code, the result is going to be a thrown `SqlException`. This is because of the wrapped managed exception handler added automatically by the SQL Engine when the code is first executed. Since SQL CLR is hosted inside of SQL Server, it makes sense that errors thrown by the SQL CLR objects are seen as errors in a format that is native to SQL Server. Currently, the SQL Engine dumbs down all errors generated from SQL CLR object with one error message in sys.messages:

```
6522-A .NET Framework error occurred during execution of user defined routine or
aggregate '%.*ls': %ls.
```

The only exceptions, no pun intended, to SQL CLR objects throwing a `SqlException` class is when the SQL Engine itself throws a SQL exception error. Earlier you experienced this when running the proc with invalid arguments, causing a batch abort. When an error trips one of the batch abort actions, then the error returned will be a SQL error. If the error is caught by .NET code using the `SQLClient` assembly, this will also appear in a `SqlException` class, and the error-handling behavior will be the same. In the commingled code sections later in this chapter, we will go into the interaction between SQL CLR code and T-SQL code to see what happens when we start using the two technologies together.

SQL CLR Error-Handling Strategies

After working with SQL CLR for a while now, as well as T-SQL and .NET, we have developed a set of best practices for handling exceptions that have worked out well. In this section, we'll go over each practice and provide some examples of what we mean. Best practices are always subjective, so feel free to consider these as suggestions and use them in your frameworks where appropriate.

SQL CLR Objects Throw Errors

SQL CLR objects throw errors. By this, we mean that SQL CLR objects are low-level objects in terms of software architectures, and it is appropriate to throw errors up the calling stack, as shown in Figure 9-4. This means that any other higher-level code calling SQL CLR routines should expect to handle such an exception. In any other place in software architecture, this could create issues, because you are effectively forcing the invoking layer to a contract of handling an error. There has to be some sensitivity to the invoking layer so that exceptions that can be handled in the lower levels are handled and only exceptions that can be acted upon are raised. SQL CLR routines are generally invoked from either a data layer or a middle-tier layer, and within these layers, it is reasonable to assume that error handling should exist and be consistent. This argument is made easier by the fact that SQL CLR routines always throw `SqlExceptions` because they are hosted in SQL Server.

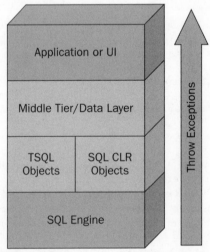

Figure 9-4

As it is not the place of SQL CLR routines to handle all errors, it may also not help to throw an error. You have to ask yourself what you can do to handle the error within the SQL CLR routine in the first place. If, by catching the error, you can perform an action such as substituting a value with a default, then do so. But if the error can not be recovered from nor resolved from within the SQL CLR routine, then allow the error to be raised. You have to rely on the calling code to catch errors and respond appropriately. If you do not raise the error, you can create bugs that remain hidden during production. Whatever you do: Do not absorb errors by coding error-handling routines like the following unless you have a really good reason that's documented in the code:

```
public static void mspDivideByZero
                    (SqlInt32 myNumerator, SqlInt32 myDenominator)
{
    try
    {
        SqlContext.Pipe.Send(Convert.ToString(
            (SqlDouble)myNumerator/(SqlDouble)myDenominator));
    }
    catch (Exception ex)
    {
        //DO NOT DO THIS...
    }
}
```

Throwing errors in SQL CLR is the same as throwing errors in .NET and can be performed by using one of these methods:

❑   Provide no error handling and the SQL Engine will throw a SqlException up to the next handler.

❑   Provide error handlers for specific exceptions other than SqlExceptions and throw that exception with additional information specific to the error.

There are arguments for either one of these options. Some think that since SQL CLR routines are low-level architectural elements, they should only generate errors, not worry about handling them. The second optinion is that possible known errors should be handled and rethrown. The advantage of rethrowing exceptions is that during the catch statement you have a chance to add additional information that can be logged or interpreted further upstream. Recoding mspDivideByZero stored procedure using this recommendation, we'd change the catch statement to something like this:

```
catch (Exception ex)
{
    string errmsg = string.Format("Numerator={0}, Denominator={1}",
            myNumerator, myDenominator);
    throw new System.DivideByZeroException(errmsg, ex);
}
```

Now we've added some important information concerning the values of the parameters at the time the exception occurred to help troubleshooting efforts in the future. It's not too terribly helpful in this example, but you get the idea. Note that you can not throw a new SqlException because it doesn't have a constructor. Instead, throw the contents of SqlException.ToString() or the SqlException itself via a new general exception, like this:

```
catch (SqlException sqlex)
{
    throw new Exception("", sqlex);
}
```

Exception Handling at Design Time

Obviously, the best policy for handling errors is to keep them from happening in the first place. Be anticipatory in your coding practices. You should be prepared for known potential exception-generating conditions: for example, end-of-file, divide-by-zero, and illegal casting. These are conditions that a well-written SQL CLR routine is expected to handle. In other words, is there is an acceptable way to handle an error condition resulting from bad inputs or unnatural events? If so, code for it.

Check Early for Error conditions

You could code your mspDivideByZero stored procedure to never generate a DivideByZeroException by checking for that condition in the SQL CLR procedure. When you code using this pattern, you have to be aware of this impact of that decision. If a zero is provided as a denominator, what do you produce as a result? Since this procedure is returning a string in the messages output, you can easily check for zero (0) as a denominator and stream the word "INFINITY" as the result. The code in the try block would then look like this:

```
if (myDenominator == 0)
{
    SqlContext.Pipe.Send("INFINITY");
}
else
{
    SqlContext.Pipe.Send(Convert.ToString(
            (SqlDouble)myNumerator / (SqlDouble)myDenominator));
}
```

This pattern can be used whenever the question "What would I do if this error occurs?" can be answered in the definitive and fits within the expected output or flow of the code.

Check for and Expect to Handle Nulls

NULLs in databases can wreak havoc on SQL CLR procedures in unexpected ways for T-SQL programmers. In T-SQL, any parameter representing primitive data types can be NULL. In .NET, this is not true. Take special attention and care when you're building SQL CLR routines that will be mapped to fields that are nullable in a database. If the parameter in the SQL CLR routine uses .NET primitive types, and the field contains a NULL, SQL will raise an exception and there will be no opportunity to attempt a try...catch.

```
[Microsoft.SqlServer.Server.SqlFunction]
public static int mfnAddNonSQLTyped(int x, int y)
{
    try
    {
        return x + y;
    }
    catch(Exception ex)
```

```
        {
            throw new Exception("Caught Error", ex);
        }
    }
```

Calling this function with NULL values as parameters generates the following result:

```
select dbo.mfn_AddNonSQLTyped(NULL, NULL)
Msg 6569, Level 16, State 1, Line 1
'msp_AddNonSQLTyped' failed because parameter 1 is not allowed to be null and is
not an
output parameter.
```

Note that this error is a pure T-SQL error. This is because the invalid parameters resulted in a batch abort from the SQL engine. This means that you didn't even get far enough into the T-SQL function prototype that wraps the SQL CLR assembly entry-point function before the statement was aborted. To avoid this situation, use SQL data types when possible for SQL CLR parameters.

The user-defined aggregate mfnSumEvenAmt that follows summarizes only evenly paid amounts of money and is a great example of how to handle NULL values. To avoid generating an error for NULL money fields, this code does two things: It uses SQL data types that can accept NULLs, and it checks explicitly for NULL values within the aggregate functions. The last thing it does is return a default of 0.00 if NULL is the final result. This utilizes the error-handling pattern of using defaults to avoid returning a nonmoney amount and to match the overall intent of the function.

```
using System;
using System.Data;
using System.Data.SqlClient;
using System.Data.SqlTypes;
using Microsoft.SqlServer.Server;

[Serializable]
[Microsoft.SqlServer.Server.SqlUserDefinedAggregate(Format.Native,
IsInvariantToDuplicates=false, IsInvariantToNulls=true, IsNullIfEmpty=true)]
public struct mfnSumEvenAmt
{
    private SqlMoney myTotalAmt;
    //This is called once per use of aggregate
    public void Init()
    {
        myTotalAmt = 0;
    }
    //This is called once per value input
    public void Accumulate(SqlMoney myAmt)
    {
        if (!(myAmt.IsNull) && ((int)(myAmt * 100) % 2 == 0))
        {
            myTotalAmt += myAmt;
        }
    }
    //This is used if SQL spawns multithreaded processes to combine results
    public void Merge(mfnSumEvenAmt ThreadedTotalAmt)
    {
```

```
            if (!(ThreadedTotalAmt.myTotalAmt.IsNull))
            {
                myTotalAmt += ThreadedTotalAmt.myTotalAmt;
            }
        }
        //return results
        public SqlMoney Terminate()
        {
            if (myTotalAmt.IsNull)
            {
                return new SqlMoney(0.00);
            }
            else
            {
                return myTotalAmt;
            }
        }
    }
```

Clean Up after Exceptions

When an exception is generated, control moves to the first available `catch` block that can handle the exception. Because the code will not return to that execution point, you need a way to clean up any significant resources like the database connection, file handles, or network connections—any resource that implements the `IDisposable` interface. One best practice is to declare these objects within a `using` statement. The advantage to using this approach is that the objects are retained in memory only as long as the scope of the statement exists. Once program control moves outside the scope of the using statement, a dispose method is called for each object to release memory and resources. This provides an automatic cleanup in the event that an exception is generated and control moves out of scope to the catch block. Use this technique to wrap the construction of your SQL connection objects and commands like this:

```
[Microsoft.SqlServer.Server.SqlProcedure]
public static void mspExample()
{
    using (SqlConnection sqlConn =
            new SqlConnection("Context Connection=true"))
    {
    }
}
```

You should also get into the habit of using a `finally` block in SQL SLR routines. The `finally` block executes after an exception is handled, or not, and even if the exception is thrown to the next handler. If the SQL CLR routine throws an exception, right before execution moves to the next handler the finally block is executed. This behavior ensures that the code in the `finally` block is run and makes an ideal spot to perform cleanup activities.

Rewriting the `mspExample` procedure, we added a `finally` statement to dispose of the `SqlConnection` and `SqlCommand` objects without the `using` statement. First, notice that you have to define the SQL objects outside the `try` statement.

```
public static void mspfinallyExample()
{
```

```
SqlConnection sqlConn =
new SqlConnection("Context Connection=true");
SqlCommand sqlCmd = sqlConn.CreateCommand();
try
    {
        sqlConn.Open();
        sqlCmd.CommandText = "SELECT 1";
        sqlCmd.CommandType = CommandType.Text;
        sqlCmd.ExecuteNonQuery();
    }
    catch (SqlException sqlex)
    {
        throw new Exception("", sqlex);
    }
    catch (Exception ex)
    {
        throw new Exception("", ex);
    }
    finally
    {
        sqlCmd.Dispose();
        sqlConn.Dispose();
    }
}
```

The `try` statement is then used to protect the connection activities, because these activities are most likely to incur an error if things go wrong. If an error were to occur, then the exception would most likely be a SQL-based exception. The `SqlException` is checked for first in an error condition, since it has this high probability. The next exception block would handle any unexpected non-SQL-based error. The `finally` block will be executed regardless of which exception is caught. It will be always be executed at the completion of the `try` block. This provides a great opportunity to structure your code so that you only have to code cleanup activities in one spot. In this example, both SQL objects are disposed of in the `finally` block.

SQL CLR Handling T-SQL Object Errors

Since SQL CLR interacts directly with the database in SQL Server, it is not long before you'll start leveraging objects already built in T-SQL. The good news is that regardless of whether exceptions are generated by data access activities, raised within the T-SQL objects themselves, or produced by batch- and statement-level aborts in the SQL engine, exceptions can be caught in the SQL CLR routines as `SqlException` types.

One of the more disappointing things about SQL CLR for some folks is that you don't get away from needing to code some T-SQL. The really disappointing thing is that the T-SQL code you embed in a SQL CLR proc is not deep-compiled or even syntax-checked. In T-SQL, if you misspell a table name, you get a batch abort. At least in SQL CLR, you get a `SqlException` that can be handled. Not that you can do anything about an incorrectly named table, but at least the batch doesn't just stop processing and you can gracefully exit a complicated stored procedure that encounters this error (hopefully, during testing processes). This error is generated if you attempt to insert a row into a table that doesn't exist:

```
System.Data.SqlClient.SqlException: Invalid object name 'NONEXISTINGTABLE'.
```

Calling a T-SQL object is a little more interesting, especially if it raises its own error. For this demonstration, we'll use a simple T-SQL stored procedure to raise a user-defined error:

```
CREATE PROC [dbo].[uspRaiseAnError]
AS
RAISERROR('Encountered an error', 16, 10)
RETURN @@ERROR
```

Then we'll call this proc from within a SQL CLR procedure:

```
[Microsoft.SqlServer.Server.SqlProcedure]
public static void mspCalluspRaiseAnError()
{
    using (SqlConnection sqlConn =
            new SqlConnection("Context Connection=true"))
    {
        SqlCommand sqlCmd = sqlConn.CreateCommand();
        try
        {
            sqlConn.Open();
            sqlCmd.CommandText = "uspRaiseAnError";
            sqlCmd.CommandType = CommandType.StoredProcedure;
            sqlCmd.ExecuteNonQuery();
        }
        catch (SqlException sqlex)
        {
            throw new Exception("", sqlex);
        }
        finally
        {
            sqlCmd.Dispose();
        }
    }
}
```

Notice that in the `catch` block we are throwing the `SqlException` class. This is because the `SqlException` class can't be rethrown as a new exception, unless you transfer the information from the class and throw a more generic exception. The `SqlException` is a custom error class that contains useful information if the invoking code needs to react to specific SQL error codes, or to simply log a complete picture of the SQL-based error. To format all the information, create a .NET helper function that you can use to format the message, like this:

```
private string FormatSqlExceptionError(SqlException ex)
{
    return ("Message: " + ex.Message + "\n" +
            "Stack Trace: " + ex.StackTrace + "\n" +
            "Source: " + ex.Source + "\n" +
            "Procedure: " + ex.Procedure + "\n" +
            "Line Nbr: " + ex.LineNumber + "\n" +
            "Inner Exception: " + ex.InnerException + "\n" +
            "Number: " + ex.Number + "\n" +
            "State: " + ex.State + "\n" +
            "Targetsite: " + ex.TargetSite + "\n" +
```

```
                    "Help Link: " + ex.HelpLink + "\n" +
                    "SQL Error Code: " + ex.ErrorCode + "\n" +
                    "SQL Severity: " + ex.Class + "\n" +
                    "Data: " + ex.Data + "\n" +
                    "Server: " + ex.Server + "\n" +
                    "Exception Type: " + ex.GetType().ToString());
        }
```

To see what the error looks like to the client, and with this organized formatting, take these following steps to build a quick Windows client that calls the `mspCalluspRaiseAnError` SQL CLR stored procedure.

1. Open Visual Studio and create a new Windows Application by selecting File ➪ New Project and choosing a Windows Application template from the .NET language you are most familiar with.

2. Add a button from the toolbox to the form. In the code-behind, add this code to call the `mspCalluspRaiseAnError` procedure and catch the impending error:

```
        private void button1_Click(object sender, EventArgs e)
        {
            using (SqlConnection sqlConn = new SqlConnection("Data
Source={YOURSERVER};Initial Catalog=CLRTESTDB;Integrated Security=True"))
            {
                SqlCommand sqlCmd = sqlConn.CreateCommand();
                sqlCmd.CommandText = "mspCalluspRaiseAnError";
                sqlCmd.CommandType = CommandType.StoredProcedure;
                sqlCmd.Connection.Open();
                try
                {
                    sqlCmd.ExecuteNonQuery();
                }
                catch (SqlException sqlex)
                {
                    Console.WriteLine(FormatSqlExceptionError(sqlex));
                }
            }
        }
```

Add the code above for the `FormatSqlExceptionError` method. This code should go under the last bracket for the `button1` click event. Using this function in the `catch` block of a client C# windows program, you can call `mspCalluspRaiseAnError` and get formatted error information that looks like this:

```
Message: A .NET Framework error occurred during execution of user defined routine
or aggregate 'mspCalluspRaiseAnError':
System.Data.SqlClient.SqlException: Encountered an error
System.Data.SqlClient.SqlException:
   at System.Data.SqlClient.SqlConnection.OnError(SqlException exception, Boolean
breakConnection)
   at System.Data.SqlClient.SqlInternalConnection.OnError(SqlException exception,
Boolean breakConnection)
   at System.Data.SqlClient.SqlInternalConnectionSmi.EventSink.
            ProcessMessagesAndThrow(Boolean ignoreNonFatalMessages)
   at Microsoft.SqlServer.Server.SmiEventSink_Default.
            ProcessMessagesAndThrow(Boolean ignoreNonFatalMessages)
   at System.Data.SqlClient.SqlCommand.RunExecuteNonQuerySmi(Boolean sendToPipe)
```

```
        at System.Data.SqlClient.SqlCommand.InternalExecuteNonQuery(DbAsyncResult
                    result, String methodName, Boolean sendToPipe)
        at System.Data.SqlClient.SqlCommand.ExecuteNonQuery()
        at StoredProcedures.mspCalluspRaiseAnError().
Stack Trace:..a repeat of information above ++
            chapter\projects\errorhandlingdemo\ErrorHandlingDemo\TestForm.cs:line 109
Source: .Net SqlClient Data Provider
Procedure: mspCalluspRaiseAnError
Line Nbr: 0
Inner Exception:
Number: 6522
State: 1
Targetsite: Void OnError(System.Data.SqlClient.SqlException, Boolean)
Help Link:
SQL Error Code: -2146232060
SQL Severity: 16
Data: System.Collections.ListDictionaryInternal
Server: HINDELL01\SQLEXPRESS
Exception Type: System.Data.SqlClient.SqlException
```

So as you can see, handling errors from either T-SQL objects or from the SQL engine is a matter of preparing to handle a `SqlException`. Now let's look at T-SQL objects and how they handle SQL CLR exceptions.

T-SQL Objects Handling SQL CLR Exceptions

T-SQL objects can also call and use SQL CLR routines, since they coexist in the same environment. Since the error handler in T-SQL only works with a scope-level error state, it makes sense that you will be restricted to the lowest level of error handling. This means that if the T-SQL objects will need to check the value of `@@Error` or wrap calls to SQL CLR code in `TRY...CATCH` blocks. Code a simple SQL CLR routine to throw an application exception that looks like the following:

```
[Microsoft.SqlServer.Server.SqlProcedure]
public static void mspRaiseAnError()
{
    throw new ApplicationException("My Manufactured SLQCLR Error");
}
```

Now, you can test this error from within T-SQL. The first test will be to try to catch the error using the `@@Error` method.

```
DECLARE @MYERR AS INT
EXEC mspRaiseAnError
SET @MYERR = @@ERROR
If @MYERR > 0
    print 'CAUGHT SQL CLR ERROR #' + str(@MYERR)
```

When you run this T-SQL code, you get the following error messages. Notice that the error is also correctly caught even though we have no choice about streaming this error message.

```
Msg 6522, Level 16, State 1, Procedure mspRaiseAnError, Line 0
A .NET Framework error occurred during execution of user defined routine or
```

```
aggregate 'mspRaiseAnError':
System.ApplicationException: My Manufactured SLQCLR Error
System.ApplicationException:
    at StoredProcedures.mspRaiseAnError()
    .
CAUGHT SQL CLR ERROR #        6522
```

Testing this again, try using T-SQL code using the TRY...CATCH block:

```
BEGIN TRY
    EXEC mspRaiseAnError
END TRY

BEGIN CATCH
    EXEC uspReportErrorInfo
END CATCH
```

In this case, use the stored procedure you built earlier to print out the detail of the values stored in the Error() functions. The output looks like this:

```
ErrorNumber ErrorSeverity ErrorState  ErrorProcedure  ErrorLine   ErrorMessage
6522        16            1           mspRaiseAnError 0           A .NET Framework
error occurred during execution of user defined routine or aggregate
'mspRaiseAnError':
System.ApplicationException: My Manufactured SLQCLR Error
System.ApplicationException: at StoredProcedures.mspRaiseAnError().
```

The SQL engine converts all CLR errors into the common .NET Framework error code 6522. From within the T-SQL objects, you can only determine whether the SQL CLR code finished without an error based on the value of @@Error, or the fact that the CATCH block is not activated. The only way to get detailed information other than the error code 6522, which occurs regardless of the error, is to parse through the Error_Message() string. This is one of the reasons that error handling at the SQL CLR level should be minimal. SQL CLR operates at such a low level in a typical development hierarchy that error handling is best left for the upper levels to interpret. The main responsibility of the SQL CLR routine is to handle conditions that are expected and throw the remainder up the call stack for the other levels of the architecture to handle.

Summary

In this chapter, we explored the multiple methods of error handling that exists now in the world of SQL Server 2005 from the @@ERROR and new TRY...CATCH error-code based error-handling methods to the structured error-handling type-based method of SQL CLR. Understanding each method helps you see the advantages and limitations of each technique and helps when developing robust code that commingles SQL CLR and T-SQL objects. In the next chapter, we'll shift from the development aspects of SQL CLR and take a look a SQL CLR from the administration and security perspective. We'll look at the code access security model and see how to restrict the activities of the SQL CLR routines. You'll also approach SQL CLR from a management perspective and get the information that you need to convince your DBAs and administrators to enable CLR for development and production use.

10

CLR Administration and Security

Being a DBA or a system administrator these days is getting more difficult. Not only do we have the responsibility of managing the day-to-day aspects of databases such as database design, back-ups, and ongoing maintenance, but we also are often on the hook for the hardware. It is common for a DBA to have system administrator-like responsibilities of installing operating systems, databases, and vendor patches to production and near-production machines. As if that is not enough, new and up-and-coming corporate and legislative mandates are taking us getting closer and closer to being responsible for the content of the data. With high-profile data leaking into pub-lic headlines on a recurring basis, and a blinding amount of change in the infrastructure due to .NET, it is understandable that DBAs are a little overwhelmed and gun shy about the concept of SQL CLR. Let's get real. Who's *officially* responsible for the "cool" technology built by vendors, consultants, or even our own developers when they are off on another project? We are.

The difficulty with being responsible for SQL Server 2005 is that there are a lot of new aspects to digest. From the new security models to T-SQL language enhancements and a revamped DTS (SSIS) environment to capabilities like the service broker and SQL CLR, these changes are over-whelming. Moreover, most, but not all of these enhancements, are designed to capitalize upon the .NET platform. This "newness" and complexity has many DBAs and system administrators uneasy about what is now running on the machines — including the new .NET icons in the admin-istrator group. As a result, many administrators do a quick search on the web and decide that the CLR integration will stay turned off. For some this is for a perceived security issue. Others will be ignore CLR because they feel that this technology has no place in a set-based database system. There are even some who will ignore it, hoping it will go away; If it were only so easy. Someone, either the vendors, consultants, or your own developers, are going to come asking about it. This chapter will get you up to speed on what you have to know from a DBA perspective, particularly as it relates to SQL Server and CLR administration. You'll look in depth at the security aspects of using SQL CLR to get an idea of the risks as well as the countermeasures you can apply. Then we'll go into the administration of stored procedures and other SQL CLR objects in your environ-ments. Before you leave this chapter, you'll know what those .NET icons in the admin program group are for, and you'll have used them to protect your servers.

.NET for the DBA and System Admin

When the feature sets for the beta versions of SQL Server 2005 were being passed around, it seemed that only the developers paid attention to the addition of the CLR integration. Even today, from the perspective of the DBA or T-SQL developer, T-SQL and our daily work in general has not been heavily impacted. There have been a few much-needed language enhancements: better paging with ordered rows, a variable TOP statement, and a new PIVOT operator. The things that are packaged as .NET enhancements to SQL Server like the new data access SQL Native Client technology, the hosting of the CLR, and the ability to configure HTTP endpoints directly into SQL Server are neat, but these capabilities are not yet being heavily adopted. Neither SQL Server nor T-SQL have been rewritten in .NET; they have only been altered to make use of the technology. What do you need to know from a DBA/Admin perspective about CLR integration? This section will cover the technical details.

Where the .NET Framework Is Located on Your Server

The .NET Framework is what most developers are referring to when they are talking about .NET. It is a set of runtime DLL libraries that define a common set of data types and system services, and it is also the sandbox that .NET code runs in — the CLR. The Framework DLLs can be located by using the Run dialog in Start ⇨ Run.

```
%windir%\microsoft.net\framework
Or
%systemroot%\microsoft.net
```

Don't be alarmed to find many directories starting with "v" here. The .NET Framework has already gone through three major versions: 1.0, 1.1, and 2.0, so each folder contains a complete set of version-based DLLs. How did they get here? Microsoft embeds Framework releases into the Windows updates and patch releases. Unlike COM, the .NET Framework was designed with the idea that the Framework would evolve, and as it does, the updates can be separated by version to minimize the impact to existing software.

To make a crude database comparison, the Framework is like the SQL engine. To be able to run a SQL query, you need to start the sqlservr.exe. This "runtime" environment loads many DLL libraries that give you the simple ability to run T-SQL statements, including access to ready-built functions like SUBSTRING. To use the SUBSTRING function, you are not required to be aware of how it is implemented. The runtime environment that empowers this capability in .NET is called the Common Language Runtime (CLR).

Only One Version of CLR Can Be Hosted in SQL Server

The one thing that we worry about with SQL CLR is that SQL Server is only capable of running one loaded version of the CLR at a time. The Common Language Runtime (CLR) is the basis, or core, of the Framework. (There are actually two versions of certain parts of the CLR for single and multiple processors.) The CLR provides the abstraction layer for common data types, or the Common Type System (CTS), and is an implementation of the common language specification (CLS). An equivalent to CLS in the database world would be the standards defined by ANSI for SQL like SQL-92 and SQL-03.

The CLR also provides a runtime component that loads the appropriate Framework, a memory manager, a Just-in-Time compiler, and a code verification that checks internal metadata against security boundaries.

If you want to find the CLR on your server, it is, as you might guess, in several different pieces. The Base Class Library portion of the CLR is a set of DLLs with names like system* and mscor* that exist in the multiple version-named folders in %systemroot%\microsoft.net. The runtime component of the CLR is not deployed in versions. There is typically one version of the runtime loader MSCOREE.DLL per machine at %systemroot%\system32. The main components of the CLR are represented in Figure 10-1.

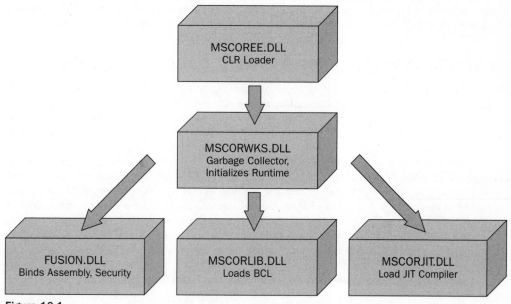

Figure 10-1

Unlike the CLR hosted in Windows, SQL Server currently only has the ability to invoke one version of the .NET Framework through the MSCOREE.DLL. The SQL engine maintains this version in metadata like everything else. You can examine this by running this query:

```
select product_version, name
FROM sys.dm_os_loaded_modules
WHERE [name] LIKE N'%\MSCOREE.DLL'
```

The results should look like this:

```
product_version   name
---------------   ---------
2.0:50727.42      C:\WINDOWS\system32\MSCOREE.DLL
```

The ability to invoke only one version of the .NET Framework may have some, as of yet unknown future consequences. As you'll notice, the first implementation of the CLR into SQL Server started with the 2.0:50727.42 version of the .NET Framework. What happens when upgrades in the next .NET Framework version provides new functionalities that you want to use, but may break existing SQL CLR code? Because SQL Server loads this one external DLL with only one Framework version for all SQL CLR code on a Server instance, it is not clear if you will be able to make a decision about which version to run when the next version of the Framework comes along. While Microsoft has been good about not breaking existing interfaces, and has so far practiced using the depreciating attribute on functionality that is going away, there is still no guarantee. To decide whether to run a patch of the Framework on your server, you are going to want to know what changes are being made to the Framework, just as you would any existing .NET project. You will need to understand the impact of all the CLR-dependent database objects on the server. This introduces a legitimate, although minor concern to the maintainability of SQL CLR routines. One bright spot is that the deployed .NET Frameworks are the same as what the developers are using for Visual Studio 2005. This at least greatly simplifies management of the server for now, but is something you'll want to pay attention to when installing Microsoft service packs and hot fixes.

How SQL Server Manages Memory Usage in SQL CLR

You may have heard developers talking about the garbage collector (GC), or garbage collection in reference to .NET development. The garbage collector is a memory management mechanism built into the CLR to monitor and optimize memory and objects located on the heap. The main benefit of the GC is to clean up behind .NET programs that may leave unused references in the heap due to error conditions, or execution paths that don't specifically release memory. Running the GC is like running DBCC FREEPROCCACHE to remove cached procedure plans, but for .NET objects instead. The big difference is that you can't control when it runs; this is up to SQL Server. This mechanism can run on separate background threads, or can be tightly integrated into the host as it is with SQL Server. SQL Server uses a parameter in the CorBindToRuntime function in the mscoree.dll to host the CLR in the same process space as the SQL engine. This provides high-speed and performance advantages, not only for garbage collection activities, but for communication interaction between the CLR and SQL databases. The advantages of hosting within SQL Server instead of using Windows include:

❑ SQL Server controls the amount of memory that CLR can use, not Windows.

❑ SQL Server controls CPU-intensive Garbage Collection operations.

❑ SQL Server can be accessed directly with an in-process data provider.

The in-process implementation of the CLR and the GC provides the best opportunity for SQL Server to control memory demands and contention between normal database operations and SQL CLR code. The other advantage is the ability to contain potential memory leakages that can be generated from SQL CLR coded objects. If SQL Server senses an abnormal amount of memory leakage, it can run the GC or control execution priorities on SPIDs. Imagine if SQL Server could have done this with your extended stored procedures. We might still be using them.

Since SQL Server 2000, it has not been typically necessary for the admin to control memory allocation. In SQL Server 2005, this has also been enhanced with the Address Windowing Extensions (AWE) API, even more so if you are using Windows 2003. SQL Server 2005 essentially works with Windows to access and then release memory as needed. To get an idea of the memory being used to run the CLR by SQL Server, use the new dynamic views and run queries in SSMS like this:

```
SELECT * FROM sys.dm_os_memory_objects WHERE type LIKE '%CLR%'
SELECT * FROM sys.dm_os_memory_clerks WHERE type LIKE '%CLR%'
```

You can also monitor CLR activity in SQL Server using the Performance Monitor. Request all counters on the .NET CLR Memory object for a log of this type of information. We'll go over the Performance Monitor in detail later in this chapter.

How to Look inside a Compiled Assembly

If you are going to allow SQL CLR development, you've probably read enough of this book to know that you are going to get an assembly from the developers to load in the database. An assembly is a DLL that is created when a .NET, CLR-compliant language solution is compiled. Unlike previous Microsoft products, the assembly is compiled into a state that is not a true binary. Yet it is not something the developer would recognize, nor is it in a native state that the CPU will recognize. This in-between state is referred to as Intermediate Language (IL). For developers, the power of IL is the interoperability between languages. For example, a stored procedure built in VB.NET can use a library function built in C# with just a reference to the assembly. The thing that unnerves some DBAs is that the idea of a DLL feels like you've got this contained object that you can't see inside. How do you know what the implementation looks like inside a DLL? Do you want to put something on your production servers between you and your clients that you don't know exactly what is does? This feeling is understandable, but these aren't your father's DLLs. An advantage to you as a DBA is that IL contains metadata that you can examine obliquely to determine what is being done within the assembly. You can use this information to decide if the assembly is a threat or is relatively harmless. We recommend that DBAs not load anything from an assembly for which you are not provided the code for reviewing purposes. However, if you are in a situation where you have no choice, the .NET CAS model can also be preset to a highly restricted state to allow you tight control over what type of code you will allow to run on the server. We'll go more into detail about it in the next section.

If you want to manually examine an assembly, download the .NET SDK or search on the Microsoft site for a utility called ILDASM.exe. This tool is an IL disassembler that allows you to look at the assembly metadata. Select menu option View ➪ Show Source Lines to be able to see all the source code. You can see the references, every callable function, and even the code in the assembly. For example, imagine being suspicious about a DLL file you've been given. Opening the DLL in ILDASM reveals something you didn't expect for a math library, the deletion of all employees in the human resource scheme. It would look like this in ILDASM.

```
.method public hidebysig static void  mspBlackBoxProcedure() cil managed
{
  .custom instance void
[System.Data]Microsoft.SqlServer.Server.SqlProcedureAttribute::.ctor() =
       ( 01 00 00 00 )
  // Code size       84 (0x54)
  .maxstack  2
  .locals init ([0] valuetype
          [System.Data]System.Data.SqlTypes.SqlString deleteSQL,
          [1] class [System.Data]System.Data.SqlClient.SqlConnection sqlConn,
          [2] class [System.Data]System.Data.SqlClient.SqlCommand sqlCmd,
          [3] bool CS$4$0000)
  IL_0000:  nop
  IL_0001:  ldstr      "delete [HumanResources].[Employee] "
```

You can make out bits and pieces about this assembly. First, it will result in a stored procedure called mspBlackBoxProcedure. You know that from the first line. The locals section shows you the local variables that are instantiated. This assembly is using a SqlConnection and SqlCommand. The locals section starts with:

```
.locals init ([0] valuetype
```

You can also see the value of the SQL string that is executing:

```
IL_0001:  ldstr      "delete [HumanResources].[Employee] "
```

If this were a stored procedure call, then you'd see the string for the stored procedure as well. If you were told this was a harmless routine, you might want to check to see why the employee table is being cleaned out. The ability of the ILDASM tool gives you more visibility to what is going on inside the DLL than you've ever had with unmanaged binary DLLs that can be currently hosted in SQL Server today as extended stored procedures.

Security and SQL Server–Hosted CLR

The issue creating the most concern about SQL CLR is a vague understanding of what it is capable of and how administrators and DBAs are going to be able to determine whether the code is safe and secure. We had the same concerns when the technology was first introduced. After working with it for a while, it became obvious that the SQL Server team knew this was going to be an issue for most of us and have built an elaborate security scheme into SQL CLR. First, you need to know that a SQL CLR routine is not a file that can run without any interaction with SQL Server. Many hurdles have to be overcome to get a SQL CLR routine to work. However, this doesn't mean that it is impossible for a SQL CLR routine to do damage, or to write a SQL CLR routine that can load and execute the contents of a file. The biggest hurdle should be you, serving as the gatekeeper for loading SQL CLR routines. You need to know how to identify what is dangerous, or at least know when to ask questions without having to learn .NET completely. This section will discuss each step taken to host a SQL CLR routine in SQL Server and will detail what you can do at each stage to harden your SQL server and Windows server.

Security Starts with Surface Area Configuration

As part of SQL Server's new security initiatives, not all features are enabled out of the box. This is a good thing, because you should be aware of when CLR integration is on. However, it would be nice if you could turn CLR integration on and off for each database, since this is where you load the assemblies. Unfortunately, it's either on or off for each server. See Chapter 2 for details about how to use sp_Configure and the Surface Area Configuration tool to turn CLR integration on.

From a security standpoint, make sure that principles and users do not have access to run the sp_Configure system stored procedure. (System procedures in the master database in general should be restricted to sysadmin level logins.) If you ever suspect that a CLR assembly is doing some harm to a server, as a last resort you could turn off CLR integration and subsequent calls to the SQL CLR objects would fail, raising exceptions to the callers. Just be aware that this would turn off access to all SQL CLR objects on the SQL instance. Note that even when CLR integration is off, one could still load assemblies into SQL Server, if not specifically denied that permission. We'll discuss hardening that area shortly.

Security by Identifying SQL CLR Code and .NET Framework Usage

What kind of damage can a developer do that you need to be aware of? The short answer is "as much as you let them." Remember that SQL CLR routines must be loaded by you into SQL Server to become active. This gives the DBA or admin a chance to look over the assembly before loading it into SQL Server. We recommend that DBAs procure source code as part of the release process. You do not have to become an expert on .NET development, but for troubleshooting, and for your own benefit, you should be able to examine the code and see what it contains for yourself.

There are many ways to figure out what is going on inside the assembly. If you have the source code, look in the first few lines at the top of the class files for statements like using System.Data; or Imports System.Data to find the namespaces that are being used. If you don't have the source, use the ILDASM tool to look into the manifest to find the assemblies. Note that you'll have to use the object browser in Visual Studio or the SQL Books Online to traverse from namespace to assembly when looking into these two very different areas.

The good things is you don't have to worry about some of the assemblies related to Windows development or compilers, because the SQL Server–hosted CLR is not hosted with all of the assemblies you'd find in the Windows host. The following sections list the assemblies loaded by default and some of the highlights of the capabilities of each. Use this information to ask informed questions about what's going on inside the assembly.

MSCorLib.dll

This assembly contains too many namespaces to list. The ones you'll want to watch are:

- ❑ `Microsoft.Win32`: This namespace contains classes to access the windows registry.

- ❑ `System`: This namespace contains the core data types used by CLR. You should expect to see this namespace in most CLR routines.

- ❑ `System.IO`: This namespace contains classes to write to and read from the Windows file system.

- ❑ `System.Security.*`: These namespaces contain classes to handle security-related settings at the assembly level. Understand that users can specifically use these libraries to bypass security settings or impersonate other logins. This is dangerous. If the assembly uses other assemblies security rights can be abnormally escalated.

- ❑ `System.Text`: Normally used for the string builder class, it contains encoding classes for text.

- ❑ `System.Threading`: This namespace contains classes to create threads and manage thread pools. You'11 want to find out why this is being used, if you see it.

System.Data.dll

This assembly contains the integration functionality required to connect the CLR to SQL Server, so naturally you should expect to see it in all SQL CLR objects. It contains several subnamespaces of importance:

- ❑ `Microsoft.SqlServer.Server`: This namespace contains the in-process data provider used to share context connections and output pipes with SQL Server. This namespace is what developers should be using if they are connecting to SQL Server.

- ❑ `System.Data.SqlClient`: This namespace contains the classes that make up the new `sqlClient` provider. These classes are functionally like the ADO.NET classes, but are specifically designed for SQL Server.

❑ `System.Data`: This namespace contains all the classes that make up what we know as ADO.NET. For example, this library contains the `connection`, `datareader`, and `dataset` objects. Be aware that this is *not* the in-process data access mechanism that is normally used to access SQL Server and could be used to connect to other data sources. Make sure you don't confuse this namespace with the assembly.

❑ `System.Data.SqlTypes`: This namespace contains the native SQL Server–type libraries to allow SQL CLR objects to set up parameters that map back to T-SQL parameter types.

❑ `System.XML`: This namespace allows structured XML data to be retrieved and stored in a `System.Data.Dataset`.

❑ `System.Data.*`: The remaining `system.data` namespaces are specific providers for ODBC, Oracle, or OLE DB. Again, if developers are using these libraries then they could be connecting to sources outside of SQL Server.

System.dll

This assembly contains the core data types and interfaces for the CLR. This assembly is required for SQL CLR routines, so you can't restrict its use.

System.Xml.dll and System.Data.SqlXml.dll

These assemblies contain the classes that make up the .NET version of the XML Document Object Model (DOM). There are also classes that provide support for things like XML Schema Definition (XSD) language and XPath queries. `System.Xml.dll` is required in SQL CLR routines for serialization purposes.

Microsoft.VisualBasic.dll

This assembly contains namespaces and classes to provide support for the MY construct, which is a shortcut library for rapid application development. This assembly is powerful and exposes some functionality that you'll want to question, but there are also financial calculation functions in these libraries that shouldn't raise any alarm. The following are some of the namespaces you should make sure you understand why they are being used in a SQL CLR routine.

❑ `Microsoft.VisualBasic.Devices`: This namespace provides access to devices such as the network, computer, and ports.

❑ `Microsoft.VisualBasic.FileIO`: This namespace allows access to the file system, including drives and folders.

❑ `Microsoft.VisualBasic.Logging`: This namespaces provides support for writing event and exception information into log listeners or files.

❑ `Microsoft.VisualBasic.MyServices`: This namespace provides proxy classes for manipulating the clipboard, the file system, and the registry.

Microsoft.VisualC.dll

This assembly contains attributes and modifiers for VisualC++. The classes allow for the examination and creation of C++ code — not a typical use of SQL CLR.

CustomMarshallers.dll

This assembly allows for interop capabilities in SQL CLR. Interop is the ability of .NET to wrap COM based components and use them. This is similar to `sp_OACreate` and similar system stored procedures. As with the system stored procedures, use of this assembly will require you to become familiar with the dependent COM objects.

System.Security.dll

This assembly contains two families of namespaces. The first is a cryptography library. The second namespace is the underpinning for CLR permission-based security. We will go over the code access security model in the next sections, but for now, know that security attributes can be programmed to allow code to perform actions that the caller does not have permissions to perform. This is not a guaranteed evil; it may make sense to create a SQL CLR stored procedure to update a specific registry key and then allow a caller without that permission to use the function. It would not make sense to create a generic SQL CLR stored procedure to update any registry key and allow any caller to execute that function. For this reason, you'll want to look for code with keywords like Assert.

System.Web.Services.dll

This assembly contains the namespaces and classes to enable the use of web services from within SQL Server. Web services are small applications that can send and exchange messages in a local, local area network (LAN), wide area network (WAN), or Internet environment. In the case of SQL CLR, this technology allows SQL Server to listen for HTTP requests and process them directly, without needing IIS. Although this seems to solve one problem of exposing the server using IIS, it uses up valuable threads, so we're not sure that exposing the database server is a better solution than the alternatives.

Although most of the time development in SQL CLR performs some sort of data manipulation, the capabilities enumerated here should make DBAs and administrators understandably nervous. These assemblies are also not the only assemblies that SQL CLR objects can use. Anything that is built as a SQL CLR routine will be given to you as an assembly. You can load just about any .NET DLL into SQL Server for use as a dependent assembly. Third-party vendors may also provide assemblies with their software. Developers may even want to use a Microsoft assembly that is not loaded by default. The important thing to remember is that any assembly than is not loaded in SQL Server by default or that you are comfortable with should be questioned. Make sure that you understand what one does before you load it.

Securing the Loading of Assemblies

A SQL CLR assembly is not referenced like a DLL file in the file system (unlike the .NET Framework assemblies). The file is actually loaded into SQL Server as metadata and then retrieved to load into memory by the hosted CLR. Since everything that is loaded, updated, or deleted as data is managed by SQL Server security, you might guess that you can control who has rights to manage assemblies. In fact, SQL Server 2005 has several new security permissions that give DBAs great control over SQL CLR code. In this section, we'll look at how you can harden SQL Server once you turn on CLR integration.

Restrict Who Can Do SQL CLR Development

Because all assemblies are located in SQL Server, you can restrict developers from doing any SQL CLR development, by hiding the assemblies from view. If the Visual Studio Reference Editor can't see the assemblies, the developer can't develop a basic project. Hide the viewing of these assemblies by not setting Grant rights to the VIEW DEFINITION server-level permission, which grants or denies access to assembly (or any) metadata. This is a complete reversal of previous installations of SQL Server, which allowed public viewing of metadata out of the box. By specifically denying rights at least of public access roles to metadata in production environments, developers will not be able to add assemblies to SQL CLR projects. They will be met with the following message:

```
The connection to the database failed for the following reason:
VIEW DEFINITION permission denied on object 'myFirstCLRAssembly', database
'CLRTESTDB'.
No server references can be added at this time, but you may continue to develop the
project.
```

This creates an interesting situation. You could restrict developers to using only the default assemblies, system.dll, system.data.dll, and system.XML.dll, just by denying rights on any server to VIEW DEFINITION. As long as they used the Visual Studio IDE, they would not be able to add any additional assemblies to their database projects. This is because the IDE needs to view SQL Server metadata to show available CLR or SQL CLR assemblies. However, this is not foolproof. This could be circumvented, by working out of the IDE, or developing at home against a personal copy of SQL Server 2005.

It may create difficulties for developers and may not be practical for you to deny VIEW DEFINITION permissions in a development server, so you may want to just leave this permission with neither GRANT nor DENY permissions. This will allow developers basic use of the tables. However, it is a best practice to specifically deny VIEW DEFINITION permissions at the production server level. You can always remove the restriction at a database or securable object level if necessary. To deny VIEW DEFINITION rights, right-click the SQL user in the security node at the server level and select Properties. On the securables page, click the Add button and select Objects for your server instance. The "View any definition" permission should be set to Deny for all metadata, as shown in Figure 10-2.

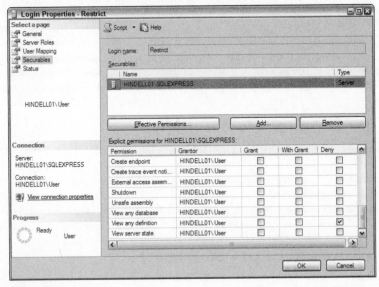

Figure 10-2

Restrict db_DDLAdmin Database Role Membership

What about loading the assembly? In Chapter 2, you learned the mechanics of loading an assembly into SQL Server. You can restrict this activity by not applying the database role of db_ddladmin or db_owner to user groups that contain developer access. If a developer attempts to load an assembly manually or through the Visual Studio IDE, they will get the following error message:

```
CREATE ASSEMBLY permission denied in database 'CLRTESTDB'.      MyAssembly
```

Typically, developers should not have access to production environments. If they do, their database role should be minimal—something like db_datareader. To ensure that all doors are closed, ensure that the public role for each database is set to the narrowest permissions possible as well. There is even a good argument for excluding this role from any permissions.

Adding Role-Based User Access to the T-SQL Prototype

Within the confines of databases in SQL Server, SQL CLR objects are not extended any special permissions related to normal SELECT, INSERT, UPDATE, and DELETE operations. When a user connects via the T-SQL entry point, the SLQCLR object executes in the context of that user. The user has to connect to the database first before they can access an entry point into a SQL CLR object. SQL CLR can't bypass this basic requirement of database user permissions.

A productivity best practice for T-SQL and now SQL CLR objects is to create database-specific roles for principles or user groups that use SQL CLR objects. Just like T-SQL objects, user groups need permission to execute the T-SQL prototype and in turn the CLR assembly. To make this easier, create a database role that has permissions to executable objects like stored procedures and user-defined functions and then assign user groups to the new database role. You can either treat all objects the same, or separate them by type or schema. If you need to separate permissions for T-SQL and SQL CLR objects, SQL Server 2005 does not provide two separate categories for easy selection. You'll have to create two separate database roles and select each of the two types of objects manually. To see an example of this, create a database role called db_ExecCLR. Select the Stored Procedure objects as the objects to secure. You'll get a list of all the stored procedures. If you have both SQL CLR and T-SQL stored procedures, you'll see why we recommend using a naming convention for the managed procedures starting with the prefix msp. It makes identification between T-SQL and SQL CLR objects much easier for the administrators. Select the procedures starting with msp and specifically set EXECUTE permissions on each.

Now every new SQL CLR and T-SQL stored procedure has to be purposely set up for EXECUTION access to appropriate user groups. If you have developer principles in the production database, you can also specifically deny EXECUTION rights to the same objects. The main point here is that you are applying security rules to SQL CLR objects in the same way you would T-SQL objects—by user.

Restricting Code at the Assembly Level

In addition to SQL Server user-based security, the CLR uses a security model that enforces restrictions based on the content and origin of the code. At first, this may seem like overkill, but if you remember all the things that the .NET Framework exposes, it isn't. Remember that SQL CLR opens up access to classes for file IO, network connections, ports, environment variables, event logs, and even the registry. So far, we've tried listing out the assemblies and namespaces so that you can use this information to prescreen assemblies before they are loaded, but if you want to shoot first and ask questions later, this is your section.

Going outside SQL Server

Although SQL CLR has the ability to code against classes that provide interaction with the world outside SQL Server, the code is not treated the same in SQL Server as code that just interacts with the database. To discover this, create a simple stored procedure that uses the `FileStream` class to write a text file to the `c:\` drive. All you need to do is open a hard-coded file handle and dump a stream into the file. Open a .NET SQL Server project and add a stored procedure class to the project. The code should look like this:

```
using System;
using System.Data;
using System.IO; //Note: Added this manually

public partial class StoredProcedures
{
    [Microsoft.SqlServer.Server.SqlProcedure]
    public static void mspWriteDatetoFile()
    {
        //open a file
        TextWriter tw = new StreamWriter("c:\\date.txt");

        //write a line of text to the file
        tw.WriteLine(DateTime.Now);

        //close the stream
        tw.Close();
    }
}
```

This is not a typical data-manipulation stored procedure. The intent is to go outside the boundaries of SQL Server to the file system to write the date into a file named `c:\date.txt`. See what happens when you try to load and execute the assembly by deploying the stored procedure through the IDE. It deploys without an error. Try to execute it. Now you should get an exception that reads:

```
Msg 6522, Level 16, State 1, Procedure mspWriteDatetoFile, Line 0
A .NET Framework error occurred during execution of user defined routine or
aggregate 'mspWriteDatetoFile':
System.Security.SecurityException: Request for the permission of type
'System.Security.Permissions.FileIOPermission, mscorlib, Version=2.0.0.0,
Culture=neutral, PublicKeyToken=b77a5c561934e089' failed.
```

In other words, this SLQCLR stored procedure is denied because of `FileIO` permissions. Does that mean that the user running the procedure is denied `FileIO` rights? That can't be the case, since you are the user and you must be able to create a text file in your own `C:\` drive, right? The problem is that you've left something out. Let's stop for a minute and gather some information about security levels for SQL CLR to see why you were stopped from running this SQL CLR procedure.

CLR Permission Levels When Hosted in SQL Server

SQL Server uses a host-level security policy for CLR in SQL Server, a modification that requires and then verifies one of three permission levels during the loading of an assembly: SAFE, EXTERNAL, and UNSAFE. These permission levels correspond to the certain uses of the .NET Framework, namespace, and even class-level activity with the SLQ CLR assemblies. An explanation of each is in the following sections.

Safe Permission Level

SAFE is the default permission set for all SQL CLR routines. It is designed for those assemblies that are not any more risky to SQL Server than T-SQL. Code set to this permissions level is not expected nor allowed to alter registry settings, call web services, or do anything that you wouldn't do in T-SQL. If you can load an assembly with this permission set and execute the entry point without a .NET CLR-based error, then the assembly probably passes the green-light test. The following table shows the two permissions that are specifically controlled when the default SAFE permission setting is used.

Permission	Assigned Permission Enforced by CLR in SQL Server
Security	Execute — This allows the assembly to execute limited security context changes (that you need to use SqlContext).
SqlClient	Only Context connections are allowed.

External Permission Level

The EXTERNAL permission level is a steep step up from SAFE. It is required for assemblies that are going to be working with any resources outside of SQL Server. By definition, this should trigger some security concerns. Although these capabilities can be controlled using the code access security model, any assemblies that you are required to load into SQL Server using this permission level can alter environment settings and files, and impersonate other users. External permission assemblies also execute under SQL Server Service account. This is why you couldn't write to the C:\ drive in the earlier example. This is also a warning to administrators that it is a good idea to know what account your SQL Server Service is running under and what rights that account has. The following permissions are available to SQL CLR routines running under EXTERNAL_ACCESS permissions. They are listed in their entirety so that you may aware of what this permission level allows.

Permission	Assigned Permission Enforced by CLR in SQL Server
Directory Services	Unrestricted access to all directory service paths.
DNS	Unrestricted access to DNS Services.
Event Log	Unrestricted access to all event logs.
Environment Variables	Unrestricted access to all environment variables.
File Dialog	Assemblies are denied access to all dialogs.
Isolated Storage File	Grant assemblies unrestricted access to file storage.
Message Queue	Grant unrestricted access to all message queues.
Performance Counter	Grant unrestricted access to all performance counters.
Printing	Assemblies are denied access to printers.
Registry	Grant assemblies unrestricted access to the registry.
Reflection	Grant assemblies unrestricted permission to discover other assemblies.

Table continued on following page

Permission	Assigned Permission Enforced by CLR in SQL Server
Security	Grants capabilities of assertion, thread control, serialization formatter, policy, domain, evidence, and principle control, remoting configuration.
Socket Access	Grants outbound connections only.
SqlClient	All Connections to SQL Server are allowed.
Web Access	Grants outbound connections only.
User Interface	Not allowed.
X509 Store	Grants unrestricted access to X509 certification storage.

Unsafe Permission Level

We cannot say this any more plainly: Do not be fooled by these SQL CLR permission level names. It is a common misunderstanding to assume that the EXTERNAL access permissions level opens up some of the permissions and then UNSAFE opens up some more. The reality is that the EXTERNAL access permission level gives away most of the operating system-level permissions. The only additional thing the UNSAFE permission level does is allow access to unmanaged code. The reason for this is that the permission sets are named from the perspective of SQL Server. Assemblies are external because they access external resources than SQL Server. Assemblies are UNSAFE because, like extended stored procedures, they can call code outside the CLR, can corrupt memory buffers in use by SQL Server (think blue screen of death), and could subvert security mechanisms. We think that most DBAs and administrators will agree that there needs to be a compelling argument to support loading an assembly marked UNSAFE into a SQL Server database—even though technically this is the same situation as extended stored procedures. The following table shows the remaining permissions that an UNSAFE assembly allows.

Permission	Assigned Permission Enforced by CLR in SQL Server
EXTERNAL	All permissions granted to the EXTERNAL permission set
Security	Grant unrestricted access to unmanaged code

Using the External_Access Permission Level

In the previous example, writing the date to a text file, you encountered the roadblock of a .NET exception when you attempted to execute the SQL CLR procedure mspWriteDateToFile. Based on the SQL CLR permission set options, you now know that you have to assign an EXTERNAL permission level to the code. How do you do that? If you are loading assemblies using T-SQL, use the WITH PERMISSION SET argument set to External_Access, like this:

```
CREATE ASSEMBLY WriteDateFile
FROM c:\prosqlclr\chapter11\WriteDateFile.dll
WITH PERMISSION_SET = EXTERNAL_ACCESS
```

If you are deploying via the Visual Studio IDE, set the permissions in the project Property form. Right-click the solution at the top of the Solution Explorer. Select Properties to bring up the project Property form. Select the database tab and set the permission level in the combo box. (See Figure 10-3). When the solution is deployed, it will use this setting to create the assembly.

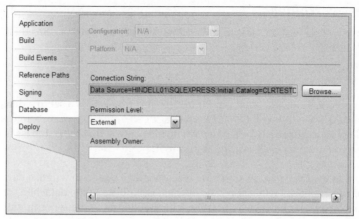

Figure 10-3

Now redeploy the procedure. You may get another exception error. A typical exception, depending upon your database access may look something like this:

```
CREATE ASSEMBLY for assembly 'WriteDateFile' failed because assembly
'WriteDateFile' is not authorized for PERMISSION_SET = EXTERNAL_ACCESS.  The
assembly is authorized when either of the following is true: the database owner
(DBO) has EXTERNAL ACCESS ASSEMBLY permission and the database has the TRUSTWORTHY
database property on; or the assembly is signed with a certificate or an asymmetric
key that has a corresponding login with EXTERNAL ACCESS ASSEMBLY permission.
```

The reason for this may have occurred to you as you went through the list of security accesses that the permission level External Access has been granted. This level is enough of a surface area risk that it requires a specific SQL Server user-based security permission to be able to load it. The idea parallels the concept behind all surface-level configuration: Features come inactivated until you activate them. To grant permissions to a user or principle to load an External Access assembly, run the T-SQL statement:

```
use master
go
GRANT EXTERNAL ACCESS ASSEMBLY to <USER>
```

You can also use the SSMS to set the EXTERNAL ACCESS ASSEMBLY securable to grant for the user that will load the assembly. Note that this security level only affects the loading or altering of an assembly, not the use of an assembly. Once the assembly is loaded, you can remove this permission and the SQL CLR routines will continue to run.

This same concept applies if you attempt to load an assembly that needs the UNSAFE permission set. The user account that needs to load the assembly must have UNSAFE ASSEMBLY rights using the following:

```
use master
go
GRANT UNSAFE ASSEMBLY to <USER>
```

The other part of the error message mentioned something about the trustworthiness of the database. Before we continue, let's discuss this setting.

Database Trustworthiness

The mechanics of getting past an exception warning you that the database has the TRUSTWORTHY flag set to OFF is simple. Run the T-SQL code:

```
ALTER DATABASE clrtestdb SET TRUSTWORTHY ON
```

However, what does this do, and what does it mean? This property is a set to a default of OFF for all databases. Before an assembly with the EXTERNAL_ACCESS or UNSAFE permission set is added to the database, the flag has to purposely be set to ON. The idea here is that the database is manually marked trusted, because you are purposely adding things to it.

The real reason that the flag is on the database is to counter a situation where a database is detached (or backed up) and can be maliciously altered by adding assemblies to the detached (or backup) database that you may not be aware of. When a database with assemblies in these permission sets is detached, the TRUSTWORTHY flag is set automatically to OFF. When the database file is reattached, the TRUSTWORTHY flag must be purposely reset to ON to continue using these assemblies. This is not a foolproof mechanism, for it is conceivable that one could script the detachment, make a malicious alteration, and then reattach the database — scripting an alteration to the TRUSTWORTHY flag. However, under most conditions this will provide a safety check to remind you to verify your assemblies before exposing your database and server. Because SQL CLR routines can't be run if this flag is ON, run a T-SQL command like this to get a quick inventory of the UNSAFE and EXTERNAL_ACCESS routines that are in the database.

```
SELECT Name as Assembly_Name,
       Permission_set_desc,
       Create_Date, Modify_Date
FROM sys.assemblies
WHERE permission_set_Desc IN
    ('UNSAFE_ACCESS', 'EXTERNAL_ACCESS')
ORDER BY ASSEMBLY_NAME
```

The results will depend upon your database, but you should be able to account for these type assemblies. If you see anything unusual in this list, do not set the TRUSTWORTHY flag until you resolve that object. The following is an example of the results this query produces.

```
Assembly_Name             Permission_set_desc   Create_Date   Modify_Date
------------------        -----------------     -----------   -----------
File Source               EXTERNAL_ACCESS       2006-07-04    2006-07-04
SubversiveAssembly        EXTERNAL_ACCESS       2006-05-29    2006-05-29
vendornetlogic            UNSAFE_ACCESS         2006-06-15    2006-06-15
WriteDateFile             EXTERNAL_ACCESS       2006-06-06    2006-06-06
XPReplacements            EXTERNAL_ACCESS       2006-06-15    2006-06-15
XPReplacements_Unsafe     UNSAFE_ACCESS         2006-06-14    2006-06-14
```

If you haven't run the T-SQL code to set the TRUSTWORTHY flag in the CLRTESTDB (or your test database), do so now. You can then redeploy the mspWriteDateToFile SQL CLR stored procedure. Now, with a successful deploy, run the stored procedure and check your C:\ drive for a file named date.txt.

If you think about it, the whole set of SQL CLR permission levels is sounding dangerous. You were able to call a T-SQL stored procedure and write a file to the c:\ drive. Now think about all the other permissions that the EXTERNAL_ACCESS permission set has. . . Scary. Before you lock down SQL Server and turn the CLR integration back off, there is a way to harden the access of SQL CLR assemblies beyond the default permission sets. In fact, you can restrict or allow a highly granular set of permissions for the SQL CLR procedures. Before we can apply this to our example, let's look at the security model of the CLR itself — the code access security model.

Securing Assemblies Using the Code Access Security Model

Code access security, or CAS, is designed for .NET developers that deal with a world where code can be downloaded and executed from network shares, an intranet, or Internet sites. The CAS is a security model embedded in the CLR and .NET Framework. It can examine the metadata in .NET code at runtime to determine where the assembly originated, whether or not the code is marked with a key by the developing entity, or if the code has a digital signature. Based on this evidence, the assembly is assigned to a code group. Code groups have names like All_Code, My_Computer_Zone, Trusted_Zone, and Internet_Zone. A policy level, typically at the Enterprise, Machine, or User level at each of these code groups, is then assigned a group of permissions that make up a security policy.

In a non-SQL CLR .NET world, this is more complicated. In SQL CLR, it is rather simple. The assemblies are in the My_Computer_Zone code group, because they originate, or are accessed from, the local machine. The policy level is also simple; it is a machine-level policy. When .NET is installed, each of these security policies is set up with defaults for each .NET Framework. To review the settings, navigate to the Administrative Tools icon in the Control Panel. You'll see icons for each Framework, titled something like Microsoft .NET Framework 2.0 Configuration. These programs are used to edit a set of XML security policy files located in the config directory of each Framework. These security policy files determine the .NET Frameworks permissions that are allowed for either all machines on an Active Directory installation (Enterprise), a Machine (current machine), or Users. Figure 10-4 shows the program opened with the Machine Security policy visible.

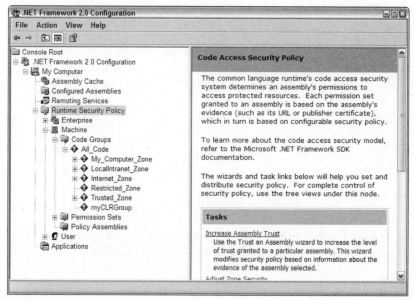

Figure 10-4

Hardening SQL CLR Assemblies Using CAS

You may have been disappointed to see that by applying the EXTERNAL_ACCESS permission set to a SQL CLR assembly, you opened up the Windows environment to the opportunity of a lot of mischief. If there were only a way you could more tightly control the definition of the permissions in the EXTERNAL_ACCESS permission set, you could regain back some control over what SQL CLR could do in environment without having to monitor every SQL CLR object. Well, you can't change the permissions set on the SQL CLR code group, but because of the way the CAS policies work together, you can create a custom policy that can also apply to enforce your own restrictions upon the SQL CLR EXTERNAL_ACCESS permission set. Within your custom permission set, you can restrict any writing to a file that is done by any .NET program to a limited set of directories on your server. Then at least you have control over where files are written.

The way CAS works is that each of these code groups are assigned a set of permissions that are bundled together into permission sets. These permission sets granularly controlled permissions at a functional level. To get an idea of what you can restrict, you'll create a permission set to restrict the 2.0 .NET Framework from writing to any directory except a specific directory. To set up a custom permission set:

1. Under the Machine Node, Right-click the Permission Sets node, and select the menu option New.

2. Select the option to Create a new permission set.

3. Type **myCLRPermissions** for the permission set name.

4. Type **Set of CLR-Specific Permissions** for the description. Click Next.

5. Take a look at the list of available permissions to assign. You can see the details by selecting a permission and pressing the Add button. Select and Add the File IO permissions.

6. Type the path **c:\prosqlclr\chapter10** into the File Path text box. Check the select, write, and append check boxes. Click OK. You'll need to go create this file path. It is not verified by the tool. The Permission Settings dialog should look like Figure 10-5.

7. Press Finish to save the permission set.

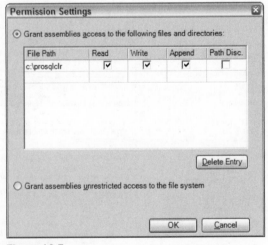

Figure 10-5

A permission set alone is harmless. To become effective, it needs to be part of an existing code group. If an assembly is part of more than one code group, the effective permissions of the assembly is an intersection of the permission at each code group. This just means that the lowest permissions apply. You can use that to your advantage to create your own code group that will allow these rules to apply, yet also be easy to remove when you are through with this example.

To create a new code group:

1.   Under the Machine node and Code Groups node, select and right-click the All code icon and select New.

2.   Select the option to create a new code group.

3.   Type **myCLRGroup** for the permission set name.

4.   Type **A CLR-Custom Code Group** for the description.

5.   Under the Membership Condition Tab, Select the Zone option. Select the My Computer Zone so that this code group applies to assemblies on the current computer.

6.   Under the Permission Set Tab, select the newly created permission set of myCLRPermissions. You'll see the File IO permission option display in the list box. Click OK to save this Code Group.

Now that you've made this change, close the Framework Configuration tool and retry your stored procedure. Because you've created a CAS code group that restricts code in the 2.0 .NET Framework to the c:\prosqlclr\chapter10\ directory, you are no longer allowed to write to the C:\ drive. The code generates an unauthorized access exception error that looks like this:

```
Msg 6522, Level 16, State 1, Procedure mspWriteDatetoFile, Line 0
A .NET Framework error occurred during execution of user defined routine or
aggregate 'mspWriteDatetoFile':
System.UnauthorizedAccessException: Access to the path 'c:\date.txt' is denied.
```

You can now go back to the SQL CLR stored procedure and change the output path to c:\prosqlclr\chapter10\ (remember to use the escape sequence \\ in the directory path) to see it work correctly.

The only downside to the way you set up this custom group is that you chose the membership requirement of My Computer. These security permissions are going to apply to any program that runs in the My Computer Zone that uses .NET 2.0. If your server environment is only running SQL Server, you may be OK. To tune this to only the SQL CLR .NET code in your shop, use strong names in your SQL CLR assemblies and map the security code group to the strong name in the Membership tab.

Feeling better? You should be able to see at this point that you have control over what you allow within these SQL CLR managed objects — even if you load an assembly with EXTERNAL_ACCESS permissions. One of the things you could do is leave the myCLRGroup Custom Code Group in place. Its policy will automatically restrict access to the registry, the environmental variable, and all the other permissions, because they were not specifically set. The only permission that has been allowed is the ability to write the specific directory. When you have the need, review the permission list earlier in this chapter on EXTERNAL_ACCESS for permissions to which you can apply this finer level of restrictive access to your custom group.

We started this section with the idea that there are many hurdles on the way before a SQL CLR routine becomes usable on a machine. Now that you have a better idea of what these hurdles are, it helps to look at this model of SQL CLR. On the right of Figure 10-6, you can now see that there is a checkpoint that must be met at almost every layer in the process.

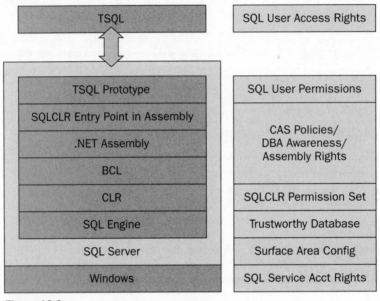

Figure 10-6

SQL CLR Assembly Metadata

SQL Server has historically stored all the information about its objects in a set of tables that are referred to as its *metadata*. This data includes detailed information about data structures, types, sizes, and even T-SQL code that defines objects. With SQL Server 2005, some of these metadata locations have changed, even have been removed to a separate resource database. Even so, this continues to be the architecture underneath SQL Server and the advent of SQL CLR this model continues. This section will help explain where SQL Server stores all the information that it uses to manage and persist SQL CLR assemblies.

Where are Noncore Assemblies Stored?

We mentioned earlier that assemblies were loaded into SQL metadata when you execute a CREATE ASSEMBLY statement. This is true for all noncore assemblies. Any assembly loaded into SQL Server using the CREATE Assembly statement can be viewed using one of the catalog views specifically for CLR assemblies. Catalog views are the recommended way to assess and view SQL Server–specific catalog metadata.

❑   Sys.Assemblies: This view reveals a storage location for each assembly in a database. Each row represents one assembly. Here you can find the CLR name that uniquely identifies the assembly, the permission set or security level, the create date, and the last modified date for each assembly.

❑ Sys.Assembly_Modules: This view reveals the classes and methods that are available in each assembly. These methods or entry points may or may not be available for binding with T-SQL DDL.

❑ Sys.Assembly_Files: This view reveals at minimum the information stored for the binary for each assembly. You can also load as many supporting files as you like for an assembly using the ALTER ASSEMBLY T-SQL statement.

❑ Sys.Assembly_References: This view reveals interassembly dependencies. The two primary key pairs are stored here to resolve which assemblies require other assemblies to run. This table is what SQL Server uses to determine if an assembly can be removed. If the assembly has a reference entry to indicate that other assemblies reference it, the dependent assemblies have to be removed first before the primary assembly can be removed.

❑ Sys.Module_Assembly_Usages: This view contains the links between assemblies and T-SQL objects like UDFs, SPs, and aggregates.

❑ Sys.Type_Assembly_Usages: This view contains the links between assemblies and T-SQL type definitions.

If you want to find where assemblies are really stored, look at the definition of the view by using the OBJECT_DEFINITION function like this:

```
SELECT OBJECT_DEFINITION(OBJECT_ID('sys.assembly_files'));
```

This returns the definition:

```
CREATE VIEW sys.assemblies AS
SELECT  s.name AS name, r.indepid AS principal_id, s.id AS assembly_id,
        qn.name AS clr_name,  convert(tinyint, s.intprop) AS permission_set,
        i.name AS permission_set_desc,
            sysconv(bit, s.status & 1) AS is_visible, -- ASM_EXPLICIT_REG
            s.created AS create_date,    s.modified AS modify_date
FROM sys.sysclsobjs s
LEFT JOIN sys.syssingleobjrefs r
    ON r.depid = s.id AND r.class = 52 AND r.depsubid = 0 -- SRC_ASMOWNER
LEFT JOIN sys.syssingleobjrefs cr
    ON cr.depid = s.id AND cr.class = 26 AND cr.depsubid = 0 -- SRC_ASMCLRNAME_QNAME
LEFT JOIN sys.sysqnames qn
    ON qn.nid = cr.indepid
LEFT JOIN sys.syspalvalues i
    ON i.class = 'ASPS'
    AND i.value = s.intprop
WHERE s.class = 10
AND has_access('AS', s.id) = 1 -- SOC_ASSEMBLY
```

This T-SQL code reveals that sys.assembly is using a set of system base tables sysclsobjs, syssingle objrefs, sysqnames, and syspalvalues. These system base tables are loaded for each database, but you will not be able to see the in the object browser. System base tables are not like pre-2005 system tables. In fact, many of the metadata tables are now stored in a new database called mssqlsystemresource. The views starting with sys are mostly in this new database. You cannot obtain direct access to these tables unless you connect to the SQL Server instance using the dedicated administrator console (DAC). You can use the OBJECT_DEFINITION function to examine the other catalog views for assemblies to find out where they really are stored. Many things have obviously changed about metadata storage in SQL Server 2005, so this information is vital if you need to know what to backup for recovery purposes.

The strange thing is that you can't back up the resource database using the normal SQL tools or SSMS. This database is not visible through these interfaces. What you can do is treat the .mdf file as a normal file-based backup or restore. You must be careful doing this not to overwrite with an out-of-date .mdf file during a restore process. The mssqlsystemresource.mdf file should be located in the default location of <drive>:\Program Files\Microsoft SQL Server\MSSQL.1\MSSQL\Data\.

You can use SQL Server metadata to create your own views. One of the things DBAs may be interested in is a complete list of SQL CLR routines deployed in a database. Using the metadata, you can create a view to list the assemblies and the corresponding T-SQL objects like this:

```
CREATE VIEW vwSQLCLR_OBJECTS
AS
--This retrieves the module-level routines
SELECT    obj.Name as SQLCLR_OBJECT_NAME,
          obj.Type_Desc as SQLCLR_TYPE,
          asm.Name as SQLCLR_ASSEMBLY,
          asm.Permission_set_Desc as SQLCLR_PERMISSION_SET,
          asm.CREATE_DATE, asm.MODIFY_DATE
FROM sys.objects obj
INNER JOIN sys.module_assembly_usages mods
    ON obj.object_id = mods.object_id
INNER JOIN sys.assemblies asm
    ON mods.assembly_id = asm.assembly_id
UNION
--This retrieves the CLR-Types
SELECT typ.name as SQLCLR_OBJECT_NAME,
          'CLR_TYPE' as SQLCLR_TYPE,
          asm.Name as SQLCLR_ASSEMBLY,
          asm.Permission_set_Desc as SQLCLR_PERMISSION_SET,
          asm.CREATE_DATE, asm.MODIFY_DATE
FROM sys.types typ
INNER JOIN sys.type_assembly_usages tau
ON typ.user_type_id = tau.user_type_id
INNER JOIN sys.assemblies AS asm
ON tau.assembly_id = asm.assembly_id
```

If you deploy this view, you'll be able to see all the pertinent information about your loaded SQL CLR objects in one query.

Where Are Core .NET Assemblies Stored?

Core assemblies like System.dll are not loaded directly into these SQL Server base tables. These assemblies are accessed like extended stored procedures. The DLL name, attributes, and physical file location are stored in SQL Server metadata instead of the contents of the DLL itself. When a DLL is used, SQL Server uses the metadata to link to the physical DLL, and loads that DLL into CLR memory. The catalog location for these assemblies is even more challenging to find. You can start by using the OBJECT_DEFINITION function with the parameter of the sys.dm_os_loaded_modules view to decompose this object.

```
SELECT OBJECT_DEFINITION(OBJECT_ID('sys.dm_os_loaded_modules'));
```

Running the previous statement gives you the body of the view, which looks like this:

```
CREATE VIEW sys.dm_os_loaded_modules AS
SELECT * FROM OpenRowSet(sysmodules)
```

The OpenRowSet call is used to access a datasource located in the new Resource database we discussed earlier that is installed with each SQL Server instance.

Managing the SQL CLR Lifecycle

Once you start the process of developing SQL CLR routines, you'll need to address how you are going to get assemblies through the various development, testing, quality assurance, and production environments. You'll need processes to deal with the fact that you are deploying a binary DLL as well as the associated T-SQL scripts. One crucial detail that you'll need to decide is whether your DBAs are going to deploy SQL CLR routines using the Visual Studio environment or via scripts. This section explains the details of the release process and provides a best practice guide to developing your own release environment and procedures.

Start by Limiting the .NET Language

When Oracle integrated Java into its database, the DBAs had an advantage: They only had to brush up on one language to debug and troubleshoot. SQL CLR routines can provide a challenge if you allow either of the currently two .NET-compliant languages. Each .NET language has its own idiosyncrasies that a DBA may or may not have enough experience to be able to troubleshoot efficiently. This potentially could require the involvement of a programmer in a production troubleshooting session. It will be more manageable in the short term to limit development of SQL CLR routines to one .NET language for the benefit of both the DBA and programmer at least until both sides become proficient in the execution of .NET code in the SQL CLR environment.

Setting Up the Environments

The best method of best developing in the SQL CLR lifecycle is to maintain two separate sets of roles, responsibilities, and machines, just as you do in T-SQL development.

Development Environments

Allow the developers their own SQL Server 2005 instance with enough permission in SQL Server to allow for efficient autodeployment capabilities of the Visual Studio IDE. They'll need to add references and to compile and redeploy in rapid development cycles. Make sure that they have VIEW DEFINITION rights to the databases on this development server to allow adding references as well as dbo_ddladmin rights (limited to specific databases) for deployment of the assemblies. We do not recommend opening up the development server for SQL CLR permission sets of EXTERNAL_ACCESS or UNSAFE by granting these rights to developer user groups as a default. These rights should be set based on a business case, not just because someone wants to use this feature set. If you have a specific CAS or role-based security policy, enforce it—even on the development machine. This way there are no surprises when the code comes to production.

Production Environments

On the production machine, developers should be specifically restricted to read-only access. If you are in a small shop, at least ensure that the dbo_ddladmin rights are denied to developers and that they do not have grant privileges to the new Control Server permissions. Developers should have the responsibility of communicating to the DBAs before developing SQL CLR routines to ensure that assemblies and namespaces they want to use will be available or even allowed in the production environment. Developers should be sensitive to the fact that DBAs will have to review the .NET code and should pick one language to use for SQL CLR development.

Promoting Source through the Environments

The DBA's deployment cycle obviously should be less frequent than the development cycle. How to deploy is the question. One option is to use the capabilities of Visual Studio 2005 to open the SQL CLR solution and deploy the solution to the production environment. Other options include using the database projects in Visual Studio to deploy the assembly and supporting files using a set of preset scripts. We'll show you how to do this if you haven't used this type of project template. f you don't have access to Visual Studio, you'll need to deploy the assembly manually. We can help you here with a set of T-SQL scripts that you can use. Your final decision rests upon whether or not the DBA has a license agreement to use Visual Studio to debug or open SQL CLR source. If you don't have Visual Studio, and you manage SQL CLR deployments, you'll have to do a little more work. If you have Visual Studio, at most you'll be more productive, at the very least you'll make some developers nervous. Many DBAs are already using database project types in Visual Studio to manage and deploy T-SQL-based changes through multiple release environments. You'll walk through a sample of the database projects in this chapter.

The basic paradigm is that developers will provide DBAs with the completed .NET solution files when testing is complete. Developers can do this by providing the physical files to a .NET solutions or by giving the DBA access into the source control environment to pull copies of and compile these files herself. This process looks like Figure 10-7, except that there may be other midstream environments between the development and final production environment. Regardless of your deployment method, DBAs need enough lead time in the change control process to validate that security policies are followed, and to look through the .NET code for use of dangerous functionalities that we have discussed in this chapter.

Scripting the Deployment of Assemblies with T-SQL

To deploy assemblies manually, at minimum you need the binary DLL file. Optimally, get all the solution files from the developers, and compile the assembly into a binary yourself. Having all the solution files makes it easier for you to load the supporting files too. You will also have an opportunity to examine the code for potential resource or security violations. If all you have is the DLL, inspect the MSIL in the DLL file using ILDASM tool that we discussed earlier in the section "How to Look Inside a Compiled Assembly."

One of the key advantages to manually scripting out SQL CLR deployments is that you have control over the process and can step through each stage.

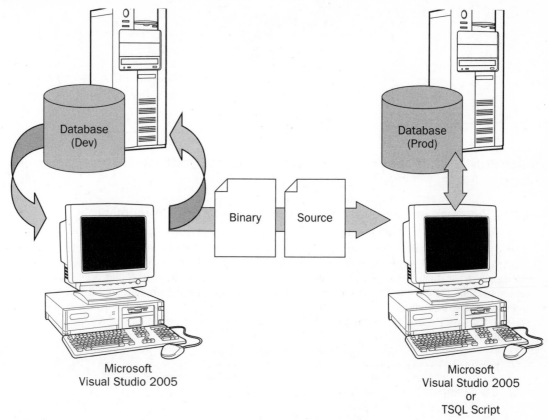

Binary   Source

Database (Dev)

Database (Prod)

Microsoft
Visual Studio 2005

Microsoft
Visual Studio 2005
or
TSQL Script

Figure 10-7

Set Up a Common Deployment Folder

On a directory that is visible, readable, and writable to your SQL Server instance, set up a deployment folder to stage your scripts that will load new assemblies. If you have an environment where each database is on different servers, you may need to create a network share that all instances in your development environment can use. The goal here is to store the source for the assemblies and the script that loads the assemblies in one place by change request. Then deploying the script to different environments just involves pointing the scripts at new server instances or databases.

Create subfolders under the deployment folder to represent a change request. Under that directory create two subfolders: one for the source files that you need to deploy and another for scripts. Your deployment directory at this point for a change request numbered REQ12345 would look like Figure 10-8.

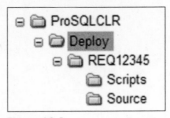

Figure 10-8

Copy all the source files from the solution for change request REQ12345 into the source directory. Just copy the structure as-is from the solution.

Scripting Preparing and Removing Permissions in the Server Environment

To deploy and load an assembly, you have to have specific rights on the Server. Safe assemblies can be loaded at any time as they are no different than T-SQL routines. Assemblies with EXTERNAL_ACCESS and UNSAFE permissions can't be loaded into a server unless you have the proper permissions. Additionally, the database to which you are loading the assembly must be in a trustworthy condition. This is a lot to remember. If you are using any assembly with these higher security requirement, use this script in T-SQL to make sure you covered all the bases. If you are only allowing SAFE assemblies, you only need to set the TRUSTWORTHY status of the database. This script should be run in the database where you intend to load the assembly.

```
/*===========================================================
  THIS SCRIPT WILL PREPARE A SERVER FOR LOADING AN ASSEMBLY
  BY GRANTING RIGHTS FOR THE CURRENT USER TO LOAD
  ASSEMBLIES OF ALL PERMISSION SETS
  AND SETTING THE DATABASE TO TRUSTWORTHY TO
  ALLOW THE ASSEMBLY TO BE LOADED INTO CLR
  NOTE: RUN IN DATABASE YOU WANT TO LOAD THE ASSEMBLY
  ===========================================================*/
DECLARE @user NVARCHAR(50)
DECLARE @tsql NVARCHAR(MAX)
DECLARE @error INT

SELECT @user = USER_NAME()
IF @user = 'dbo'
  SET @user = '[BUILTIN\Administrators]'

PRINT 'STEP PREPARE SERVER AND DATABASE FOR ASSEMBLY LOADING'
PRINT 'SERVER  :   [' + @@SERVERNAME + ']'
PRINT 'DATEBASE:   [' + db_name() + ']'
PRINT 'USER    :   ' + @user
PRINT 'START TIME: ' + convert(varchar(max), getdate())

PRINT ''
PRINT 'GRANT PERMISSION TO LOAD EXTERNAL_ACCESS ASSEMBLIES'
SET @tsql = 'USE MASTER ' + char(13) + char(10) +
                   'GRANT EXTERNAL ACCESS ASSEMBLY TO ' + @user + ''

EXEC sp_ExecuteSQL @tsql
SET @Error = @@Error
```

```
      IF @Error <> 0
        BEGIN
          PRINT 'ERROR OCCURRED: ' + CONVERT(varchar(50), @error)
          PRINT 'GRANTING EXTERNAL_ACCESS LOADING PERMISSIONS'
          PRINT 'TO ' + @user
        END
      ELSE
        BEGIN
          PRINT 'GRANT PERMISSION TO LOAD UNSAFE ASSEMBLIES'
          SET @tsql = 'USE MASTER ' + char(13) + char(10) +
                             'GRANT UNSAFE ASSEMBLY TO ' + @user + ''

          EXECUTE sp_ExecuteSQL @tsql
          SET @Error = @@Error
          IF @Error <> 0
            BEGIN
              PRINT 'ERROR OCCURRED: ' + CONVERT(varchar(50), @error)
              PRINT 'GRANTING UNSAFE LOADING PERMISSIONS'
              PRINT 'TO ' + @user
            END
          ELSE
            BEGIN
              PRINT 'MARK DATABASE ' + db_name() + ' SO ASSEMBLIES CAN RUN'
              SET @tsql = N'USE MASTER ' + char(13) + char(10) +
                     'ALTER DATABASE ' + db_name() + ' SET TRUSTWORTHY ON '
              EXEC sp_Executesql @tsql
              SET @error = @@ERROR
              IF @error <> 0
                BEGIN
                  PRINT 'ERROR OCCURRED: ' + CONVERT(varchar(50), @error)
                  PRINT 'MARKING DATABASE ' + db_name() + ' SAFE TO RUN ASSEMBLIES'
                END
            END
        END
    END
  PRINT ''
  PRINT 'STEP COMPLETED'
  PRINT 'END TIME: ' + convert(varchar(max), getdate())
```

After you load an assembly, you may want to restrict the permission of the deploying user to ensure that you maintain good controls for who is loading assemblies with these higher security requirements. Use this script if you are using change control personnel to deploy assemblies as the last step in a deployment process to deny the current user's rights to load future assemblies.

```
/*============================================================
  THIS SCRIPT WILL HARDEN A SERVER TO DENY LOADING
  OF ANY ASSEMBLY WITH EXTERNAL_ACCESS OR UNSAFE
  PERMISSION SETS--EVEN ADMIN
  BY DENYING RIGHTS FOR THE CURRENT USER TO LOAD
  NOTE: ONLY RUN IN DATABASE YOU ARE DEPLOYING ASSEMBLIES
  ============================================================*/
DECLARE @user NVARCHAR(50)
DECLARE @tsql NVARCHAR(MAX)
DECLARE @error INT

SELECT @user = USER_NAME()
```

```
IF @user = 'dbo'
  SET @user = '[BUILTIN\Administrators]'

PRINT 'STEP REMOVE LOADING PERMISSIONS'
PRINT 'SERVER  :   [' + @@SERVERNAME + ']'
PRINT 'DATEBASE:   [' + db_name() + ']'
PRINT 'USER    :   ' + @user
PRINT 'START TIME: ' + convert(varchar(max), getdate())

PRINT ''
PRINT 'DENY PERMISSION TO LOAD EXTERNAL_ACCESS ASSEMBLIES'
SET @tsql = 'USE MASTER ' + char(13) + char(10) +
                'DENY EXTERNAL ACCESS ASSEMBLY TO ' + @user + ''

EXEC sp_ExecuteSQL @tsql
SET @Error = @@Error
IF @Error <> 0
  BEGIN
     PRINT 'ERROR OCCURRED: ' + CONVERT(varchar(50), @error)
     PRINT 'DENYING EXTERNAL_ACCESS LOADING PERMISSIONS'
     PRINT 'TO ' + @user
  END
ELSE
  BEGIN
     PRINT 'DENY PERMISSION TO LOAD UNSAFE ASSEMBLIES'
     SET @tsql = 'USE MASTER ' + char(13) + char(10) +
                     'DENY UNSAFE ASSEMBLY TO ' + @user + ''

     EXECUTE sp_ExecuteSQL @tsql
     SET @Error = @@Error
     IF @Error <> 0
       BEGIN
          PRINT 'ERROR OCCURRED: ' + CONVERT(varchar(50), @error)
          PRINT 'DENYING UNSAFE LOADING PERMISSIONS'
          PRINT 'TO ' + @user
       END
  END
PRINT ''
PRINT 'STEP COMPLETED'
PRINT 'END TIME: ' + convert(varchar(max), getdate())
```

Scripting the Dropping of an Assembly

Before you can load an assembly, any current versions of the assembly will need to be removed. If this assembly is being used by other SQL CLR routines, it will not be able to be removed and updated until all the depending assemblies are removed. This will create some coordination issues if you are developing any core assemblies with the intent of having them be a shared library of common utilities. Just be aware that you'll have to unload and reload all the dependent assemblies. That's why storing the source and the scripts to load the source in a deployment location are a good idea. To drop an assembly, use this script:

```
/*============================================================
  THIS SCRIPT WILL REMOVE AN EXISTING ASSEMBLY AND ANY
  SUPPORTING FILES: PDB, CS, .*
  NOTE: IF ASSEMBLY HAS OTHER DEPENDENT ASSEMBLIES YOU WILL
```

```
       NEED TO REMOVE THOSE ASSEMBLIES FIRST
       USAGE:
       INSERT THE ASSEMBLY NAME THAT YOU NEED TO DROP
       SET @ASSEMBLYNAME = N'sampleassembly'
       =========================================================*/
       DECLARE @ASSEMBLYNAME NVARCHAR(50)
       SET @ASSEMBLYNAME = N'YourAssembly'
/*=========================================================
       THEN RUN THE ENTIRE SCRIPT
       =========================================================*/
       DECLARE @user NVARCHAR(50)
       SELECT @user = USER_NAME()
       IF @user = 'dbo'
         SET @user = '[BUILTIN\Administrators]'

       PRINT 'STEP DROPPING ASSEMBLY '
       PRINT 'SERVER  :   [' + @@SERVERNAME + ']'
       PRINT 'DATEBASE:   [' + db_name() + ']'
       PRINT 'USER    :   ' + @user
       PRINT 'START TIME: ' + convert(varchar(max), getdate())
       PRINT N'DROPPING ASSEMBLY ' + @ASSEMBLYNAME

       /* Drop the assembly */
       IF EXISTS (SELECT name FROM sys.assemblies WHERE name = @ASSEMBLYNAME)
         BEGIN
           DECLARE @error int
           SET @error = 0

           /* Drop the assembly user defined aggregates, triggers, functions and
              procedures */
           DECLARE @moduleId sysname
           DECLARE @moduleName sysname
           DECLARE @moduleType char(2)
           DECLARE @moduleClass tinyint
           DECLARE assemblyModules CURSOR FAST_FORWARD FOR
             SELECT t.object_id, t.name, t.type, t.parent_class as class
               FROM sys.triggers t
               INNER JOIN sys.assembly_modules m
               ON t.object_id = m.object_id
               INNER JOIN sys.assemblies a
               ON m.assembly_id = a.assembly_id
               WHERE a.name = @ASSEMBLYNAME
             UNION
             SELECT o.object_id, o.name, o.type, NULL as class
               FROM sys.objects o
               INNER JOIN sys.assembly_modules m
               ON o.object_id = m.object_id
               INNER JOIN sys.assemblies a
               ON m.assembly_id = a.assembly_id
               WHERE a.name = @ASSEMBLYNAME
           OPEN assemblyModules
           FETCH NEXT FROM assemblyModules
           INTO @moduleId, @moduleName, @moduleType, @moduleClass
           WHILE (@error = 0 AND @@FETCH_STATUS = 0)
           BEGIN
```

```
DECLARE @dropModuleString nvarchar(256)
IF (@moduleType = 'AF') SET @dropModuleString = N'AGGREGATE'
IF (@moduleType = 'TA') SET @dropModuleString = N'TRIGGER'
IF (@moduleType = 'FT' OR @moduleType = 'FS')
   SET @dropModuleString = N'FUNCTION'
IF (@moduleType = 'PC')
   SET @dropModuleString = N'PROCEDURE'
SET @dropModuleString = N'DROP ' + @dropModuleString +
      ' [' + REPLACE(@moduleName, ']', ']]') + ']'
IF (@moduleType = 'TA' AND @moduleClass = 0)
BEGIN
   SET @dropModuleString = @dropModuleString + N' ON DATABASE'
END
IF NOT EXISTS (SELECT name FROM sys.extended_properties WHERE major_id =
               @moduleId AND name = 'AutoDeployed')
BEGIN
   DECLARE @quotedModuleName sysname
   SET @quotedModuleName = REPLACE(@moduleName, '''', '''''')
   RAISERROR(N'The assembly module ''%s'' cannot be re-  ' +
               ' deployed because it was created outside of ' +
               'Visual Studio.  Drop the module from the database ' +
               'before deploying the assembly.', 16, 1,
                     @quotedModuleName)
   SET @error = @@ERROR
END
ELSE
BEGIN
   EXEC sp_executesql @dropModuleString
   FETCH NEXT FROM assemblyModules
      INTO @moduleId, @moduleName, @moduleType, @moduleClass
END
END
CLOSE assemblyModules
DEALLOCATE assemblyModules

/* Drop the assembly user defined types */
DECLARE @typeId int
DECLARE @typeName sysname
DECLARE assemblyTypes CURSOR FAST_FORWARD
   FOR SELECT t.user_type_id, t.name
     FROM sys.assembly_types t
     INNER JOIN sys.assemblies a
     ON t.assembly_id = a.assembly_id
     WHERE a.name = @ASSEMBLYNAME
OPEN assemblyTypes
FETCH NEXT FROM assemblyTypes INTO @typeId, @typeName
WHILE (@error = 0 AND @@FETCH_STATUS = 0)
BEGIN
   DECLARE @dropTypeString nvarchar(256)
   SET @dropTypeString = N'DROP TYPE [' +
     REPLACE(@typeName, ']', ']]') + ']'
   IF NOT EXISTS (SELECT name FROM sys.extended_properties
     WHERE major_id = @typeId AND name = 'AutoDeployed')
   BEGIN
     DECLARE @quotedTypeName sysname
```

```
          SET @quotedTypeName = REPLACE(@typeName, '''', ''''''')
          RAISERROR(N'The assembly user defined type ''%s'' ' +
          'cannot be preserved because it was not automatically ' +
          ' deployed.', 16, 1, @quotedTypeName)
          SET @error = @@ERROR
      END
      ELSE
      BEGIN
        EXEC sp_executesql @dropTypeString
        FETCH NEXT FROM assemblyTypes INTO @typeId, @typeName
      END
    END
    CLOSE assemblyTypes
    DEALLOCATE assemblyTypes

    /* Drop the assembly */
    IF (@error = 0)
        EXEC(N'DROP ASSEMBLY [' + @ASSEMBLYNAME + N'] WITH NO DEPENDENTS')
  END

  If @Error is null or @Error = 0
  BEGIN
    PRINT 'COMPLETED SUCCESSFULLY'
  END
  ELSE
  BEGIN
    PRINT 'DID NOT COMPLETE AS EXPECTED '
    PRINT 'RETURNED ERROR CODE ' + CONVERT(NVARCHAR(MAX), isnull(@error, 0))
    PRINT 'PLEASE CHECK THE RESULTS '
  END
PRINT 'END TIME: ' + convert(varchar(max), getdate())
```

Script the Loading of the Assembly

Adding the assembly loads the contents of the assembly DLL straight into SQL Server metadata. To add an assembly, you need to know the name of the assembly. Right-click the project in Visual Studio and look in the property pages for the Application settings to get the assembly name or require that the developer provide the assembly name to you. You'll also need to know what permission set to apply to the assembly. The developer should provide this for you as well. Find the path to the assembly by looking in the solution folder hierarchy for a file folder named \BIN or by using the location that you copied the binary DLL file. With this information, you are ready to load. Run this script in the database that you want to install the assembly:

```
/*===========================================================
  PROVIDE THE ASSEMBLY NAME AND THE ASSEMBLY PATH
  THAT YOU WANT TO LOAD INTO A DATABASE
  USAGE:
  SET @ASSEMBLYNAME = 'sampleassembly'
  SET @ASSEMBLYFILEPATH = '<FILE PATH TO ASSEMBLY>.dll'
  SET @PERMISSION_SET = 'SAFE | EXTERNAL_ACCESS | UNSAFE'

  NOTE: RUN IN THE DATABASE YOU WANT TO LOAD THE ASSEMBLY
  ===========================================================*/
```

```
DECLARE @ASSEMBLYNAME       VARCHAR(50)
DECLARE @ASSEMBLYFILEPATH NVARCHAR(100)
DECLARE @PERMISSION_SET    NVARCHAR(50)

SET @ASSEMBLYNAME = N'sampleassembly'
SET @ASSEMBLYFILEPATH = N'C:\ProSQLCLR\YourDeployDir\YourAssembly.dll'
SET @PERMISSION_SET = N'SAFE'
/*===========================================================
THEN RUN THE ENTIRE SCRIPT
===========================================================*/
DECLARE @user NVARCHAR(50)
DECLARE @tsql NVARCHAR(MAX)
SELECT @user = USER_NAME()
IF @user = 'dbo'
  SET @user = '[BUILTIN\Administrators]'

PRINT 'STEP ADDING ASSEMBLY '
PRINT 'SERVER  :   [' + @@SERVERNAME + ']'
PRINT 'DATEBASE:   [' + db_name() + ']'
PRINT 'USER    :   ' + @user
PRINT 'START TIME: ' + convert(varchar(max), getdate())
PRINT N'ADDING ASSEMBLY ' + @ASSEMBLYNAME +
    ' WITH PERMISSIONS ' + @PERMISSION_SET


DECLARE @Error INT
SET @tsql = N'CREATE ASSEMBLY ' + @ASSEMBLYNAME +
'  FROM ''' +
  @ASSEMBLYFILEPATH +
  '''  WITH PERMISSION_SET = ' +
  @PERMISSION_SET + ''

PRINT @tsql
EXEC sp_executesql @tsql
SET @error = @@ERROR
IF (@error <> 0)
BEGIN
  PRINT 'ERROR OCCURRED ' + CONVERT(VARCHAR(MAX), @Error)
  PRINT 'ASSEMBLY ' + @ASSEMBLYNAME + ' FAILED TO LOAD '
END
ELSE
BEGIN
  EXEC sp_addextendedproperty 'AutoDeployed', N'no','ASSEMBLY', @ASSEMBLYNAME
  EXEC sp_addextendedproperty 'SqlAssemblyProjectRoot', @ASSEMBLYFILEPATH,
      'ASSEMBLY', @ASSEMBLYNAME
END

PRINT 'END TIME: ' + convert(varchar(max), getdate())
```

Scripting the Addition of Supporting Files

We've discussed the merits of loading support files in the database with the assemblies. However, if you were maintaining a copy of the solution in a deployment directory, this would be an unnecessary step. The concern was that the DBA would need this content to troubleshoot an error in a production situation.

Since the source could be found in the deployment location, the DBA could use these files for trouble-shooting. The only file you may want to add as a supporting file is the PDB file for the assembly. This file contains pointers to the source of the DLL to allow for debugging of the SQL CLR routines. Obviously, you would not want to do this in a production deployment. The script for loading supporting files into SQL Server is:

```
/*============================================================
  PROVIDE THE INFORMATION OF THE SUPPORTING FILES THAT YOU
  NEED TO LOAD INTO THE DATABASE AND RELATE TO AN EXISTING
  ASSEMBLY
  USAGE:
  SET @ASSEMBLYNAME = 'sampleassembly'
  SET @SUPPORTFILEPATH = '<FILE PATH TO SupportFilePath>.xxx'
  ============================================================*/
  DECLARE @ASSEMBLYNAME    NVARCHAR(50)
  DECLARE @SUPPORTFILEPATH NVARCHAR(MAX)

  SET @ASSEMBLYNAME = N'YourAssembly'
  SET @SUPPORTFILEPATH = N'C:\ProSQLCLR\YourDeploy\YourFile.xxx'
/*============================================================
  THEN RUN THE ENTIRE SCRIPT
  ============================================================*/
  DECLARE @user NVARCHAR(50)
  DECLARE @tsql NVARCHAR(MAX)
  SELECT @user = USER_NAME()
  IF @user = 'dbo'
    SET @user = '[BUILTIN\Administrators]'

  PRINT 'STEP ADDING SUPPORTING FILES'
  PRINT 'SERVER  :   [' + @@SERVERNAME + ']'
  PRINT 'DATEBASE:   [' + db_name() + ']'
  PRINT 'USER    :   ' + @user
  PRINT 'START TIME: ' + convert(varchar(max), getdate())
  PRINT N'ADDING SUPPORT FILE ' + @SUPPORTFILEPATH
  PRINT N'TO ASSEMBLY ' + @ASSEMBLYNAME

  DECLARE @error INT
  SET @error = 0

    IF (@@TRANCOUNT > 0)
    BEGIN
      SET @tsql = N'
        ALTER ASSEMBLY [' + @ASSEMBLYNAME + ']
        ADD FILE
        FROM ' + @SUPPORTFILEPATH+
        'AS ' + @ASSEMBLYNAME

      EXEC sp_executesql @tsql

      SET @error = @@Error
      IF @Error <> 0
        PRINT 'ERROR LOADING FILE: ' + @SUPPORTFILEPATH
    END
  ELSE
```

```
      BEGIN
         PRINT 'ASSEMBLY N' + @ASSEMBLYNAME + ' DOESN''T EXIST IN ' + db_name()
      END

   PRINT 'END TIME: ' + convert(varchar(max), getdate())
```

Scripting T-SQL DDL to Wrap Assembly Entry Points

We've talked about loading the assemblies, but how do the T-SQL objects get mapped to the assembly entry points? You'll need to provide the normal T-SQL DDL that maps a T-SQL object to the assembly entry point. The mapping simply points the implementation from a batch of T-SQL statements to an external assembly. The T-SQL looks could like this for an example stored procedure implementation.

```
CREATE PROCEDURE mspWriteDatetoFile
AS
EXTERNAL NAME
[WriteDateFile].[StoredProcedures].[mspWriteDatetoFile]
```

At this point, this is simple T-SQL object creation, so you can add grant statements as your security model dictates. How do you know the three sets of names to plug into this statement? They essentially map to the following:

```
[ASSEMBLY NAME].[CLASS NAME].[ASSEMBLY METHOD]
```

You can find the assembly name in the `sys.assemblies` catalog view once the assembly is loaded or you can look in the project property pages under the Application tab. You can find the class and method by looking up the assembly in the `sys.assembly_modules` catalog view or using the following T-SQL procedure:

```
CREATE PROC usp_DisplayAssembly_EntryPoints
   (
        @AssemblyName as varchar(100)
   )
AS

SELECT   asm.[Name] as [Assembly Name],
         mod.Assembly_class as [Class Name],
         mod.Assembly_method as [Assembly Method],
         asm.permission_set_Desc as [Permission Set]
FROM sys.assemblies asm
INNER JOIN sys.assembly_modules mod
ON asm.assembly_id = mod.assembly_id
WHERE asm.[Name] = @AssemblyName
```

The results would look like the following for the `WriteDateFile` assembly you built earlier in this chapter.

```
Assembly Name Class Name        Assembly Method     Permission Set
------------- ----------------- ------------------- ---------------
WriteDateFile StoredProcedures  mspWriteDatetoFile  EXTERNAL_ACCESS
WriteDateFile StoredProcedures  mspWriteDatetoFile  EXTERNAL_ACCESS
```

Using this information, you could build the T-SQL DDL to look like this:

```
ALTER PROCEDURE [dbo].[mspWriteDatetoFile]
WITH EXECUTE AS CALLER
AS
EXTERNAL NAME [WriteDateFile].[StoredProcedures].[mspWriteDatetoFile]
GO
```

If you are using any role-based security, you can add these permissions here by executing a regular T-SQL GRANT statement like this:

```
GRANT EXECUTE on dbo.mspWriteDatetoFile TO <Your_SP_Role>
```

Structuring These Scripts in a Database Project

These scripts are like any of your current change control scripts. They can get a little hairy to keep track of and to run in the right order. One way to organize them is name and save them somewhere in a template folder like this:

- ❑ Step 1. Prepare Server and Database.sql

- ❑ Step 2. Drop Existing Assembly.sql

- ❑ Step 3. Add Assembly.sql

- ❑ Step N. Add Supporting Files.sql

- ❑ Step Z. Remove Loading Permissions.sql

- ❑ Step ZZ. Create T-SQL DLL.sql

When a deployment is imminent, just copy these scripts into your deployment folder, update the parameters, and they are ready to load and run. As you load them into the SSMS query window, you'll need to log into the server instance and database that you want the assembly to be deployed to.

Visual Studio provides a great way to keep track of scripts like this and allows for easy deployment to different environments by just changing a connection. To see what this would look, like open Visual Studio. Select File ➪ New Project. In the project templates, select the node Other Project Types and Database. Select the Database Project, and save the solution in your deployment directory under the release\source directory structure. Add these template scripts to the project. Your completed project should look like Figure 10-9.

Notice that the solution has two database references stored in the solution. You can add all your change control databases up front as references. To deploy these scripts into each database, just right-click on the project node DeploymentExample and select the menu option Set Default Reference. The Database selection window will then allow you to point to and click on the environment to which you want to deploy the scripts. You can also right-click on a script and select the menu option Run On. Then select the database connection on which to run the script.

To run a script, just right-click on a script and choose menu option Run. The script will then execute on the default database connection.

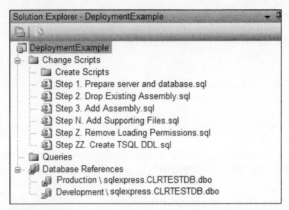

Figure 10-9

Deployment Using Visual Studio

If you are using Visual Studio for deployment, life is much easier. Visual Studio compiles, deploys, and loads all supporting files for an assembly for you automatically if set up properly. Visual Studio also creates the T-SQL DDL as well. This can reduce your deployment time drastically. If you've got a copy of the whole solution in the deployment staging area, all you need to do is open the solution, change the database that it is pointing to, and redeploy the solution. To change the database location, right-click on the project properties to access the Database tab. Press the browse button to either make a new or select an existing connection to the environment in the database connection dialog.

Typically, development work produces a debug version of the assembly. You can deploy debug, or release versions of your project depending upon the likelihood that you may need to deploy in the environment. Check the project properties build configuration to determine the last compile and deploy options to make sure they are both set to deploy in the build that you want for the project assembly. Figure 10-10 is an example of the build properties of the project set to build a release version of the assembly.

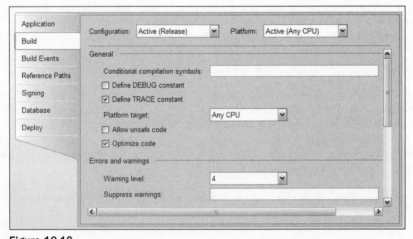

Figure 10-10

Compiling and deployment can be done in two separate steps. You should at least attempt one compile before actual deployment to avoid any surprises. Compiling can be done by selecting the menu option Build ➪ Rebuild. You should see that the assembly builds into the `release` subdirectory under the project `bin` directory.

```
Compile complete -- 0 errors, 0 warnings
Target CopyFilesToOutputDirectory:
    Copying file from
        "obj\Release\WriteDateFile.dll" to "bin\Release\WriteDateFile.dll".
```

Deployment is also a one-button step. Select the menu option Build ➪ Deploy when you're ready to deploy. A stream of information is generated into the output window that looks similar to this:

```
------ Build started: Project: WriteDateFile, Configuration: Release Any CPU ------
Build started 5/24/2006 10:14:50 PM.
Target CopyFilesToOutputDirectory:
    WriteDateFile -> C:\prosqlclr\admin chapter\projects\WriteDateToFile\
            WriteDateFile\bin\Release\WriteDateFile.dll

Build succeeded.

Time Elapsed 00:00:00.21
Drop assembly: WriteDateFile.dll ...
------ Deploy started: Project: WriteDateFile, Configuration: Release Any CPU -----
Deploying file: WriteDateFile.dll, Path: C:\prosqlclr\admin
chapter\projects\WriteDateToFile\WriteDateFile\obj\Release\WriteDateFile.dll ...
Deploying file: mspWriteDatetoFile.cs, Path: C:\prosqlclr\admin
chapter\projects\WriteDateToFile\WriteDateFile\mspWriteDatetoFile.cs ...
Deploying file: Properties\AssemblyInfo.cs, Path: C:\prosqlclr\admin
chapter\projects\WriteDateToFile\WriteDateFile\Properties\AssemblyInfo.cs ...
========== Build: 1 succeeded or up-to-date, 0 failed, 0 skipped ==========
========== Deploy: 1 succeeded, 0 failed, 0 skipped ==========
```

As a best practice, we recommend that you save this information into a text file and store it as one of the supporting files for the deployment. This information can document the deployment and ensure that the correct files were deployed.

Promoting Supporting Files

As part of the turnover process, not only should the binary assembly be loaded into SQL Server, but the source as well. If you are using the recommendation of a staged scripting location, you will not need to load this information into the database unless you just want to. This protects everyone since the code can be retrieved for troubleshooting, backed up with the database, and referred to easily if a server needs to be evaluated for the impact of a .NET Framework enhancement to SQL Server.

If you are using the Visual Studio IDE to deploy SQL CLR assemblies, you can have either all files, or only certain supporting files loaded automatically. The setting to control this is in the project Properties. Look in the Deploy tab of the project Properties form. A check box appears on the form under Deployment Options that you can select to Deploy Code. If the check box is checked (see Figure 10-11), all files necessary to recompile the code will be loaded into the assembly files metadata. If the check box is not checked, only the DLL (and PDB file if you're deploying debug assemblies) will be loaded. If the

Configuration combo box is set to a Debug option to indicate that the assembly is being compiled with debug information, then a public debug file will also be loaded with assembly metadata. For production assemblies, you would want this setting set to Release.

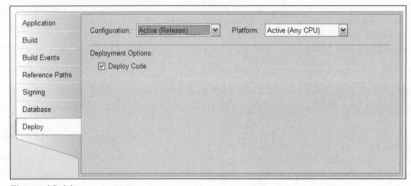

Figure 10-11

Some examples of typical supporting files are shown in the following table:

File Extention	File Description
Csproj	C# project files
Vbproj	VB.NET project files
Cs	C# class files
Vb	VB.NET class files
Pdb	Program debug database file (if deploying DLLs with debug info)
Txt	Supporting information
Doc	Release documentation

To load supporting information other than the code, you'll have to use the TSQL ALTER ASSEMBLY statement. To do this, you'll need to alter the assembly to add the source files. The ALTER ASSEMBLY statement supports arguments to allow the loading of the supporting files. A sample statement looks like this:

```
ALTER ASSEMBLY myfirstclrassembly
ADD FILE 'c:\FirstCLRRoutine.cs'
```

The file argument doesn't require that the supporting file be on the local machine. The same statement loading the file from a remote machine would look like this:

```
ALTER ASSEMBLY myfirstclrassembly
ADD FILE '\\remoteserver\FirstCLRRoutine.cs'
```

If you want to load all the supporting files in one swoop, then do this:

```
ALTER ASSEMBLY myfirstclrassembly
ADD FILE FROM  '\\remoteserver\FirstCLRRoutine.cs', 'c:\FirstCLRRoutine.cs'
```

Just remember if you ever need to refresh the assembly by loading a new binary, all the supporting files will also have to be removed. If you forget to do this, the ALTER ASSEMBLY statement will generate an exception to force you to remember. If you enforce the provision of new copies of supporting files with new binaries, keeping synchronized will not be an issue. If these supporting files are not loaded, DBAs will only have access to the binary. That only leaves the ILDASM tool to decompile an assembly to troubleshoot issues with SQL CLR routines. Chapter 2 provides an example of how to build an SSIS package to extract files from the sys.assembly_files view if you need this capability.

Backups

Assemblies are loaded into base system tables in specific databases. Because they are associated directly with a database, they get backed up with them as well. However, during backup processes, if you have assemblies marked with EXTERNAL_ACCESS and UNSAFE permission sets, the database TRUSTWORTHY flag is set to FALSE during the backup. Upon restore, you'll need to reset the TRUSTWORTHY flag to be able to use these assemblies.

Monitoring and Troubleshooting SQL CLR

Once you have SQL CLR code running, how can you monitor its behavior and troubleshoot issues when they occur? You can view SQL CLR objects in the same light as T-SQL objects, but there are some differences and specific things to look for when monitoring them in SQL Server.

Monitoring with SQL Server Profiler

Use the SQL Server Profiler the same way you would normally to look at the details of T-SQL events in the SQL Server database engine. A new addition to the profiler is the CLR Assembly Load event. This event reports details on the loaded assembly like the name, object ID (assembly_id), version, and public key token. You can also see if the assembly is having problems loading. If you implemented the CAS permissions to restrict IO to only the c:\prosqlclr\ directory, and an assembly attempted to write to a location other than that directory, you'd see details like this:

```
Assembly Load Failed for requested assembly system.enterpriseservices,
version=2.0.0.0, culture=neutral, publickeytoken=b03f5f7f11d50a3a,
processorarchitecture=x86 with Error code: 0x80070002.
```

Why is this information is stored in the ObjectName column? This assembly is the one throwing the exception when the misbehaving assembly is attempting to write to an unsecured location.

However, you'll be disappointed to know that you can't track the SQL Statement event classes to see what code is being executed as you can with a T-SQL-based stored procedure. The following is a sample of the event classes generated while executing the mspWriteDatetoFile stored procedure. Note that all the T-SQL and stored procedure event classes are selected for display.

```
Event Class            Text Data
------------------     ---------------------
SP:CacheMiss           exec mspWriteDateToFile
SQL:BatchStarting      exec mspWriteDateToFile
SQL:StmtStarting       exec mspWriteDateToFile
SP:Starting            exec mspWriteDateToFile
SP:Completed           exec mspWriteDateToFile
SQL:StmtCompleted      exec mspWriteDateToFile
```

Here you see that both the stored procedure and the T-SQL events just report the calling of the T-SQL prototype. No further insight to what is occurring within the assembly is visible in the profiler. However, the profiler is still useful in determining how these SQL CLR objects are being called and monitoring CPU and IO usages.

Using Dynamic Management Views

In SQL Server 2005, the kernel layer (SQL OS) has been rebuilt to expose some of the internal structures and data through a set of dynamic management views, or DMVs. These DMVs are designed to reduce the need to produce physical memory dumps of SQL Server process memory by providing the same type of granular information. For Administrators and DBAs, this information can also be useful to monitor SQL CLR effects on SQL Server 2005. These views may require either VIEW SERVER STATE or VIEW DATABASE STATE permissions to see rows.

What Assemblies Are Loaded?

Once an assembly is loaded, it is up to SQL Server to unload it. Loaded assemblies have an advantage in that subsequent calls to the assembly will not invoke the load event we traced using the SQL Profiler. This means that the DLL will not need to be located in sys.assembly_files and loaded into memory. To view the assemblies that are loaded for a server, use the DMV sys.dm_clr_loaded_assemblies. It will be a little easier to read if you join to the sys.assemblies view to retrieve the assembly name and to the DMV sys.dm_clr_appdomains to retrieve the Appdomain name like this:

```
select   datediff(mi, lasm.load_time, getdate()) as [Assembly Load Time (min)],
         asm.Name as SQLCLR_ASSEMBLY,
         asm.Permission_set_desc as SQLCLR_PERMISSION_SET,
         appd.Appdomain_Name as APPDOMAIN,
         datediff(mi, appd.Creation_time, getdate()) as [AppDomain Load Time (min)]
FROM sys.dm_clr_loaded_assemblies lasm
INNER JOIN sys.assemblies asm
ON lasm.assembly_id = asm.assembly_id
INNER JOIN sys.dm_clr_appdomains appd
ON lasm.appdomain_address = appd.appdomain_address
```

If you want to get an idea of the T-SQL objects that can benefit from this caching, use this T-SQL query:

```
SELECT   obj.Name as SQLCLR_OBJECT_NAME,
         obj.Type_Desc as SQLCLR_TYPE,
         asm.Name as SQLCLR_ASSEMBLY,
         asm.Permission_set_Desc as SQLCLR_PERMISSION_SET,
         asm.CREATE_DATE, asm.MODIFY_DATE
FROM sys.objects obj
INNER JOIN sys.module_assembly_usages mods
```

```
      ON obj.object_id = mods.object_id
INNER JOIN sys.assemblies asm
      ON mods.assembly_id = asm.assembly_id
INNER JOIN sys.dm_clr_loaded_assemblies lasm
ON lasm.assembly_id = asm.assembly_id
```

How Much Memory Is the CLR Using?

SQL Server 2005 has been reworked to become almost hands-free in terms of memory configuration for a system administrator. Typically, SQL Server will acquire and release memory as needed — even up to several megabytes each second. The current design calls for SQL Server to maximize a buffer pool of memory to reduce the amount of IO required, but also to manage this buffer pool so that the operating system has enough memory to operate effectively. Because CLR is integrated into SQL Server, it is possible for the SQL engine under significant memory pressure to abort threads from the CLR until finally even unloading the Appdomain and the assembly itself. You will know you are experiencing this type of memory condition when exceptions occur that report that the .NET Framework execution was aborted because of an out of memory condition.

If you are having memory related issues, use one of the DMVs to monitor memory usage while you run load tests using the SQL CLR objects. Memory in SQL Server is divided up into a three-tier hierarchy. For any SQL component like CLR to access memory, it has to go through a memory clerk, which manages memory at the lowest levels of the hierarchy. To get an overall look at the heap memory usage, start first with a look at the sys.dm_os_memory_clerks DMV. This view shows you in the single_pages_kb column the amount of memory that the single page memory allocator is taking directly from the overall SQL memory pool in KB. This number, combined with the amount of memory taken by the virtual allocator (CLR Host) outside of the memory pool in the multiple_pages_kb column, gives you an idea of the total amount of heap allocated memory used by each memory clerk. You can get a look at this memory information for CLR by using this query:

```
select type as MemoryClerk_Type,
       single_pages_kb,
       multi_pages_kb,
       virtual_memory_reserved_kb,
       virtual_memory_committed_kb,
       page_size_bytes
from sys.dm_os_memory_clerks
where type like '%clr%'
```

One of the things you should expect to happen is that virtual_memory_committed_kb plus single_pages_kb memory should increase to a point and then trigger the garbage collection in the CLR. To free the memory used by CLR it is not necessary to reboot the server or restart SQL Server. You can clear cache using the normal DBCC command DBCC FREESYSTEMCACHE. However, if you have to do this often, or if the values in these columns continue to increase, or errors occur rapidly, it is possible that you may need to examine your assembly for static variables, which are persisting in memory or the use of finalizers, which put pressure on garbage collection activities. To dig into detail that is more granular, you may look at the memory modules themselves by using a similar query:

```
SELECT mo.[type] as MemoryObj_Type
     , sum(mo.pages_allocated_count * mo.page_size_in_bytes/1024)
           AS N'Current KB'
     , sum(mo.max_pages_allocated_count * mo.page_size_in_bytes/1024)
```

```
            AS N'Max KB'
FROM sys.dm_os_memory_objects mo
WHERE mo.[type] LIKE '%clr%'
GROUP BY mo.[type]
ORDER BY mo.[type]
```

The information is only the tip of the iceberg in terms of what you now have to troubleshoot memory-related issues. For more details on SQL Server internal metrics and statistics, look up the other dynamic management views in the Books Online.

What Is the Impact of SQL CLR on the CPU?

Even though you'll find that SQL CLR uses less CPU than T-SQL for complicated logic constructs, looping, or calculations, it is possible that SQL Server can become a performance bottleneck if it is expected to perform database and service-level tasks. SQL Server is not so easily load balanced and scalable as a middle tier. One of the DMVs that you can use to evaluate CPU load is the `sys.dm_clr_appdomains` DMV. This view provides a nebulous column cost to measure the CPU cost of hosting and unloading the Appdomain. This column is nebulous because the exact definition can not be located within any of the public Microsoft documentation. According to the Books Online, this is a relative indicator. Higher-cost values increase the probability that the Appdomain is putting the server under memory pressure. Look at this value before starting a load test to get an idea of the impact on the CPU by running a query like this:

```
select appdomain_name,
       datediff(mi, Creation_time, getdate()) as [AppDomain Load Time (min)],
       state,
       cost
  from sys.dm_clr_appdomains
```

Admittedly, this is not the best information to help determine CPU usage. There is always the system stored procedure that can provide overall CPU statistics, called sp_monitor. Running this procedure provides information like this:

```
last_run                current_run             seconds
---------------------   ---------------------   -----------
2006-05-26 14:43:26.060 2006-05-26 14:44:10.363 44

cpu_busy                io_busy                 idle
---------------------   ---------------------   -------------------------
24(0)-0%                2(0)-0%                 62307(42)-95%

packets_received        packets_sent            packet_errors
---------------------   ---------------------   -------------------------
513(3)                  2026(22)                0(0)

total_read          total_write          total_errors         connections
------------------  -------------------  -------------------  -------------------
1013(5)             135(1)               0(0)                 913(0)
```

For even more data, we need to dig into Performance Monitor.

Monitoring Counters with Performance Monitor

The performance monitor, or the PerfMon, can be used to track resource usage information for the server. Since normally the PerfMon utility is an OS-level monitor, the monitor can track only CLR Total Execution Time for each SQL Server instance. However, since SQL CLR is using the .NET Framework on the machine, all other counters related to the .NET can be captured globally for each server in the categories beginning with `.NET CLR*`. You can load a settings file `SQLCLR Performance Log.htm` from the Wrox website that contains all the categories preset to profile all CLR activity. You can also create the capture parameters yourself. To open the PerfMon utility, type **perfmon** into a command line or in a Run window.

Under counter logs in Figure 10-12, you'll notice the SQL CLR performance log. This was created by loading the precached settings. A performance log captures objects. The most useful of these categories are:

❑ **.NET CLR Data:** `sqlClient` connections and pooled connections.

❑ **.NET CLR Exceptions:** Handled and unhandled exceptions thrown by CLR assemblies.

❑ **.NET CLR Interop:** Counters on calls to COM-wrapped objects.

❑ **.NET CLR JIT:** Usage of JIT compiler.

❑ **.NET CLR Loading:** Loading, unloading, and failures to load assemblies by app domain.

❑ **.NET CLR LocksAndThreads:** Locks and threads used by CLR.

❑ **.NET CLR Memory:** Memory usage and garbage collection activity.

❑ **.NET CLR Networking:** Network resource usage.

❑ **.NET CLR Remoting:** Usage of any object outside a caller's app domain.

❑ **.NET CLR Security:** Verification and checks of code against code access security (CAS) model.

❑ **.NET Data Provider for SQLServer:** .NET SQL Server connections and pooled connections.

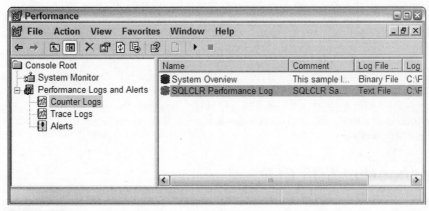

Figure 10-12

Within each object is a set of counters. If you double-click on an item in the Counters list view you can see what counters are being recorded for each object. In Figure 10-13, you'll notice that all counters were selected for each object. Within the Add Counters form (not shown) you'll be able to get detailed information about each counter that is being captured by clicking the Explain button for each counter.

Figure 10-13

One of the counters you may pay attention to is the % Time in GC. This counter reports on the amount of CPU cycles spent in garbage collection activity since the last GC activity ended. If this counter shows a high value, something is going on with memory that is requiring a lot of garbage collection activity — time to look into the assemblies using the most memory. Another counter to watch is the # Induced GC value. This counts the times that the garbage collector is specifically called and could indicate a bad programming practice, since the GC is CPU-intensive.

There are more counters than we could cover that you'll find useful when administering SQL Server with SQL CLR objects. Take some time to become familiar with them and create your own counter logs. To run one of these logs, select it. Right-click and select Run from the pop-up menu. Use these logs to monitor specific situations. We don't recommend leaving them running for long periods of time except in extraordinary situations.

Troubleshooting SQL CLR

If you have turned on the SQL Server Profiler, and executed some of the SQL CLR procedures, you can watch some of the raw T-SQL and see the contents of the executing statements. To turn on Profiler, navigate to Start ➪ Programs ➪ Microsoft SQL Server 2005 ➪ Performance Tools ➪ SQL Server Profiler. Make sure that you select a stored-procedure-based trace that enables you to see the contents of the procedure that is executing. What you may have discovered is that even though you can see the loaded of the assembly and the calling of the T-SQL statements, you are in the dark in terms of seeing what is going on inside the assembly. So how in the world can you get inside the SQL CLR routine to see what is going on? This is the primary reason that we recommend that you store source in the `sys.assembly_files` metadata. One way to troubleshoot is to look into the code of the assembly within SQL Server and see if you can visually find the issue. Another method is to load the code into Visual Studio in a test or QC environment and walk through the code to the issue. We'll cover both.

Examining SQL CLR Already Loaded in a Database

If you establish a practice of loading source, it is easy to display this information as if you had right-clicked onto a T-SQL stored procedure in the object browser and requested to script the procedure into a query window. The object browser simply retrieves the information from `sys.comments` and displays it. Chapter 2 goes over one method of extracting supporting files using an SSIS package, but you can also look at the contents of C# and VB.NET SQL CLR objects by using this T-SQL stored procedure utility to display class files into the query window. (For best results, change your query window to output results to text or to a file instead of a grid.)

```
CREATE PROCEDURE usp_DisplayAssemblyClasses(
     @ASSEMBLYNAME VARCHAR(100)
     )
AS
DECLARE @CONTENT VARCHAR(MAX)
DECLARE @FILEPERMTYPE VARCHAR(100)
DECLARE @NAME VARCHAR(260)

SELECT @FILEPERMTYPE = PERMISSION_SET_DESC
FROM sys.assemblies
WHERE [NAME] = @ASSEMBLYNAME

DECLARE rsASSEMBLYFILES CURSOR FOR
SELECT f.[NAME], [CONTENT]
FROM SYS.ASSEMBLY_FILES f
INNER JOIN SYS.ASSEMBLIES a
on f.Assembly_ID = a.assembly_ID
WHERE a.[NAME] = @ASSEMBLYNAME
AND right(f.[Name], 2) IN ('vb', 'cs')
AND left(convert(varchar(max), content), 1) <> 'i'
ORDER BY [FILE_ID]

OPEN rsASSEMBLYFILES

FETCH NEXT FROM rsASSEMBLYFILES
INTO @NAME, @CONTENT

-- Check @@FETCH_STATUS to see if there are any more rows to fetch.
WHILE @@FETCH_STATUS = 0
BEGIN

    -- Concatenate and display the current values in the variables.
    PRINT '//' + replicate('=', 80)
    PRINT '//SQLCLR Assembly: ' + @ASSEMBLYNAME
```

```
        PRINT '//Supporting File: ' + @NAME
        PRINT '//Permission Set : ' + @FILEPERMTYPE
        PRINT '//Scripted        : ' + convert(varchar, getdate())
        PRINT '//Content: (NOTE: THE LINES ABOVE ARE NOT PART OF THE ORIGINAL CODE)'
        PRINT '//' + replicate('=', 80)
        PRINT CONVERT(varchar(Max), @CONTENT)
        PRINT CHAR(13) + CHAR(10)

        -- This is executed as long as the previous fetch succeeds.
        FETCH NEXT FROM rsASSEMBLYFILES
        INTO @NAME, @CONTENT
    END

    CLOSE rsASSEMBLYFILES
    DEALLOCATE rsASSEMBLYFILES
```

Once the code is displayed in the output portion of the query window, it is easily read and can be used to troubleshoot the easier exceptions.

Using Visual Studio to Debug

Debugging using Visual Studio is possible because it is tightly integrated into SQL Server. This means you can literally walk through each line of code to see the error as it occurs. This capability is what many have wished were part of the T-SQL coding environment and will influence many others to attempt to use SQL CLR over T-SQL for lengthy stored procedures. We do not recommend this technique of debugging against a production database, because it is resource-intensive. This technique will also not be helpful if you are attempting to track an intermittent error that doesn't involve a software issue.

Open up a project in Visual Studio and make sure that the database connection is against a nonproduction database. After opening a class object, click in the left-hand margin on a line of executable code to create a debug breakpoint. This breakpoint will be the point where the code will stop executing when run in debug mode.

The twist to debugging SQL CLR projects is that you have to create something that can execute or start the assembly. In a normal console application, you'd fire up the command-line interface, or in a Windows application, you'd designate a form as the startup point. For SQL CLR, you execute an assembly using a T-SQL command. Create a T-SQL script to call the entry point in the assembly, assuming that the assembly will load and create the T-SQL prototype automatically. Add this script to a file in the Test Scripts node of the project explorer. To call the SQL CLR UDF in Figure 10-14, you'd need a T-SQL statement like this:

```
SELECT dbo.mfnCalcLoanPayment(15000, 48, .07)
```

Add this to the default Test.sql file added for you automatically when the SQL CLR project was created. To start debugging, select the menu option Debug ⇨ Start Debugging, or press F5. The assembly will compile and redeploy (another reason to not debug in production) before stopping on the breakpoint.

You may wait a few minutes for the debug session to be created between SQL Server and Visual Studio, but when it stops, the IDE should look something like Figure 10-14. The yellow highlighted area shows that execution was halted upon reaching the breakpoint.

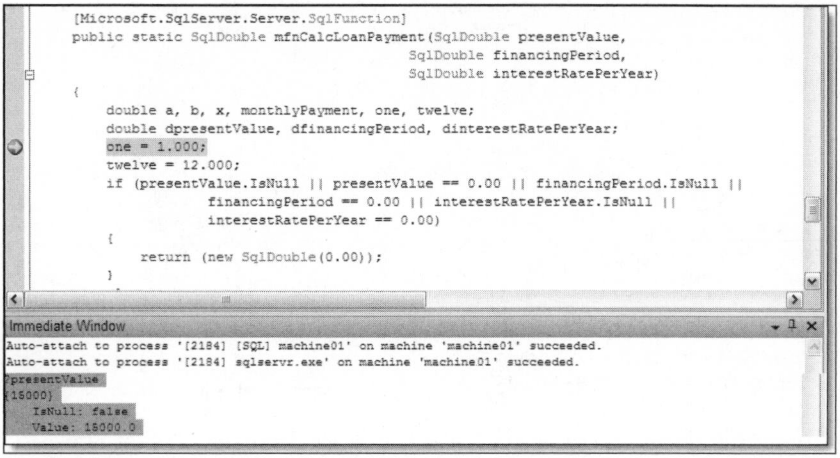

Figure 10-14

In this debug mode, you need only to move the mouse over a variable to see the value of it in real time. An alternative is to print the values of items into the immediate window. You can see an example of this in the lower half of Figure 10-14. The contents of the value type `presentValue` is printed using the statement `debug.print` or the shortcut symbol (?). The two values are printed below in the immediate window. To continue to walk line by line through the code, press the F11 button. The code will continue to execute until it leaves the scope of the test defined in the `Test.sql` file, or if you press Shift-F5 or the Stop Debugging button. Techniques like this can help DBAs determine what the problems are with code that runs incorrectly and are great advances to dealing with complex T-SQL code.

Summary

In this chapter, we covered the SQL CLR enhancement to SQL Server 2005 by starting with a quick refresher into the .NET Framework and what it means to system administrators and database administrators in terms of security, release cycles, and finally troubleshooting and performance. We covered how the CLR works and how you can harden your environment to limit the capabilities of SQL CLR to your own comfort level. We learned how by digging into the CAS security model and by learning all the security provisions that the Microsoft SQL Server team built into SQL Server 2005.

To get you ready for the SQL CLR code that you'll be asked to load into the database, we went over the basics of .NET development so that you can get a heads-up on the things to look for that might be dangerous. We discussed the release environments and went over techniques of deployment depending upon whether you have the Visual Studio IDE, or not. We even went over the .NET administration icons for the administrators. We hope after you've had a chance to take this closer look at SQL CLR, you'll be able to see that this technology is worth more than a quick search on Google, and we hope you'll turn on CLR Integration when you see an appropriate use of it.

Now, we will put all this together and look at a case study that solves a business problem using both T-SQL and SQL solution patterns. This case study will give you the perspective from conception to deployment that is hard to experience when working small examples.

11

Case Study

How many hours do we have? It is a common business need to calculate the amount of time it takes to perform a task. In many industries, it is acceptable to calculate the difference between two dates and report the result in days. In other industries, the need is magnified, if only by degree, to reporting the amount of time in hours, minutes or seconds. In many of today's highly demanding business scenarios, this linear way of looking at time is not enough. Things happen within the boundaries of a start and stop time: employees arrive late and leave early, factory floor machinery is turned off for maintenance outages or reconfigurations for an outgoing customer shipment, and there are just times when work does not occur due to holidays and weekend schedules. In these instances, you may find yourself under the demand to produce a calculation of time with an element of relativity. Dates in general and date calculations specifically have always been a bit of a challenge in T-SQL. In this case study, you'll see how you can approach date calculations differently using SQL CLR. In the end, you are going to develop a business availability calculation to apply to real-world scenarios.

While there are undoubtedly more intricate case study topics, we think this example speaks to the heart of the appropriate use of SQL CLR. Before SQL Server 2005 introduced the ability to host .NET for use in T-SQL-based problem solving, we all had a fixed solution template when it involved accessing date and performing data calculations. If the going got tough and you were comfortable, you'd code logic in T-SQL to parse strings and iterate through cursors. For those who have been burned by T-SQL or who are not as comfortable in the eccentricities of the language, the knee-jerk reaction has been to pull the data down into the application using ADO, or ADO.NET, to perform the same tasks. Having worked with SQL CLR since the first beta versions, we feel that while SQL CLR certainly is not a replacement for T-SQL, there is a place in your development arsenal where it just as clearly fits. For the complex and ordinary date calculations you will develop in this chapter, you can use SQL CLR to take advantage of the .NET Base Class Libraries and array structures to solve the problem incrementally and gain some performance benefits as a side advantage. So follow along while we walk through a complete end-to-end real-world problem of calculating total business availability from the statement of the problem to the maintenance of the solution.

Business Case

In several industries, you'll find the need to report a time-based metric in relationship to business availability. In the introduction, we discussed two applications of this need. One need is with project-based human resources allocation, and another with operations that rely on combinations of people and machinery uptime. So, exactly what are we talking about? We need to develop a solution to calculate the amount of time between two dates, but one that takes into account all the operation downtimes that occur during that same time frame.

Figure 11-1 demonstrates four scenarios that you'll typically find, measuring business availability between two dates July 4, 2006 and July 5, 2006. The first timeline in the figure simply looks at a starting and stopping time and reports the time difference as 24 hours. The second timeline shows working shifts superimposed onto the timeline to demonstrate how working shifts interact and affect the amount of time available. Considering these shifts allows for reporting possible business availability of 24 hours for activities occurring during the shift work, as opposed to the 8 working hours available to tasks that require use of office personnel. The third timeline is the same as the second, except that you can see how holidays also affect work schedules. These first three timelines are obviously more applicable to human resources allocation. The last timeline is more applicable to the manufacturing industry where machines run 24 hours a day, 7 days a week except for maintenance, outages, occasionally a reconfiguration activity, and rarely, but possibly, for holidays.

Any metrics that measure the performance of a business task and that consider these real-world exceptions will obviously have more meaning. For instance, a package sort time from start to finish in 6 hours looks different when done between 4 hours of sorting equipment downtime for maintenance. An employee working 8 hours a day would seem acceptable until evaluated against a shift that calls for a 12-hour work week. For this case study, the focus will be limited to the two domain applications of employees and package sorting, but you'll build SQL CLR objects that are generic enough to apply to many domains. What we'd like to do is simply provide a time range and retrieve the business availability within that range.

To keep our terminology generic, instead of talking about employee shifts or sorting runs, we'll refer to a *timed segment* as a period of the business day that can be timed. Timed segments should be named in a meaningful way for our problem domains. Examples of timed segments are 12HRSHIFT1, 8HRSHIFT, and CONVEYOR1. In turn, each of the timed segments could have several dimensions, represented by time segment types. Examples of time segment types are DEFAULTHRS, HOLIDAY, WEEKENDOFFHRS, and OUTAGE. Of course, you could build more types, but one that will have special meaning is the DEFAULTHRS time segment type. It is the time segment type needed to define default start and stop times for a timed segment. This could mean a normal work day or default machine uptime. Once you know this normal business time period, you only need to take into account weekend schedules to properly enumerate the number of business days in a given period. Weekend schedules are defined by the WEEKENDOFFHRS segment type and provide special instructions on how you should consider the two days Saturday and Sunday. All other time segment types are simply exceptions to the normal, default business schedules.

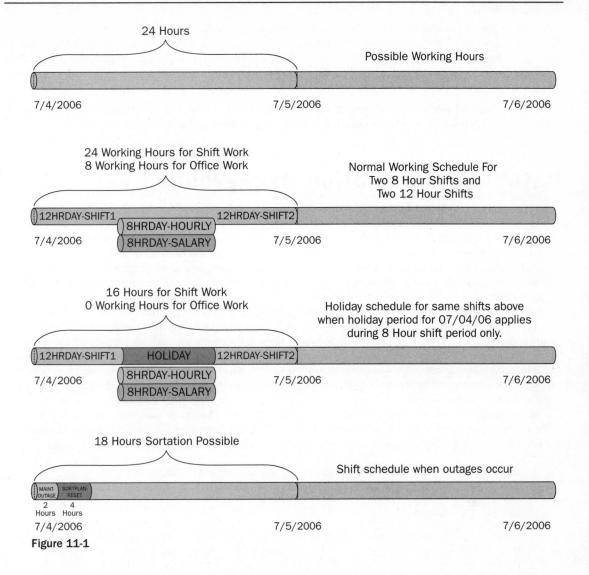

Figure 11-1

The requirements for the business availability calculation look like this:

❑ The function should accept a start and end date expressed in seconds as the lowest level of granularity. If a start date does not include seconds, the default of 00:00:00 will be used. If an end date is not expressed in seconds, the default of 00:00:00 will also be used.

❑ The function should normally grant the ability to provide a series of timed segments for specific consideration for a given time period. If no timed segment is provided, or if more than one timed segment is provided and overlapping occurs, then the intersection of these time segments will be merged and eliminated to produce the longest continuous time segment period.

❑   The function should allow for the ability of what-if calculations by accepting a list of paired start and stop times that mark custom time exclusion periods that should not be included in the business availability final calculation. Again, if these custom segments overlap with any existing segments, the segments will be merged. If a series of exclusion periods are provided, then these periods will be the only periods considered for calculation.

❑   The final solution should provide the ability to calculate business availability for one discreet set of parameters or generate multiple results across a set-based series of parameters.

DateTime Calculation Background

Business-date calculation functionality doesn't exist natively in the .NET or T-SQL core date-calculation functions, so first we should look at current date math capabilities. Performing date math is one of the areas that programmers seem to struggle with, particularly when using T-SQL. We suspect that part of the confusion occurs because the SQL Server team made the decision to combine date- and time-based data storage into two flavors, but not the two flavors that you might expect. Programmers familiar with MS Access and other databases wrongly assume that the smalldate data type is the flavor without the time component. Actually both can store time data. Datetime data types store time-based data to the detail of one three-hundredth of a second, but smalldatetime data types limit time storage to the accuracy of minutes. It is common to find errors in T-SQL code from unexpected conversions, improper boundaries in WHERE clauses, and misunderstandings of DatePart calculations. We suspect that part of the problem lies in having to learn two different date handling systems, one in T-SQL and another in a separate programming language. The advantage of building stored procedures and user-defined functions in SQL CLR is that you'll be able to code the date calculations where, regardless of the .NET language used, you'll be using the same datetime and timespan classes in the core .NET assemblies. As a result, your date calculations should be more accurate and less error-prone. As a prerequisite to starting the case study, examine these SQL CLR solutions to common T-SQL programming errors in date calculations. Use the following T-SQL script to create a sample date table for these next examples:

```
CREATE TABLE MyDate(myID INT, mySmallDate smalldatetime, myDate datetime)
GO
insert into myDate SELECT 1,  '07/01/06 00:00:00', '07/01/06 00:00:00'
insert into myDate SELECT 2,  '07/01/06 08:00:00', '07/01/06 08:00:00'
insert into myDate SELECT 3,  '07/01/06 09:00:00', '07/01/06 09:00:00'
insert into myDate SELECT 4,  '07/01/06 10:00:00', '07/01/06 10:00:00'
insert into myDate SELECT 5,  '07/01/06 20:00:00', '07/01/06 20:00:00'
insert into myDate SELECT 6,  '07/01/06 21:00:00', '07/01/06 21:00:00'
insert into myDate SELECT 7,  '07/01/06 23:00:00', '07/01/06 23:00:00'
insert into myDate SELECT 8,  '07/01/06 23:59:59', '07/01/06 23:59:59'
insert into myDate SELECT 9,  '07/02/06 00:00:00', '07/02/06 00:00:00'
insert into myDate SELECT 10, '07/02/06 00:00:01', '07/02/06 00:00:01'
```

This script, and all the code in this chapter, can be found in the Chapter 11 folder of the book's code files, which you can download from this book's web page at www.wrox.com.

Implicit Casting Issues

One of the first things you'll notice about the sample table entries is that some date and times are converted when saved into the smalldatetime column. Use this query to examine this for yourself:

```
SELECT * FROM MYDATE WHERE myID = 8
```

The results show 07/01/06 23:59:59 being converted to 07/02/06 00:00:00 — a completely new day.

```
myID          mySmallDate              myDate
-----------   ----------------------   -----------------------
8             2006-07-02 00:00:00      2006-07-01 23:59:59.000
```

Fortunately, this hidden implicit conversion occurring exactly at the last second of the day may not be critical for most industries. If it is critical for you, change the data type of the column to datetime to capture that last second. Otherwise, know that the smalldatetime data type is not capable of storing seconds, and casting will occur. Another more common instance of this error happens when implicit casting occurs in the WHERE clause of a query. How many rows do you think this T-SQL statement returns using your test data in the myDate table?

```
--INCORRECT QUERY FOR ALL ROWS DURING 07/01/2006
SELECT *
FROM myDate
WHERE mySmallDate >= '07/01/2006 00:00:00'
  AND mySmallDate <= '07/01/2006 23:59:59'
```

If you answered 10 rows, then you'd be right. The intent may have been to grab all entries up and until the last second of the day, but this query will return even the first entry of 07/02/2006 00:00:00. This is because the mySmallDate field is a smalldatetime data type, and the outer boundary is converted to the same by rounding up to the next day — 07/02/2006 00:00:00. To make sure that you choose the right data type for data storage, use the following table for a quick reference.

Real World	T-SQL	.NET
TIME (hh:mm)	smalldatetime	System.DateTime
TIME (hh:mm:ss)	datetime	System.DateTime
DATE only	smalldatetime	System.DateTime
DATE and TIME or TIMESTAMP	datetime	System.DateTime

Did you notice in this table that .NET uses the same structure for all dates and times? This is not an accident. You may disagree with combining both date and time data into one structure, but the advantage is that the experience of working with it will be consistent regardless of the time component or the significance of that measure. We'll dig into this DateTime structure in a minute and explain how to avoid this issue in your parameters when using .NET SQL CLR procedures.

Storing Time in Date-Only Fields

Another of the common areas of miscalculation of date-based data occurs when the intent to store only date information is undermined by allowing a time component to also be inserted in the field. This can create errors when retrieving data for reporting, or date calculations based on assumptions about the data. You can see an example of the effect of this in the following T-SQL query:

```
--TIME DATA IS INADVERTENTLY ALLOWED IN DATEONLY FIELDS
SELECT *
FROM myDate
WHERE mySmallDate = '07/01/06'
```

The argument in the WHERE clause assumes that the data in the mySmallDate field does not contain time elements. This results in automatically adding the equivalent of 00:00:00 to the date. Only one row matches this date and time exactly. This problem can be resolved by truncating the time component from your date fields using a convert statement like this:

```
convert(datetime, convert(varchar(8), @MYDATE, 112))
```

The style value of 112 is an International Organization for Standardization (ISO) format for dates only, which has this format: yyyymmdd. This format incidentally is the way all dates are stored within SQL Server, regardless of localization. The hour, minute, and second values are truncated by the conversion and set automatically to 00:00:00. By converting and removing the time component from the date, the query now would retrieve rows matching the original intent.

Otherwise, alter how you construct the WHERE clause in the query. This example also takes into account international date format considerations by converting the arguments into the standard SQL Server storage format for comparison. This gives you the ability to compare apples to apples.

```
DECLARE @StartDate datetime
SET @StartDate = '07/01/2006 00:00:00'

SELECT *
FROM myDate
WHERE mySmallDate
   between convert(smalldatetime, @StartDate, 112)
   and convert(smalldatetime, (dateadd(mi, -1, @StartDate + 1)), 112)
```

The BETWEEN clause is inclusive of each boundary. Notice that the outer boundary of the BETWEEN clause adds a day and subtracts one minute. The statement @StartDate + 1 is a shortcut to adding a whole day and had the same effect as another dateadd function using a day datepart. This is best way to retrieve all possibilities of time for a day for a shortdatetime data field. If you want to perform the same action for a datetime that includes seconds, the outer boundary is the same, but instead subtract one second instead of a minute.

The .NET DateTime Class

The .NET language uses one structure to represent and store the value of a moment in time. This class, or DateTime value type, is similar to the T-SQL datetime data type in that the date and the time component are rolled up into the class. The .NET DateTime is a value type, and the class must be created, or instantiated, to use it. In the constructor, there are many overloaded options available to initialize the date structure by specifically setting each date and time component. Another way to populate a date structure is by using the convert class to translate and map the date and time components from a string to the DateTime class. Each method can be seen in these C# code snippets:

```
//Initialize using one of the constructors
DateTime startDate = new DateTime(2006, 7, 1, 0, 0, 0);
```

```
//Initialize by conversion of a string
//But Error to catch is general
DateTime endDate = Convert.ToDateTime("07/01/2006");

//Initialize by conversion of a string
//Generates a specific FormatException
DateTime endDate = DateTime.Parse("07/01/2006");
```

The advantage to the DateTime structure is that you've got all the date and time components available, whether you use them or not. There is not one DateTime structure for seconds and another for just month, day, and year. The tradeoff for reducing the confusion of choosing between small and normal data types means carrying a larger storage requirement than you may actually need. For example, you'll still have to deal with carrying around a default date when you only want to store a time attribute. A common practice for the default is to use the date 01/01/1900.

How do you make sure that an incoming string is a properly formatted date before you attempt to convert or cast? If you are using VB.NET, you have access to an isDate() function that is functionally similar to the T-SQL isDate() function. However, in C#, for prior versions of the framework you were are on your own. The common practice was to create a custom Static method in your utility or helper class that accepted a string and returned a true of false based on whether parsing that string into a DateTime structure threw an error. Interestingly enough, this is the same methodology underneath the VB.NET isDate() function. The issue you'll encounter is that dates like 01/01/450 will return as a valid date, because this is within the acceptable range of the .NET DateTime data type. You may need to add your own domain-based date verification to this basic isDate validation function.

```
/// Checks whether or not a date is a valid date.
public bool isDate(string sdate)
{
    DateTime dt;
    try
    {
        dt = DateTime.Parse(sdate);
        return true;
    }
    catch(FormatException)
    {
        return false;
    }
}
```

The 2.0 .NET framework includes the method TryParse() on the DateTime class. You can use this method to test the value and return either a default or a properly cast version of your string date and time value in one shot. Here is an example of how to use the TryParse() method in the Main() method of a console application:

```
string mStr = "baddate";
DateTime dt = new DateTime();
DateTime.TryParse(mStr, out dt);
Console.Write("Value of {0} converted to date is {1}\n",
    mStr, dt.ToString());
mStr = "01/01/2006";
DateTime.TryParse(mStr, out dt);
```

```
                    Console.Write("Value of {0} converted to date is {1}\n",
                        mStr, dt.ToString());
                    mStr = "01/010111";
                    DateTime.TryParse(mStr, out dt);
                    Console.Write("Value of {0} converted to date is {1}\n",
                        mStr, dt.ToString());
                    Console.Read();
```

The results are:

```
    Value of baddate converted to date is 1/1/0001 12:00:00 AM
    Value of 01/01/2006 converted to date is 1/1/2006 12:00:00 AM
    Value of 01/010111 converted to date is 1/1/0001 12:00:00 AM
```

When using this method, treat any datevalue of 01/01/0001 12:00:00 AM as a nondate value. This is equivalent of the isDate() method returning a value of false.

The .NET TimeSpan Class

The TimeSpan structure calculates the duration between moments in time. In a way this is a lot like the T-SQL DateDiff function. Where the TimeSpan class excels is that once duration has been calculated, the interval can be restated in any time dimension. The methods in .NET are also strongly descriptive, so the chance of confusing date part abbreviations is not likely. Here is an example of calculating the duration in minutes between two dates in T-SQL and .NET. Notice the use of the method TotalMinutes to provide the duration in minutes. This is a more direct and less error-prone approach than needing to know that datepart parameters mi or n are needed to report the duration in minutes.

```
/*T-SQL CALC OF MINUTES BETWEEN DATES*/
DECLARE @StartDate datetime
DECLARE @EndDate datetime

SET @StartDate = '07/01/06 00:00:00'
SET @EndDate = '07/01/06 23:59:59'

SELECT DATEDIFF(n, @startDate, @endDate)

/*C#.NET CALC OF MINUTES BETWEEN DATES*/
DateTime startDate = new DateTime(2006, 7, 1, 0, 0, 0);
DateTime endDate = new DateTime(2006, 7, 1, 23, 59, 59);

/*TimeSpan structure calculates the duration and stores*/
TimeSpan mySpan = endDate.Subtract(startDate);
Console.WriteLine(mySpan.TotalMinutes.ToString());
```

However, if you are used to the T-SQL version of duration calculation, you may be in for a bit of a surprise with the results of the .NET TimeSpan calculation. You may have intended to calculate the duration in minutes, but since seconds are provided in the dates (notice the seconds in the previous example), and the result is returned as a whole number with a fractional part representing the seconds. The T-SQL version of the number of minutes in a day returned a whole number 1,439. The .NET version returned 1,439.98333333333. You could round this result after the fact of course, but this could introduce new errors. When making a calculation of this sort where only the whole number portion of the minute is significant, make the decision to round or truncate the datetime value prior to calculating the duration, like this:

```
private static int DateDiffMinutes(string sstartDate, string sendDate)
{
    /*C#.NET CALC OF MINUTES BETWEEN DATES*/
    DateTime startDate = DateTime.Parse(sstartDate);
    DateTime endDate = DateTime.Parse(sendDate);

    TimeSpan mySpan = endDate.Subtract(startDate);
    Debug.WriteLine(mySpan.TotalMinutes.ToString());
    //1,439.98333333333

    /*REDEFINE THE DATE BY TRUNCATING THE SECONDS*/
    startDate = new DateTime(startDate.Year, startDate.Month,
            startDate.Day, startDate.Hour, startDate.Minute, 0);
    endDate = new DateTime(endDate.Year, endDate.Month, endDate.Day,
            endDate.Hour, endDate.Minute, 0);

    mySpan = endDate.Subtract(startDate);
    return(mySpan.TotalMinutes.ToString());
    //1,439
}
```

If you want to run this code, cut and paste it in a standard Visual Studio Stored Procedure project template over the default function. You can see how the startDate was restated to exclude seconds by inserting zero into the second parameters or the optional constructor of the DateTime class in this code snippet.

```
/*REDEFINE THE DATE BY TRUNCATING THE SECONDS*/
startDate = new DateTime(startDate.Year, startDate.Month,
        startDate.Day, startDate.Hour, startDate.Minute, 0);
```

You could also make your own decisions about rounding here as well. Use this technique of recasting the datetime structure to ensure that dates passed into SQL CLR objects don't run into the implicit casting issues that we discussed earlier in this section.

Finally, notice that when you calculate the number of minutes in a day, using the outer boundary of the time 23:59, you get a result of 1,439 minutes in a day, but this doesn't seem to check out when you work out the calculation by multiplying 24 Hours × 60 Minutes = 1440. We've lost a minute between 23:59 and 24:00. The reason why may become obvious if you change the output to look at the total days over the same time, and see the result of 0 days. Monday is not a full day until it is Tuesday. The date boundary is not breached until we go from the time of 23:59 and cross over to 00:00. The day then ends and the additional minute is calculated. This seems to unsettle folks because when you query for the data wanting only the saved date and time values up to and until Tuesday, the time values can only be 23:59 with smalldatetime data before they are the next day and of no concern. Just remember that when you are calculating durations for dateparts, you have to look at the whole picture of days, hours, minutes, and seconds instead of only one of these dimensions. The minutes may be 1,439, but the seconds could be 59. This is the obvious advantage of using .NET SQL CLR for any of your date math calculations. The DateTime and TimeSpan classes reinforce the concept that all these dimensions belong together, instead of leaving you to perform DateDiff calculations on your own.

Solution Approach

For this case study, you are going to solve this business continuity problem using T-SQL and SQL CLR to demonstrate how SQL CLR really alters how you approach and structure a solution to a business problem. To keep the solution generic and flexible, we are using a database table to store a set of default times for normal working hours, and exceptions to these normal hours. Back in the "Business Case" section of this chapter we discussed timed segments, and they will allow you to separate the different modes of business that occur during the day that you want to keep track of. These segments could be machine or people schedules. These segments are going to be loaded into a table called businessCalendar. Each segment will contain starting and stopping time details about both the default and exception timed segments. Two of the timed segments are fixed so they can be used to calculate default business hours and weekend hours. These segments will look like this:

TimeSegmentType	Description
DEFAULTHRS	Start and stop times considered default business hours
WEEKENDOFFHRS	Start and stop times for default weekend hours

All other timed segments are used to calculate period exceptions and can use any label for the timed segment or time segment type that makes sense in the business domain. Some examples that are considered exceptions to normal business hours are OUTAGE, HOLIDAY, or SCHEDULEOFF. In addition to these exceptions, custom exceptions can always be provided as a comma-delimited list of time pairs to this function.

At this point regardless of whether you build the solution in T-SQL or SQL CLR, the basic tasks for solving this problem are the same:

❑ First, you need to validate that the minimum required input parameters of start date and end date are provided, and that they represent a valid period. You should also examine the optional parameters to ensure that they are provided in the proper format.

❑ To know what constitutes a business day, check the business calendar table to review the default business hours for the timed segments that are provided. Remember that each timed segment represents either a shift or manufacturing line, so it is possible to be provided a series of timed segments. In any case, return the longest continuous time possible without time overlaps.

❑ For each calendar date that is touched by the date range provided, evaluate whether the day is a normal working day or a weekend day, and check to see if any exceptions exist in the business calendar table for default weekend hours. An exception would have a timed segment type of WEEKENDOFFHRS and result in the defined time frame being a nonbusiness period for calculation purposes.

❑ For each calendar date in the date range provided, evaluate whether any exceptions exist for that business day. Many exceptions exist may exist within a day. If more than one is provided, or is possible with overlapping time exceptions, then calculate and apply the longest continuous time exception possible.

Just to make sure we are all on the same page on these overlapping calculations for exceptions and default business hours, examine Figure 11-2, which represents two calculations for a typical work day in a manufacturing operation. The first graphic shows a typical pair of 12-hour shifts where one starts and the other stops at 7:00 a.m. and 7:00 p.m. If you were concerned with the total number of working hours for SHIFT1 and SHIFT2, the answer would be 24 total hours. Since there are no overlaps in the two shifts, the business availability for this day is calculated by adding the total hours for both shifts.

Let's look at arrangements that are more complicated. Consider an office shift in this example that starts at 7:00 a.m. and ends at 4:00 p.m. If you were asked only about the total working hours available for both the 12HRDAY-SHIFT1 and the 8HRDAY-HOURLY shift, the total hours in Calculation 1 would be 20 Hours. Since the normal office timed segment starts after the first 12-hour shift, the total business hours for the two timed segments would be the total of both.

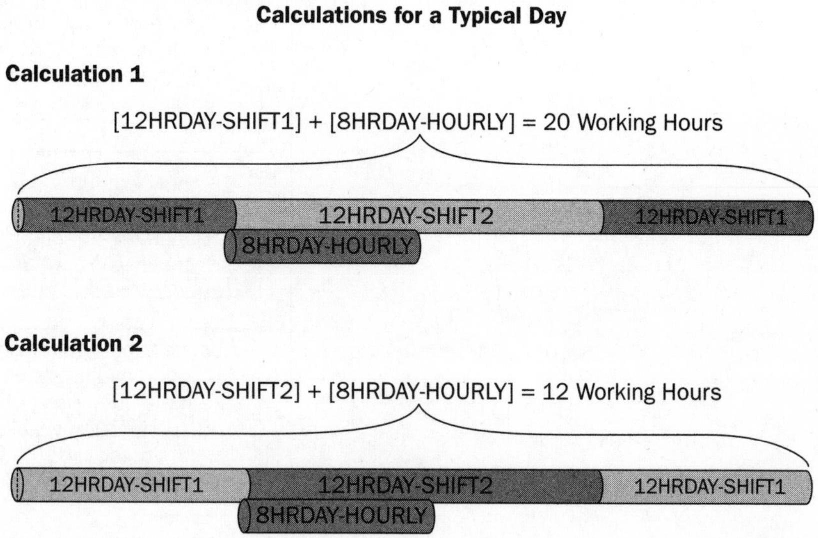

Calculations for a Typical Day

Calculation 1

[12HRDAY-SHIFT1] + [8HRDAY-HOURLY] = 20 Working Hours

Calculation 2

[12HRDAY-SHIFT2] + [8HRDAY-HOURLY] = 12 Working Hours

Figure 11-2

In the second calculation, if you are asked what are the business availability hours for the 8HRDAY-HOURLY and the 12HRDAY-SHIFT2, you only have 12 working hours. This is because the 8-hour timed segment starts but ends in the middle of a 12-hour timed segment. The overlap in time is removed from the total time to calculate the total continuous working hours.

Finally, since we are working in a business context and not a scientific context, it is only necessary to calculate time at the granularity of seconds. Calculations will be made at this level and then reported in a `datetime` variable that contains a full time component, including hours, minutes, and seconds. The overall solution approach will look like Figure 11-3.

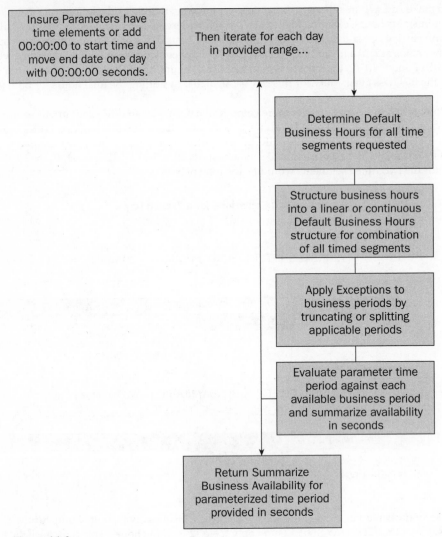

Figure 11-3

Solution Prerequisites

To get started, you'll need a database in which to work. In this chapter, we'll be using a database called CLRTESTDB. If you worked through Chapter 2 or any of the other examples, you should have created this database earlier. Feel free to create these prerequisites in the default database that may be installed with SQL Server 2005 AdventureWorks. We recommend that you also have a copy of Visual Studio 2005. You may be able to work through the case study without it, but the deployment aspects are much easier using the tools within the Visual Studio IDE.

To persist the default business and weekend schedules as well as the exceptions in our timed segment data, you'll need to create a table called businessCalendar. Although we've kept this solution structure simple, you could easily extend it to handle situations in the real world like the addition of a client dimension. Create the businessCalendar by executing the following T-SQL in the CLRTESTDB:

```
USE [CLRTESTDB]
GO
GO
CREATE TABLE [dbo].[BusinessCalendar](
   [TimedSegment] [char](15) NOT NULL,
   [TimeSegmentType] [char](15) NOT NULL,
   [SegmentStart] [datetime] NOT NULL,
   [SegmentEnd] [datetime] NOT NULL,
 CONSTRAINT [PK_BusinessCalendar] PRIMARY KEY CLUSTERED
(
   [TimedSegment] ASC,
   [TimeSegmentType] ASC,
   [SegmentStart] ASC,
   [SegmentEnd] ASC
)WITH (IGNORE_DUP_KEY = OFF) ON [PRIMARY]
) ON [PRIMARY]
GO
```

Add the following rows to simulate a manufacturing conveyor line that runs 24 hours a day, 5 days a week. You'll use these timed segments for creating a basic solution to the business time availability calculation, then we'll expand the example for more complicated timed segments.

```
INSERT INTO BusinessCalendar
SELECT 'CONVEYOR1', 'DEFAULTHRS', '00:00:00', '00:00:00'
GO
INSERT INTO BusinessCalendar
SELECT 'CONVEYOR1', 'OUTAGE', '07/04/2006 10:00:00', '07/04/2006 12:00:00'
GO
INSERT INTO BusinessCalendar
SELECT 'CONVEYOR1', 'OUTAGE', '07/04/2006 16:00:00', '07/04/2006 18:00:00'
GO
INSERT INTO BusinessCalendar
SELECT 'CONVEYOR1', 'MAINTENANCE', '07/08/2006 22:00:00', '07/09/2006 02:00:00'
GO
```

T-SQL-Based Solution

Any time you attempt to approach a solution using T-SQL, you should always start with the idea that a set-based approach is achievable. This is, after all, a database language, so you should be prepared to work with sets of data. With this business problem, you could almost produce a set-based solution using subqueries if the start and stop time segments were linear and were not allowed to overlap. The overlapping is one of the reasons that you need to abandon a set-based approach and use a logical approach. The other reason is that you have to recalculate the actual business schedule for each day. This requires examining each day, starting first with the default business hours for that day and then removing the exception periods to end up with a number of business availability start and stop periods. Once you have those availability periods, use the parameterized period provided to the function against this schedule. If the parameterized period completely includes a day, then all of the business availability periods should be included. If the period bisects one day then only the applicable business hours for that day will be summarized.

T-SQL Object Type Decision

We'll start is by defining what type of T-SQL object you are going to need to create. Because the end results of this business availability calculation will be the number of seconds between two periods, you know that the return value can be an integer. You don't need to return partial seconds, because in the problem domain this is not meaningful. T-SQL objects that return integers can be either user-defined functions (UDFs), user-defined aggregates (UDAs), or stored procedures. Even though stored procedures can be used to return solution results in the return values, this is not a recommended design. Typically, a return in a stored procedure should occur via output parameters. Because one of the business requirements states that you need to be able to perform this calculation across a set of rows, a stored-procedure-based solution can be eliminated, because it wouldn't lend itself to in-line placement at a row level. User-defined aggregates would be a great candidate for this calculation, since the summarization could occur across a row or series of rows level. The issue with the UDA for now is that it can only be performed on one column, and you'll need two. This problem will have at the minimum a start and stop time for a period that you want this business availability calculated. The only choice left is to build this solution as a user-defined function. A UDF will provide the capability to pass in parameters of two columns while processing a rowset, and will return a scalar value that is a result of the calculation made using the parameterized time period.

T-SQL Optional Parameters

You would like to build a T-SQL function that will be used in-line or for a specific scalar calculation, that accepts required and nonrequired parameters. In T-SQL stored procedures, you can easily define parameters as optional by providing default settings for each optional parameter. In T-SQL user-defined functions, parameters are always required. The parameters can be purposely set to a NULL or an empty string, but a placeholder for each parameter must be provided when the function is called. To create a user-defined function that meets your business requirements, you'll need two parameters for the requested date period, one optional parameter for a set of timed segments, and an optional parameter for a custom exclusion periods that need to be applied against normal business hours. You want to be able to make the business availability calculation based on more than one timed segment. For example, you may want to know how many hours both conveyors were online and operational during a time period. In this case, each conveyor may have its own timed segment entry, since each is on- or offline based on specific circumstances. You may be interested in how many billable hours could have been achieved across two work shifts. These are both examples of paired requests, but you can see that they could be escalated into calculations involving more than two timed segments. Instead of attempting to determine a fixed number of allowable segments and defining multiple timed segment entry parameters to handle a finite number of timed segments, define one parameter to accept a large NVARCHAR string that is expected to be a comma-separated list of string values. These values should correspond to an entry in the BusinessCalendar data table by a matching attribute in the TimedSegment column. This parameter could also be set to ' ' or NULL by the caller with the intent that all timed segments should be considered. The function parameters should look something like this:

```
@start datetime,              --beginning of sampling period
@end    datetime,             --end of sampling period
@timedSegmentList nvarchar(800),  --OPTIONAL comma separated timed segments
@timeExclusionList nvarchar(1000) --OPTIONAL date/time exclusion date pairs
```

Since you are going to use the values provided in the `timedSegmentList` variable to look up default business days in the `BusinessCalendar` table, you are either going to select specifically or select all, so it doesn't matter what this default is. You could set the default to `'ALL'`, and then interpret the value of `'ALL'` as the logical trigger to select all entries with the `TimeSegmentType` of `DEFAULT` to get the default business hours. The problem is that the caller of this function would need have the domain knowledge to know that this default is required. This usually results in having to deal with NULL anyway, so there is no point in creating an artificial default. What you really care about is: Did the caller pass in a timed segment or not? Just be prepared to test the parameters in the body of the function to treat empty strings and NULL values as the equivalent of a default parameter. It is much easier to perform this one check then to check additionally for an artificial default string.

The last parameter here is the `timeExclusionList`. The business function is designed to work with a business calendar table where all actual or scheduled exceptions are located. Normally, the function will just look up the exceptions to the timed segment business hours in this table. However, the business requirements also request that client callers have the capability to provide a series of time-value pairs for what-if analysis. Our agreed-to assumptions on this input is that it will come into the function as a value-pair comma separated string as well. Expect this default to also be set to NULL or `' '`, because if an exceptions list is not provided, the function should consider all table-based exceptions to business hours for the timed segment provided.

Validation of Date and Time Input Parameters

The first real task to perform in the solution diagram is to validate the `datetime` parameters provided to the function. The first validation that we can perform is to make sure that the parameters are not NULL. Even though the parameters are not defined as optional, this only means that some value has to be provided for the parameter. NULL is a value (even if it represents an absence of value), so you should check for that. The date range should also be validated to ensure that the end date occurs after the start date. This validation is easily performed with equality operators.

The problem with `datetime` data, as we explained earlier, is that the type can hold either date data or time data or both, so there is no way to enforce that date *and* time data should always be provided. You know to calculate accurately the total number of seconds in a day that you need to measure starting on one date up to the next date, but this is going to be hard to enforce on the client caller. If the parameters 07/04/06 and 07/04/06 are provided, you can properly infer that the intent is to calculate the business availability of the date 07/04/06. You know, however, that to calculate this accurately you have to calculate the amount of time between 07/04/06 and the start of 07/05/06 at 00:00:00. We will assume that if a date is provided without a time element that the intent is to measure the entire day. The end date will be recalculated to match the caller's presumed intent. If the end date has a time component, then no change to the end parameter will be made.

This first calculation will convert the end period parameter if the two dates are the same with no time attribute:

```
IF convert(varchar(8), @end, 108) = '00:00:00'
   SET @End = convert(datetime, @end + 1, 112)
```

This second statement will then evaluate the two boundaries of the time parameters to ensure that the function can proceed to calculating business availability:

```
SET @totalworkseconds = 0
...
If (@start is not null and @end is not null) AND
  (@start <= @end)
BEGIN
   --START BUSINESS DEFAULT CALCULATIONS
END
```

If this test is not met, the function will report the total of the currently calculated value of
TotalWorkSeconds, which is set to 0 at the start of the function.

Designing around Variable-Based Cursors

The next task in the solution approach is to iterate through a period of calendar dates defined by the
input parameters and calculate for each day the default business availability for that one day. The
default business availability is the normal excepted working hours for a timed segment. The data is
stored in the BusinessCalendar table without a date dimension because our assumption is that our
business hours are consistent and are only occasionally altered for unusual events. This way, you don't
have to store the actual business hours for each day and need only worry about storing the exceptions.
You may include this level of complexity if you would like, after completing the case study. The problem
at the moment is that you need the ability to pull the default business hours for each day for a series of
timed segment types. What you'd like to be able to do is this:

```
--THIS IS NOT A VALID T-SQL STATEMENT
DECLARE rsBusinessDefaults CURSOR FOR
     SELECT SegmentStart, SegmentEnd
     FROM businessCalendar
     WHERE TimeSegmentType = 'DEFAULTHRS'
     AND TimedSegment IN (@timedSegmentList)
     ORDER BY SegmentStart ASC
```

You'd think that all you would have to do is get the @timedSegmentList restated with the proper tick
marks around each item of the segment. However, this is an attempt to mix dynamically generated and
fixed T-SQL, which will not work. T-SQL doesn't have an array structure that you can pass around, and
the closest structure that it has, a table, can't be passed around either. The only way to work around
this is to break the comma-separated string into a table using a user-defined table-valued function that
works similar to the string assembly split function. This will allow the passing of a string into the function and the retrieval of a table representation of each of the values in the tokenized string. Then your
cursor-building statement will look something like this:

```
DECLARE rsBusinessDefaults CURSOR FOR
     SELECT SegmentStart, SegmentEnd
     FROM businessCalendar
     WHERE TimeSegmentType = 'DEFAULTHRS'
        AND TimedSegment
        IN (SELECT PARSEDVALUE
              FROM dbo.fn_Split(@timedSegmentList, ','))
     ORDER BY SegmentStart ASC
```

By setting the variable @timedSegmentList to 'CONVEYOR1,CONVEYOR2', this cursor will return a
rowset that looks like this:

TimedSegment	TimeSegmentType	SegmentStart	SegmentEnd
CONVEYOR1	DEFAULTHRS	1900-01-01 00:00:00.000	1900-01-01 00:00:00.000

There is only one entry because a timed segment named CONVEYOR2 doesn't exist in the business calendar yet, but at least you have the ability to generate a variable-based cursor to build the business default hours structure, and you'll use this later.

You can solve the variable-based cursor for the exception periods the same way. For exceptions from the businessCalendar table, you just need to select all entries that are not the default nor weekend timed segments. If the exceptions are provided as a comma-separated list, you need the ability to turn that list into a table with start and stop times. These requirements are a little different than just returning the tokens separated by the comma character. You need to be able to pair up the arguments into date ranges and ensure that you are dealing with dates. For this application, you'll create a separate function called fs_CustomExceptions. This function is similar to the first, but expects date-value pairs in an input string and will return a two-column set of exclusion periods. Building this cursor will result in a similar approach to the default business-hours cursor.

```
DECLARE rsBusinessExceptions CURSOR FOR
    SELECT TimeSegmentType, SegmentStart, SegmentEnd
    FROM dbo.fn_CustomExceptions(@timeexclusionlist)
    WHERE (SegmentStart >= @start and SegmentEnd <= @End)
    ORDER BY SegmentStart ASC
```

Defining cursors is a tricky business from a design perspective, because you can only define the cursor once in a T-SQL batch. What you'd like to do is add the variable of the current date in the parameterized period to the cursor so that you are only looking at the business exclusions for the currently iterating date. Since you can't redefine the cursor, you have to pull every exception for each day in the entire parameterized period and reposition the cursor to the date that you are iterating. The following pseudo-code explains what you'd like to do and what you must do in T-SQL.

```
--PSUEDO-CODE
--WHAT YOU'D LIKE TO DO...
FOR EACH DAY IN [PARAMETERIZED PERIOD]
    GET CURSOR OF EXCEPTIONS USING CURRENT DAY
    CONSOLIDATE INTO BUSINESS HOUR STRUCTURE

--WHAT YOU HAVE TO DO
FOR EACH DAY IN [PARAMETERIZED PERIOD]
    GET CURSOR OF ALL EXCEPTIONS

  IF CURSOR DAY = CURRENT DAY
      CONSOLIDATE INTO BUSINESS HOUR STRUCTURE
```

This means that even though this code operates inside the SQL engine and the distance is short, you still have to pull back unnecessary rows for each day to weed through. If the date range were large, this could have a significant impact on latency. You'll see later how you can get around this restriction using SQL CLR.

Creating the Table-Valued Functions

To have the ability to use one parameter in a user-defined function that can be used to pass a number of key values, you need to be able to separate the tokens out. To facilitate using the multiple values in an IN clause of a cursor definition, you need to be able to represent them in a table or list format. In the previous section, we discussed building two separate functions: fn_split and fn_CustomExceptions to accomplish this task. There are several different approaches to solving this problem. Examples include:

❑ Passing the comma-separated data into a table-valued function that builds and returns a dynamic T-SQL statement.

❑ Passing in XML instead of a comma-separated list and using XQuery or OPENXML to return the nodes as a list.

❑ Using an iteration pattern to parse the tokens from the comma-separated data.

❑ Using a table of numbers to generate a set of positional references for each character from 1 to the length of the parameter string. This set of positional references is used in a table to compare and parse each position on the string to find the required delimiter.

As you might expect, each of these options has benefits and downsides. Building a dynamic T-SQL statement is not a good idea because of SQL injection. Passing in XML is a viable option, but may be overkill for the simple lists in this case study. Using the iteration pattern is not the fastest method, but is really intuitive and performs perfectly fine for the small number of timed segments that we expect in this function. The table-of-numbers approach is the fastest but may be difficult to grasp and maintain. This approach is also more difficult to use with the date-value pairs for the multiple exceptions that can be provided as parameters. What we'll do is use the table-of-numbers pattern with the timed segments parameter, and then an iterative approach with the exclusions parameters and let you compare.

One thing that both patterns require is a knowledge of the length of the incoming string. Not that this trips up too many folks, but another eccentricity of T-SQL is that the LEN function doesn't really return the length of a string. If you were to check the length of the string "123 " (notice the trailing space) in .NET, you'd do something like this:

```
string mystring = "HEY ";
System.Diagnostics.Debug.WriteLine(mystring.Length.ToString());
```

You'd expect the length of this string to return 3 letters + 1 space = 4 characters. If you run a similar bit of logic in T-SQL you'll get a different result.

```
DECLARE @mystring NVARCHAR(10)
SET @myString = '123 '
SELECT LEN(@MyString)
```

The results return a count of 3 characters. The issue is that the LEN function ignores trailing spaces. This could be an issue with logic that requires precise positional information in a string. One way to avoid this is to use the RTRIM function on the parameter in the body of the function. The second option is to use the DATALENGTH function that counts the bytes in the string. The only caveat is that you'll need to divide by 2 to get the total number of characters in the string, like this:

```
DECLARE @mystring NVARCHAR(10)
SET @myString = '123 '
SELECT LEN(@MyString)/2
```

Which returns the proper result of 8 bytes or four characters. Idiosyncracies like this in T-SQL aren't difficult to grasp but may sometimes be hard to remember. One of the advantages of coding in .NET is this length behavior is consistent across all the .NET languages, so there is nothing different to remember when developing in SQL CLR.

Creating the TVF for Parsing Timed Segments

The first table-valued function to build is the one that returns the parameterized timed segment values. This is a simple value list on which you can easily implement the table-of-numbers methodology. Since cracking a delimited string into a table of values is an abstract task, name the function and set the parameters to accept a string and a variable delimiter. The function should also return a table of the parsed values. This can be done by setting the return value on the function as a table definition like this:

```
CREATE FUNCTION [dbo].[fn_Split](
        @DelimitedString nvarchar(4000),
        @Delimiter nchar(1)
)
RETURNS  @ArrayList TABLE (ParsedValue nvarchar(4000))
AS
```

In the body of the function, a default delimiter is set, the incoming string parameter is trimmed to properly calulate its length, and then a series of integers, one for each character of the string, is inserted into a table variable.

```
BEGIN
  DECLARE @LEN INT
  DECLARE @START INT
  IF @Delimiter IS NULL or @Delimiter = ''
    SET @Delimiter = ','
  SET @START = 1
  --So That LEN=LEN Remove Trailing spaces
  SET @DelimitedString = rtrim(@DelimitedString)
  SET @LEN = LEN(@DelimitedString)
  --Make string uniform by wrapping with delimiter
  If left(@DelimitedString, 1) <> @Delimiter
    SET @DelimitedString = @Delimiter + @DelimitedString

  If Right(@DelimitedString, 1) <> @Delimiter
    Set @DelimitedString = @DelimitedString + @Delimiter

  --Fill a table of serial numbers = length
  DECLARE @TABLEOFNUMBERS TABLE(Number INT)
  WHILE @START <= @LEN
    BEGIN
      INSERT INTO @TABLEOFNUMBERS
      SELECT @START
      SET @START = @START + 1
    END
```

The remainder of the function performs the parsing using a set-based method against the table of numbers that is used to parse the string by position, looking for the delimiter character at each position. The results are generated in a set and inserted into an additional table variable @Arraylist, defined earlier in the function prototype. The function then returns the @Arraylist table of timed segments.

```
        INSERT INTO @ArrayList
        SELECT rtrim(ltrim(substring(@DelimitedString, Number + 1,
            charindex(@Delimiter, @DelimitedString, Number + 1) - Number - 1)))
            AS ParsedValue
        FROM    @TABLEOFNUMBERS
        WHERE   Number <= len(@DelimitedString) - 1
        AND   substring(@DelimitedString, Number, 1) = @Delimiter

        RETURN
    END
```

Cut and paste each of these code snippets together, and run the T-SQL DDL in the CLRTESTDB database to create the fn_Split function.

Creating the TVF for Parsing Exception Datetime Pairs

The second table-valued function that you need to base the Business Exceptions cursor on will be the result of cracking another string of datetime paired values. You can use the table-of-numbers methodology on this function as well, but after performing the additional date verifications on each token, the time saved is outweighed by the simplicity of the iteration method. Since providing an exception datetime series is an infrequent use of the function, the choice of the easier iteration method to produce the resultset will have little impact on performance.

This TVF will return a slightly different table structure. When the custom exceptions are not provided, the function normally uses the BusinessCalendar table to retreive the exceptions. In this table, not only are the start and end datetimes of the segment reviewed, but the TimeSegmentType is also expected in the resultset. To keep this symetrical, you'll need to add a field in the returned table structure to contain a default TimeSegmentType. Since you know any custom exception parameter value should qualify as an exception, you can just return a generic string labeled "exception." In the remainder of this section we'll build this function piece by piece. The function prototype for this TVF will look like this:

```
    CREATE FUNCTION [dbo].[fn_CustomExceptions](
                @delimitedExceptions NVARCHAR(4000),
                @delimiter NCHAR(1))
    RETURNS  @customExceptions TABLE (
                        TimeSegmentType NVARCHAR(15),
                        SegmentStart datetime,
                        SegmentEnd datetime)
    AS
    BEGIN
```

Notice that the returned table contains three columns. This is not an abstract task. The naming of the function aligns it to a specific purpose. The next section sets up a series of variables that you'll use in the iterator pattern to move character by character through the string to parse of each token by delimiter.

```
    DECLARE @nLen int,
            @nStart int,
            @nEndIndex int,
            @sDelim char(1),
            @sSegStart varchar(20),
```

```
                    @sSegEnd varchar(20),
                    @nLoopCtr int

        SELECT @nStart = 1
        SET @nLoopCtr = 0

        SET @delimitedExceptions = rtrim(@delimitedExceptions)
        SELECT @nLen = Len(@delimitedExceptions)

        IF @delimiter is null or @delimiter = ''
            SET @delimiter = ','
```

The last statements perform the equivalent of setting a default for the delimiter to a comma if this parameter is empty or set to NULL. The remainder of the function parses the tokens by looping through each instance of the delimiter. For each pass of the loop, the tokens are saved in either a start or an end period variable, depending upon whether the pass is odd or even. When an even pass is reached, the two values are tested for date validation. If the tokens are dates, they are inserted into the table variable @customExceptions that will be returned by the function. The added functionality to check dates and convert them would be difficult to perform in the other methods of parsing strings.

```
        WHILE @nStart <= @nLen
          BEGIN
          SELECT @nEndIndex = charindex(@delimiter, @delimitedExceptions, @nStart)

          IF @nEndIndex = 0
              SELECT @nEndIndex = @nLen + 1

          IF @nLoopCtr % 2 = 0
              SET @sSegStart = (ltrim(substring(@delimitedExceptions,
                                                @nStart, @nEndIndex - @nStart)))
          ELSE
             BEGIN
                SET @sSegEnd = (ltrim(substring(@delimitedExceptions,
                                                @nStart, @nEndIndex - @nStart)))

                IF isDate(@sSegStart) = 1 and isDate(@sSegEnd)=1
                    INSERT INTO @customExceptions
                    VALUES ('EXCEPTION', Convert(datetime, @sSegStart),
                                          Convert(datetime, @sSegEnd))
             END

        SELECT @nStart = @nEndIndex + Len(@delimiter)
        SET @nLoopCtr = @nLoopCtr + 1
      END
      RETURN
    END
  GO
```

Cut and paste each of these code snippets together, and run the T-SQL DDL in the CLRTESTDB to create the fn_CustomExceptions function.

Creating and Calculating the Business Default Hours Structure

To make a problem easier to solve, it is sometimes easier to look ahead to the solution. What you need is a series of rows to represent the valid business periods for each day with start and stop times. After taking into account the boundaries of the supplied date parameters, you could then simply summarize the number of total business seconds for each segmented business period. For example, a business default period for a conveyor that is expected to run 24 hours a day with outages from 12:00:00 to 15:00:00, and 18:00:00 to 22:00:00 would generate a structure that looks like this:

```
BusinessDay    SegStart                    SegEnd
2006-07-04     2006-07-04 00:00:00.000     2006-07-04 12:00:00.000
2006-07-04     2006-07-04 15:00:00.000     2006-07-04 18:00:00.000
2006-07-04     2006-07-04 22:00:00.000     2006-07-05 00:00:00.000
```

If the parameterized period is for the whole date of 07/04/06, then you just add up the differences between the segment end and start times for each of these business periods. If the parameterized period is only from 13:00:00 to 23:00:00, you'd just change your structure to remove invalid periods and truncate the remaining periods like this:

```
BusinessDay    SegStart                    SegEnd
2006-07-04     2006-07-04 13:00:00.000     2006-07-04 18:00:00.000
2006-07-04     2006-07-04 22:00:00.000     2006-07-05 23:00:00.000
```

The end result for this day can be determined by adding up the differences in these segments as well. If you build this structure for each day and summarize the results, you'll easily be able to report the results. This matches the method spelled out in the solution approach.

The trick in T-SQL to building this type of structure is to use some form of a table definition. A table is the closest array-like structure native to T-SQL. Using a table on small set of data like these will provide the ability to run a summary operation against the results of the table in one statement instead of iterating through the structure or holding counter balances. For purposes of early development, we like using a temp table, because it allows for reviewing the results of the latest state of the data if something goes wrong. The other option is to use a table variable, which we like to use later in development, for small datasets, but it is harder to troubleshoot. Once it goes out of scope, the state and contents of the table are lost. In later development cycles, temp tables are easy to convert to table variables and you can add some temporary select statements to report the results to a log table or convert the function to a script by commenting out the function definition.

The data you need to store in this structure is limited. The final table variable structure will contain the segment start and end datetimes and a flag for deletion. This flag will allow for the identification of overlaps and then can be used to circle back to remove the rows from the structure. A completed table definition will look like this:

```
DECLARE @tmpBusCalendar TABLE(segstart datetime, segend datetime, delflag bit)
```

To determine the default hours for the timed segments provided, query the BusinessCalendar table looking for time segment types of 'DEFAULTHRS'. By definition, these data represent the time periods that are considered the normal business hours. If the entries were enforced by an application to always be linear and didn't overlap, you could just query and dump these entries into a temp table variable. But since this function is used to examine business availability across overlapping shifts, you have to be able to consolidate the shifts as you process them. The cursor that gets built will depend upon what is provided in the `timedSegmentList` parameter. In the following code, you can see how the `rsBusinessDefaults` cursor is defined based on the value of this input parameter:

```
--CURSOR DEFINITION FOR DEFAULT BUSINESS HOURS
--IF @timedSegmentList is not provided then assume all should be considered.
--Looking here for the contiguous business periods while removing overlap...
IF @timedSegmentList is NULL or @timedSegmentList = ''
BEGIN
    DECLARE rsBusinessDefaults CURSOR FOR
        SELECT SegmentStart, SegmentEnd from businessCalendar
        WHERE TimeSegmentType = 'DEFAULTHRS'
        ORDER BY SegmentStart ASC
END
ELSE
BEGIN
    DECLARE rsBusinessDefaults CURSOR FOR
        SELECT SegmentStart, SegmentEnd FROM businessCalendar
        WHERE TimeSegmentType = 'DEFAULTHRS'
        AND TimedSegment IN
            (SELECT PARSEDVALUE FROM dbo.fn_Split(@timedSegmentList, ','))
        ORDER BY SegmentStart ASC

END
```

As you process each row in the set of business defaults in ascending order, you are looking specifically at the start and stop dates for each timed segment. If the row is the first row, you want to add that to the structure for later comparisons. For each additional row, you only have to look forward in time to determine if the new time segment increases the trailing edge of the current time segment, or if the time segment is a new segment altogether.

```
--LOOKS AT THE LAST RECORD IN STRUCTURE
IF (0 = (SELECT COUNT(*)
            FROM @tmpBusCalendar))
    INSERT INTO @tmpBusCalendar(segStart, segEnd)
    SELECT @rsStart, @rsEnd
ELSE
    BEGIN
        SELECT @tmpStart=MAX(isnull(SegStart, '00:00:00'))
        FROM @tmpBusCalendar
        SELECT @tmpEnd=MAX(isnull(SegEnd, '00:00:00'))
        FROM @tmpBusCalendar
        If @rsEnd > @tmpEnd AND @rsStart <= @tmpEnd
            UPDATE @tmpBusCalendar
            SET SegEnd = @rsEnd
        Else IF @rsStart > @tmpEnd
            INSERT INTO @tmpBusCalendar(segStart, segEnd)
            SELECT @rsStart, @rsEnd
    END
```

The result of this logic is a table with consolidated time periods for all the specific timed segments requested.

Altering Business Default Hours Structure with Exceptions

Exceptions to normal business default hours have the same characteristics as the issues you had with the business default hours. Exceptions overlap and occur with start and stop periods that aren't linear. This requires iterating through another cursor to punch holes in the normal default business schedule. The Business Exceptions cursor `rsBusinessExceptions` is declared the same way, based on the value of the `@timeexclusionlist` parameter. It is not necessary to display that part of the code here; you can see it in the code download for this chapter on this book's web site at www.wrox.com.

One added twist to applying exceptions to business schedules is handling weekends. A weekend is simply an exception to a normal business schedule. A weekend could mean that the entire day is considered a nonworking time, or a weekend could mean that the work day is shortened by a few hours. It is a predictable, repeatable event driven by the representative offset of the day of the week. As each pass is made iterating through the days in the parameterized date range, check to see if the day is a weekend day and apply the weekend special exception periods accordingly. The checking is done with this piece of code:

```
--NEED TO CHECK FOR WEEKEND
IF ((@rsTimeSegType = 'WEEKENDOFFHRS' AND
    datepart(WEEKDAY, @currDay) IN (1, 7))
```

Be careful with what part you use with the `datepart` function. It is not a guarantee that Sunday will always be returned with a `datepart` of 1. Each day of the week has an enumerated, fixed value from 1 to 7. Sunday is actually an enumerated day value of 7. The `datepart` for `WEEKDAY` returns the position of a day relative to a defined first day of the week. If the value of the system variable `@@TEFIRST` is defined as 7-Sunday, using the `SET DATEFIRST` statement, a date falling on Sunday will return a `datepart` of 1 for `WEEKDAY`. If `@@TEFIRST` has been set to 1, then a date falling on Sunday will return a `datepart` of 7 for `WEEKDAY`. If it is a possible scenario that you'd have to deal with this, use the system function `@@TEFIRST` to retrieve the numeric representation of what is considered the first day and work from that offset to calculate the day of the week as you intended to interpret it.

The other thing you have to do to make the final action of summarization possible is to look at the weekend schedule in the current day's context. The weekend schedules are like the business default schedules in that they are stored with meaningful time elements only. You don't want to have to provide an entry for each weekend schedule for the rest of time. It is easier to store only the time element and as you iterate through each day, just merge the current date with the weekend times as an exception for the day. This is done by casting the date to pull out the time element and the date elements, merging each piece together and recasting back as a `datetime` value, like this:

```
SET @rsStart = convert(datetime, convert(varchar(8), @currDay, 112) + ' ' +
                       convert(varchar(8), @rsStart, 108))
```

Now the weekend exception schedule can systematically appear the same as a regular exception for the day that is being evaluated. This will make your exception consolidation logic easier to manage.

The hard part is going through each exception in `datetime` order and evaluating the impact of the exception to a consolidated business schedule. If a working business period is completely encompassed by an exception period, then the default business period did not occur as expected and that period is removed from the temporary business hours structure like this:

```
DELETE FROM @tmpBusCalendar
WHERE segStart >= @rsStart
AND segEnd <= @rsEnd
```

If an exception starts and stops within an existing business time segment, then the segments have to be split into pieces. Because the action of splitting a business time segment takes three steps, you will mark the conflict first to use as a reference. Here are the three steps you must take to split a time segment with an exception:

1. Add the first half of the new business time segment that ends where the exception starts.

2. Add the second half of the new business time segment that starts where the exception ends.

3. Remove the original business time segment.

This code handles the splitting of a business time segment:

```
--IF EXCEPTION IS CONTAINED BY BUSINESS PERIOD
--THEN BUSINESS PERIOD SPLIT INTO TWO PIECES
UPDATE @tmpBusCalendar
SET delFlag = 1
WHERE segStart <= @rsStart
AND segEnd >= @rsStart

IF @@ROWCOUNT > 0
    BEGIN
        --PUT NEW FIRST PIECE IN
        INSERT INTO @tmpBusCalendar(segStart, segEnd)
        SELECT segStart, @rsStart
        FROM @tmpBusCalendar
        WHERE delflag = 1

        --PUT NEW SECOND PIECE IN
        INSERT INTO @tmpBusCalendar(segStart, segEnd)
        SELECT @rsEnd, segEnd
        FROM @tmpBusCalendar
        WHERE delflag = 1

        --REMOVE ORIGINAL ENTRY
        DELETE
        FROM @tmpBusCalendar
        WHERE DelFlag = 1
    END
```

If an exception starts within a business time period or ends within a business time period, you only need to truncate either the starting or ending portion of the business time segment. This logic performs this task.

```
--UPDATE CALENDAR WHEN EXCEPTION
--MAY ALTER THE FOWARD BOUNDARY
UPDATE @tmpBusCalendar
SET segStart = @rsStart
WHERE segStart <= @RsStart
```

```
        AND segEnd >= @RsStart

        UPDATE @tmpBusCalendar
        SET segStart = @rsEnd
        WHERE segStart <= @RSend
        AND segEnd >= @RSend
```

Of course, the last possibility is that the exception doesn't occur in a business time segment because the time segment has been cut already from previous exceptions. If an exception doesn't start or stop within a business time segment, then it is just ignored.

Considering the Parameterized Time Period

The last time segments to apply are the ones provided to the function as parameters. If a business period is determined to be from 08:00:00 to 17:00:00, and the parameters are querying about the availability between 13:00:00 and 14:00:00, then the answer is 3600 seconds or one hour. An easy way to look at the parameterized time period is to view it as a reflection of the way you handled the exception period. The convenient part of the part of the logic is that the parameterized time period is linear. All portions of the business time segments not within the linear boundaries of the parameters are removed to leave only the true business time segments.

This logic is made simpler by the fact that you only need to check the two endpoints of the business hours structure. At each point, there are only three possibilities:

❑   If the parameterized time period starts after a business segment ends, or ends before a business time segment starts, that segment can be completely removed.

❑   If the parameterized time period starts or ends in the middle of a business segment, then the segment should be truncated by replacing the starting or ending point of the business segment with the parameterized boundary.

❑   If the parameterized time period starts before a business segment starts, or ends after a business segment ends, this is considered immaterial and no action is taken.

Since there is nothing new to point out in this part of the code, we'll save the space here and let you review the code by downloading it from this book's page at www.wrox.com.

Calculating the Business Availability

Don't lose track of the fact that you are iterating through each day of the parameterized date range provided as input to the function. For each day, you are calculating the business default working hours, applying all the exceptions, and finally applying the endpoints of the parameterized dates. For each iteration, this temporary structure needs to be examined and calculated into a running total. Summarizing the time depends on what you are timing. Since you are calculating business availability, you can assume that seconds are the most granular time frame that you should consider. For other applications, you may want to calculate time segments in milliseconds. Back when we were considering how to solve this problem, we chose to save state in a table variable. This decision makes this last step the easiest of all. You can test for existence of entries and summarize this table variable structure by iteration using simple T-SQL statements. The final calculations seem almost anticlimactic.

```
IF EXISTS(Select * FROM @TmpBusCalendar)
    SELECT @totalworkseconds = @totalworkseconds +
                sum(datediff(ss, segStart, SegEnd))
            FROM @TmpBusCalendar
```

If the test for the existence of rows returns TRUE, then the running total of seconds is increased by the summarization of the work seconds that represent the business availability of one of the days in the parameterized date range. All that is left is to clean up the cursors and return the final value of the running total seconds.

```
RETURN @TotalWorkSeconds
```

The next section will post the code for the T-SQL version of the business availability calculation — fnGetBusinessAvailability. To get a preview of how this works we'll use the default entries that you inserted into the businessCalendar in the "Solutions Prerequisites" section of this chapter. These entries should look like Figure 11-4.

	TimedSegment	TimeSegmentType	SegmentStart	SegmentEnd
1	CONVEYOR1	DEFAULTHRS	1900-01-01 00:00:00.000	1900-01-01 00:00:00.000
2	CONVEYOR1	OUTAGE	2006-07-04 10:00:00.000	2006-07-04 12:00:00.000
3	CONVEYOR1	OUTAGE	2006-07-04 16:00:00.000	2006-07-04 18:00:00.000
4	CONVEYOR1	MAINTENANCE	2006-07-08 22:00:00.000	2006-07-09 02:00:00.000

Figure 11-4

If you look at the business availability for 07/04/06, you'll notice that the default business hours reflect a 24-hour shop. However, there are two recorded outages that total 4 total consolidated linear hours. The actual business availability for 07/04/06 then should be 20 hours or 72,000 seconds. Run the same parameters using your new business availability function to see if you get the same calculation we ran mentally.

```
select dbo.fnGetBusinessAvailability('07/04/06', '07/04/06', 'CONVEYOR1', '')
```

The results are as you should have expected 72,000 seconds. Once we have the results in seconds the calling application can convert this value into whatever time frame makes sense.

SQL CLR-Based Solution

A SLQCLR-based solution to this business availability problem has the same goals as the SQL-based solution. You can mimic the SQL-based solution, creating a similar logic structure, to get a SQL CLR solution to work. SQL CLR is clearly capably of performing the mechanics of retrieving recordsets and executing SQL statements in the SQL engine, but what we want to do with this section is reinvent the solution from a .NET development perspective. As a .NET developer, you approach this problem differently. First, you might identify the abstractions, and then note any opportunity of code reuse, and finally you may tweak the pulling of data to use memory-based collections to iterate these small date-based collections. You may even solve parts of the problem out of sequence, isolating a portion of the logic to concentrate on a calculation. Deciding when to use SQL CLR to solve a problem and when to go back to T-SQL is part of the debate of the usefulness of this new SQL Server feature. By working through this case study, you'll give SQL CLR a real-world workout and will be able to judge the advantages and disadvantages in a way that might be easier with up close experience. In the end, you'll be able to make your own judgment about when using this technology is appropriate.

Setting up a .Net Studio Solution and Database Projects

To begin your solution, first you need to create a directory structure. We'll be using the `c:\prosqlclr\` folder we set up in Chapter 1 and 2 as a root for this solution. Throughout this book, we have created one-project, one-class solutions resulting in single-assembly SQL CLR examples. Obviously, the smaller projects are a better forum to focus on the implementation details within SQL CLR objects or routines, but in this solution, you will build a more practical and involved example. There are things that you'll want to consider like assembly reuse and testing, that will drive how you put these solutions together. We'll examine these things as you put together the .NET version of this business availability solution. By habit, we like to start our .NET development by creating a blank solution and add any projects later to the solution. To get started follow these few steps:

1. Add a subfolder called `chapter11` to the `c:\prosqlclr\` directory.

2. Create a .NET empty solution by opening up Visual Studio 2005 and clicking File ⇨ New Project.

3. Find the Other Project Types node and click the Blank Solution template under Visual Studio Solutions.

4. Name the solution **BusinessAvailability** and set the location to the root of the `c:\prosqlclr\` `chapter11\` directory.

5. Save and close this solution. We will come back to this later.

You may prefer to download the entire project from this book's web page at www.wrox.com.

Adding Nondatabase Projects to SQL CLR Solutions

Unlike a typical .NET project that allows you to use all the different project templates, you have a restriction with SQL CLR solutions. SQL CLR solutions can only include the .NET-based database project template for building solutions. This is an area of some confusion. Some think that because they can't add a regular .NET Class Library project to a SQL CLR or database solution, that you must not be able to use your current non–SQL CLR assemblies. This is not true. The reason that you can't bring a regular .NET Class Library project into a SQL CLR solution is that the projects are fundamentally different in terms of where the CLR is located. You may notice that when you add a reference to a SQL CLR project that the references don't look the same as the references that you'd find in a normal .NET project. (See Figure 11-5.) In SQL CLR projects, the references are located in the database instead of the framework file path in the file system of your machine. Currently, solutions can only link to one CLR reference or the other.

You cannot create and deploy a CLR-based project or solution in SQL Server that has a reference to an assembly that is not or will not be loaded into SQL Server with your current solution. This means that if you have a regular .NET Class Library project, you can't just add the project into the solution, compile, and deploy the assembly into SQL Server. Well, that's not completely true. You can compile the solution, but when you attempt to load the assembly, you'll get a message that informs you that your assembly was not found in the SQL Server metadata for assemblies. This is because the regular .NET Class Library project is not marked with the hooks that the SQL CLR deployment process needs to create and load the assembly into SQL Server metadata. So, from this you can gather that unless an assembly is loaded into

SQL Server, you won't be able to use that solution within your SQL CLR project. To get your assembly loaded you can do one of two things:

❑ Create a new .NET Database project and copy your classes into either an existing or a new project. The .NET Database or SQL CLR projects come with the hooks that are needed to automatically load assemblies. When you compile and deploy the project, the dependent assemblies will be loaded as well. You can use this route if you don't mind duplicating your .NET source or having two projects point to that source. You may also have to take this route if your .NET assembly contains dependent assemblies that are considered Unsafe from a SQL Server perspective. See Chapter 10 for a discussion of these limitations.

❑ Take your normal .NET project, compile it, and load your compiled assembly from its `bin` directory into SQL Server. This is the recommended method, because you aren't recreating copies of code to maintain. You will have to perform this step manually, but it is simple to do. You may have done this in Chapter 2 as an exercise using the `CREATE ASSEMBLY` TSQL DDL statement: We'll show you how to create a regular .NET assembly and use it in this solution later in this section.

Either way, once an assembly is loaded into SQL Server, you will be able to create a reference to it within your SQL CLR–based .NET projects.

One of the things that will make working with more involved solutions easier is to plan the structure of how the projects will be pulled into the solution. For this case study, we are going to use a precompiled helper assembly for some common date and SQL-based functionality. This will help you get an idea of how to implement code reuse in SQL CLR development. We are also going to separate out the logic for the business availability calculation to have smaller, more manageable pieces, and to be able to test those functionalities with a .NET console application. Note that a .NET console app causes no reference problems within your solution because it is not referenced by the solution. During deployment, it will simply be ignored. However, to test the logic in the assemblies, the .NET console needs references to them. Since the console application can't retrieve references from the SQL host, you can just point the console references to your development `bin` directory instead. This way you can test your assemblies during development without having to resort to T-SQL-based testing methods. A generic diagram of what you are going to build can be seen in Figure 11-6.

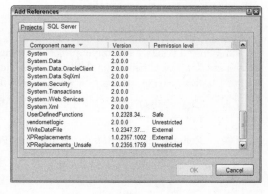

Figure 11-5

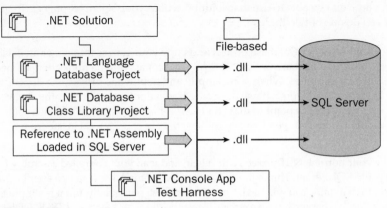

Figure 11-6

The other planning point to note in Figure 11.6 is that you'll separate the business availability logic into a separate assembly. The only reason for this is that you may have other classes for similar calculations that you may want to deploy into this assembly. The final assembly at the top of the hierarchy is the SQ CLR interface to all this logic. You can now implement any type of relevant SQL CLR object in this assembly or other assemblies.

Building the Corp.Core.Utilities Assembly

This assembly project will simulate an assembly that you may find yourself creating in your development shop. Structurally and architecturally, it is just like your normal .NET development projects. There are certain generic functionalities that you'll use repeatedly and can benefit from creating and storing these routines in an assembly that you can reuse. In this project, there are a few things that you'll need to specifically address. Remember that one of the business requirements is that a literal string can be provided that indicates a series of exception dates. You'll also need to test each token in that string to make sure that it is a valid date. If you are using VB.NET, you'll have access to an isDate() function that can validate dates, and you can use the TryParse() method C#. We'll build an isDate() function to demonstrate utility based methods in this assembly.

1. Create a .NET empty solution by opening up Visual Studio 2005 and clicking the menu option File ⇨ New Project.

2. Find your C# or VB.Net project templates. Select a normal Class Library project template. Name the project **Corp.Core.Utilities**, and click OK. When the project opens, check the project properties to make sure that the namespace and assembly names both are Corp.Core.Utilities.

3. Change the name of the default class file to Utilities.cs. Remove the default class1 definition from the class.

4. Remove the default System.Collections.Generic and System.Text assemblies from the class.

5. Save the project to the root of the Chapter11 directory. It should be the default if you already created the blank solution.

Now you are ready to implement the isDate() function. To keep all these related utility-type functions together, you'll create a class definition for this function. You may recall that we built this function earlier in the ".Net DateTime Class" section. Add this class definition and then copy the function definition into this class. Without the isDate() implementation, which would be redundant, the class file should look like Figure 11-7.

```
using System;
namespace Corp.Core.Utilities
{
    public class DateUtilities
    {
        isDate to check whether or not a date is a valid date.
    }
}
```

Figure 11-7

The other problem that you are going to have to solve is being able to parse the delimited input that represents the business timed segments for the business availability calculation. A function that can crack the tokens in the delimited string and convert them into a T-SQL compliant IN clause will make the retrieval of this information easy. You'll add a utility to perform this function. Instead of putting this function inside the current DateUtilities class structure, in your Utilities class file, just add a new public class structure called TSQLUtilities. The class definition should look like this:

```
public class TSQLUtilities
{}
```

Notice that the class definition is public. This separation of functionality into classes now enables an organizational structure to allow the addition of future T-SQL utilities. Dealing with delimited strings in .NET is trivial. The Split function can break a delimited string into tokens that you can iterate through and add the proper T-SQL formatting to create a string that can be substituted into an IN clause. The function buildINClause looks like this.

```
public static string buildINClause(string delimitedstring,
                                   char delimiter)
{
    string[] tokens = delimitedstring.Split(delimiter);
    string inClause = string.Empty;
    delimitedstring.Replace("'", "");

    if (delimitedstring != string.Empty)
    {
        foreach (string s in tokens)
        {
            inClause = inClause + "'" + s.Trim() + "',";
        }
        if (inClause.EndsWith(","))
            inClause = inClause.Remove(inClause.Length - 1, 1);
    }
    return inClause;
}
```

Notice that the delimiter is added to the function so that you can use this same function in other projects. Add this function within the bracket of the TSQLUtilities class.

The last set of utility functions that you need is some utilities to convert SqlDataTypes into base types. The reason for this is that SQLDataTypes are nullable, and you need to have a rule for how you are going to handle that situation for conversion. Otherwise, you'll have to duplicate that logic throughout the solution. Create a class structure named ConvertUtilities like the TSQLUtilities class you created earlier. Add a namespace to the top of the Utilities class file for System.Data.SqlTypes. You'll then add the two conversion utilities that you need for this project. The first function that you'll create is a string conversion function ConvertSQLString(). This function will check to see if the incoming SqlString is NULL and convert it to an empty string. Otherwise, the string will be converted to the base string type and returned. This function looks like this:

```
public static string ConvertSqlString(SqlString myString)
{
    if (myString.IsNull)
    {return string.Empty;}
    else{return (string)myString;}
}
```

The last function will convert SqlDateTypes into base DateTime structures. Again, you have to deal with the possibility of NULL values. This implementation is up to individual preference. One natural value to use for clear communication between calling functions and this internal implementation is to use the DateTime.MinValue value. This allows the calling function, as long as it is a .NET assembly, to specifically test for this condition. The ConvertSqlDateTime() function looks like this:

```
public static DateTime ConvertSqlDateTime(SqlDateTime myDate)
{
    if (myDate.IsNull)
    {return DateTime.MinValue;}
    else
    {
        DateTime myNewDate = (DateTime)myDate;
        return new DateTime(myNewDate.Year, myNewDate.Month, myNewDate.Day,
                myNewDate.Hour, myNewDate.Minute, myNewDate.Second);
    }
}
```

Now you are ready to compile this assembly. In the menu, select the Build option and compile the assembly. You should see a DLL named Corp.Core.Utilities in your bin directory, located in your project hierarchy. If you used the suggested directory structure and are compiling a debug version of your assembly, you'll find this DLL in this location:

```
C:\ProSQLCLR\Chapter11\Corp.Core.Utilities\Corp.Core.Utilities\bin\Debug\
```

If your project is set up to compile a release version, the last subdirectory will be named release\. (You can check your build properties in the project properties build tab.) This takes care of creating a simulation of an assembly that you may have in your development shop that you may want to extend to use in SQL CLR projects. Next, you'll create another assembly for utility functions that are more SQL CLR based.

Building the Corp.SQLCLR.Utilities Assembly

To demonstrate that you can share assemblies from other SQL CLR–based projects, you'll build a simple `DataTable` retrieval utility that you can pass a `SELECT` T-SQL statement to, and returns a `DataTable`. We'll use a .NET database project instead of a regular .NET project for this, since it provides the hooks for deployment and contains the assemblies that you need to have access to the SQL Server context connection objects that you need for efficient connectivity. To get started, follow these steps:

1. Create a .NET empty solution by opening up Visual Studio 2005 and clicking File ⇨ New Project.

2. Navigate to the Database templates under either the C# or VB.NET language nodes. Select SQL Server Project Template.

3. Name the project **Corp.SQLCLR.Utilities**. Press OK to create the project. You will get a dialog to connect to a database. This is because the .NET database projects need a reference to the CLR in the server and the other assemblies in the database you wish to develop the project against. Connect to the CLRTESTDB database that you have been using for this book.

4. Save the project to the root of the `Chapter11` directory. It should be the default if you have already created the blank solution.

Now you have a project that, when compiled and deployed automatically, knows that it should be deployed into the SQL CLR database. To add your implementation details, right-click it in the Solution Explorer and select Add ⇨ New Item. Select the class item template and set the name to `DataHelper.cs`. Because you are going to perform a retrieval of data using the SQL `Context` connection, replace all the namespaces with these:

```
using System;
using System.Data;
using System.Data.SqlClient;
using System.Data.SqlTypes;
using Microsoft.SqlServer.Server;
```

Add this function into the `DataHelper` class that will convert a T-SQL `SELECT` statement into a `DataTable`:

```
Public class DataHelper
{
    #region GetDataSetWithSQL
    public static DataSet GetDataSetWithSQL(string mySQL, string myConnStr)
    {
        SqlDataAdapter sqlDa = new SqlDataAdapter();
        DataSet sqlDs = new DataSet();
        using (SqlConnection sqlConn =
           new SqlConnection(myConnStr))
        {
            SqlCommand sqlCmd = new SqlCommand(mySQL, sqlConn);
            sqlCmd.CommandType = CommandType.Text;
            sqlDa.SelectCommand = sqlCmd;
            sqlDa.Fill(sqlDs, "TABLE");
            sqlConn.Close();
        }
        return sqlDs;
    }
    #endregion
}
```

Notice that we are passing in a connection string to this utility function. Since we are building a SQL CLR solution, you may wonder why we don't just leave this hard-coded to "Context Connection=True". We could, but this makes testing more difficult later. We'll explain in later when we create some unit tests for the SQL CLR solution. You'll also notice that in this function there is no error handling. Typically, in these low-level utilities we allow the error to bubble up to the caller where it can be handled. This function doesn't have enough information to decide what to do if an error occurs retrieving this data.

You may also wonder why we are not using a DataReader in this scenario, since it would be more efficient and more lightweight for retrieval purposes. Unfortunately, SQL CLR objects can't have more than one active SqlContext connection at a time. To build a generic routine, you have to use an object that can be created, disconnected, and closed before it is passed around.

Deploying the Corp..Utilities

Because you have two different project types, you'll have two different deployment techniques. For the last Corp.SQLCLR.Utilities assembly, you only need to build and deploy this solution to SQL Server. The project, because it is a SQL Server project template, has all the hooks to perform dropping existing copies of the assembly and loading the new copy. You should see the assembly in the SSMS solution explorer under the CLRTESTDB assemblies, like Figure 11-8.

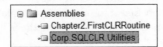

Figure 11-8

Deploying the Corp.Core.Utilities assembly will be a manual process. You'll execute a T-SQL command in the SSMS query window to load this binary assembly into SQL Server. Execute this T-SQL to load this assembly:

```
USE CLRTESTDB
GO
CREATE ASSEMBLY [Corp.Core.Utilities] FROM
'c:\ProSQLCLR\Chapter11\Corp.Core.Utilities\Corp.Core.Utilities\bin\Debug\Corp.Core
.Utilities.dll'
WITH PERMISSION_SET = SAFE
```

Check SSMS to verify that both these assemblies are now loaded, as shown in Figure 11-9.

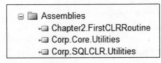

Figure 11-9

Now you have examples of both a regular .NET assembly and an existing SQL CLR .NET assembly that you can use to build your solution upon. Let's turn now to building the business availability solution.

Creating the Corp.SQLCLR.Scheduling Assembly

For most of the examples in this book, we have created single-project implementations of SQL CLR objects. This is for the simplicity of example purposes. In the real world, you will have scenarios that make this unacceptable. Take, for example, your need to create this business availability calculation. What if this calculation is one of several that you want to group together? Wouldn't you like to group these functions in one place where finding them is easy? What if you wanted to get rid of one of the SQL CLR functions that use these calculations? If the SQL CLR object definitions are mixed into the implementations, you'll have to drop all of them to update just one of them. You can see that this could cause some issues.

The better way to build these SQL CLR objects for production maintainability and testing purposes is to separate the SQL CLR object definition from its implementation. Of course, you should do this only if it makes sense. A one-off function here or there will not be a big deal. This advice applies to problem solving in a business domain where the potential of having several similar calculations exists. Relative to this case study, you could have a calculation that returns the number of business days within a date parameter. This calculation is very similar to what you are going to build in this case study and could take advantage of some of the programming methods that you build. It makes sense that these two calculation functions could be co-located in one assembly, and then multiple SQL CLR objects can be built to use those method entry points. In this methodology, it is easy later to add, change, or delete a SQL CLR object without affecting the others that use this assembly. The downside is that changes to the core assembly will cause a ripple effect for the SQL CLR objects. To make this easier to manage, we recommend that a solution should be built so that all the dependent SQL CLR object definitions are contained within it — including a reference to the core assembly. This allows the DBA to open up the solution and quickly redeploy to core assembly and all the dependent SQL CLR object definitions using the hooks within each project. This is a lot easier then manually removing each dependency and recreating them.

Setting Up the project

You are going to use this separation methodology in this example. The first thing we have decided is that we are going to create a core assembly for all our scheduling calculations. It will be called Corp.SQLCLR.Scheduling. This name allows for quick identification that the assembly is:

❑ Owned by Corp

❑ Generalized to a SQL CLR–based class expected to be hosted in SQL Server

❑ Contains implementation for scheduling-type business logic

To build this assembly, first you'll need to shut down all your open projects and reopen the blank solution in c:\prosqlclr\chapter11\businessavailability.

1. With the empty BusinessAvailability solution open, select the menu option File ➪ Add ➪ New Project. Select the SQL Server Project template under either the C# or VB.NET project templates database node.

2. Name the project Corp.SQLCLR.Scheduling. Leave the location as c:\prosqlclr\chapter11\businessavailability. This will create a folder under the current solution folder with the same name. It will also define the default namespace and assembly name.

3. Connect to the CLRTESTDB database.

4. Add a class to the project by right-clicking on the `Corp.SQLCLR.Scheduling` project and selecting Add ➪ New Item. Select the class item template. Change the name to **Business.cs**.

5. Add references to the `Corp.Core.Utilities` and `Corp.SQLCLR.Utilities` assemblies into the `Corp.SQLCLR.Scheduling` project. The references should be in SQL Server. The Add References dialog and final solution should look like Figure 11-10.

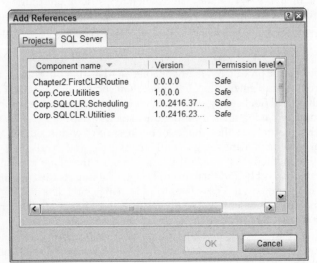
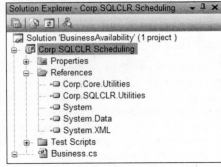

Figure 11-10

6. For the `Corp.SQLCLR.Scheduling` project to use these assemblies, you must add the namespaces to the class that you'll be coding. Since the assemblies were given the same names as the namespaces, this will be easy. Replace the default namespaces in the `Business.cs` class file with the following:

```
using System;
using System.Data;
using System.Collections;
using System.Data.SqlTypes;
using Corp.Core.Utilities;
using Corp.SQLCLR.Utilities;
```

The last thing you want to check is the visibility of the referenced classes and methods. If you set up public classes and methods, you should be able to see them here. The easiest way to check this is to use the menu option View ➪ Object Browser to bring up the Object Browser. This shows all the assemblies, namespaces, classes, and methods available within the solution. You should see the classes we are exposing in each project here, like Figure 11-11.

One of the common issues that you may discover at this point is that the classes may not be visible. This is because they are probably not public. Go back, review the previous section, and make sure that these class definitions are public to external assemblies. This basic project is then ready for the implementation logic. This is covered in the next step.

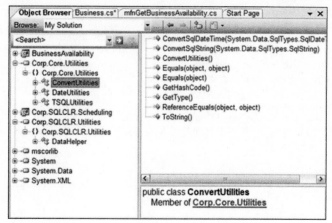

Figure 11-11

Defining a TimeSegment Class

One of the core differences between problem solving in T-SQL versus a full-featured programming language is that some aspects can be abstracted into separate classes. One such opportunity is the `TimeSegment` class. If you followed along in the lengthy T-SQL version, you may have noticed that you had to perform several specific operations with date and time attributes. These common operations include:

❑   Ensuring that dates were valid.

❑   Converting user intent to machine requirements. An example of this is when a date range is provided from 07/04/06 to 07/04/06. Humans intend this to mean the whole day. The machine considers this to be 0 seconds. You need to consistently handle this end date and convert to machine understanding.

❑   Converting any date range to calculate the real number of days, instead of a fractional rounding of days. This requires a conversion of the end date regardless of time to the next day at 00:00:00 to ensure we get an accurate day count.

❑   Because `BUSINESSDFTHRS` and `WEEKENDOFFHRS` are two time segment types that are dateless, you need the ability to apply the current day that you are evaluating to these time components.

These operations are needed all over the place, so the first task is to create the `TimeSegment` class. You can use either a separate class file or the same class file. We'll go through each line of the class so you can see all of it and explain it in sections.

1.   Create the public class definition in the `business.cs` file under the business class definition.

2.   Add private variables to hold a start date, and end date, and a time segment type. These attributes match up to the database definition except for the `TimedSegment`. Create public `get` and `set` properties for these private variables. The start of the class and the properties are here:

```
#region TimeSegment Class Definition
public class TimeSegment
{
    private DateTime mStart;
```

```
private DateTime mEnd;
private string mtimeSegmentType;
public enum SpecificDateParm { start, end, both };

//Properties of TimeSegment
public string TimeSegmentType
{
    get { return mtimeSegmentType; }
    set { mtimeSegmentType = value; }
}
public DateTime Start
{
    get { return mStart; }
    set { mStart = value; }
}
public DateTime End
{
    get { return mEnd; }
    set { mEnd = value; }
}
```

3. Next, create the two outer boundaries of any two start and stop dates. Create two additional properties with private variables named `StartMin` and `EndMax`. These properties are read only and return calculated values based upon their corresponding `Start` or `End` date properties. The `StartMin` should always return a timeless start date. The `EndDate` should always return a timeless date one day more than the actual `EndDate`. The code in the two properties looks like this:

```
public DateTime StartMin
{
    get
    {
        return new DateTime(mStart.Year, mStart.Month, mStart.Day,
                            0, 0, 0);
    }
}
public DateTime EndMax
{
    get
    {
        DateTime workdate = new DateTime(mEnd.Year, mEnd.Month, mEnd.Day,
                            0, 0, 0);
        workdate = workdate.AddDays(1);
        return workdate;
    }
}
```

4. When you create the constructor, you'll realize that there are two ways to use this class. In one way, you are receiving information that may need to be altered as it is accepted. In another way, you need to accept the data as is with no changes. If, for example, the date and time stamps are coming from the business calendar table, you can assume that the date and times are properly set. If date and time boundaries are coming from external inputs, you may need to adjust the end date to make the right calculations. To handle this optional situation, you'll have two constructors. One handles a parameter that will restate the end date, if it has no time component, to be the whole day. The other constructor will simply store provided dates.

```
//CONSTRUCTORS
public TimeSegment(DateTime mystart, DateTime myend,
               string mytimeSegType, bool CheckforEndDateAdjustment)
{
    if (CheckforEndDateAdjustment)
    {
        //If both parm are same day convert end date to next day 00:00:00
        if ((mystart.Equals(myend)) &&
               (mystart.Hour == myend.Hour && mystart.Minute == 0 &&
                              mystart.Second == 0))
        {
            myend = new DateTime(myend.Year, myend.Month,
                              myend.AddDays(1).Day, 0, 0, 0);
        }
    }
    this.Start = mystart;
    this.End = myend;
    this.TimeSegmentType = mytimeSegType;

}
//CONSTRUCTOR
public TimeSegment(DateTime mystart, DateTime myend, string mytimeSegType)
{
    this.Start = mystart;
    this.End = myend;
    this.TimeSegmentType = mytimeSegType;
}
```

5. The remaining logic pertains to the setting of dates on a time segment to match the current date that you are interested in. Because you'll have many scenarios that use this functionality, you need to be able to control the granularity of the transaction. You'll see an additional parameter that is actually an enumeration to provide the different methods of altering the start, end, or both of the dates when required. The enumerations are found in the first section of the previous code.

```
public void SetDateForTimeOnlyProperties(DateTime myDate,
                                      SpecificDateParm DateParmPos)
{
    if (SpecificDateParm.start == DateParmPos ||
          SpecificDateParm.both == DateParmPos)
    {
        DateTime newStart =
               new DateTime(myDate.Year, myDate.Month, myDate.Day,
                              mStart.Hour, mStart.Minute, mStart.Second);
        mStart = newStart;
    }

    if (SpecificDateParm.end == DateParmPos ||
          SpecificDateParm.both == DateParmPos)
    {
        DateTime newEnd =
               new DateTime(myDate.Year, myDate.Month, myDate.Day,
                              mEnd.Hour, mEnd.Minute, mEnd.Second);
        mEnd = newEnd;
    }
```

```
        if (mEnd == mStart && ((mEnd.Hour + mEnd.Minute + mEnd.Second) == 0))
            mEnd = mEnd.AddDays(1);
}
```

6. The remainder of the class contains a `ToString()` method that can be used during testing to dump the contents of the class.

```
public override string ToString()
{
    return "Start Value      : " + Start.ToString() + "\n" +
           "Start Min Value: " + StartMin.ToString() + "\n" +
           "End Value        : " + End.ToString() + "\n" +
           "End Max Value    : " + EndMax.ToString() + "\n" +
           "Segment Type     : " + TimeSegmentType.ToString() + "\n";
}
}
#endregion
```

You'll notice from this point on that this class structure is heavily used in the project. You can stuff the beginning and end dates into this structure and they travel together throughout the solution. This provides great flexibility and assurance of logic consistency. The full commented code is available online at this book's page at www.wrox.com. The #region and #endregion tags are real useful here in separating the logic boundaries. Click on the first tag to roll this code up and out of view while you continue on to the logic in the business class.

Defining the Rest of the Business Class

From here on out we are just going to code through a .NET implementation of the BusinessAvailability calculation. Our steps are mapped out in the Solution Approach section we covered earlier. But to see a sneak peek at what your finished solution will look like see Figure 11-12 for the stubbed out regions that we are going to fill in.

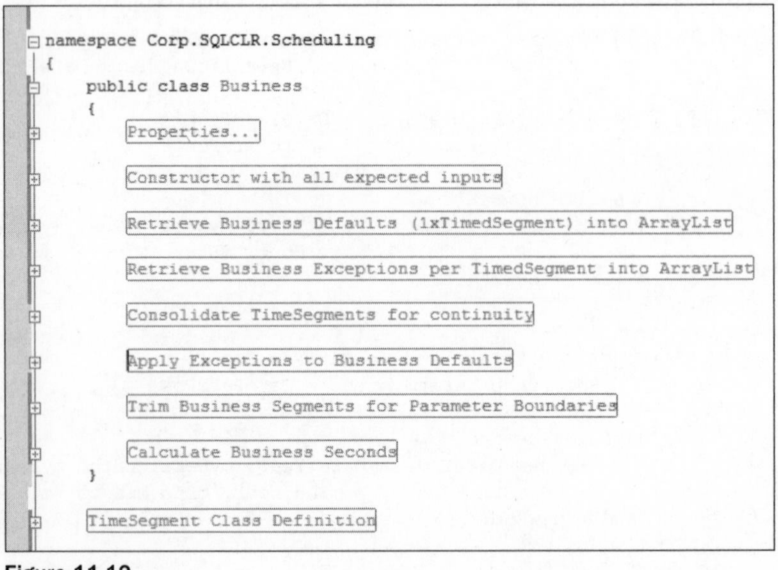

```
namespace Corp.SQLCLR.Scheduling
{
    public class Business
    {
        Properties...

        Constructor with all expected inputs

        Retrieve Business Defaults (1xTimedSegment) into ArrayList

        Retrieve Business Exceptions per TimedSegment into ArrayList

        Consolidate TimeSegments for continuity

        Apply Exceptions to Business Defaults

        Trim Business Segments for Parameter Boundaries

        Calculate Business Seconds
    }

    TimeSegment Class Definition
```

Figure 11-12

Each of these regions (except for the properties) represents a portion of logic that we'll be covering in the next sections. These sections each represent a method that you will be adding to the implementation of the `Business` class structure in the `Corp.SQLCLR.Scheduling` assembly.

Creating and Calculating the Business Default Hours Structure

In the T-SQL version of this solution, you may recall that we had a few issues to deal with in our solution. The first issue is that a cursor definition is immutable, meaning the definition can't be changed on the fly. Parameters can be substituted, but the statement can't be altered in the definition. This difficulty is easily overcome in .NET, since you can build a SQL string or call a T-SQL or SQL CLR function or stored procedure to build the cursor.

This brings up another point. Developers are much more comfortable with the idea of building resultsets to solve programming problems. When it comes to doing the same thing in SQL Server, this seems more difficult. This is partly because cursors are difficult to pass around to other routines. This type of programming is routine in languages like .NET.

In the `GetBusinessDefaults()` method, you are expecting to retrieve a list containing many `TimedSegments`, or perhaps a singleton. This timed segment is used to build and retrieve the default hours for the timed segment(s) provided. We'll set up the method for these requirements to look like this:

```
#region Retrieve Business Defaults (1xTimedSegment) into ArrayList
public static ArrayList GetBusinessDefaults(string TimedSegments,
                                            string myConnStr)
{
    //Start with new working array
    ArrayList workingArrayList = new ArrayList();
```

Notice the use of the `ArrayList` class. This is similar to the data tables that you created in the T-SQL version. However, unlike a table variable, you can pass these structures around from inside this method back out to the controller that can send it to other methods to combine the exceptions. This makes the testing of each part of the solution easier to manage.

You'll build this `SELECT` statement based on what you have in the input string. This would be better implemented as a call to a stored procedure, but building a generic stored procedure routine is not as practical as returning the content of a T-SQL string.

```
string mySQL = "SELECT SegmentStart, SegmentEnd " +
               "FROM businessCalendar " +
               "WHERE TimeSegmentType = 'DEFAULTHRS' ";
//NOTE: TimedSegments already in proper INSTR format...
//      or are singleton entries
if (TimedSegments != string.Empty)
    mySQL = mySQL + "AND TimedSegment IN (@INSTR) ";

mySQL = mySQL + "ORDER BY SegmentStart ASC ";
mySQL = mySQL.Replace("@INSTR", TimedSegments);
```

The next line uses the utility class in your `Corp.SQLCLR.Utilities` assembly to retrieve a `DataSet` using the `SQLContext` connection.

```
//Uses the Corp.SQLCLR.Utilities Assembly..
DataSet ds = DataHelper.GetDataSetWithSQL(mySQL, myConnStr);
```

Then all that remains is to loop through the results of the `DataSet` and load up the array.

```
foreach (DataRow dr in ds.Tables[0].Rows)
{
    TimeSegment newSegment = new TimeSegment
        (Convert.ToDateTime(dr[0]),
            Convert.ToDateTime(dr[1]),
            "DEFAULTHRS", false);
    if (newSegment.Start == newSegment.End &&
        newSegment.Start.Hour == 0 &&
        newSegment.Start.Minute == 0 &&
        newSegment.Start.Second == 0)
        newSegment.End = newSegment.EndMax;
    workingArrayList.Add(newSegment);
}
return workingArrayList;
```

Notice that you create a `TimeSegment` class structure for each entry. This allows you to use the business logic encapsulated in the `EndMax` field under specific circumstances. If the business default hours are stored as 07/04/06 00:00:00 and 07/04/06 00:00:, then the end date is restated as the max end date or 07/05/06 00:00:00. The array list is then returned to the `BusinessAvailability` controller method.

Retrieving and Calculating the Exceptions Structure

One of the issues you had with calculating the exceptions structure in the T-SQL version was not being able to look at business exceptions one day at a time. The T-SQL version was restricted because of the limitations of being able to restate the cursor definition for each day in the parameters loop. This resulted in unnecessarily having to examine all exceptions for each day instead of being able to target your examination to the specific day in the parameter loop.

```
#region Retrieve Business Exceptions per TimedSegment into ArrayList
public static ArrayList GetBusinessExceptions(string TimedSegments,
                                string timeExclusionList,
                                TimeSegment ts,
                                string myConnStr)
{
    //Create a working array structure
    ArrayList workingArrayList = new ArrayList();
```

You'll notice that this logic is broken out into a function called `GetBusinessExceptions()` and you can accept a date parameter to this function to use to retrieve targeted exceptions. Since a date range fits into the standard rules for a `TimeSegment`, you can make use of this structure here as well. You can use the encapsulated `StartMin` and `EndMax` properties to pull a bounded date range for each date in the parameterized date range.

```
//If there is a time exclusion list then it is a custom list
//otherwise the list requires pulling SQL Data based on a time
//segment start and end.
if (timeExclusionList == string.Empty)
```

```
    {
        //If no custom exceptions and want all timedsegments
        string mySQL = "SELECT SegmentStart, SegmentEnd, "
                "TimeSegmentType " +
                "FROM businessCalendar " +
                "WHERE ((TimeSegmentType <> 'DEFAULTHRS' " +
                "AND (" +
                "(SegmentStart between '" + ts.StartMin.ToString() +
                        "' and '" + ts.EndMax.ToString() + "') " +
                "OR (SegmentEnd between '" + ts.StartMin.ToString() +
                        "' and '" + ts.EndMax.ToString() + "') " +
                ")) " +
                "OR (TimeSegmentType = 'WEEKENDOFFHRS'))";

        if (TimedSegments != string.Empty)
        {
            mySQL = mySQL + " AND TimedSegment IN (@INSTR) ";
        }
        mySQL = mySQL + "ORDER BY SegmentStart ASC";
        mySQL = mySQL.Replace("@INSTR", TimedSegments);

        DataSet ds = CLRUtilities.GetDataSetWithSQL(mySQL, myConnStr);
        foreach (DataRow dr in ds.Tables[0].Rows)
        {
            TimeSegment newSegment = new TimeSegment
                (Convert.ToDateTime(dr[0]),
                    Convert.ToDateTime(dr[1]),
                        Convert.ToString(dr[2]).TrimEnd(), false);
            if ((newSegment.Start.Year == 1 ||
                    newSegment.Start.Year == 1900)
                && (newSegment.Start.Month == 1)
                && (newSegment.Start.Day == 1))
            {
                newSegment.SetDateForTimeOnlyProperties(ts.StartMin,
                            TimeSegment.SpecificDateParm.both);
            }
            workingArrayList.Add(newSegment);
        }
    }
}
```

The other thing of interest here is the use of the SetDateForTimeOnlyProperties() method. Because the time segment type of WEEKENDOFFHRS is stored as a time-only attribute, you have to apply the current date provided in the time segment provided as an input parameter. This function will turn a stored WEEKENDOFFHRS setting of 01/01/1900 08:00:00 to 01/01/1900 17:00:00 into 07/04/06 08:00:00 to 07/04/06 17:00:00 when the input TimeSegment parameter is set to a start date of 07/04/06.

The exception function also has to deal with the fact that the exceptions period could be provided by a comma-delimited input string that represents a series of date ranges. In the T-SQL version, you had to write a T-SQL table-valued function that turned that input into a set of rows that you could use in a T-SQL statement. In the SQL CLR version, you only need to parse that delimited string into tokens and check for proper dates. This is made easier by using the .NET library Split() function. Basically, all you have to worry about is testing the date, which is handled by the corp.core.utilities DateUtilities isDate() function.

```
    else
    {
        //If provided an exclusion period list then parse it out
        string[] timeList = timeExclusionList.Split(',');
        DateTime dtHold = new DateTime(1900, 1, 1, 0, 0, 0);
        for (int i = 0; i < timeList.Length; i++)
        {
            if (DateUtilities.isDate(timeList[i]) == true)
            {
                if ((i % 2 != 0) && (i != 0) ||
                    (i == (timeList.Length - 1)))
                {
                    TimeSegment newSegment =
                        new TimeSegment(dtHold,
                                DateTime.Parse(timeList[i]),
                                "CUSTOMEXCEPTION", true);
                    workingArrayList.Add(newSegment);
                }
                else
                { dtHold = DateTime.Parse(timeList[i]); }
            }
            else
                break;
        }
    }
    return workingArrayList;
}
#endregion
```

Because this information is coming from an external source that you do not control, the assumption is that you could be fed date ranges that need to have the end date examined for calculation purposes. Notice that the constructor used in the `TimeSegment` class creation for each entry has the Boolean parameter of `CheckforEndDateAdjustment` set to true. This allows the `TimeSegment` class to apply business logic to the end dates on each date range according to the business rules needed for correct date calculations. Finally, we return the contents of an array that contains the business exceptions for the date provided to the method.

Consolidating Time Segments for Continuity

Both the business-default-hour and business-exception-hour storage structures need to be consolidated so that calculation routines can be made on the total continuous time frames. In the T-SQL version, you had to use a iterator pattern and calculate as you moved through the cursor. This had to be performed individually for each structure. You can now contemplate this logic once and use it for both structures. This ensures better software consistency, for this case study, or for any future time-based calculations, you may need to add to your `Core.SQLCLR.Scheduling` assembly.

In the `ConsolidateTimeSegments()` method, you accept an array list of `TimeSegments` and perform the same iterator pattern as you did in the T-SQL version.

```
#region Consolidate TimeSegments for continuity
public static ArrayList ConsolidateTimeSegments(ArrayList myTS)
{
```

```
                //Make the longest continuous time segments possible
                ArrayList newTS = new ArrayList();
```

The code then goes through an iteration of segments in datetime order to build an entirely new ArrayList of TimeSegments that consolidate and remove time segment redundancy. One of the things that helps in building logic like this is to create a visual model of what you are attempting to do and continually bounce your logic off of this model. For this portion of the logic for both the T-SQL and SQL CLR versions, we used the visual model shown in Figure 11-13.

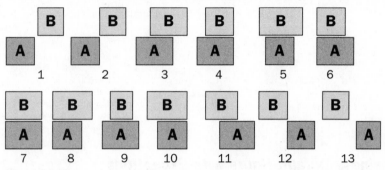

Figure 11-13

This visual model represents the possibilities of each segment against another. You want to make sure that you have prepared for each possibility in your programmed solution. The logic to combine the blocks in scenario 2 in the figure would result in a superset of the starting boundary of time segment A and the ending boundary of time segment B. This logic can be found in the remaining body of the method.

```
            TimeSegment b = null;
            foreach (TimeSegment a in myTS)
            {
                //On first pass nothing to do but
                //save an entry
                if (b == null)
                { }
                else
                {
                    if ((a.Start < b.Start &&
                        a.End < b.Start) || a.Start > b.End)
                    {
                        newTS.Add(new TimeSegment(b.Start, b.End, "CONSOL"));
                        newTS.Add(new TimeSegment(a.Start, a.End, "CONSOL"));
                    }
                    else if (a.Start <= b.Start && a.End >= b.Start
                            && a.End <= b.End)
                    {
                        newTS.Add(new TimeSegment(a.Start, b.End, "CONSOL"));
                    }
                    else if (a.Start <= b.Start && a.End > b.End)
                    {
```

```
                            newTS.Add(new TimeSegment(a.Start, a.End, "CONSOL"));
                    }
                    else if (a.Start >= b.Start && a.Start <= b.End
                            && a.End > b.End)
                    {
                            newTS.Add(new TimeSegment(b.Start, a.End, "CONSOL"));
                    }
                    else if (a.Start >= b.Start && a.Start <= b.End
                            && a.End <= b.End)
                    {
                            newTS.Add(new TimeSegment(b.Start, b.End, "CONSOL"));
                    }
            }
            b = a;
        }
        if (newTS.Count == 0)
            newTS.Add(b);
        return newTS;
    }
#endregion
```

Altering Business Default Hours with Exceptions

The logic in the `ApplyExceptionsToBusinessSchedule()` uses Figure 11-12 heavily, but in a different way. The consolidation routine looks to combine segments, and the exception routine works to remove nonworking business-hour exceptions from the normal working hours for each parameterized date in a date range. For efficiency, you only need to pull the business default hours once. To preserve this data, you make a copy of the `TimeSegment`s in the array of business default hours. You should also note that reference types like array lists can be altered within the body of the method even though value-type variables are copied by value. You'll see the copying of the array as one of the first steps in this routine.

```
#region Apply Exceptions to Business Defaults
public static ArrayList ApplyExceptionsToBusinessSchedule(
                                ArrayList BusDefaults,
                                ArrayList BusExceptions,
                                DateTime currDayChecking)
{
    ArrayList workingBusDefaults = new ArrayList();
    foreach (TimeSegment wts in BusDefaults)
    {
        workingBusDefaults.Add(
            new TimeSegment(wts.Start, wts.End, "COPY"));
    }
```

The main reason you need to copy this array is that you are going to alter the array contents within this method as you apply each business-exception time segment to each business-default-hour time segment. Because you are iterating over the `ArrayList`, you do not want to alter the array item by removing `TimeSegment` objects from the list. Instead, you move the start dates forward or end dates backward in each business-default-hour `TimeSegment` as exceptions eat into the business hours. If a business-hour segment is cut off in the middle, you throw the isolated section of the bisected segment into a new structure to be added back in the end, advance the forward boundary of the business hours, and keep going. This is illustrated visually in Figure 11-14.

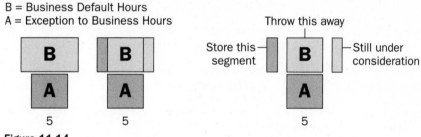

B = Business Default Hours
A = Exception to Business Hours

Figure 11-14

The only other complication is to consider the weekend hours. Weekend exceptions are only applicable on weekend days. In the T-SQL version, you had to worry about converting the time-based weekend exceptions to the current day. In the SQL CLR version, the `TimeSegment` class has done that for you. You only have to focus on the logic, which is: For each usiness exception, only apply weekend exceptions if the current day is a weekend date. The logic that performs this task is:

```
ArrayList newItems = new ArrayList();
foreach (TimeSegment a in BusExceptions)
{
    //BusinessException can't be null And
    //Apply if a weekend exception AND it is a weekend date
    //or the exception is not a Weekend exception
    if (a != null && (
        (a.TimeSegmentType == "WEEKENDOFFHRS" &&
         (currDayChecking.DayOfWeek == DayOfWeek.Saturday ||
         currDayChecking.DayOfWeek == DayOfWeek.Sunday))
        || (a.TimeSegmentType != "WEEKENDOFFHRS")
        ))
    {
        foreach (TimeSegment b in workingBusDefaults)
        {
            if ((a.Start < b.Start && a.End <= b.Start))
            {
                //Exception doesn't impact the business
                //++ hours to newitems/end business period
                newItems.Add(
                    new TimeSegment(b.Start, b.End, "COPY"));
                b.Start = b.End;
            }
            else if (a.Start <= b.Start && a.End >= b.End)
            {
                //Exception fully removes the business hours
                b.Start = b.End;
            }
            else if (a.Start <= b.Start &&
                    a.End >= b.Start &&
                       a.End <= b.End)
            {
                //Chopping off the front of the time period
                newItems.Add(
                    new TimeSegment(a.End, b.End, "ADDED"));
```

```
                b.Start = a.End;
        }
        else if (a.Start > b.Start &&
                    a.End < b.End)
        {
            //Exception Splits the time period
            //changes the ending time
            newItems.Add(
                new TimeSegment(b.Start, a.Start, "ADDED"));
            b.Start = a.End;
        }
        else if (a.Start > b.Start &&
                a.End >= b.End)
        {
            //Truncates the end
            newItems.Add(
                new TimeSegment(b.Start, a.Start, "Added"));
            //effectively ends the business period
            b.End = a.Start;
            b.Start = a.Start;
        }
    }
    }
}
```

Because you are just winding the business default date forward, and keeping track of isolated business hours, you have the possibility that a valid business-default-hour segment still exists at the end as well. You need to add that remaining segment to the newItems collection of isolated TimeSegment objects. The remainder of the code handles these TimeSegments as well as weeding out the ones that have been made inert by setting the start and end dates to the same date and time.

```
//In the foreach statement we'll be iterating through the remaining
//time segments in the workingBusDefaults to see if any business time
//periods remain after applying exclusions.
ArrayList AddItems = new ArrayList();
foreach (TimeSegment ts in workingBusDefaults)
{
    if (newItems.Count == 0)
    {
        AddItems.Add(ts);
    }
    else
    {
        foreach (TimeSegment newts in newItems)
        {
            if ((newts.Start == ts.Start &&
                    newts.End == ts.End) ||
                (ts.Start == ts.End)) { }
            else
            {
                AddItems.Add(ts);
                break;
            }
        }
    }
```

```
        }
    }
    //The remaining business time segments are added to those
    //that were isolated by business exceptions
    //the remaining structure is returned to the controller..
    foreach (TimeSegment addts in AddItems)
    {
        newItems.Add(addts);
    }
    return newItems;
}
#endregion
```

When the `newItems ArrayList` is returned to the calling method, you are left with a set of valid business hours for a date. Now you need to apply the boundaries of the parameterized time period provided at the beginning of this problem. In other words, if you determine that the business was available from 09:00 to 17:00, but you are asked what the business availability was between 13:00 and 14:00 the answer is constrained by your parameterized period.

Considering the Parameterized Time Period

One way to look at the parameterized time period is as another set of exclusions. Originally, we had planned to simply run the remaining business hours back through the same `ApplyExceptionsTo BusinessSchedule()` method using the hours of the parameters as the exclusion period. We quickly realized that the parameterized time period is the opposite of an exclusion period. (See Figure 11-15.)

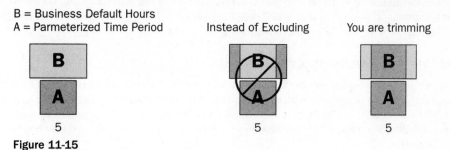

Figure 11-15

In Figure 11-14 the grey represents the segment that the exclusion would remove. In the case of the parameter time segment, you want to keep that section. The only way to get this result is to calculate the two outer periods to send in as exclusions. Reluctantly we realized that we'd not be able to reuse the `ApplyExceptionsToBusinessSchedule()` method for this task. Instead, we created a new method, `TrimBusinessSegmentsbyParms()` that performs this task. It is shown here:

```
public static void TrimBusinessSegmentsbyParms(ArrayList businessCombined,
                DateTime start, DateTime end)
{
    foreach (TimeSegment busTs in businessCombined)
    {
        if (start > busTs.End)
        {
```

```
                    //removes time segment from consideration
                    busTs.End = busTs.Start;
            }
            else if (start >= busTs.Start &&
                        start <= busTs.End)
            {
                busTs.Start = start;
            }

            //if (busTs.Start > end)
            if (end < busTs.Start)
            {
                //removes time segment from consideration
                busTs.End = busTs.Start;
            }
            else if (end >= busTs.Start &&
                        end <= busTs.End)
            {
                busTs.End = end;
            }
        }
    }
    #endregion
```

The end result is that only the business periods that belong within the parameterized time segment have a date range that can be calculated. These separate time segments are represented by the objects of type TimeSegment in the array businessCombined that is passed into this function. Notice that this function doesn't return an ArrayList. That is not necessary because the ArrayList is altered by reference, and this is the last logic process other than calculating the final results.

Calculating the Business Availability

The last utility method calculates the time difference between the start and end dates of each TimeSegment object in the array. To perform this calculation, you just iterate though the array and perform the calculation for each TimeSegment. The TimeSpan .NET class provides the structure to store the results and report the total seconds that you need to report ultimately back to the caller. The completed function is simple and looks like this:

```
#region Calculate Business Seconds
public static double CalcBusinessAvailabilitySeconds(
                    ArrayList businessCombined)
{
    double totalSecs = 0;
    foreach (TimeSegment ts in businessCombined)
    {
        TimeSpan t = ts.End.Subtract(ts.Start);

        totalSecs += t.TotalSeconds;
    }
    return totalSecs;
}
#endregion
```

Although this last routine is simple, it is not as simple as its equivalent in the T-SQL solution. As you may recall, at this point all you needed to do was run a T-SQL summary query against a table — one line of code. As we complete the example, we'll step back for a more objective examination. Now the only thing left is to create a constructor for this version of the business availability calculation.

Coding the Business Availability Constructor and Driver Method

With all the utility methods in place, you still need to code the constructor for the Business class. This method acts as the driver or controller method that calls the utility methods in the right order to generate a business availability calculation. The design approach calls for a separation of the SQL CLR T-SQL object definition and this class, so you can expect that the parameters passed to the SQL CLR object will be coming into this Business class. This class will be best encapsulated if you accept those parameters as is and perform any validation within the class, instead of expecting external validation. This means the constructor will need to be written with SqlDataTypes as parameters — especially since you are deploying ultimately as a T-SQL scalar UDF. These UDFs are typically run against sets of data that you cannot expect to be filtered for non-NULL data values. The prototype for the constructor looks like this:

```
#region Constructor with all expected inputs
public void BusinessAvailability(SqlDateTime sqlstart,
                                 SqlDateTime sqlend,
                                 SqlString sqltimedSegmentList,
                                 SqlString sqltimeExclusionList,
                                 string myConnStr)

{
```

The next lines of the BusinessAvailability() constructor are designed to validate the date parameters. If the values are NULL, or if the range is not a valid range, the function will return the default of 0 business availability.

```
//TEST IF YOU SHOULD EVEN ATTEMPT TO PERFORM CALCULATION
if ((!sqlstart.IsNull && !sqlend.IsNull) && sqlstart <= sqlend)
{
```

The next lines convert the SqlTypes to .NET data types using the Corp.Corp.Utilities assembly. The end date is also updated if it missing a time element. Because of the date calculations arithmetic, this must be converted to the next date with a time element of 00:00:00. The two parameters of specific business segments and exclusions are also converted with the referenced assembly to a .NET string type, using an empty string if the value is NULL.

```
//CONVERT NULLABLE TYPES
DateTime start = ConvertUtilities.ConvertSqlDateTime(sqlstart);
DateTime end = ConvertUtilities.ConvertSqlDateTime(sqlend);

//Correct the end date to date + 1 00:00:00
//for calculation purposes
if (end.Hour == 0 && end.Minute == 0 && end.Second == 0)
    end = end.AddDays(1);

//Strings converted using Corp.Core.Utilities
String timedSegmentList =
        ConvertUtilities.ConvertSqlString(sqltimedSegmentList);
String timeExclusionList =
        ConvertUtilities.ConvertSqlString(sqltimeExclusionList);
```

To build the T-SQL clause, we used the `TSQLUtilities` class in the `Corp.Core.Utilities` assembly to convert the delimited string into a proper T-SQL `IN` clause.

```
//Convert a delimited string to proper IN Clause
TimedSegments = TSQLUtilities.buildINClause(TimedSegments, ',');
```

The incoming parameters are stored in a `TimeSegment` object to be used throughout the method. The business defaults are retrieved once for efficiency and then consolidated. A `TimeSpan` calculation is made against the parameter dates to determine how many days the function needs to evaluate.

```
TimeSegment parmTimeSegment =
        new TimeSegment(start, end, "PARM-HRS", true);
end = parmTimeSegment.End;

ArrayList businessDefault = GetBusinessDefaults
                                  (timedSegmentList, myConnStr);

//Should be date-less at this point
businessDefault = ConsolidateTimeSegments(businessDefault);

//Determines the number of real days in parameter date range
TimeSpan days = parmTimeSegment.EndMax.Subtract
                    (parmTimeSegment.StartMin);
```

The remainder of the controller iterates through each day in the parameter range and calculates the business availability for each day, summarizing the total business availability in seconds. The `foreach` loop is used to reset the business default `TimeSegment` array so that the date portion of the business defaults reflect the same day that the exclusions are being pulled. Remember that the business default hours is stored as a time-only value, so this action is required. Otherwise, the utility methods are being called in the order prescribed by our solution approach.

```
//for each day in parameter date range we have to calculate
//the business time segments and the exception time segments
//then apply the exception time segments to the business segments
for (int i = 0; i <= days.TotalDays - 1; i++)
{
    //Set the current defaults to the current date
    //because defaults are stored as times only
    foreach (TimeSegment tsloop in businessDefault)
    {
        tsloop.SetDateForTimeOnlyProperties(
                parmTimeSegment.StartMin.AddDays(i),
                TimeSegment.SpecificDateParm.both);
    }

    //Create the daily timesegment for each loop
    TimeSegment ts = new TimeSegment(
                parmTimeSegment.StartMin.AddDays(i),
                parmTimeSegment.StartMin.AddDays(i + 1),
                "PARAMETERDATES", true);

    //Get Business Exceptions for that day
```

```
ArrayList businessExcepts =
        GetBusinessExceptions(timedSegmentList,
            timeExclusionList, ts, myConnStr);
//Consolidate the time segments
businessExcepts = ConsolidateTimeSegments(businessExcepts);

//Remove the exceptions from the normal business
//hours for the day...
ArrayList businessCombined =
        ApplyExceptionsToBusinessSchedule(
            businessDefault, businessExcepts,
            parmTimeSegment.StartMin.AddDays(i));

//Remove business hours not in parameters of
//the requested date range
TrimBusinessSegmentsbyParms(businessCombined, start, end);

//Summarize the number of seconds
TotalSeconds +=
        CalcBusinessAvailabilitySeconds(businessCombined);
            }
        }
    }
#endregion
```

Notice that the return on this method is of type `void`. This method could return the results of the business availability calculation, but we are using a public instanced property to show that instance classes and variables can be used in SQL CLR in the lower hierarchies. The exposed property is `TotalSeconds` and is implemented in the first line of the `Business` class (above the prototype for the method) like this:

```
#region Properties...
private double mtotalSeconds;
public double TotalSeconds
{
    get { return mtotalSeconds; }
    set { mtotalSeconds = value; }
}
#endregion
```

To make sure that everything is working properly, you should compile the solution now to see if you get a clean build. Common problems here could arise from upper/lowercase letter issues or incorrect references to assemblies.

Creating the SQL CLR Object

When we were approaching the T-SQL version of this solution, we decided to create a SQL user-defined function to perform this business availability calculation. We'll do the same thing in the SQL CLR version. The first thing you need to do is add a SQL CLR .NET database project to this solution. In this project, you are going to provide the function prototype definitions that SQL Server will use to create a T-SQL object upon deployment.

1. With the empty `BusinessAvailability` solution open, select File ⇨ Add ⇨ New Project. Select the SQL Server Project template under either the C# or VB.NET project templates database node.

2. Name the project **BusinessAvailability** as well. This will create a folder under the current solution folder named `businessavailability`.

3. Add a user-defined function to the project by right-clicking on the Solution Explorer and selecting Add ⇨ New Item.

4. Change the name of the class to `mfnGetBusinessAvailability.cs`. This results in renaming the physical class file and will result in the naming of the first method of the class as well.

5. Add an attribute to the function to indicate that this routine will request and perform data access in SQL Server. This attribute should look like this:

```
[Microsoft.SqlServer.Server.SqlFunction(DataAccess=DataAccessKind.Read)]
```

6. Add the SQL CLR static method that will be used as a T-SQL entry point. It is expected that this method can be used across sets of data that could contain NULL values. This prototype is prepared for that scenario by including the nullable `SqlDataTypes`. The method parameters should look like this:

```
public static double mfnGetBusinessAvailability(
                      SqlDateTime sqlstart,
                      SqlDateTime sqlend,
                      SqlString sqltimedSegmentList,
                      SqlString sqltimeExclusionList,
```

7. The business availability calculation will be deferred to the `BusinessAvailability` class in the `Corp.SQLCLR.Schedule` assembly. This is done with by instantiating the class using a constructor that expects, upon creation, to receive the parameter values required to make the calculation. This logic looks like this:

```
Business ba = new Business();
string myConnStr = "Context Connection=True";
ba.BusinessAvailability(sqlstart, sqlend,
                     sqltimedSegmentList,
                     sqltimeExclusionList,
                     myConnStr);
return ba.TotalSeconds;
```

8. If you were to attempt to build the solution at this point you'd see that an assembly reference is missing. You need to instruct this SQL CLR object definition class where to find the assembly reference to the `Corp.SQLCLR.Scheduling` assembly that contains the real `BusinessAvailability` calculation class. For this assembly, you are going to add a project reference. Right-click on Solution Explorer and select Add ⇨ Reference. In the Add Reference dialog, select the Projects tab and click the `Corp.SQLCLR.Scheduling` project reference.

9. To complete the reference, add the namespace to your SQL CLR object definition class `UserDefinedFunctions`. Remember the namespace and assembly names were set to the same name.

```
using Corp.SQLCLR.Scheduling;
```

10. The last task is to return the total seconds of business availability. This is set within the businessavailability class and can be retrieved by the SQL CLR object in the TotalSeconds property. The SQL CLR object will return this value like this:

```
return ba.TotalSeconds;
```

At this point, the solution should look like Figure 11-16.

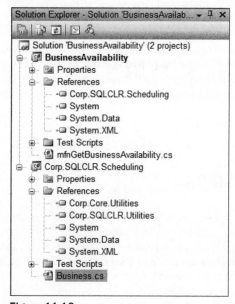

Figure 11-16

To complete the development of the .NET version, build the solution and deploy it to the CLRTESTDB database.

Calculating the Business Availability

Although it was far from being a full featured test, we looked at a quick example at the end of the T-SQL version of this function. Let's look at that example again. You ran this scenario in T-SQL:

```
select dbo.fnGetBusinessAvailability('07/04/06', '07/04/06', 'CONVEYOR1', '')
```

The results you expected and obtained were 72,000 seconds. To test this same example in the SQL CLR version of the same logic, run this in SSMS in a query window.

```
select dbo.mfnGetBusinessAvailability('07/04/06', '07/04/06', 'CONVEYOR1', '')
```

The results are the same.

Solution Comparisons

If you've walked through both of these solutions, you have spend some serious time digging into the details of T-SQL and SQL CLR—especially as they relate to date and time calculations. You've probably learned more than you want to know about calculating business time segments. What is your impression about using either method? We chose this example for a case study because it really gets to the heart of the matter. It shows two solutions using typical language-specific approaches. Is it easier to code the .NET solution or the T-SQL solution? Is it easier to debug the .NET solution or the T-SQL solution? Which has better performance? Which is easier to maintain? Which has more gotchas? We're willing to bet that most people will have a response to one or the other and what they do every day in the technology arena will probably drive that response more than the capabilities or lack of them in either case. The point is that we've provided this case study to show that there is now more than one way to do something in the database. In this section, we'll drill down into some of these comparisons to bring out some of the details that we may not have been able to discuss while you were developing the two solutions.

> We have also built a more advanced, alternative T-SQL-based solution that doesn't use cursors, which you can download for this chapter on this book's web site at www.wrox.com for comparison.

Testing and Debugging

Since both routines result in T-SQL user-defined functions, it is easy to test the outcome of each solution. One our favorite testing mechanisms is a T-SQL batch that is designed to test the boundaries of the solution responses. Typically, this T-SQL batch is created prior to the full development of the solution and appended as the development continues. The structure of each statement in the batch is designed to provide either a PASS or FAIL response to an expected result of a known test. This is similar to a Debug.Assert programming approach. Structure the test statements like this:

```
--NORMAL DAY WITHOUT EXCEPTIONS
select [TEST:DAY W/O EXCEPTIONS]=
    case when 86400 =dbo.fnGetBusinessAvailability(
      '07/05/06', '07/05/06', 'CONVEYOR1', '')
        then 'PASS'
    else 'FAIL' end
```

This test returns a column that clearly states the purpose of the test. The parameters are set to return an expected result. That result is validated in the case statement. The results of this type of testing scripts look like this:

```
TEST:DAY W/O EXCEPTIONS
-----------------------
PASS
```

This type of testing works well at the later stages of development, but when things are going wrong, testing the T-SQL statement gets a little difficult. The normal approach is to turn the function into a script by commenting out the definition and return statements and adding a declare statement to the parameters like this:

```
/*ALTER FUNCTION [dbo].[fnGetBusinessAvailability]
(*/
DECLARE
```

```
      @start datetime,              --beginning of sampling period
      @end    datetime,             --end of sampling period
      @timedSegmentList nvarchar(800),   --OPTIONAL comma separated timed segments
      @timeExclusionList nvarchar(1000)  --OPTIONAL date/time value pair exclusion
                                    --periods
/*)
RETURNS INT
AS
BEGIN*/
    <<BODY OF FUNCTION HERE>>
/*
   RETURN @TotalWorkSeconds
END*/
```

This allows you to run the script, but then you need to add little scripts within the batch to dump out values of variable and the temporary table variables to get an idea of the values as the batch is running. Testing the T-SQL version in process looks like Figure 11-17.

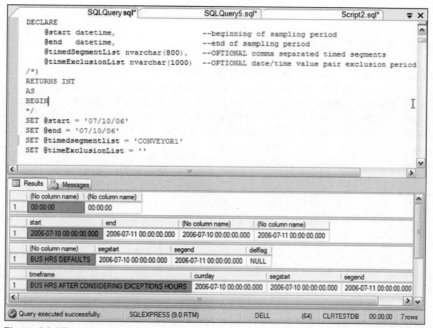

Figure 11-17

Compare this to testing in SQL CLR. Put a breakpoint in the Business class at the point in the constructor where the businessDefault ArrayList is first populated with the values of the business default hours. Then add this T-SQL code in the Test.Sql file in the TestScripts node of the SQL CLR BusinessAvailability project.

```
select dbo.mfnGetBusinessAvailability('07/04/06', '07/04/06', 'CONVEYOR1', '')
```

387

Press F5 or select Debug ⇨ Start Debugging. The solution will deploy, run, and then stop at your break-point. Press F10 to complete the method call. Then you can view the contents of the businessDefault ArrayList, as shown in Figure 11-18.

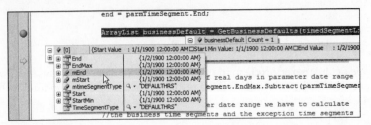

Figure 11-18

Accessing this level of information will speed up the development process of a complicated logical pro-cedure. It is amazing that you get all this detail without adding one line of testing code. As you can see, there are ways to debug in T-SQL and SQL CLR.

Adding a .NET Console Test Harness

Testing T-SQL routines in parts is somewhat difficult and many times impossible. Imagine what you would have to do to set up an isolated test of the logic of one small section of this calculation. Because the SQL CLR solution was able to break up the task into smaller utility methods, we can use traditional test-based development methods on these utility methods. One of the methods used is to add a .NET console application to the solution. This console application will contain several unit tests that you can perform against the utility methods to insure that they are working properly before they are added to the larger solution and become unmanageable to troubleshoot.

To create a sample .NET console test harness for the BusinessAvailability solution:

1. Add a .NET console application to the opened BusinessAvailability solution by selecting File ⇨ Add ⇨ New Project.

2. Click the Windows node under your .NET language. Select the Console Application project tem-plate. Change the name to **TestHarness**. Leave the location pointed to the root of the business availability solution: C:\ProSQLCLR\Chapter11\BusinessAvailability.

3. The console application needs references to the utility methods of the Corp.SQLCLR.Scheduling assembly, but the console app can't connect to retrieve the assemblies loaded in SQL Server. But the test harness can be used against the file-based binaries located in the project folder hierarchy. To connect to these references, right-click on the references node in the TestHarness project in the solution explorer. Browse and add the references to these assemblies located in the following directories:

```
C:\ProSQLCLR\Chapter11\Corp.Core.Utilities\Corp.Core.Utilities\bin\Debug\Corp.Core.
Utilities.dll
C:\ProSQLCLR\Chapter11\BusinessAvailability\Corp.SQLCLR.Scheduling\bin\Debug\Corp.
SQLCLR.Scheduling.dll
C:\ProSQLCLR\Chapter11\Corp.SQLCLR.Utilities\Corp.SQLCLR.Utilities\bin\Debug\Corp.
SQLCLR.Utilities.dll
```

4. Change the namespaces in the Program default class to the following:

```
using System;
using System.Collections;
using System.Data;
using Corp.Core.Utilities;
using Corp.SQLCLR.Utilities;
using Corp.SQLCLR.Scheduling;
```

5. Add this default testing code to the `Program` class main method. This code will run the two test methods that we'll write and send the responses to the console window.

```
try
{
TestTimeSegmentAutoEndDateConversion();
TestTimeCalculation();
TestGetBusinessDefaults()
}
catch (Exception ex)
{
    Console.WriteLine(ex.ToString());
}
Console.Write("Press Enter to finish ... ");
Console.Read();
```

6. Add these static testing methods to the body of the `Program` class. The first test is used to check the validity of sending two dates in with the same day to see if the `TimeSegment` class will convert the end date to the next day with no time element.

```
public static void TestTimeSegmentAutoEndDateConversion()
{
    TimeSegment ts = new TimeSegment(DateTime.Parse("01/01/1900"),
            DateTime.Parse("01/01/1900"), "SAMPLE", true);

    Console.WriteLine("TEST OF END DATE CONVERSION AUTOMATICALLY");
    Console.WriteLine(ts.End == DateTime.Parse("01/02/1900 00:00:00"));
}
```

The next test is used to build an array of business availability and send it specifically to the calculation method to see if it works properly.

```
public static void TestTimeCalculation()
{
    ArrayList myList = new ArrayList();
    double results = 0;
    TimeSegment ts = new TimeSegment(
                DateTime.Parse("07/04/06 10:00:00"),
                DateTime.Parse("07/04/06 12:00:00"), "TEST");
    myList.Add(ts);
    TimeSegment ts1 = new TimeSegment(
                DateTime.Parse("07/04/06 12:00:00"),
                DateTime.Parse("07/04/06 12:01:00"), "TEST");
    myList.Add(ts1);
    TimeSegment ts2 = new TimeSegment(
                DateTime.Parse("07/04/06 12:01:00"),
```

```
                                DateTime.Parse("07/04/06 12:01:01"), "TEST");
        myList.Add(ts2);
        results = Business.CalcBusinessAvailabilitySeconds(myList);
        Console.WriteLine("Total for dates: " + "\n" +
                            "is " + results.ToString() + " seconds...\n" +
                            "Total Expected: \n" +
                            "is 7261 seconds....");
    }
```

The last test is used to test the loading of the business defaults to see if the interaction with SQL Server is loading this structure properly.

```
public static void TestGetBusinessDefaults()
{
    string myConnStr = "Data Source=HINDELL01\\SQLEXPRESS;" +
                    "Initial Catalog=CLRTESTDB;" +
                    "Integrated Security=SSPI;" +
                    "Persist Security info=False";
    ArrayList al = new ArrayList();
    al = Business.GetBusinessDefaults("'CONVEYOR1'", myConnStr);
    foreach (TimeSegment ts in al)
    {
        Console.WriteLine("Default Business Hours for\n" +
                    "TimeSegment Type: {0}\n" +
                    "Start:    {1}\n" +
                    "End:      {2}\n", ts.TimeSegmentType,
                    ts.Start.ToString(),
                    ts.End.ToString());
    }
}
```

7. Set the TestHarness project to the startup project by right-clicking the project and selecting Set as Startup Project.

With this set up, you can run the test harness by pressing F5 or selecting Debug ⇨ Start Debugging. The Console application will run the two expected tests and return a standard output window like Figure 11-19.

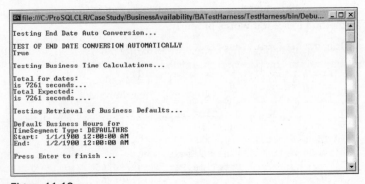

Figure 11-19

The great part about this is that you can set the `BusinessAvailability` SQL CLR project back to the `StartUp` project, build and deploy the solution without any deployment of the Console application. This allows the `TestHarness` project to hang around for the next iteration of development and testing. By setting up your data access methods in this solution to accept connection strings, you were able to test the worker methods using the assemblies without hosting them in SQL Server. This saves you from having to create T-SQL-based testing procedures and enables you to use automated testing tools for SQL CLR development. However, when you test the SQL CLR function `mfnGetBusinessAvailability` you'll have to deploy the solution and test using the T-SQL this function passes the SQL Context connection string. You can use this as an example of how to use a console application to unit test your SQL CLR code.

Deployment and Administration

The T-SQL version of the Business Availability calculation is easier to deploy into another database environment, without a doubt. A simple T-SQL script can transfer the function to another database. The SQL CLR solution, as we have presented it, is a little more difficult. With the dependent assemblies, you can get into trouble if the assemblies are not loaded in the right order. The one assembly that loaded into SQL Server from a regular .NET project had to be loaded manually. This could create an opportunity for a mistake to occur during deployment.

Regardless of the level of experience you have with .NET, it is safe to say that the deployment of a T-SQL object is easier, but what about the administration? This depends upon the skill level of the DBA for sure, but there are some facts that make administering production issues more complicated under SQL CLR. For one, you can't run the Profiler on the activities that occur in the CPU or memory of the database server. Since SQL CLR spends much time in these areas, you can only guess where something may be going wrong in the logic. T-SQL has the same problem, but the solutions are mostly data-centric, leaving most of the activity traceable in the Profiler.

If a problem is found in the SQL CLR solution, the DBA will need to be able to troubleshoot the body of the SQL CLR object. This means he or she may be able to extract the code from the assembly metadata tables or may have to go back to the developer to review the implementation details. This is not as fast as querying the `syscomments` table for `TSQLobject` metadata. In the short run, T-SQL has an edge in the deployment and administration comparison category.

Performance

To compare the two business functions from a performance perspective, we used the methodology established in Chapter 5 to compare and contrast several aspects of T-SQL versus SQL CLR scenarios. We ran both functions repetitively through 10 sets of 1,000 calls and compiled the results of each into two main graphs for total time and total CPU time. The graphs in Figure 11-20 show the results of these benchmarks.

You can see clearly that the SQL CLR version of the solution excels in making this type of elaborate calculation. The SQL CLR version is taking less CPU time, and less total time to complete the business availability calculation. T-SQL is spending more time in the CPU performing the iterations that are not its specialty. These results show that for some activities you can achieve a performance gain by refactoring your T-SQL code into SQL CLR code.

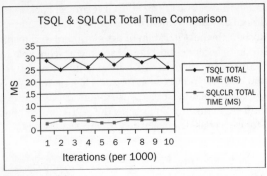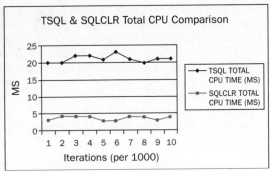

Figure 11-20

Development Perspective

You may be wondering why we didn't create the business availability method as a static method. A static method would have allowed us to call it without having to instantiate a copy of the Business class first. This was purposeful. If you start experimenting with these SQL CLR objects, you'll find out quickly that instance methods and types can't be in that outer .NET class that functions as the SQL CLR object definition class. These classes are for static or non-instance variables and methods only. We've found that some developers think this limitation applies across the board and have stopped looking at the reuse possibilities of the SQL CLR. If you've already got .NET classes and assemblies, we designed this case study for you to see that integrating these assemblies into SQL CLR objects is not only possible, but easy.

In this case study, you integrated a regular .NET assembly, a SQL CLR binary assembly, two SQL CLR projects, and a console application for a test harness. From a development perspective, SQL CLR feels a lot like a typical development process. You have to remember that the references are in SQL Server not in the file system. But the ability to break down the problem into smaller parts is what make these solutions feel like development projects.

Summary

We've done our part. We've dug into the details of the new features of SQL CLR and exposed them via a direct comparison to T-SQL to solve a problem of calculating business availability. If you were following along and working the case study with us, you have had the opportunity to make a direct apples-to-apples comparison of these two methodologies. The issues with immutable cursor definitions and the lack of ability to pass table variables around created some difficulties with implementing this solution in T-SQL. In the end, we were able to complete the task. The .NET solution creates some issues with deployment and level of complexity. Developers may find that this solution is straightforward and the T-SQL solution to be convoluted. T-SQL developers may see things the reverse way.

So, what did you think? Does the ease of debugging and the possibility of code reuse interest you enough to make SQL CLR a part of your SQL Server development toolkit?

Index